M000222908

Tuning the
Therapeutic Instrument

Tuning the
Therapeutic Instrument

Affective Learning of Psychotherapy

JILL AND DAVID SCHARFF

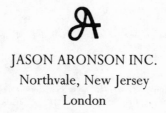

JASON ARONSON INC.
Northvale, New Jersey
London

The authors gratefully acknowledge permission to reprint material from the following sources:

"Teaching and Learning: An Experiential Conference," by David E. Scharff and Jill S. Scharff, *Journal of Personality and Social Systems* 2(1):53–78. Copyright © 1979 A. K. Rice Institute, Evanston, IL.

"Father," by Fay Chiang, from *In the City of Contradictions.* Copyright © 1979 by Sunbury Press. Quoted by permission of the author.

This book was set in 11.5 pt. by Alpha Graphics in Pittsfield, NH, and printed and bound by Book-mart Press, Inc. of North Bergen, NJ.

Library of Congress Cataloging-in-Publication Data

Scharff, David E., 1941–
    Tuning the therapeutic instrument: affective learning of psychotherapy / by David E. Scharff and Jill Savege Scharff
      p. cm.
    Includes bibliographical references.
    ISBN 0-7657-0245-2
    1. Psychotherapy—Study and teaching . 2. Affective education. I. Jill Savege Scharff. II. Title.
RC336.S36 2000
616.89'14'071—dc21   99-048775

Printed in the United States of America on acid-free paper. For information and catalog write to Jason Aronson Inc., 230 Livingston Street, Northvale, New Jersey 07647-1726, or visit our website:www.aronson.com

For Jay

Contents

Preface and Acknowledgments   ix

Contributors   xiii

Part I
Affective Learning

1   Firsthand Accounts   3
    Overcoming Fears of Uncertainty   3
    Dealing with Displacement of the Transference
      in Supervision   6
    Applying Group Dynamics in Teaching   10
    Understanding Cultural Pressures on Women   15

2   The Affective Learning Model   21

3   Individual, Group, and Chaos Theories   45

4   The Rocky Road of Affective Learning   71

5   Intensity, Brevity, and Focus   85

6   Therapeutic—but Not Therapy   99

7   The Group Unconscious and the Individual Dream   109

Part II
Affective Learning in the Small Group

8   Reflections by Students   127
    The Mother as a Desired Object   128
    Letting Go and Holding On   131
    Poor Indeed, If Only Sane   133
    The Student as Teacher   136
    Resonance with Self and Objects   138

9   The Affective Learning Small Group   143

10   The Individual and the Couple as Objects in the Group Dynamic   161

11   On Being Open to a New Object   173

12   One Student's Experience in Many Small Groups   183

13   The Course of a Small Group in a Five-Day Conference   203

Part III
The Shared Experience of Teaching and Learning

14   Preparing for a Presentation   237
       Selecting the Presenter   237
       Mentoring the Presenter   239
       Preparing the Clinical Presentation   240
       The Effect on the Preceding Small Group   245

15   The Presentation   249

16   Reflections on the Presentation   265
       The Impact on the Presenter's Subsequent Small Group   265
       The Learning Process in the Other Small Groups   268
       The Presenter's Reflections   273

Part IV
Leading from Affective Experience

17   The Role of the Chair   279

18   The Small-Group Leader as Chair   297

19   Supervision in the Learning Matrix   313

20   The Internal Couple in the Group Mind   333

21   Risks, Advantages, and Applications   355

Epilogue   369

Appendix   Teaching and Learning: An Experiential Conference   373

References   403

Index   413

Preface and Acknowledgments

Tuning the Therapeutic Instrument: Affective Learning of Psychotherapy describes an innovative psychotherapy training design for teaching and learning object relations theory and practice. Written for therapists who are interested in their own learning and who want to teach others, it shows how studying concepts, confronting resistances, and learning from experience in a group combine to develop the therapist's self as a sensitive instrument for therapy, supervision, and teaching. Only by being open with ourselves can we hope to be responsive to patients, clients, and students.

The group affective learning model is based on a simple observation: As therapists read, listen, study together, and discuss in a group setting, they engage in a group learning process that develops, reflects, and amplifies the concepts being taught. In addition to enhancing comprehension and emotional responsivity, the group process transforms the therapist's way of thinking and working with emotional experience. At the heart of the model lies the small affective learning group in which therapists work together with help from their small group leader to learn from their experience. In the small group they integrate intellectual understanding and emotional responses to theoretical and clinical presentations, and then apply their learning to clinical practice.

Traditionally, psychoanalytic theory and technique have been learned in three ways: by being a patient in therapy, by working as a supervised clinician, and by augmenting clinical skills with knowledge of theory acquired from reading and seminars. All these methods for learning are of value, but their effectiveness has been limited by the degree of separation between the tracks. The affective learning design offers an alternative that bridges the gap between therapy, supervision, and seminar.

The affective learning model is based on object relations theories of the individual and the group. In the therapeutic relationship, we find displayed the internal object relationships of patient and therapist as they coconstruct and recover from transference. In the affective learning group, we find that displays of internal object relationships occur as therapists teach and learn together. Then we can study the internal object relationships firsthand.

Within the learning matrix, internal object relationships interact with others in small and large group settings that are porous to examination. This reduces the likelihood of intense individual transferences being displaced from personal therapy and psychoanalysis into the learning setting. Even so, the therapist-as-student is inclined to substitute a healing task for a learning task. Traditionally, this has been ignored or referred back to the therapist's analyst.

In the affective learning model, however, we acknowledge reverberations caused by internal object relationships. We work with them openly so that they do not muddy the group's grasp of the concepts. Then we find that they actually illuminate our primary task of teaching and learning the theory of psychoanalysis and the technique of psychotherapy. Like transference in therapy and the countertransference it evokes, the group process both expresses a resistance and provides a medium for learning and growth.

This book is in four parts. Part I begins with firsthand accounts of experiencing and applying affective learning. Then we outline the affective learning model and its theory base in individual, group analytic, and chaos theories. We illustrate its use in group settings varying in size, duration, and leadership; discuss how the affective learning small group differs from therapy; and present our way of adapting it to time-limited teaching modules.

In the first chapter of Part II, therapists who are in the student role reflect on their learning experiences, each one representing a point along the continuum from cognitive to affective modes of learning. The following chapters describe the authors' thinking about their groups' openness to learning from experience and their way of working in small groups of short and long duration, including an international student's view of his growth through participation in many small groups. The concluding chapter of that section follows the course of a week-long small group over seven sessions, showing how the didactic material is metabolized in the group process.

Parts III and IV bring together the individual, group, and institutional elements of the learning matrix. Focusing on a student-as-teacher presentation and small group responses to it, the chapters in Part III explore an institution-wide teaching and learning experience during a single weekend conference. In Part IV, the impact of leadership on teaching and learning is addressed in chapters on the role of the chair, the effect of the learning matrix on the supervisory process, and the unconscious reverberations of the internal couple in group life. We conclude with a discussion of risks, advantages, and applications of the affective learning model. In the epilogue, David Scharff as the program director has the last word.

Tuning the Therapeutic Instrument: Affective Learning of Psychotherapy is the result of a cooperative teaching and learning venture among students, faculty, and international guest faculty of the International Institute of Object Relations Therapy where we continue to use, develop, and test our model. This book, like the affective learning program it describes, shows that we value the continuing education of the teacher as much as of the learner and gives voice to the opinions of students and faculty members alike. In using the term *student*, we do not mean to minimize the competence of the therapists who study with us, and who are recognized professionals in counseling, education, pastoral counseling, psychiatric nursing, psychiatry, psychology, and social work. Many are already experienced in psychotherapy, some are trained in psychoanalysis, and some are teaching other mental health professionals. We use the term *student* simply to denote the therapist in the learning role. By the concluding chapter, we hope to have demonstrated the advantages of affective learning and to raise the issue of its adaptation for use in the basic training of psychoanalysts and psychotherapists in traditions other than object relations. In the appendix we have reprinted our account of an early version of our model in educational settings at the university and secondary-school levels. We think that it could be applied in elementary schools, teacher training, marriage enhancement workshops, and life-skills training as well.

Only those faculty and students who submitted material for this book are acknowledged on the page that lists the contributors. We thank them for their ideas and wonderful examples and for letting us mix and match them to create the final product. Others have also contributed to the refinement of the affective learning model reflected in this book. We are grateful to Jack Hartke, Sheila Hill, Kent Ravenscroft, Paula Swaner, and Walt Ehrhardt for their participation as faculty; to Tom Kapacinskas for his leadership in the Fellows program; to Daniel Goldberg, Jaedene Levy, Helen Meek, Louis Reed, and Charles Schwarzbeck for their advice; and to Jason Aronson, Dennis Blumer, Yvonne Burne, Dickson Carroll, Lorna Goodman, Kent Morrison, and Tappan Wilder for their support and guidance as Board members. There would be no institution for affective learning without the superb administrative skills of Anna Innes and her assistant Mary Thomas. To all these people we are deeply grateful for working with us as colleagues and for their friendship.

At the publishing house, our excellent editor Judy Cohen was as usual a delight to work with, and Juliann Popp and Roberta Riviere dealt with the marketing and publicity in the widely circulated *Psychotherapy Book News*, while Russell Perna ensured a lively presence for the book on the Aronson website. Norma Pomerantz was helpful in facilitating our communications with the publisher. Most of all, we are indebted to Jason Aronson for commissioning this book based on his belief in the value of this approach. We thank all of them for representing our work so beautifully.

We would like to thank guest speakers and colleagues at the leading edge of object relations theory for working with us intensively, supporting our venture, encouraging the development of the model, and contributing to its development. These include Joan and Neville Symington (Australia); Ernst Falzeder (Austria); Ross Lazar (Germany); Imre Szecsödy (Sweden); Danielle and Jean-Michel Quinodoz (Switzerland); Anne Alvarez, Robin Anderson, Ronald Britton, James Fisher, Jeremy Hazell, Roger Kennedy, Stanley Ruszczynski, Elizabeth Spillius, and Gianna Williams (United Kingdom); and Salman Akhtar, Glen Gabbard, Ted Jacobs, Joseph Lichtenberg, Mike Nichols, and Joan Zilbach (United States). Returning guest speakers whom we especially want to thank are Christopher Bollas for inspired teaching and faithful support; Earl Hopper for friendship and program development ideas; Anton Obholzer for his loyalty over the years, his outstanding consultation, and his discussion of the model recorded in Chapter 21; and Arthur Hyatt Williams for his much appreciated, lively teaching year after year. We have been fortunate to have Glen Gabbard and Tom Ogden expressing enthusiasm for our work, Otto Kernberg participating in conferences even when traveling as President of the International Psychoanalytic Association, and Henry Friedman and Joe Silvio encouraging us to discuss our model at the American Psychoanalytic Association and the American Academy of Psychoanalysis. We are grateful to all of them, and to many others who lectured occasionally, including David Bell, Dennis Duncan, Steve Ellman, Peter Fonagy, Martha Papadakis, Allan Schore, Mary Target, and Vamık Volkan.

Last but not least, we are grateful to our students, especially those who return as graduates and fellows to enrich the culture of the teaching institution. We have enjoyed their collaboration and their commitment to learning from experience. Where it has been necessary to refer to individuals in order to illuminate a group process report, we have protected their anonymity by changing identifying details, by using pseudonyms both for students and faculty, and by not revealing the authorship of each vignette. Although discretion prevents us from giving detailed credit chapter by chapter, we gratefully acknowledge and value each contributor to *Tuning the Therapeutic Instrument: The Affective Learning of Psychotherapy.*

Jill Savege Scharff
David E. Scharff

Chevy Chase, Maryland
www. iiort.org
February 28, 2000

Contributors

Charles Ashbach, Ph.D., is a faculty member of the Institute for Psychoanalytic Psychotherapies in Philadelphia, PA where he is a psychologist in private practice in Philadelphia and Wyndmoor, PA. He is co-author of *Object Relations, the Self and the Group*. He is on the faculty of IIORT Washington, (the International Institute of Object Relations Therapy in Washington, DC), editor of the IIORT bulletin, and chair of IIORT Philadelphia.

Gaye Ayton, M.A, President of the North Coast Association of Mental Health Professionals, is currently in private practice specializing in long-term psychoanalytic psychotherapy in Eureka, CA. She is a graduate of the two-year object relations theory and practice program at IIORT Washington.

Carl Bagnini, M.S.W., B.C.D., is on the faculties of Suffolk Institute of Psychotherapy and Psychoanalysis and St. John's University Post-graduate Family Therapy Training Program. He is in private practice in Port Washington, NY. He is co-chair of the couple, child, and family therapy program at IIORT Washington and chair of IIORT Long Island.

Karen Fraley, M.S.S., B.C.D., received her degree from Bryn Mawr Graduate School in Social Work. A board certified diplomate in clinical social work, she is in private practice in Exton, PA. She is a graduate of the two-year program in object relations theory and practice and a Fellow at IIORT Washington.

Michael Kaufman, L.P.C., M.A., is in private practice in Charlottesville, VA. He is on the faculty of IIORT Washington and coordinator of the Charlottesville program in object relations theory and technique, IIORT Charlottesville.

Patricia Lindquist, Ph.D., a psychologist in private practice in San Diego, CA, trained at the Anna Freud Center in London and the Washington School of Psychiatry. She co-authored *Psychological Abuse of Children in Health Care*, and writes on psychological management of children's physical illness. She is a faculty member of IIORT Washington and chair of IIORT San Diego.

Anton Obholzer, B.Sc., M.B. Ch.B., D.P.M., F.R.C. Psych., a psychiatrist and psychoanalyst who trained at the Tavistock Clinic and the Institute of Psychoanalysis, London, is chief executive of the Tavistock and Portman NHS Trust. Co-editor of *The Unconscious at Work*, he writes on unconscious processes in organizations. He is distinguished guest faculty, IIORT.

Kyung Soon Park, Ph. D., is a candidate at NYU Psychoanalytic Institute. She received her Ph.D. in psychology from Korea University Graduate School where she was associate researcher and lecturer in the department of psychology. She has studied couple therapy at IIORT Washington.

Samuel Pinzón, Ph.D., president of the Panamanian Psychological Association, is a clinical psychologist in the private practice of psychoanalysis in Panama and a professor at the Universidad de Panamá. His books include ¡*Vive Mejor!*, *Quattuor*, and *Un Psicólogo en la Escuela-La Experiencia Freinet*. He is on the faculties of IIORT Washington and IIORT Panama.

Judith M. Rovner, M.S.W., is a clinical assistant professor of psychiatry at Georgetown University, adjunct faculty at Georgetown Counseling Center, and consultant faculty at the Clinical Social Work Institute. She is in the private practice of psychotherapy in Chevy Chase, MD. She is a faculty member of IIORT Chevy Chase, and is the chair of the clinical application program and chair of the supervision program, IIORT Washington.

Elizabeth A. Rundquist, M.A., A.T.R.-B.C., is an art therapist in the private practice of psychotherapy in New York City where she also teaches and supervises art therapy. She exhibits her artwork in New York City and the Northeast. She is a graduate of the two-year program in object relations theory and practice at IIORT Washington.

Kate Scharff, M.S.W., is the founder and director of Washington Services for Relationships in Transition and is in the private practice of child and adult psychotherapy in Washington, DC. A graduate of Columbia University School of Social Work and the Institute for Child, Adolescent, and Family Studies in New York City, she is about to graduate from the two-year program in object relations theory and practice at IIORT Washington.

Nell Scharff, M.A., teaches English at Hunter College High School in New York City. She is a doctoral student in education at New York University where her research is on the application of group theory to classroom teaching. She has studied Bion and Freud at IIORT Washington.

Lea de Setton, Ph. D., is a professor at University Santa Maria La Antigua, Republica of Panamá and she is in the private practice of family and couple therapy in Panama. She is on the faculties of IIORT Washington and IIORT Panama.

Stephen Skulsky, Ph.D., is a clinical psychologist in the private practice of individual, group, and couple psychotherapy in Omaha, NE. He is a faculty member of IIORT Washington and chair of IIORT Omaha.

Michael Stadter, Ph.D., is a clinical psychologist in private practice in Bethesda, MD and is on the faculty of the Washington School of Psychiatry. He is the author of *Object Relations Brief Therapy: The Relationship in Short-Term Work*. He is on the faculty of IIORT Chevy Chase and is the Dean of Students at IIORT Washington.

Stanley A. Tsigounis, Ph.D., is on the faculty of the Tampa Institute for Psychoanalytic Studies and is a clinical psychologist in private practice in Sarasota and Tampa, FL. He is on the faculty of IIORT Washington and is chair of IIORT Tampa.

Yolanda Varela, M.A., past president of the Panamanian Psychological Association, is a clinical psychologist with a masters degree in educational psychology. She is in the private practice of individual, child, couple, and family psychotherapy in Panama City, Republic of Panama. She is on the faculty of IIORT Washington where she chairs the summer institutes of the two-year program, and she is chair of IIORT Panama.

David E. Scharff, M. D., co-director of IIORT, is a clinical professor of psychiatry at Georgetown University and at the Uniformed Services University of the Health Sciences, and a teaching analyst at the Washington Psychoanalytic Institute. He received his medical degree from Harvard, his psychotherapy training at Massachusetts Mental Health Center, Boston and the Tavistock Clinic, London, and his psychoanalytic certification from the American Psychoanalytic Association. He is in the private practice of psychoanalysis and psychotherapy with adults, children, couples, and families in Chevy Chase. He is the author of

The Sexual Relationship, Refinding the Object and Reclaiming the Self, and editor of *Object Relations Theory and Practice, Fairbairn Then and Now*, and *Freud at the Millennium*. With Jill Scharff, he co-authored *Object Relations Family Therapy* and *Object Relations Couple Therapy*. He is chair of IIORT Chevy Chase and Manhattan, and he directs the two-year program in object relations theory and practice at IIORT Washington.

Jill Savege Scharff, M. D., co-director of IIORT, is a clinical professor of psychiatry at Georgetown University, and teaches child analysis at the Washington Psychoanalytic Institute. She received her medical degree from the University of Aberdeen, and her psychotherapy training at the Royal Edinburgh Hospital, Edinburgh and the Tavistock Clinic, London, and her certification in adult and child psychoanalysis from the American Psychoanalytic Association. She is in private practice in Chevy Chase, working in psychoanalysis and psychotherapy with adults, children, couples, and families. She is the author of *Projective and Introjective Identification and the Use of the Therapist's Self* and editor of *Foundations of Object Relations Family Therapy*, and *The Autonomous Self: The Work of John D. Sutherland*. With David Scharff, she co-authored *Object Relations Therapy of Physical and Sexual Trauma, A Primer of Object Relations Therapy*, and *Object Relations Individual Therapy*. She is on the faculty of IIORT Chevy Chase, and she chairs the couple, child, and family therapy program at IIORT Washington.

I
Affective Learning

In Part I, students and faculty join us in introducing our model for the affective learning of psychotherapy. In Chapter 1, vivid personal examples re-create the experience of affective learning and demonstrate its usefulness. This sets the scene for Chapters 2 and 3 in which we present the theory of the affective learning model and its theory base in individual object relations, group analytic, and chaos theories, integrated with findings from research in neurobiology and affect regulation. Chapter 4 illustrates the model with a small-group leader's account of her small group over the course of a weekend as its members work on well-known object relations concepts and unfamiliar chaos theory, individual and group responses, and dreams. Returning to theory and technique, Chapters 5 and 6 show how principles of brevity, intensity, and focus sharpen the effectiveness of the method in both short-term and longer-term groups and how affective learning groups differ from therapy groups. Chapter 7 concludes Part I with an example of an affective learning group dealing with defenses of splitting and rejection and organizing the underlying unconscious themes in relation to an individual's dream.

1

Firsthand Accounts

To set the scene, a therapist, a clinical supervisor, an educator, and an international post-graduate student give voice to their experience of affective learning.

OVERCOMING FEARS OF UNCERTAINTY

The first time I attended a conference for the affective learning of psychotherapy as a student, I thought of the weekend experience as a block of time for learning blocks of stuff, together with people who were also blocks of stuff to deal with—funny, boring, tyrannical, warm, stiff, exciting, challenging, whatever—simply stuff. I wanted to be seen in a concrete way that confirmed me as reliable and responsible, a good person for clients to identify with in psychotherapy, and a strong professional self undisturbed by personal anxieties. My own personal therapy had taught me to have a solid sense of my self through which I hoped to contribute to solid ego structures for my patients. In order to do this, I placed a high value on my own secure sense of individuation, separateness, and self-sufficiency. I came to the affective learning of object relations theory to confirm that sense of professional certainty and solidness as a therapist. That, however, is not what I found.

Affective learning required me to bring out my capacity to deal with uncertainty and mystery, with the as-yet unknown and the unknowable, with the fluidity and unpredictability of the human unconscious. I could no longer think of learning in terms of stuff to take in and be sure of. I had to think of myself in interaction with the experience, flowing to the end of the time allowed by the weekend format, each weekend like the tributary of a river that gathered momentum as it became fuller and deeper.

I didn't like to experience myself in fluid terms because I was afraid of regression. I preferred to feel stable and secure and to think of myself in static terms. The intimacy in the small affective learning group offered me some of the security I sought. When I had to give that up to join the large group in the plenary review meeting, I felt uncomfortable. I hated the large group. The measly allotment of time for a weekend conference made me feel as if I'd landed on an island whose denizens were as yet unknown.

My new concept of the We-self-as-a-river-of-life-process contradicted my idea of I-self-as-invincible-stuff. The We-self is all about change, growth, and learning from others. The I-self is my essential reality. I still think that my I-self is a strong part of me, but the affective learning group showed me that it is also a burden that kept me from sharing at the deepest levels of unconscious communication. Gradually I became better at letting go and joining the experience until one day I was asked to be a group co-leader.

When I first accepted the task of co-leading a group, I was surprised to find that I fell silent. I felt adrift on a vast sea of something I couldn't quite grasp. I now recognize that feeling as a sign of my terror of the deep and all the psychological and sexual stuff lurking there. There's that word "stuff" again—I wanted to package up and submerge what I couldn't understand. I wanted to be in touch with my perceptions of what was occurring in the group, but that would require relinquishing my treasured certainties and fantasies of solidity, and I felt afraid of that.

To become a group leader, I had to reshape the defenses that let me feel solid and supported without letting them cripple me and wall me off from group processes. Too often I blocked my reception of the group's communications. If I did not block them off, I felt them too intensely. I caught myself trying not to let them affect me. I had to look at my personal history with groups and unlearn a lifelong pattern so that I could get to the point of welcoming and naming projective identifications of me as the group leader.

I got a jump start on this when examining my aversive responses to the manuscript for Chapter 20 of this book. It includes a report on a faculty discussion that deals with the learning of material taught by a couple and conveys the striking difference between conscious and unconscious responses to the same situation in a teaching setting. At the cognitive level, I was interested in the content of the reported discussion which clearly made the point that learning is affected by unconscious factors. At the emotional level, I was repulsed. I didn't want to read a faculty discussion that shows all the world what is done in private. I was revolted by the part where the program directors revealed their dread of opening the door to examination of the impact of their being a couple on the learning process. I found both of these accounts odious. I wanted to scream, "SHUT THE DOOR!" I immediately recognized my responses as primal scene reactions, but it took another month for the strength of my reaction to make sense, a whole month before I let the door open on its resonance with my own experience as a therapist, a group leader, and a woman in my own family.

I'm a minister's wife. For years, my husband and I have not infrequently been assaulted by projective identifications from individuals in our Christian parish community. Projections of hate and envy leave us feeling annihilated. Having only just survived a few of these painful encounters with parishioners, I now maintain a hawk-like protectiveness about our privacy as a couple. I am vigilant as can be. While trying to be kind, attentive, and resourceful, I nevertheless build a moat around us in order to repel projections of hate and envy.

Living in a large parish is like living in a small town, where individuals, couples, and families are often obsessed with what is not there: acknowledgment, security, reassurance, control, faith, health, obedient children, loving parents, money. These worries about what is missing feed on themselves until they mutate from grumbling anxiety into convulsive group crises to which the minister must attend. Individual and group lacks and losses claw at my husband's consciousness and at his unconscious anxieties. There can be so many demands on him that I choose to absent myself from the overload in order not to be absent from him. I am his partner, not theirs, except on a carefully delineated basis.

Living as the head couple in that provisional space, where the minister both speaks for God and is the humblest servant of the parish, leaves a barely discernable column of air for us as a private couple. So I make space, on purpose, for both of us when he cannot or will not. I refuse to extend my Christianity to a place where I am sucked up and spat out as he is so frequently. I deal with attacks and demands by delineating myself apart from him and his calling, and by protecting us as a couple from them.

Reading Chapters 20 and 21, it clicked with me that my techniques for living as a minister's wife are careful defenses against group process that I have found necessary for years. As a therapist myself, a teacher of psychotherapy, a student, and a faculty member leading groups, I'm now involved in the affective learning of psychotherapy where the culture insists that group process is ultimately dependable and enriching, not immature and destructive. In the affective learning culture, I've been trying to experience myself as part of the collective "We-self" of the group instead of walling myself off as an "I-self." But over the years as the minister's wife, I've become deft at being an "I-self" rather than a "We-self." This seemed to help me in the parish, but it hampered me as the leader of an affective learning group.

As a group leader, I, like the minister's wife, was not confronting projections that were aimed at me. My I-self was preventing me from dealing with these projections as well as I would like. What I've learned in the affective learning group is that my behavior in groups was based on a view that this group process would kill me, as my sharing of ministry has threatened to do.

Comparing my group experience of multiple pairings for learning psychotherapy with my life experience in a single couple led me to re-evaluate the need for privacy. It has been a mystery to me for a long time how on the one hand I need my moat and on the other I need *koinonia*, the fellowship that the parish life provides. I have discovered that what I hate in parish life is also what I love and need. My hatred of some of its elements makes the moat necessary. The hunger that hate creates brings me back to the fellowship that is truly encircling.

After all this time living with and supporting my husband in his work, and honing my clinical skills in affective learning groups, I've discovered that my own couple stance with my minister-husband is impossible. It's non-relational. The very behavior I valued so highly I now see as a defense against uncertainty. I no longer want this to shield me from the fullness of experience as a therapist or as a minister's wife. I have to mingle myself concretely and metaphorically in order to integrate myself within an encircling group. Learning the theory and practice of object relations from experience in the affective learning group, I've found a way to understand my role as a co-leader in the religious community as well as in the affective learning institution. Using this insight, I'm preparing to lead affective learning groups more courageously, and to relinquish treasured certainties within the parish as well.

DEALING WITH DISPLACEMENT OF THE TRANSFERENCE IN SUPERVISION

I've recently been appointed to work with my own supervisee, Harry. I've supervised psychotherapists in other settings, but this is my first time supervising someone in the affective learning program, and I'm interested to see how that context amplifies my understanding. Harry is a nice guy with a successful practice, a stable married life, and a respected place in his community. He asked for supervision so that he could work in greater depth, address the transference more consistently, and stop dodging issues of aggression. His assessment of his need was consistent with the impression that he gave in the affective learning small group setting. When segments of the group expressed anger, he tended to defuse the feeling with his use of empathy and intellectual explanation. He came across as a sensitive, responsive, mature, and well-related person in groups, but perhaps he may have been in retreat from his own aggression there as well. All in all, other students liked him very much. Now that I know him as a therapist in supervision, I find him well-informed, empathic, experienced, sensitive, and emotionally connected to his patients.

Harry brought to supervision his individual therapy work with Gladys, a divorced woman who is a fourth-grade teacher. Gladys experiences black moods in which she feels ashamed of herself, cut off from herself, and wordless. As a child she was shamed by a mother who rejected her displays of emotion. Gladys attends regularly and pays her bill on time. She says what is on her mind, and she brings in dreams that Harry likes to work with. She has a good therapeutic alliance with Harry, but she always has another relationship with a man to turn to. These other relationships are illicit, confessional, and may even be sexual. They violate the man's professional boundaries, and they always end in disappointment for Gladys.

> Harry reported to me that Gladys had developed a new sexual relationship with a man who was a doubly forbidden object: he was her supervisor in the school system and he was married. Like him, Harry is married and has a professional relationship to Gladys, two factors that preclude a dating relationship. The displacement of feelings about Harry to the lover was obvious to me. Then Harry told me that this new boyfriend is actually called Harry! I pointed out to him the urgent need to interpret the displacement of the transference, and he said to me, "No, I want to let it build. The relationship is gratifying to Gladys when she's so lonely. I don't want to trigger her into emptiness."

My job was to help Harry see that these relationships represent a displaced transference that expresses Gladys's rejection of him and her longing to be loved and found exciting by him. He could easily see that idea, but he did not object to the series of illicit relationships as enactments. Harry agreed that his response was typical of the way he backs off.

Backing off is not typical of me, but I found that I couldn't insist on my point of view. So I took this problem to the faculty meeting. I told my colleagues that Harry reads his patient well, follows her unconscious themes, and is thor-

oughly engaged with her, but her positive and negative reactions in the transference to him go largely uninterpreted. I said that I had agreed with Harry's
intention to let the transference develop in the displacement, but that I also told
him repeatedly that it needs to be gathered and interpreted in terms of the therapeutic relationship.

My faculty colleagues supported that idea, and asked me what happens
when I explain this to Harry. I told them he argues that Gladys will feel anger
and shame if he comments because she experiences interpretation as a criticism
of what she is not doing or has not seen. She thinks she should do everything for
herself. She feels she cannot ask for her needs to be met because she doesn't
want to be a burden. He calls this her omnipotent streak, and he feels that he
must leave it alone, or she will be ashamed and angry, and will lose her empathic connection with him. One faculty member thought that, like Gladys,
Harry must feel he has to do everything himself. My colleagues wanted to know
how Harry responds to my offer of help and how I feel when I suggest a more
assertive or even a direct comment for Harry to make. I told them Harry counters
that the patient clams up or says "Yes, but."

Theoretically Harry wants to work on changing, but he has a well-argued
reason not to, based on his awareness of the patient's shame and his exaggerated
sensitivity to the possibility of inflicting the sense of shame on her. In contrast to
Harry, I feel as if I'm too direct. I remind myself that Harry as the therapist is
closer to the situation than I am as the supervisor. I end up thinking that maybe
he's right to avoid a calamity. Instead of seeming hard-hearted, I back off.

I said that Harry says he wants to work on confronting aggressive issues, but doesn't do it, and I end up feeling that it's better to be reticent—which
I don't believe is empathic at all. My colleagues said to me quite directly, "You're
identifying with Harry in being overly responsive to the issue of avoiding shame.
Think over your reasons for that, and then see how it goes with Harry."

This approach made sense, but when I was with Harry listening to his
next session with Gladys, I found myself behaving like him again. Now I was
the one who wanted to say, "Yes, but!"

> Harry reported a session in which Gladys had been mostly wordless.
> He said to me, "Gladys's body was straining as if she was trying to get
> some sounds out. I said to her, 'You seem to be telling me that words
> or even sounds are not all right to express here.' I was trying to help
> Gladys put her pain in words. Gladys began to hit the couch. When I
> did not object, she hit it harder. She was crying and at the same time
> holding her breath and making some muffled, straining sounds.

"Then Gladys said, 'You make it so hard for me because you don't have the right hard and soft objects.' She was silent for the rest of the session."

Harry did not explore the significance of this striking phrase, "the right hard and soft objects." I noticed it, and then I forgot about it, as he went on to describe the next therapy session:

"Gladys said she couldn't stand how she had been feeling since the last session, and yet she didn't call because she had a male friend staying at her house—not her lover Harry, but her former lover Seamus. Gladys said she was worried about how few sessions remained before my absence, which she assumed was to attend a conference. She expected to feel rejected. She got very quiet for a moment and then released a flood of dreams of falling apart, going places, and being in abandoned buildings. She waited for me to interpret the dreams, and I found it easy to read them. Here's what I said about them. . . ."

Harry felt positive about Gladys releasing affect, about his ease of understanding her dreams, and about her having an improved capacity to take in his interpretations. Indeed, I thought his dream interpretations were on the mark. But he seemed oblivious to the fact that Gladys had felt like falling apart after he had encouraged catharsis and regression, and at a time when he was about to be absent, and so she had gone to Seamus, an object for holding that was the alternative to Harry. By Harry's not pointing out the diffusion of her feelings of neediness into other relationships, this time with Seamus, I thought that he was aggressively colluding with Gladys's tendency to displacement. Harry disagreed with me. He saw his therapeutic task as one of interpreting blocks arising from experience in her family of origins so as to encourage individual expression and release her capacity for relating. He didn't want to confront Gladys with the aggressive aspects of eroticizing and displacing the transference.

I didn't diminish the value to Gladys of this session, but I tried to show Harry that his choices were defusing his working in the transference, which is what he came to me to learn. I felt unable to get through to him.

Again I took my concerns to the faculty meeting. My colleagues picked up on Gladys's complaint that Harry did not have "the right hard and soft objects." This suggested to them that what Gladys needed from Harry was the right combination of hardness and softness. They said that Gladys had found an excellent soft object in Harry, but she needed a hard object to come up against as well—and she had to find it in Harry. Harry also needed a hard object—and he needed to find it in me as his supervisor.

With their support, I went back to Harry with renewed firmness and conviction. I admitted the unhelpfulness of my previous softness and went on to face him with many examples of his avoidance of being the hard object. He said that he mostly agreed with my perceptions, but that it was "hard" to see his avoidance so directly. More determined, he went back to Gladys and helped her to accept him as a therapist who, as he put it, dealt with her straight on.

APPLYING GROUP DYNAMICS IN TEACHING

No one spends more time teaching, learning, and being in groups than a teacher. Teachers, however, are generally unaware of the value of group theory. We rarely go beyond a vague awareness of a mysterious class dynamic. I've been a high school English teacher for nine years, but I became aware of group theory only three years ago when I was team-teaching a teachers' education course, the purpose of which was to enable future teachers to become more reflective about their own learning histories. I was struck by the inability of our teaching team to reflect in any constructive way on the problems in our teaching relationships and to recognize how our conflicts, primarily those about power and authority, were echoed in the class response. I felt frustrated about having neither a language with which to discuss problems in the teaching team nor a framework within which to examine how the team's problems mirrored struggles in the administration and played themselves out among our students. So I looked for readings and conferences devoted to the impact of group dynamics on teaching and learning.

I studied Freud and Bion at conferences using the affective learning model. I read about the use of the affective model and group relations in the classroom and in adolescent development (D. Scharff 1975a,b, D. and J. Scharff 1979). I sought consultation on how to apply the affective learning model to the high school classroom, and I attended A. K. Rice conferences on group relations. At affective learning-based conferences, I explored the conscious and unconscious individual and group processes involved in teaching and learning psychoanalytic theory. In group relations conferences, I joined in the intense experiential exploration of the unconscious workings of groups.

Both conference settings refer to the work of Bion (1961) on groups. I found two of Bion's central ideas useful: that every group has its own character or personality, greater than and different from the sum of its parts, and that every group has both a conscious work group and an unconscious life dominated by subgroupings that he called *basic assumptions*, which can either impede or facilitate the conscious task. Every teacher has experienced Bion's point: each class has a unique character, and there are days when it can't get its work done for mysterious reasons. Another critical concept, introduced by Bion (1961) and elaborated by Leroy Wells (1985), is *the group-as-a whole* phenomenon. According to Wells, individuals often act not just on their own behalf, but on behalf of the group. This is an unconscious process in which the group-as-a-whole colludes in having certain feelings and behavior expressed by particular members so that others can disown corresponding parts of themselves.

With others in my small groups, I tried to understand unconscious dynamics as they unfolded in the temporary institution of the conferences. In the small and large group events, two cornerstones of both conference models, individuals comment on and analyze their personal experience in the here and now. By studying and sharing their experience and learning from others' efforts, they hope for insight. As a member of these groups, I became aware of the tremendous difficulty—but also the possibility—of connecting across difference. I gained an experiential understanding, rather than a purely theoretical one, to support my earlier sense of the power of parallel process. I experienced and examined in depth with others who cared as much as I did how conflicts and patterns operative at one level of the institution are echoed in others. Most important, perhaps, through personal experiences that were painful, exhilarating, and everything in between, I began to hone my ability to recognize the unconscious at work. I began to tease out, for example, when individuals were acting on their own behalf and when they were not. And I began to apply this learning to my work as a teacher.

I had always thought about my students psychologically, but when I attempted to take their individual psychology into account, my job became completely impossible. How could I do this when I faced 135 students every day, each with different psychological needs? Yet how could I not consider psychological factors when I was now more convinced than ever that a child's ability to learn depends largely on what is occurring at the unconscious level? I hoped that my new knowledge of group theory would help me on my return to the classroom.

After my first and second conferences, I felt excited about the possibility of seeing each class anew. At the same time, I felt overwhelmed at the thought of dealing with the enormous complexity that I now knew to exist in the room, whether or not I could see it. My head had been spinning in a conference group of seven members when our sole task had been to study our own small group. How much more complex an understanding of group process would be when dealing with five groups of twenty-seven students every day! In addition, I'd be responsible for teaching academic content, not just learning it, and without any colleagues who shared this interest or knowledge. It would be a lonely business but a thrilling challenge as well.

First, I found that, as a result of my experience at the conferences, I brought to my students a deeper empathy for their experience. Teachers may chastise students for not respecting one another, or criticize their tendency to self-segregate along racial and gender lines. But how can teachers help students move beyond respect as anything more than a buzz word if we ourselves have not faced our own prejudices and our capacity for cruelty? Experiential groups offer teachers a powerful opportunity to own these aspects of themselves and to make a real connection with a person or group that may have been the object of hatred or fear.

Second, I brought the group-as-a-whole perspective. By my third conference, I had absorbed this concept deeply enough in my bones that I had what for me has been a revolutionary insight: my classroom group is not just an aggregate of individuals, each with his or her own personal psychology. Of course it is that, but it is also something more. It is a *group*, an entity all its own.

Thinking of each class as a group entity, I've been able to take the group unconscious into account, and that has enabled me to move forward with the entire group in mind. Teaching subject matter, it is not my primary task to lead the class in studying the group process, except where attention to the dynamics of the teaching and learning process in the class facilitates the students' present and future learning. So, often but not always, my interpretations remain unspoken hypotheses that I arrive at as to how the class is functioning and why. This then helps me design a teaching intervention that frees the class to learn collaboratively so that each member has a fair chance of learning the academic content.

Here is an example. I teach in a large, urban, public school that has a rigorous entrance exam. Students enter in the seventh grade, and, having excelled easily at their old schools, are often terrified when they find themselves among a group of students who are equally achieving. Suddenly, many feel stupid and afraid. At the end of the first week of school last year, I began a poetry unit with my seventh graders by handing out copies of the previous year's seventh-grade literary magazine. I asked each child to pick a favorite or a least favorite poem and to write about why he or she made this selection. Then I asked the students to form into groups of four, read each poem aloud, choose one poem according to their own criteria, and select a representative to read it to the re-convened class. The plan was to see whether there were commonalities in what they liked and didn't like so as to generate ideas about what makes a good poem.

On this particular day, I noticed that although every child spoke in the small group, the six children who read as representatives of their groups were all white. This was striking, particularly because the class was almost half Asian. (There were no black or Hispanic students in the class, which was indicative of a larger, systemic problem that I will not get into here.) Before learning about group process from personal experience at conferences, I would have understood this situation to be a result of cultural norms, individual personalities, and coincidence. With group relations heavily on my mind and increasingly under my skin, I saw a group-as-a-whole phenomenon unfold before my eyes. This time I had a language and a framework that helped me organize the experience in a new way.

I realized that, as a group, all of the students had a vested interest in having the white students speak for the class. In permitting them to continue, I had unconsciously colluded in creating this dynamic. In a group relations conference, this interpretation would have been spoken, so that if it rang true, participants could have reclaimed the part of themselves they had let others carry. But in the group relations conference context, the participants would have signed on for that type of learning, and so the group leaders would have felt authorized to address these issues from the beginning. What I might have done in the classroom setting would have been to share my observation, hoping that pointing out the imbalance would invite children who had been silent to speak up. This didn't seem appropriate because I didn't have a relationship with the new class that would allow me to articulate this, not to seventh graders during their first week in a new school. If I were to state my observation, it would be strange to them, and it would not be effective in helping them accommodate to the new community or in facilitating their learning, certainly not in the time we had available, and particularly not with a population so deeply committed to meritocracy.

If I were to make my observation explicit with children of this age at this early point in the year, it would be heard as criticism by all. White students would feel attacked and accused of doing something wrong. Asian students, some of whom were already sensing enormous cultural barriers, would feel exposed. Once a secure student–teacher relationship had become established, teaching the class directly about group dynamics could certainly be an aspect of my work with them if I thought it would facilitate the learning. At this point in the term, however, I simply wanted to *do* something to change the dynamic quickly before it established itself as the norm. So I made an intervention based on my unspoken observation.

The next day I brought in "Father," a poem by Fay Chiang (1979), a Chinese-American writer. The poem is a beautiful description of the author's father guiding her "young hand" as she holds a bamboo brush and learns to write her name in Chinese characters. Certain phrases in the poem refer to the meanings of the separate parts of the characters that make up her name: "Green, heart, three dots of water, woods." When I asked the questions I felt were necessary for us (me included) to understand this poem, the Asian students, many of whom had knowledge of Chinese characters, became our experts. Their hands sailed into the air. One usually quiet boy came to the board to write his Chinese name for us, and to explain how characters are constructed. Once we had this information, we could discuss the universal issues raised by the poem: memories of fathers, what it's like being raised in a country with a language different from one's parents', the importance of our names. Throughout the discussion I noticed that many who had been silent the day before seemed to feel welcomed into the conversation in a qualitatively different way.

I think of that moment when white students spoke for the class as a coming together of many factors. White students may have felt more authorized than non-white students due to a perceived affiliation with me, their white teacher, especially if I seemed to be more comfortable with their thoughts, their culture, and their experiences, those being familiar to me and maybe actually like mine. The likelihood of my being viewed as more able to relate to white culture was exacerbated by the fact that the faculty and administration of my school are predominantly white. And beyond that, the culture of the school is consistent with that of many white, middle-class, educated households.

My school and the city it serves value speed and assertiveness, unlike many Asian communities that value politeness and reserve. Admittedly, most Asian parents who choose to send their children to this highly competitive school want them to fit in to its academic culture, but there is still a conflict between values at school and values of the local community. Many students whose home culture is apparently different from my own and from the predominant culture of the school are searching for inroads toward fitting in. Students might assume that I, who represent the school's standards, endorse this fast-paced, competitive culture. On the contrary. I'm searching for ways to make equal room for all cultures, to encourage students to slow down and savor the value of working together and building a learning community.

What I've described refers to one moment in one day in the ongoing life of a class. It would be a gross simplification to say, based on what I learned that day, that the most useful way for me to think about these students generally was along racial lines, or even to make the generalization that Asians were the more silent members of the class. As the year progressed there were shy students who were white and outspoken students who were Asian. My point is that at that moment in the life of our class, the group-as-a-whole lens clarified the situation and shaped my course of action that leveled the playing field and allowed all students to be more fully present.

Prior to learning about the group dynamics of teaching and learning, I might have responded to a similar situation in a similar way, but the thinking process getting me to that place would have been different. I would have viewed the situation from a theoretical perspective, emphasizing individual agency and responsibility. In doing so I would have played into my students' sense that they as individuals are entirely responsible for their own destinies and that they make their choices freely. I know now that the reality is infinitely more complex.

I still struggle with how best to incorporate group theory into my teaching, especially with the question of how much should be stated explicitly to students and when. The work is sometimes so mystifying and confusing that I am eager for colleagues in education with whom to share ideas. Many of them are interested, but not yet well informed. So far, however, most of my fellow students have been therapists whose primary task is different than mine. My task is education; the therapist's task is healing. Yet both of us are working on making the unconscious conscious when it furthers our separate tasks, and both of us have to use tact and timing in choosing the right moment and method for intervening. Because my concern with development overlaps with theirs, I'm comfortable for now learning psychoanalytic theory, child development, and group process among therapists. But I'm on my own when it comes to application in the educational setting.

In addition to using my knowledge of group process in the classroom, I'd like to integrate here-and-now group experiences into teacher education programs. Would many teachers want such training? I wonder. If they were to realize its benefits, as I've done, my feeling is that many would.

UNDERSTANDING CULTURAL PRESSURES ON WOMEN

I come from a country on the Pacific rim where there is a dearth of training in object relations theory and therapy. Cognitive therapy was recommended as a substitute by my professor, but I found it boring and not as useful to me as object relations in my research on depression in married women. So I've had to study object relations without a teacher. I'm writing my dissertation on the interaction of housewives' depression with marital conflict and its treatment by a psychotherapeutic approach based on object relations. Only a few books on object relations are available and those are in English, and so I've been translating object relations theory papers into my language on my note-book computer to share with fellow students, but I feel the need to learn more with others who can discuss it knowledgeably with me. One day I happened to read the chapter on psychoanalytic marital therapy in the *Clinical Handbook of Couple Therapy* (J. Scharff 1995), and it was like a beacon in the misty sea to me. Following the beacon, I traveled many miles to the United States to attend a week-long institute on object relations couple therapy to give me more ideas for completing my thesis.

On the first day, I found I had more trouble understanding spoken English than I had expected. In addition I was jet-lagged. I could only follow the lecturers by reading up on the topics ahead of time or reading while they spoke. In the small group I had a hard time participating in the discussion. It was stressful for me, going from the lecture setting to the small group. I experienced quite a culture shift. I needed time to settle in and follow the conversation. I wasn't sure I understood everything that was being said, but I had no trouble understanding what the participants were feeling.

On the second day, the group members noticed that I wasn't saying much and they asked me how I was doing. I said that I was just listening. I was quiet because I needed a time for transition from the world of the seminar to the world of the small group room, from outside to inside, before I could say what I was thinking. I didn't tell them that I felt helpless, as if trying to crack a giant rock with an egg.

A woman looked at me impatiently. She insisted that she should be able to speak without waiting for me or anyone else to cross the transition. Then she said angrily that she had to wait so long that she had forgotten what it was she meant to say. Some other woman spoke about needing time to adjust, the same thing I was feeling. She was afraid of being judged for what she said and afraid of making people angry. The first woman immediately said that that is the very thing she was going to say. I felt relieved. Everyone nodded sympathetically and I realized that we had the same fears and feelings and that we could express them as part of our work in the group.

I suddenly felt terribly overwhelmed with feeling I couldn't find the words to describe. I didn't want anyone to see. I hid in the bathroom, and I must have stayed there a long time. The group leader knocked on the door. I came out with my hands over my eyes. I couldn't stop sobbing, and I curled up on one end of a couch like a baby. Another foreign student, a kind man who felt sympathy for me, sat beside me and comforted me, and I was gradually able to find some words for my distress.

I explained to the group that I had felt upset to receive understanding. I could never have told my family, or even my husband—even though he is kind and gentle, more than most husbands—anything and everything I feel, as I and everyone else in the group was allowed to do. A woman in my country is not supposed to show anger, ambivalence, or ambition. She is expected to compete in the areas of beauty and marriage, studying only in night school. Because of this suppression of women's feelings and strivings, there's a lot of marital conflict that can't be expressed. My research finds that this leads to depression in women, the housewife's tragedy. I could hardly believe it when women in this small group were making complaints and talking about their needs without feeling ashamed of themselves. I wished I could have stayed for more learning from experience like this, but I had to go home again, back to reading and using what I'd learned that week. I felt sad about going home to my culture. My tears fell like rain on dry leaves.

Oriental society depends on the stability of the family system. To maintain a strong family bond, there are many cultural traditions, expectations, and rules, all of which both support and suppress the individual. In Hyo thought, respect and obedience toward parents is absolute, anger toward them is strictly forbidden, and endurance of repression is a virtue in women. Filial piety is automatic. Children must respect their ancestors and are absolutely forbidden to disobey or even oppose their parents. In the past, when our society was totally patriarchal, a woman married into her husband's family. She lived in his family house and belonged to his family, where three or four generations might be living together. She had no authority. In fact, according to the proverb, the new bride should be deaf for three years and dumb for three years. Male and female roles were clearly separate: the man took care of the financial needs of the family and the wife took care of the children. Most couples didn't sleep separately from their babies at night until after the birth of the second child, or the husband slept apart from his wife so that she could take care of and sleep with the baby. This father-husband absence was the conventional virtue. At the same time preference was shown toward the son.

While the history of the ancestors flows away like a river, the waters re-circulate and continue to influence the next generation near the banks of the river. There is still a relative lack of contextual holding by the father, which leaves the mother distressed and drives her closer to her child. It also means that there is a prolonged period of symbiosis, especially for the boy as the future head of the family, and the idea of son-preference is still firmly rooted. This child-rearing practice means that it is difficult for the parents to re-establish a good sexual relationship, and I think that this may be what drives husbands to extramarital affairs, as if the old social convention of permitting one husband multiple wives were still in place.

The young woman desperately devotes herself to her child, especially her son, which is exactly what her mother-in-law does with her own son even though he is now an adult, a husband, and a father. The three of them are entangled in a jealous triangle. The mother-in-law acts as if the young woman is like a second wife, depriving her of her son. The son is still caught up with his mother, and his wife is caught up with her too. The young wife feels more like a daughter-in-law than a wife, and she gets depressed. The daughter-in-law who follows the proverbial advice to remain blind and dumb while suffering this painful situation in her youth is the one who becomes a notorious mother-in-law in later years when she can endure no more. The cycle continues and results in mother-in-law and daughter-in-law conflict, marital conflict, and female depression, except that nowadays some young women do not agree to suppress their aggression and, not knowing how to deal with their feelings, run to divorce.

I became interested in object relations theory, because it deals with the influence of the mother–child relationship on the development of the Oedipus complex and on future couple relationships. Here's how it helps me think of what is happening in the Asian marriage where the wife gets depressed. The mother-in-law projects her exciting object into her son and her rejecting object into her daughter-in-law, who is depriving her of her son. The husband projects his exciting ego into his mother and his rejecting ego into his wife, who is fighting with his beloved mother and who is too preoccupied with the children. So the wife has a double projection of rejecting objects into her. She may then amplify the rejecting system by projecting her rejecting objects into her inattentive husband and her possessive mother-in-law, and her exciting objects into her children. Filled with bad objects, the wife gets depressed. When the projections are intense, she has a major depression.

I see this projective identification system as the mechanism causing *Hwa-byung*, also called housewife depression, a syndrome that affects middle-aged Asian women, especially Korean and Japanese women. Hwa-byung is described in Appendix 1 of the *DSM-IV* as a culture-bound syndrome caused by the suppression of anger. *Hwa* means fire and is a good word for the slow-burning rage and suddenly spurting anger that women are not supposed to express. These feelings, however, are fueled by the rejecting objects that they have introjected into themselves without a word of complaint, but which they nevertheless protest with symptoms of depression, panic, pain, and fears of impending death.

I am surprised but grateful to find that Oriental culture can be understood in terms of Western object relations theory. Fairbairn's (1952) models of object relations have given me a way of thinking about Hwa-byung, depression, marital conflict, and the triangular system of object relationships involving the wife, her mother-in-law, and the husband/son. Winnicott (1965) convinced me that a ruthless relation to the breast—unimaginable according to traditional Oriental values of filial piety—is nevertheless essential to establishing the child's capacity to apprehend and use the external world. Dicks's (1967) concept of unconscious fit in marriage is helping me understand that paradox of the couple relationship in which the same projective identificatory system that drives the attraction of the courtship period is the source of conflict in the marriage, and then shows up in the wife's symptoms of depression. Klein's (1946, 1952, 1975) descriptions of phantasy in the internal world convey the woman's view of the Oedipus complex, and her concept of envy is relevant to understanding the wife's depression in dealing with a husband who remains first and foremost a son, and a mother-in-law who prefers her son over his wife. For me, reading Scharff and Scharff (1991) about the process of family therapy and seeing a couple's transferences in the children's play was breathtaking, like looking into the Grand Canyon. I could see to where the cupid's arrow flies and I could feel what it longs for.

When I returned home, everything was good and I felt happy. Maybe I couldn't understand much at the institute, but I could feel a lot. Now I would like to tell you how I felt about the institute and why I went there.

At the institute there are many trees. In my childhood, there were many trees—not fresh and green, but cut for human needs. My childhood home was a wood factory with many workmen and many machines. In order not to be swept into the chaos, I used to keep to my room. Many things were forbidden to me in my family, in my school, in society, the same for me as for my friends. So my room was my safety, my shelter, my happiness. There, through my imagination, I could fly anywhere. Sometimes I climbed up to the roof where I looked over the wall of the Catholic church at a nun who lived with others, but who was alone. Sometimes I sat behind the house, near the kitchen, listening to my mother rustle the dishes. This gave me a peaceful feeling but I never imagined a future for me in the kitchen.

Married to a warm and permissive husband, I was happy, but all was not well with my inner life. I was then able to face the kernel of unhappiness. One day I felt as if I were sitting on the riverside. Not in the river, but on the riverside. Not swimming in the river, but on the riverside. I could never, never take off into the river. I thought of the saying, "The river is the mother of nature, the breast of nature." I wanted to approach the river, but I could not do it because of anxiety. I desperately denied the unconscious truth of my object relationships, because of loyalty to my mother, who consciously devoted herself to us, like any other mother of our culture. I am used to being alone, but I want and need others.

At the institute I revisited my paranoid-schizoid and depressive positions as I struggled to overcome my deafness and dumbness in the strange situation of the affective learning small group. Once I finish my Ph. D., I'll return to learn more about object relations to help women in my culture. This was my first long journey, my first time to leave my country, and my first adventure free as the wind, free as the butterfly.

Object relations may become my life-long task. This is just the beginning.

2
The Affective Learning Model

THE AFFECTIVE LEARNING MODEL

The affective learning model is a teaching and learning method for psychotherapists and psychoanalysts who want to learn object relations theory. In this model, object relations theory of the individual and the group is both the subject being taught and the medium for teaching and learning it. Therapists who come to learn about the theory in terms of self and other also teach themselves and others while learning with them. The teacher learns and the learner teaches as they engage in role in the learning process. The affective learning model is built on a few key concepts:

- Affects are the motivating and integrating engine of self-object organization at all levels—in the mind, in the neuropsychological functioning of the brain, in relationships, and in groups.
- The internal relationship of self and object is the basic unit of the structure and functioning of the psyche as the organizer of external relationships.
- Individual psyches communicate with others through unconscious processes of projective and introjective identification.
- Unconscious processes lead individuals to combine spontaneously with others to form subgroups that express shared unconscious concerns.
- Following the affective landmarks of subgroupings and learning from the experience is more effective than cognition alone in arriving at understanding.
- The processes of learning in the group provide illustrations of the psychoanalytic concepts that are being learned.

The Site for the Affective Learning of Psychotherapy

At the International Institute of Object Relations Therapy, we have created a site in which to develop the affective learning model, an alternative to the way psychoanalytic theory and therapy are generally taught. This has been possible only because of freedoms and conditions that we have allowed ourselves. For example, we are inclusive rather than exclusive. We do not try to preselect our applicants or postselect our membership because we do not try to evaluate standards of competence. We are not trying to teach or certify analysts exclusively. Our students are not analytic candidates but rather psychotherapists and analysts who want to know more about psychoanalysis in the object relations tradition. We are not trying to maintain an elite, and we have nothing to lose. This leaves us free to develop an alternative model of teaching and learning psychoanalytic theory and the practice of psychoanalytic psychotherapy.

THE EDUCATIONAL PROGRAM
FOR AFFECTIVE LEARNING

The Design of the Program

The two-year program of instruction takes place in a modular immersion format consisting of two week-long immersions in a basic curriculum of theory and eight three-day weekends of presentations at the leading edge of the development of theory. The first week-long immersion in basic curriculum covers the object relations theories. In the second year, the week-long immersion deals with infant research, infant observation, and their links to countertransference. The curriculum of the four weekends in each of the two years is not fixed but features new ideas in object relations and other contemporary psychoanalytic theories. The method of instruction includes lecture, video, case presentation, and large- and small-group discussion. There are also optional electives: An additional weekend or week-long conference is usually offered with a cosponsor in another city or country, and a week-long institute on psychoanalysis applied to couple and family therapy is given annually. For students who enroll in the two-yeaar program to learn theory, there is no requirement for treatment or supervision, although some participants elect to have both.

For students who want more clinical training in psychotherapy, we have extended the two-year core program by an advanced program of two additional years of attendance at weekend conferences or at study groups organized by faculty in their home cities or convened by conference call or video link. Students enrolled in this clinical application program are required to have individual and group supervision in person or by telephone with a faculty member. Treatment is also a requisite for those in the advanced clinical program, but it may be undertaken with any analytically oriented analyst or therapist, usually not a member of the faculty. This policy on treatment arose because many of our students commute from afar, but it has the additional advantage that treatment remains a private matter untrammeled by institutional politics, and education is not complicated by intense transferences to the training analyst or therapist. We do not require completed cases because we do not judge the therapist's competence by the patient's goals. Instead, the supervisor rates the student's therapeutic skills on a standard scale in terms of twenty-one items. We also ensure that the supervision component is equally specifically evaluated by the supervisee. Supervision dilemmas are discussed at a supervision meeting by all supervisors and faculty members who have worked with the student. In this setting, each student's supervisory experience is related to learning behaviors throughout the program.

With no major revisions to the basic model over the years, but with frequent minor adjustments, the model has worn well. Students report a high degree of satisfaction with it, although it has to be noted at the outset that it is not for everyone, only for those who have a sustained commitment to learning from experience, a tolerance for intense affective engagement, and a capacity for personal openness as they review the information presented, their personal present experience and its resonance with the past, their professional clinical experience, and their here-and-now involvement in personal and group processes.

The Philosophy of the Model

We make our teaching contract with the individual. Each is responsible for his or her individual learning. We present the concepts in a range of formats so that students have a better chance of relating to the material and learning it in their own style. Individual needs for learning, anxieties about learning, and defenses against learning in the various formats then become as much the subject of study as the material being presented. But the individual learns in the large-group setting—in a lecture, in the median-size group of a week-long institute, and in the small group that meets for discussion at a more intimate level. We find that the concepts being studied affect the person and the group, so that the concept gets illustrated in the behavior of the group. This allows for far greater understanding than the purely cognitive reception of material and so greatly enhances the applicability of theory to the therapy practice of the individual therapist. We believe that all important learning occurs in the environment of the relationships each individual has: external, current relationships to teachers, parents, peers, and children and internal object relations that represent the record of past such relationships. The new findings from neuroscience about early development and infant research on attachment patterns not only support the concepts of object relations theory but also point to the value of the affective model for teaching and learning that we are describing.

It is not enough to provide lectures and readings about the affective core of psychic structure. When teaching about internalization, for instance, we need a setting in which internalization can occur, not merely to understand the concept of internalization intellectually but to learn it from experience as well. Reading and listening provide a cognitive map, which, without an emotional experience, can only be logically convincing at best. It will lack depth and resonance. Even though some students like theory and can relate well to the philosophical logic and internal consistency of a theoretical system, none of them gets a complete understanding from reading and listening or even from discussion alone. All students need a personal experience of encountering phenomena to which theory can only refer. This gives affective credibility to concepts that then become more digestible and comprehensible. To accomplish this, the learning has to occur in an intellectual climate that has affective resonance with what is being taught.

We learn *about* relationships through being *in* relationships to study. We learn how to be civilized human beings by living in relation to important individuals and groups. And from that life experience, we build a system of internal object relationships. So, if we are trying to learn about self and other in the external world; ego, affect, and object in the internal world; and how the two worlds are interrelated, we will learn most efficiently and thoroughly from studying the relation of self and other as we experience it individually and in groups. The experience of *individuals studied in groups* and the experience of *groups studied by individuals* gives here-and-now evidence for the validity of concepts of self and other, ego and object. The group itself is a practical application of the theory to be taught.

The group affective model rests on a planned mixture of learning vehicles and formats to provide for as many channels and types of group learning situations as possible. But what distinuishes the group affective learning model is less the mixture of modalities than the focus on learning from experience with others in a group setting. We keep an eye on the nature of relationships that underlie and illuminate the learning process in the lecture, the small group, or individual supervision. The program is designed to offer a range of teaching relationships with different tasks which, however, have some degree of overlap: lectures, including dialogue between guest experts, faculty, and students; large-group workshops; midsize unstructured group plenaries; and small-group meetings for intensive work on integration. Plenaries and small groups especially link the intellectual to the affective in the experience of individual students as they learn, and of faculty members as they teach, the theory and practice of object relations.

Contrast with Traditional Psychoanalytic Education

In the traditional model for psychoanalytic or psychotherapy training, an individual training analysis, or personal analytic therapy, is supposed to provide the affective resonance for the individual. But how these confidential treatments are tied to learning the theory (and even to learning technique) is unclear. It is usually taken as a matter of faith that once analysts are accredited as training analysts, the conduct of their analyses of candidates can be left outside the educational review and evaluation process (J. S. Scharff and D. E. Scharff 1999a,b, 2000).

Successful self-analysis of one's own dreams *was* the qualification for becoming an analyst in the early years of psychoanalysis. Later, therapeutic analysis with an established analyst *was* the training. According to Falzeder (1999), it was Jung who first recommended that a formal training analysis be required of every new analyst. Incidentally, René Spitz and Emil Oberholzer preceded Jones in being the first to seek training analysis before it was a requirement—Spitz in 1911 with Jung and Oberholzer in 1912 with Freud (Falzeder 1999). Acknowledging the merit of the training analysis, Freud endorsed Jung's recommendation as an educational principle, and it has been followed ever since.

Over the years, there was debate about the amount of teaching that should occur during the training analysis. The consensus is now that a training analysis should be therapeutic rather than didactic. Gradually, training was delegated to institute committees, with varying amounts of feedback from the training analysts about the suitability and readiness of their analysands for the profession. Over time, many trainees resented the interference of this feedback, and a number of training analysts became uncomfortable with reporting on educational progress from the perspective of a clinical situation of trust (Arlow 1972). A literature grew up concerning the difficulty, and perhaps impossibility, of getting or giving a valid analysis under the constraint of divided loyalties between the clinical needs of the analysis and the standards of the training institute (Lifschutz 1976). While it is essential that confidentiality be maintained, the overvaluing of the role of training analyst is demeaning to the educational task of the training institution. The closed nature of the work of the training analysis engenders an atmosphere of paranoia there (Kernberg 1986).

In many places, the feedback from the analyst was attenuated or ended, but if it was not, it continued to be a source of frequent bitterness and debate. Even where reporting ended, unoffical communications through look and gesture during meetings or informal discussions could take its place. When this occurred, it created an atmosphere of suspicion among those not privy to what was being inferred. The training analysts as a group with special analyst/candidate pairings not open to process and review became the in-group, who represented the real analytic work, while the teachers and the seminar program became devalued and excluded, like an oedipal child from the parents' sexual life (Dorey, quoted in Kernberg 1986). As the training analysis became separated from the formal educational process, nothing arose to replace the concept of an integrated personal and professional experience where affective and intellectual experience was shared by teachers and trainees, except in supervision, which, like analysis itself, remained hidden.

The traditional Eitingon (1923) model was introduced at the psychoanalytic institute in Berlin which Eitingon founded and where he was the only supervising analyst. The Eitingon model spread from Berlin to dominate psychoanalytic education. It consists of three components: training analysis, supervision of control cases, and theoretical seminars and clinical conferences. It is also characterized by careful preselection of candidates, a restricted pool of authorized training analysts, and a standard, required, conservative curriculum through which candidates proceed year by year. According to Falzeder (1999), the model arose as a defensive reaction against the countless boundary violations and confused, affect-laden role relationships that were prevalent in the first years of psychoanalysis. Useful modifications over the years included the introduction of elective courses, contemporary psychoanalytic theories, democratic selection of training analysts, and the cessation of feedback from the training analyst regarding the analysand's progress. Nevertheless, according to Bernfeld (1962), the Eitingon model is inherently destructive and leads to regression and infantilization of candidates.

The French-speaking societies developed an alternative model. According to Kernberg (1998), the French model is the major alternative to the Eitingon model at this time. The French model gives the candidate more autonomy and control over the selection of the analyst, there being no designated training analysts and no required curriculum. Various ongoing seminars feature institute faculty and society members working together. The candidate participates in whichever seem most interesting, and there is no evaluation of performance or progress. This model has the advantage of conferring freedom in intellectual decision making and spurring innovative, collaborative thinking, but it has drawbacks as well. The candidates may not feel infantilized, but on the other hand they may feel adrift. Not that there is no evaluation at all, but it comes in the form of feedback from the supervisor who then becomes as powerful a figure as the training analyst. The supervision style is to work with parallel process, in which experiences in the supervisory relationship are addressed as reflections of the transference and countertransference. Final selection for membership occurs at the end point of training. This end-stage selection process generates anxiety and creates wastage.

In a seminal article on psychoanalytic education, Arlow (1972) noted that despite advances in psychoanalytic thinking since Freud, the organization and content of the training program remained largely unchanged because of a tendency to cling to the past. He held that transmitting knowledge cannot be achieved by cognitive teaching alone and that identification with models of working is important and central in educational programs. Because of the charismatic position of training analysts in the educational system, however, candidates identify with them as heroic figures, and conservatism or rebellion develops rather than mutual respect. Identification with heroic figures based on unanalyzed idealization and fantasies of family romance infuse the training program with a mythology that unfortunately leads to a ritualization of the training program and prevents innovation.

Arlow pointed to the need for standards and quality control to be issued by institutes and committees of the American Psychoanalytic Association. Focusing on the training analysts, he advised that they be aware of the mythology operating at the institutional level and revealed in the candidates' unconscious fantasies. In this way he hoped to control the negative effects of unanalyzed social unconscious processes on the primary task.

Kernberg (1986) also addressed the issue of problems in psychoanalytic education. He noted symptoms of malaise in psychoanalytic institutes, including feelings of paranoia, irrational idealization of senior colleagues, and inhibition of independent thinking. He pointed to a number of underlying problems, among them the exclusion of psychoanalytic teachers who are not training analysts from the center of information, devaluation of the educational task, lack of objectivity due to political influence affecting assessment of clinical competence and readiness for promotion, and the substitution of power for sapiential authority. He pointed to the separation of the training analysis task from the educational task of the psychoanalytic institute as necessary for preserving confidentiality but inimical to developing a shared commitment to the primary task of training analysis. Kernberg's proposals for remedy included improving the conceptualization of the primary task, creating better organizational structures, and, most important, ensuring open process and review of the clinical work of teachers and training analysts as well as of candidates. This last provision addresses the need to defuse the hidden impact of the training analyst and the closed hierarchical system.

The Training Model in Allied Professions

As the training analysis became separated from the formal educational process, nothing arose to replace the concept of an integrated personal and professional experience where affective and intellectual experience was shared by teacher and trainee. The only place such an experience occurred was in the allied, but also very different and vastly separate, worlds of group and family therapy training, where training groups were part of the course. In the 1960s and 1970s, experience in the sociotherapeutic communities expanded the use of such groups not only in training but also in management. These became places where shared experiences could be learned from and staff differences understood (Jones 1952). The encounter group movement gave further fuel to this fire, but it did not touch the analytic communities, which regarded with suspicion, with some justification, the "let-it-all-hang-out" approach. Distrust and disapproval of the regressive aspects of that group process may be why the analytic community largely overlooked the more rigorous group analytic model developed in Great Britain by S. H. Foulkes (1964), spawning a group therapy model (Pines 1979), and by W. R. Bion (1961, 1962), leading to the "Tavistock" group relations training in relation to leadership and authority, developed by A. K. Rice (1965) and colleagues in Great Britain and spread by Margaret Rioch (1970a,b) and colleagues in the United States.

The Call for Innovative Models

Recently, Kernberg (1998) reviewed the Eitingon and French models of training and their modifications and concluded that neither one was free of regressive, authoritarian, and infantilizing features. He does not imagine that there is such a thing as an ideal model, but he thinks that the flaws in the existing models are such that there should be experimentation with alternative models more likely to generate new psychoanalytic knowledge. He called for the development of innovative models of training that "provide an intensity of experiential as well as academic learning" (p. 28) and that "provide an atmosphere of excitement and freedom" (p. 32). Kernberg (1986) pointed to ignorance of organizational structure and group dynamics as a source of misery and paranoia found in training institutions where the various parts operate in a vacuum. Given that psychoanalytic training relies heavily on Freud's canon, it is not surprising that there is ignorance and avoidance of group dynamics when Freud (1921) left only one article on group psychology and one that gives a fearful appraisal of the power of the group to constrain the autonomy or fuel the aggression of the individual. Kernberg (1986) realized that the "exploration of the dynamic unconscious carried out in multiple therapeutic analyses within a social organization increase the regressive potential of group processes" (p. 815). His point was that analysts should recognize this problem, learn about the impact of group processes, develop more open organizational structures, and experiment with new models of psychoanalytic education. We agree wholeheartedly.

Taking this idea a step further, we think that a training organization needs to harness the group processes and learn from the regressive potential instead of trying to avoid it, which only makes it more destructive. From studying the group process that is stimulated while learning analytic concepts, we have arrived at a new model. This model relies on individual and group analytic theory presented for intellectual discussion, affective response by the individual and the group, reflection, integration, and clinical application. We call it *affective learning*.

Background for the Development of the Model

Early in our careers, we each experienced as members and consultants the Bion-Rice "Tavistock" model, which focuses on the experience of leadership and authority. While at the Tavistock Institute of Human Relations from 1972 to 1974 conducting research with secondary school students and teachers, we adapted the Tavistock model to give school-leaving students and teachers a group learning experience focused on the object relations of growth and development (Savege 1974a,b, D. E. Scharff 1975a,b, 1980, Scharff and Hill 1976). In the mid-1970s in Washington, DC, we tried out a conference model with high school and college teachers and students focused on the object relations of teaching and learning (D. E. Scharff and J. S. Scharff, 1979; reprinted as Appendix 1). As our interest moved toward the training of psychotherapists and especially toward students in object relations family therapy, we modified our model again to fit the needs of this group. In 1988, we applied the model to the training of students in individual object relations psychotherapy. Since then we have been refining it into its present form as the affective learning model.

The new affective learning model developed from an amalgam of experience with individual psychoanalysis, psychoanalytic groups, psychotherapy groups, couple and family therapy groups, psychoanalytic reading seminars, study groups, work groups, school consultation groups, and groups for the study of authority and leadership. Working in all these areas, it became obvious that there is interaction, complementarity, and continuity between the individual and the system: Group concepts of psychological space, defensive patterns, and shifts in levels of functioning within the group matrix resonate with the individual therapist's familiar ways of understanding the individual's inner world, defenses, and shifts from paranoid-schizoid to depressive position functioning (Ashbach and Schermer 1987). Affective learning in groups brings together psychoanalytic theories of the individual influenced by object relations theory and psychoanalytic theories of the group influenced by systems theory to create an educational methodology that is consonant with the subjects being taught. The major theory bases come from individual object relations theory and group analytic theory, augmented by contemporary research on affect and brain development.

   The resulting affective learning model is a unique integration of psychoanalytic theories of the individual influenced by object relations theory (Fairbairn 1952, Klein 1946, Winnicott 1965), research on affect and brain development (Schore 1994), psychoanalytic theories of organizations influenced by general systems theory (Bertalanffy 1950, Jacques 1955, Menzies 1960, Miller and Rice 1967), theories of group therapy (Foulkes 1948, 1974, Foulkes and Anthony 1957, Pines 1979, Yalom 1970), group psychoanalysis (Ezriel 1950, 1952, Wolf and Schwartz 1962), group consultation (Bion 1961, 1962), schools research (Salzberger-Wittenberg et al. 1983, Savege 1974a,b, D. E. Scharff 1975a,b, 1980, Scharff and Hill 1976, D. E. Scharff and J. S. Scharff 1979), community psychiatry (Jones 1952, Savege 1973), and chaos theory (Gleick 1987).

Learning from Experience in the Group

   The group size for teaching and learning using the affective model varies from small groups of five to ten members and median groups of fifteen to twenty to large groups of thirty to a hundred. The median group of twenty to thirty people has a distinctly different set of functions and organization than the small group of five to ten, the fairly large group of forty to a hundred, and the very large group of a few hundred members. The small group tends to reflect needs for affiliation and dependency, while the median group draws out fears of isolation, and the really large group induces fears of merger or chaos. The individual is driven to relate in the small group by love, while in the median and large groups the connection is made through hate. The small group tends to reflect family and peer experiences, the median group echoes experience in institutions, and the large group represents the wider culture. The task in the small group focuses on the *affective* understanding of the intellectual exchange. In contrast, in the larger groups, *intellectual* formulation of the affective exchanges is the focus and the link to institutional and cultural experience.

The Large Group

The combined membership of faculty and students meets for lectures, workshops, clinical case presentations, and discussion in the large group. Compared to the groups of 500 that convene to explore large-group dynamics in group therapy association meetings, our groups can hardly qualify as large in a technical sense. Our conference membership is usually a smallish large group of forty to a hundred members, but we use the term *large group* to distinguish it from the small groups.

The large group exists in two forms in the program, depending on the affective learning model. The first form is the workshop group of approximately forty to a hundred members listening to lectures and participating in workshops in a cathedral or classroom seating format. Faculty, seated among the group, take turns with students to contribute. Discussion comes from the floor, as members contribute their thoughts, perhaps in response to one another or, more usually, in response to the presenter. Here we encourage a groupwide conversation, but that does not always occur.

There is a second, occasional arrangement occurring perhaps one weekend in ten. On this weekend, the task is the study of object relations applied to group therapy and institutional consultation. The large group meets in a special arrangement specifically for the study of large-group process. The group meets in three or more concentric circles to highlight issues that arise when members are unable to see everyone or be seen. This replicates the experience of being in a large group of more than 100 people in which dynamics of fusion, massification, aggregation, and chaos are likely to emerge. The group meets a few times in this way during the weekend to study the application of object relations theory to group dynamics.

The Median Group

In the group therapy literature, de Maré and colleagues (1991) described a twenty- to thirty-member group as a median group, an intermediate structure whose function has been explored only in the last twenty years. The group in the summer institutes and in the weekend plenary review meetings is usually of median size. Two examples from the median group, one from a summer institute and one from a weekend conference, are given in Chapters 18 and 20.

For the plenary review meeting, the large group often splits into two groups, one consisting of two-year program participants and the other consisting of weekend-only participants. The two plenaries are usually the size of median groups, in each of which students and faculty are sitting together in a circle facing each other or students are together facing faculty. Sometimes the choice of seating arrangement is determined by the limitations of the room in which the meeting is held, but in general we like to include both options over the course of a year. The circle is most conducive to thinking together in a collaborative, egalitarian way. The student group facing the faculty in a row is more able to get in touch with envy, criticism, and rebellious attitudes to authority.

In the plenary, the task includes airing of problems to be solved and issues to be understood. The group raises administrative problems and programmatic criticisms and suggestions while thinking about the experience that has led to these comments. A free-form dialogue, which is the large-group counterpart of free association, moves the group toward the understanding of the median group and the institutional experience. The task is multilayered and complex. Students, teachers, and administration are on the same footing from the standpoint of contributing to dialogue and meaning, a task in which we value understanding both for each individual and for the overall institutional culture, where we recognize diversity of experience but also bear in mind the health and viability of the institution. In this sense, we aim to achieve what de Maré and colleagues call *koinonia*, a Greek word referring to the fellowship that fosters discourse and understanding for mutual benefit.

The Task in the Large and Median Groups

In the *group to study large-group dynamics*, interpretation of the group process is the main activity. In the *large workshop* group, interpretive comments about group process are used only occasionally to address impediments to learning or to illustrate the substantive process being studied in that presentation. In the *plenary* group, interpretive comments are used frequently by both faculty and students in their shared attempt to establish the meaning of shared and individual events. This free-form median group studies the institution and the relationship of individuals to the institution and to the wider culture. The plenary component of our learning task shares equal priority with individual and small-group learning.

Informal Subgroupings

During the breaks for lunch and dinner, students are on their own. This is free time, and they may choose to be alone, to study, or to socialize, sometimes with members from their own small group, and sometimes with friends or family members. Coffee breaks and receptions, however, are integral to the program. They are designed to attract the whole membership to the hall and so facilitate unstructured, free-form interaction with faculty and students. In that space, students may bring out behavior that is relevant to the learning process and that has been inhibited in the formal parts of the program. For example, a student may have difficulty respecting the boundary around the work group and may try to use the coffee break to get extra one-on-one time with a faculty member for discussing matters that are not social but that properly concern the group. We consider this informal time an important component of the learning process and subject to process and review.

Learning from Experience in the Small Group

Small-group work is the cornerstone of the program. We design each training module to include a series of small-group discussions with an integrative task. The small group consists of five to ten students and a faculty member committed to the task for two years. Students committed for four three-day weekends meet with their group and its leader twenty times over seven or eight months, while students enrolled only for one three-day weekend meet five times. Students enrolled for the two-year program have seventy sessions with the same small group and leader. Sometimes circumstances result in one group having as few as four members, and on occasion we assign two faculty members as leaders of one group for coleading experience.

The individual's task in the small group is to discuss the theoretical and clinical material that has been read or presented and at the same time to examine intellectual and emotional responses to it. As each member attempts to do this, discussion follows, and a group process develops.

The group's task is to facilitate its members' learning from all levels of experience. While studying the theoretical and clinical material that is provided, the group examines its own process to discover how the individual's inner world combines with the personalities of others to illustrate the concepts and to foster or impede the learning.

The small group of five to ten members has a special standing representing the intimate nuclear family experience and at the same time the peer group. In this size of group, members have experience that can be processed by all of them in the immediacy of the moment, and yet, because the size is larger than most nuclear families in our culture, they reach a broader perspective from multiple individual understandings of shared experience. The small group is the place to integrate learning from didactic lectures and workshops, reading, and clinical experience with personal experience (inner world and outer world). It is the place to explore the impact of the learning experience itself on what is being learned. In this way, *learning about* object relations is amplified by *experience of* object relations. Learning occurs at all levels of scale, and the differences between the levels are subject to examination.

Through discussion, the small-group members might discover that a concept concerning self and other that seemed clear to one person is confusing to another, and so the concept is revealed in its complexity. A moment of closeness enjoyed by two members could be felt as painfully exclusive to a third member and yet might seem pathetically shallow to a fourth. Group members can examine individual and shared transferences to their group leader, and they can see how and why they join in an unconsciously organized group mode to support or subvert the learning task. They can test whether the various intellectual and emotional implications of a member's communication apparent to each group member were the ones that were indeed intended and, if not, what individual and group factors led to partial understanding and misunderstanding.

This complex task is at once so ambitious and so ambiguous that its full realization is impossible. Our goal is simply to provide a living experience of the learning task in action. When group members have heard a lecture or participated in a workshop on projective identification, they are primed to study the manifestations of their own projective identifications. Here is an example of how this might develop.

The group members might discuss an elusive concept, the different ways it has been explained in the literature, and the clinical example presented by the lecturer to illustrate it. A man may offer a clinical vignette that seems to support the concept, and a woman may see it differently. The two might enter into a lively argument that becomes highly intellectual. During this discussion, another group member may remember a personal event that penetrates the intellectualized content of the discussion. Then the group might turn to the leader, asking him as a faculty member to clarify a murky or contested point. The leader might decide that the greatest opportunity for learning rests with his simply clarifying the point in question.

On the basis of his countertransference at this point, the leader might, however, decide that it is time for an interpretation. If he feels pressured to come up with the answer as if no other member of the group is in possession of knowledge, he might interpret the process of the group's turning to him as a projective identification of power and knowledge into him and a concomitant depletion of competence of the group as a whole. Thinking of a *because clause* (Ezriel 1950), he might then interpret the group dependency on him as a defense against differentiation and autonomy or an attempt to create a pair with him so as to avoid noticing the group envy of the two members of the group who had been paired in a lively exchange.

Interpretation is not the leader's responsibility alone. The woman mentioned earlier might note that the male leader seemed uncomfortable as she expounded on the ideas the lecturer had developed. She might suggest that she was living out or enacting the group's projective identification of knowledge and authority into her and that she identified with this because of her wish not to depend on him. Such an interpretation might come from a sophisticated group member, herself functioning at that moment as a teacher from whom others (including faculty) can learn, but equally it might come from a sensitive novice. Another group member might notice that the leader had begun to act to impart knowledge rather than to foster its discovery as before.

What we hope to convey here is that the group culture values all areas of experience, investigates them, dissects them, gives them shape, and integrates them as knowledge. The group develops a capacity for *negative capability*—"being in uncertainties, mysteries, doubts without any irritable reaching after fact and reason"—a quality described by Keats and recommended by Bion for achieving understanding of unconscious processes (Keats quoted Bion 1970, p. 125). The group values the capacity to suspend knowing what is already known in order to investigate what is not yet understood. It values the moments when intellectual thought and affective experience come together as knowledge, and it values letting go of that knowledge to make room for future needs to know.

This blend of exploration and experience leads to a process of search and discovery. The group shares moments of puzzlement, drowning in affect and distancing from it, freezing in fear, and benefiting from multiple perspectives taken from different points of view. The group offers each individual the opportunity for growth in knowledge and in personal experience and the chance to share and teach from each of these positions. Many illustrations of small-group work can be found in Parts I and II.

The Regressive Pull

Small-group participants are not seeking personal help. They are not suffering as patients are. They sign up for a growth experience, not for healing. This correctly limits the extent of revelation they expect of themselves and others. Furthermore, the integrative task demands that the group attend to the cognitive aspects of the experience as well as to the emotional aspects. This means that we expect less regression than in a therapy group. Nevertheless, some participants may in fact be hurting psychologically in ways known or unknown to them, and some may undergo trauma and loss while traveling to a two-year program away from their home supports. So there will be times when the group functions more like a therapy group. The stance of the group leader is an important factor in setting the tone for the group. Nevertheless, we find that each small group (even with the same leader) interprets the task somewhat differently. Each group strikes its own balance between emphasis on the personal and the group issue, the intellectual and the emotional, and the regressive and the progressive.

The regressive pull in these small groups occurs because their size primes the members to look for an intimate experience akin to family life. At times, they function *as if* their tasks were to offer therapy for individual members. This tendency is the target of the most frequent criticisms from outside faculty and guest presenters, from critics of our method, and from ourselves. We remain alert to dynamic processes that tend to pervert the task, but we do not avoid the possibility by eliminating small groups or structuring them to meet a simple aim. Most learning designs cut off access to internal individual experience while we consciously maintain an open avenue to it.

We take the view that the tendency to regression is inevitable and must be the constant object of study, but it is not an inherent flaw in the method. It is not *in* the way; rather, it *is* the way. Transference and countertransference in psychoanalysis used to be thought of as resistance and then came to be seen as the manifestation of the problem and the method for its resolution. Similarly, in the learning group, struggling with this tension between the learning task and the tendency to personal regression—more specifically the pull to act as if the group existed to contain and transform individual affect and conflict—is the principle task of the group leader. This pull to raw emotional experience requires constant balance by the application of intellectual understanding to achieve integration. For more discussion on this topic, see Chapter 6.

The Group Leader

The small-group leader's task is the maintenance of balance between cognition and affect, between individual needs and group process. The group leader, as faculty delegate from the program to the group, embodies this task and attempts to keep it constantly in mind, just as a therapist does for a patient. But to a greater extent than for a therapist with an individual patient, the group leader is not alone in having professional competence in analyzing dynamics. Members of a small group each carry their own experience in learning and teaching, in analyzing and understanding personal and clinical experience, and in teaching one another and learning from other group members. We value the teacher and learner in each person—the teacher each group member carries within and the learner in each faculty member. We value reciprocal interaction—helping others learn something new while learning from them. We value openness to new experience and reflectiveness. Self-analysis of the self in action with others in the work of learning about the self and others is the hallmark of object relations therapy—and of our teaching and learning model.

Group leaders have their own work group: The faculty group is a place for them to review and think about the small-group experience. Membership in the working faculty group connects the small group to the institutional task and keeps the institution in touch with the group and its individuals. For examples of the work of the faculty group, see chapters 13, 19, and 20.

The Faculty Small Group

Regular faculty meetings review the process of the program, the small groups, and the large groups they have experienced together. The faculty group is the course director's small group. From his experience with the faculty, he constructs a view of the course as a whole. These faculty group meetings are central to the process of the affective learning program. The meetings themselves exhibit small-group process, as faculty members and the faculty group leader work together, blending discussion of each small group with review of the faculty process, to understand the progress of the whole group.

Review of the small groups is the focus of the faculty meeting, but while doing this, the faculty uses its own process to aid in the understanding of how each group approaches the integrative task and how together they reflect the effectiveness of the whole program. New faculty and experienced faculty, acting as their own small application group in consultation with the course director as faculty group leader, study the way in which the concepts and the affective learning occur through the unfolding pattern of each small group over the course of each weekend and over the longer course of the two-year program.

These meetings have a supervision element in that the program director or another faculty member charged with the role of faculty group leader exercises responsibility for the competence of each faculty member and for the fulfillment of the educational objectives. In addition, new faculty members require supervision to help them learn the model. At the same time, they find their voice and their place by working together on shared issues of group leading technique. This is not a hierarchical sort of supervision, however. The intent is to create a matrix in which learning and teaching occur.

Although the course director embodies the task of understanding and integrating these matters, the faculty shares the job. Thus, a faculty tries to develop its own *group mind* in order to understand the learning process as it applies to each individual student and to the institution as a whole. In this process, the affective experience of faculty members in leading and trying to understand their small groups and in participating in their faculty group becomes the main source of information. Countertransference in teaching and learning is the most important guiding instrument, just as it is in the therapy being taught.

Multiple Faculty Roles: Chairing, Presenting, Tutoring Students

We want faculty to experience and learn from multiple roles within the educational institution. *Chairing* single sessions gives faculty a chance to develop skills in managing boundaries and in creating a nonstressful environment for the presenter and the student. *Presenting* gives faculty the opportunity to improve their functioning as didactic teachers of theory and clinical practice. *Cochairing* weekend events enables faculty to demonstrate or develop skills in planning the format and in *tutoring* students to present cases or papers during the event. The weekend cochair tutors the student in preparing an effective clinical presentation by focusing on the intellectual content and the student's affective response in anticipation of the presenting task, alternately shaping the material the student will present and discussing the student's anxieties about presenting. At the individual level, the student presentation serves to prepare the student for a teaching role, and at the institutional level, it creates a learning vehicle for the larger group.

When faculty members chair plenary and workshop sessions, they learn to set boundaries, facilitate exchanges between guest presenters and participants, organize learning events, and exercise personal authority in pursuit of the learning task. All these roles are reviewed by the faculty group, who are supportive of one another's need to learn and refine a variety of skills and who work together to analyze the constraints against learning. For more discussion of the role of the chair and its effects on the small-group leader, see Chapters 17 and 18.

BEYOND THE WEEKEND CONFERENCES AND WEEKLONG INSTITUTES

Supervision

Supervision is a common and central component of psychoanalytic and psychotherapeutic education. The relationship with the supervisor is the central mentoring relationship through which skills traditionally have been passed on. At its best, supervision provides trainees with safe, growth-promoting relationships where vulnerabilities of trainees can be explored without judgment or retribution as professional (and incidentally personal) growth is promoted.

At its worst, supervision constitutes a penetrating exposure of vulnerable and exposed trainees whose shortcomings and failings are held against them and whose progress is blocked by the superior attitude of the supervisor. At its best, supervision is supportive and confrontational without the downside of control and humiliation. Not that the need for a supervisor's judgment should be done away with: Judgment about student and faculty effectiveness and growth is central to any model of education. But questions about how to tie judgment to facilitation of growth must be studied and modified if the institutionalization of a repressive, antigrowth culture is to be avoided by the construction of a culture of progressive understanding.

We work toward this by creating a supportive context for supervision review. Individual supervision respects the privacy of the individual, but ongoing evaluation by both supervisor and supervisee is openly discussed by faculty to implement improvements. Supervision, though bounded in the conduct of each session, is linked to the institution so that it does not tend to become isolated. We do this in several ways that are amplified in the next section. Supervision teaches the concepts of technique, and it does so by focusing on transference and countertransference as the core of object relations therapy. Supervision may explore the supervisee's personal affective reactions or prior personal experiences since they are part of countertransference, but it will not be a place for conducting psychotherapy of the trainee (see Chapter 19).

Paired and Group Supervision

Students convene in groups of two to five members in order to reflect on the clinical encounter. Contributions from peers offer multiple perspectives on clinical process and problems, and the space for thinking that develops counters the erroneous idea that there is only one right way of conducting therapy. When group supervision is not possible for geographic or logistical reasons, we encourage trainees to have an experience of paired supervision locally or by telephone. Peer supervisory situations have a value in addition to the individual supervision setting, and so all students are encouraged to have both individual and group supervision where that is possible.

Faculty Study of Supervision

The faculty meets regularly to study supervisory roles and processes. When we began this practice, we quickly discovered that we could look meaningfully at supervision of individual students only by linking it to our experience of them throughout the program. We worried that this meant that we would be exposing and judging private vulnerabilities of trainees in the light of our prejudices about them, but the advantages of a thorough consideration of each student's supervision clearly outweighed the risks. We found that educational blocks could be more easily understood in the context of our wider knowledge of students and ourselves as we exposed our supervision decisions and conflicts in the faculty group (see chapter 19).

These meetings proceed by describing the process and problems of supervising a student and then explore our overall experience of that student elsewhere in the program, especially in the small- and large-group learning settings. The network of information about a student weaves the various experiences of several members of the faculty into a richer fabric than could be accomplished by the review from the single perspective of one or even several individual supervisors. Having established a broad image of the student, our focus moves on to the supervisor. Most of the discussion is geared at increasing the supervisor's skill in assessing the nature of the student's clinical difficulties, in making interventions with tact and timing, and in evaluating progress. Faculty review focuses on the skill of the supervisor, just as individual supervision focuses on the growth of the therapist, not the patient. We become aware of the strengths and vulnerabilities of various faculty members. This allows a more informed view of the role and difficulties of supervision within the context of the overall program. We then use our shared group experience to strengthen the skills of faculty not only in their supervisory role but also when teaching in all modalities of the program.

Satellite Faculty Roles

Each faculty member is also involved in running or teaching local study groups, carrying out individual and group supervision, and linking individual students to various aspects of the core program. The same principles of affectively based learning are applied to these functions carried out in different cities with local variation. The center of the satellite programs is the weekly or monthly study group, which combines the same elements of content-based learning of theory and therapy, clinical study, and personal experience blended into the learning group. Local programs are designed to provide integration with the core program and the weekends but also to provide a stand-alone experience for students who wish to participate only in the local study groups or courses in individual, family, or group therapy.

PRACTICALITIES OF THE PROGRAM

The Student Membership

We admit all qualified applicants who still seek admission after we have discussed the program with them. To the extent possible in advance of actually experiencing the program, we want them to understand what they are getting into in the group segment. Then, provided that they have basic clinical training or work experience in a clinical setting, we admit them. We would discourage and might even turn away someone whose physical or mental stamina seemed insufficient to the demands of the group learning task.

In practice, we have not had to turn someone down, although several students have not proceeded with the program—some after talking with us before enrollment and others who found out later that it was not for them. If things go well, they discover this within a few days of beginning. We refund their fees, and the parting is relatively agreeable. On a few occasions, students have struggled with the experience for some time before deciding that it does not offer what they expected. They depart, usually with pain for them, their small-group members, and the faculty, but the group goes on. In many years of leading small groups, there was only one group struggle that we could not resolve. A nidus of trauma led to the exodus of one member after another until only a pair of students remained, thus revealing the underlying rageful fantasy about an envied couple from whom the others felt excluded and who failed to create a magical union that would give birth to a savior to lead the group to a better place.

The result of our open admissions policy is that we have classes of mixed ability and level of experience by design. A typical group will contain students a year out of their basic degree (masters in social work; doctorates in psychology, education, and pastoral counseling; or masters in family therapy, counseling, or nursing) alongside students with many years in the field of psychotherapy, including some with psychoanalytic credentials. We find that students whose age, background, and training run the gamut can teach and learn from one another much as family members at different developmental stages, peers and cross-age friends do. Even an infant who cannot speak teaches its parents even as it learns from them. The student who is a newly trained therapist learns from the more experienced therapist as well as from the faculty member and at the same time brings a fresh voice to temper the understanding of the seasoned professional for whom familiar concepts may have lost their vitality. This nonselective policy was chosen deliberately to ensure representation of a mixture of life and professional experience and thus to create a rich educational matrix. Each participant, faculty and student alike, is there in the role of teacher, learner, evaluator, and program redesigner.

The Faculty

Our faculty are psychoanalysts and analytic psychotherapists, all interested in object relations theory and practice with significant training and experience in applying object relations theory to clinical practice and to group process, either within our program or in human relations training conferences. While all the faculty have adult training, most are also interested in some special populations or modalities: group, family, children, addictions, employee assistance, or sexual disorders. Several are interested in other approaches, such as Jungian analysis; cognitive, behavioral, or sex therapy; and institutional consultation. The faculty shares a conviction that learning from experience is crucial to a clinician's growth and that the group affective model of learning forms the core of the students' experience. As a faculty, we have also found that working this way with these groups of students and our own experience as a working faculty group that studies its own process provide the core experience for our own learning and growth.

Evaluation

Students evaluate every weekend or weeklong conference. They are the most important consultants in the continual re-evaluation and modification of the training program. They complete an extensive evaluative form, rating each component on a numbered scale, and provide more elaborate commentary on those points that they think need attention. Their written evaluations keep the program in touch with the educational and training needs of students and faculty. In addition, we invite evaluative discussion in large-group meetings whenever relevant and especially in the plenary meetings of the program. In these meetings, we aim for consensus on the issues that need rethinking and redesign. We tell participants (and remind ourselves) that our training can be effective and relevant only through faculty response to continued evaluation. This open system policy produces some discomfort and some scrambling to change course in mid-event when indicated, but it ensures continual discourse, which is essential for a vital model of teaching and learning object relations theory and practice.

In this chapter, we have presented the basic concept of affective learning of object relations theory and practice for psychotherapists and psychoanalysts. The next chapter, by two male co-leaders, summarizes this understanding of the model and its use in their small group. The remaining chapters in Part I elaborate on theoretical considerations and illustrate methodology.

3
Individual, Group, and Chaos Theories

In this chapter, we revisit the object relations approach to teaching and learning. We show how our our model of affective learning derives from group analytic theory informed by systems theory and from individual object relations theory augmented by findings from brain research on affect and neurobiological development and set against the background of chaos theory, also known as complexity theory. Having summarized group analytic theory and individual object relations theory, the two pillars on which this group affective learning model rests, we conclude with a brief explanation of the relevant principles from chaos theory and how they illuminate the process of learning to apply psychoanalytic theory in clinical practice with individuals, couples, families, and groups.

THE OBJECT RELATIONS OF
TEACHING AND LEARNING

Learning occurs for an infant when a neurological and physiological substrate in the infant is prepared to accommodate and be shaped by experience. From the first, these experiences relate to a primary person, usually the mother. Infants rely on the mother, the father, and the family to give them secure attachment from which they can safely separate. Many things are learned in the process of a close attachment, but many others have to be learned in the process of a separation that allows the young individual to go his or her own way in order to explore, make sense of new experience, and then come back to a primary relationship. The mastery of knowledge seems to be a human motivational system in its own right, but we also come to treasure knowledge because it is a part of those we love and because it lets us take care of ourself, lets us give to others, and do for those we love.

In the process of teaching and learning, attachment bonds are often strengthened when two people—mother and infant—are learning together. As two grown-ups or a group of adults experience the mutuality of learning together, they draw on their early relationships. Learning together, adults experience feelings of gratitude and self-worth. This mature interdependence is the successor to infantile early dependence.

Often, however, the relationship between personal attachment and the facilitation of learning is subject to the forces of destruction. For example, a student or younger person can envy a teacher or adult's knowledge, or a teacher can envy a student, perhaps for youth, intelligence, or unfettered potential. These anxieties and defenses regularly affect the pursuit of knowledge and may even cause an impasse. By noticing these blocks to learning, we open ourselves to a widening circle of knowledge.

In teaching and learning about emotional experience, we must take into account the history of relationships at the center of emotional experience. We mean to include not only the history of early relationships and the present actual relationships that are their inheritors but also the whole internal world of object relationships. These internal objects guide each person through life. They are themselves modified by learning from experience with new objects during the course of life. Internal objects resonate and interact with new experience, confirm existing perceptions, or modify and rebuild the original version of the object. In the affective learning group, this complex process guides our study and is itself the object of study.

The relationships of each person to others are at the center of the study task. The person's internal object relations set determines the capacity for conducting psychotherapy and psychoanalysis. We study these processes in the group, where they both facilitate and limit our working toward understanding.

THE GROUP THEORY BASE: GROUP ANALYSIS

What Is a Group?

In Neri's (1998) review of the literature and in his own thinking, the group is described as a common ground, a shared space for listening and for whatever may emerge, a transpersonal and suprapersonal container for thoughts and feelings. The group is seen as a medium, a matrix, a communication network, and a collective mentality. It has been established as an initial condition for development, a situation of transit to other conditions, and a place of transformation and change. The group is a living organism with moods and atmosphere communicated verbally and nonverbally. It is a protomental system, a functioning multiplicity and a unity, an organized system of mental forms, and a system of synchronicity and interdependence. The group is variously likened to a star formation or a constellation, a wheel, a field, a pool, and the interior of the mother's body, each simile referring to an aspect of group life.

A few quotes from Neri (1998) amplify these views: "The group is 'a special space or relational and mental container' in which emotional transformations and thought operations are carried out" (p. 17) and where "passions, knowledge and relationships are thrown into dynamic collation" (p. 109). The group members assume "an active role and a joint responsibility for all that concerns living, experiencing and thinking about everything that happens in the common field" (p. 16). "The group as a whole is not simply a turn of phrase, it is a living organism, as distinct from the individuals comprising it. It has moods and reactions, a spirit, a feeling and an atmosphere" (p. 21). The "group constitutes a sort of model of 'functioning multiplicity,' not only because of the presence of several people, but also of the multifaceted and global aspects of its thought" (p. 147). These views immediately make the point that a group is far more than a collection of individuals. It is a complex organization of component relationships.

The group has temporal and physical boundaries. It exists in physical space, defined by its size and the arrangement of chairs. The small group of five to ten members meets in a circle. The medium-size group of fifteen to thirty members (called the median group) may meet in a circle or a double-row circle. The large discussion group of thirty to one or two hundred members may be seated theater style or in concentric circles, depending on the task. The group exists in time, bounded by the beginning and end of each session, by the number of sessions and by the event within which it takes place. It has a beginning, a middle, and an end. It has a past, a present, and a future. The group has a membership and a leadership that remains constant over the period covered by the event. The group has continuity and develops a history. It continues to exist in the mind of the individual after the group is over.

Complementing these spatial and temporal boundaries, the group has a *group skin*, created by the distinctive culture of this group separating it from other groups (Anzieu 1988). The group culture includes the structure of members' voices and patterns of interaction, subgroup formations, attitudes toward the leader, and the task, all of which define its identity and differentiate it from other settings that may seem to be less defined in comparison. Within its skin, the group has a body and a mind. The body may seem to be a female body, like the maternal body that the members wish to suck on, explore, and enter, or whose cavernous spaces they dread. Or it may be like a male body that has a hard edge and a powerfully penetrating capacity. The group has a *group mind*, a mind of its own that goes its own way. The group takes on a life of its own. It becomes an entity, an external object that becomes an internal object for its members. This internal object is then related to as an object to be feared, longed for, hated, deprecated, revered, appreciated, and so on.

Individual problems in understanding the material are projected outside the self into the space of the group, where they acquire a new dimensionality as each member resonates with the index problem that has been brought to the group's attention. The group perspective transforms the individual problem into a shared issue that the individual can now see better because it is outside himself (Pichon-Rivière 1977, Searles 1965a). The individual learns about herself from her impact on others and how they view her and deal with her. And the individual brings to the group a focus for its collective work.

The group's leader relates to the group as a whole. Within that collective image, each individual contributes thoughts, feelings, and interactions with others to the group life and is affected by the group process. Neri (1998) introduced the term *commuting* to describe the shift in levels in group interaction. The group *commutes* between the focus on figure and ground, individual and group, cognition and affect, and knowledge and passion to arrive a comprehensive view of the group as a complex living system subject to dynamic flow.

The individual creates turbulence in the group process, and the group creates turbulence in the individual, a situation of mutual feedback and dynamic flow that pushes toward change and rearrangement of ideas and affect regulation. The group functions as an organizing system that appears to create a level of chaos at the same time that it is draws meaning out of chaos. Chaos, continual feedback, and self-organization give rise to the creative and transformational properties of groups.

Small-, Median-, and Large-Group Characteristics

So far, all that we have said applies whether the group is large or small. There are differences between small and large groups, nevertheless. The small group of five to ten members resonates with family experience, preoedipal and oedipal issues, and interferences with love, intimacy, and individual development. The median group of fifteen to thirty members is a place to explore the connection of the members to the wider culture. In the large group chaos, isolation, and mob dynamics dominate (Hopper 1977, Kreeger 1975, Springmann 1976, Turquet 1975). While small groups thrive on the need for affiliation and dependency, median and large groups take hate as the starting point. This happens because hate is stimulated when affiliative wishes are frustrated by the size of the group.

The Small Work Group and the Basic Assumption Group

Our model for affective learning in groups is heavily influenced by the work of Bion on small working groups. In *Experiences in Groups*, Bion (1961) noted that a small group has a work group mentality, but it also has subgroups devoted to seeking gratification. He introduced the term *basic-assumption group* to describe the instantaneous combinations of various group members into these subgroup formations. He found that these subgroupings tend to cluster around three main themes: dependency on the leader, fight against or flight from the authority vested in the leader, and pairing as a defense against the frustration of being a member of a group and an expression of hope for the conception of a better leader to take the group out of its dilemma.

Bion noted that the basic assumption group often subverts the task. Dependency, fight/flight, and pairing may be used defensively to throw the group off course and so to avoid the anxiety of getting on with the job. For example, in the family, children who remain at home supported through their young adulthood create a subgroup that blocks the family from doing its job of releasing them to autonomous living. Soldiers deserting a platoon create a flight subgrouping that disables the military effort. Teenagers who harass their teachers form a subgroup that fights against authority instead of facing the anxieties of learning complex material. In a dysfunctional family, a parent and child may bond intensely and exclusively so that the other parent feels jealous rather than the child and the task of oedipal resolution cannot proceed.

Equally, Bion found that the basic assumption group also suppports the task. Members join the group through their shared need to affiliate. The dependency subgroup formation supports their remaining affiliated to the group. The fight/flight subgrouping enables the individual to maintain a degree of autonomy while engaging in group activity and subscribing to a group identity. Pairing can lead to creative ideas that go beyond what the individual can produce alone and yet develop faster than when the whole group is in on the discussion. If the group leader is not adequate to the task, the emergence of a substitute leader from the membership may indeed be needed.

Bion used the Kleinian concept of projective identification to explain the unconscious communication of these shared group transferences to the leader. Recognizing the impact of these group processes and interpreting them in the light of the countertransference gives the leader a way of conceptualizing the group processes and making them conscious. This interpretive activity clears the way for the group to proceed with its task. If basic assumption groups obtrude on the work group and are ignored, little intellectual activity is engaged in. But if the group learns to recognize and understand them, "intellectual activity of a high order is possible" (Bion 1961, p. 175).

We have followed Hopper (1977) in adding a fourth basic assumption to Bion's original three (J. S. Scharff and D. E. Scharff 1998d). It refers to defensive subgroup formations involving merger or splintering. Hopper calls this basic assumption *massification/aggregation*. Some groups act as an aggregate of individuals with no shared purpose or mental life, while others act with a mass mind, the individuals appearing to be fused. Massification and aggregation are the poles of the fourth basic assumption. A sporting crowd united in protest against defeat or a family joined in grief are temporarily in a state of massification. A group of students who should be working as a team instead become an aggregate when each one pursues the project independently. Like the other basic assumption groups, massification/aggregation may support or undermine the group task.

The Median and Large Group

Through hate, the individual joins the median and large group. The size of the group absorbs and defuses the attack. Hate, like hunger, signifies an absence of something ardently desired. Hate is neither creative nor destructive per se but is a form of ego energy not to be subdued or denied but to be affirmed, cultivated, and transformed. Too often, guilt arises as an attempt to disguise and deny hate, as a kind of reaction formation. This makes it difficult to study the primary experience of feeling excluded by the presence of the large group or to reach the underlying wish for belonging. The group's purpose is to help transform hate into dialogue, serial dialogue, and multilogue, a groupwide conversation that reveals the richness of multiple points of view (de Maré et al. 1991). Through this process, meaning is created out of chaos.

Feelings of exclusion and hate form the initial affective bridge to the large group. As small increments of meaning emerge, the group moves on to

establish and then understand the culture of the large group and its connection to the wider culture in which it exists. Just as *affectively* understanding intellectual interchanges is central to the work of the small group, so *intellectually* understanding the affective exchanges of the large group becomes
the medium of discourse and provides the link to institutional and cultural
experience.

Differences between Small and Median or Large Groups

To summarize the difference, in small groups the individual is the object of focus, and the group is the main agency (Foulkes and Anthony 1957). In
the larger group, it is the group that is the object, and the individual is the agency
(de Maré et al. 1991). Nevertheless, since our whole endeavor is a training one,
we then must reverse the process once again to note that we are offering an
experiential education of the large group, from which we expect our *individual
members* (both students and faculty) to learn, even though at the same time we
may actually be trying to understand, and thereby improve, the institution in
which the teaching and learning are occurring.

THE GROUP AND THE WIDER CULTURE

All work groups reflect, resist, digest, and metabolize the influence of
the institutions and the wider society in which they exist and work. Similarly,
the family conveys social and cultural influences to its individuals and especially
to its children. In the affective learning institution, the small group is influenced
by the large group, and the whole institution is affected by the culture in which
it operates. In addition to approaching their affective learning groups with the
more familiar "here-and-then" transferences based on past personal experience,
individuals also approach their groups with "there-and-now" transferences based
on reactions to societal attitudes and events of universal impact (Hopper 1996,
J. S. Scharff and D. E. Scharff 1998c,d). Hopper describes these shared reactions
to experience in society as the *social unconscious.*

In the affective learning institution, we make conscious one aspect of
the social unconscious. We consciously present for examination a specific element of the wider professional culture in that we regularly and purposefully
introduce new ideas conveyed by our guest and faculty presenters through pre-
paratory readings and presentations to the large group. The absorption, digestion, and integration of material from outside the institution is done in the large
group first and continues in the small groups.

The Small Affective Learning Group

The affective learning small group is for teaching and learning concepts, not for therapy. The affective learning model has similarities to group therapy in terms of the use of affect, countertransference, and interpretation of unconscious processes in the group, but the educational context and contract establish the difference. Nevertheless, the model draws on group theory from the fields of both group therapy and group relations. With substantial modifications, the recommendations regarding group therapists' technique apply in the educational context (see Chapter 8).

In a teaching and learning group, as in a small therapy group, the leader's attitude toward the group is crucial in establishing the culture that will be productive for learning. She thinks of the group as a whole, her mind resonating with the descriptions and images that we mentioned previously. She does not impose structure on the group beyond the temporal and spatial frame. She lets the discussion develop and interprets emerging blocks to the flow of associations much as an individual analyst would.

The leader uses specific techniques to encourage the effective functioning of the group. She actively seeks to hear from the members of the group. If any are silent, she asks what is being held in the silence. She listens to words, notices gestures, and maps the kinesic interaction among group members. She attends to the quality of silences, lapses, breaks, and hesitations in dialogue. She senses the atmosphere. She follows the unconscious theme of the group. If a dream is given as the product of an individual's unconscious, she nevertheless works with the associations of all members of the group and so deals with it as a reflection of the group mind. She thinks about the group process and comments on it. The leader *commutes* between relating to the members as individuals with their unique perceptions, thoughts, and feelings and relating to the group as a whole with its unique patterns, atmosphere, and group mind.

She notes repeating patterns of interaction, conceptualizes them in terms of their defensive function, and helps the group tolerate the underlying anxieties. Through her containing function, she metabolizes these anxieties until they become thinkable. The group identifies with her containing function and itself becomes a working container for holding, processing, and transforming anxiety-provoking, affectively charged mental and relational material. She thinks about the group process and comments on it. Identifying with and sharing in her containing function, the group finds that meaning emerges from experience.

The Institutional Matrix

Last but not least, each small group comes to appreciate that it exists in a matrix along with other groups, including the large group of the entire conference membership. The character of one group affects the other. Small work groups may identify selectively with aspects of the faculty. Each small group resonates with a split-off part of the total institution. All groups in the matrix need to be considered to approach a more complete under-standing of the material, the responses to it, the teaching and learning objec-tives, and the nature of the institution in which students and faculty teach and learn.

INDIVIDUAL OBJECT RELATIONS THEORY

The individual theory base draws from the British object relations theo-rists Fairbairn, Winnicott, and others (Sutherland 1980), attachment research (Ainsworth et al. 1978, Fonagy et al. 1991, Main and Solomon 1986, Slade 1996), and neuroscience (Schore 1994). Our integration of object relations theories rests on the organized, systematic object relations theory of the endo-psychic situation provided by Fairbairn. We then enrich this basic theory by the ideas of Winnicott and apply it to the interpersonal situation by patching in the concepts of Klein and Bion (D. E. Scharff 1996). Since Fairbairn's theory is centered on the mother–infant relationship, it transfers easily to the study of transference and countertransference in the therapeutic relationship and is ap-plicable to understanding the dynamics of couples, families, and groups (Dicks 1967). Since it is systematically argued, it provides a coherent base from which to extend our ideas with contributions from Winnicott, Balint, Bollas, Guntrip, Ogden, and Sutherland and from theorists of other schools of contemporary psychoanalysis.

We concentrate on object relations because, of all analytic ap-proaches, we have found it to be the most adaptable across the range of thera-peutic modalities (D. E. Scharff and J. S. Scharff 1987, 1991, J. S. Scharff and D. E. Scharff 1998, Stadter 1996). We also find in it the basis for the teach-ing and learning design. To orient the reader to our blend of object relations theories and to tie it to our understanding of groups and to our philosophy of teaching and learning, we give the following brief overview of object rela-tions theory, concentrating on the work of Fairbairn, Klein, Winnicott, and Bion.

Fairbairn

Fairbairn (1952) took as the basis for infant development the need to be in a relationship with a mother. He wrote that as a dependent infant relates to the mother (the external object), the infant finds the experience of depending on the relationship inevitably frustrating compared to uterine bliss, in which needs were met automatically. The infant has to come to terms with frustrating aspects of the experience. If the level of frustration is intolerable (whether because the mother is neglectful or the infant has low tolerance or intense needs), the infant deals with it by introjecting the object (the internal object). The mind, which is a pristine ego at birth, is structured by internalizing the object and splitting it into parts that correspond to the particular way in which the object was perceived as frustrating. The object is split into a satisfying, a need-rejecting, and a need-exciting part. To the extent that the external object was experienced as satisfactory, the corresponding satisfactory internal object remains available to central and more conscious function as the ideal object shorn of elements that might create distress. To the extent that the external object was frustrating, a part of the internal object is split off and repressed. Depending on whether the frustration took the form of exciting need or rejecting need, the internal object is then further split into an exciting object and a rejecting object, respectively.

The ego (or self) is structured by its relation to these objects. A central part of the ego remains close to consciousness in relation to the internal ideal object. Then this central part of the ego defends itself from overwhelming affect by splitting off two parts of itself: the libidinal ego, corresponding to the repressed exciting object, and the antilibidinal ego, relating to the repressed rejecting internal objects. These aspects of the ego are repressed in association with the objects, together with the corresponding affects of longing and rage. Affects lead to and characterize internal central, rejecting, and exciting relationships between parts of the ego and its internal objects. Ego, affect, and object are the components of the *internal object relationship*.

In the rejecting object system, the antilibidinal ego's relationship to a persecuting part-object may be characterized by both an angry feeling attributed to the object and a hang-dog feeling of the victimized ego. In the exciting object system, the libidinal ego's relationship to a tantalizing part-object might be characterized by longing, sexualized arousal, and the accompanying anxiety of impending let-down. If the longing is too painful, the rejecting object system then clamps down on the craving and augments the central ego's repression of the exciting object system. The central ego, which is the more reasonable part of the ego that remains close to consciousness, has its own internal part-object (the ideal object), which is more or less satisfying and not overly rejecting or exciting. The affects of this central internal object system are flexible, reasonable, and satisfiable in response to manageable levels of stimulation from external relating.

Fairbairn's student and biographer, J. D. Sutherland (1963,1989), emphasized that the fundamental unit of mental structure, the internal object relationship, consists of a part of the ego attached to a part of the object, characterized by a telltale affect. The three systems—the conscious central self and the repressed libidinal and antilibidinal internal object relationship systems—are all in dynamic relation.

Klein

Klein (1975) retained the Freudian view of instincts as the basis for infant development. She described an infant propelled through the period of dependency by the force of constitutionally determined life and death instincts. The force of the death instinct threatens the self with annihilation and makes the first few months a highly anxious time. To deflect the anxiety and aggression arising from the death instinct, the infant projects aggression into the mother, misidentifies her as being like the feelings projected into her, experiences her as persecutory, and defends himself from this frightening object by taking it back into the self and identifying with it. To keep the life instinct safe from destruction by proximity to the death instinct inside the self, the infant also projects good feelings emanating from the life instinct into the mother, identifies her as a caring object, and then takes that in as well. Klein (1946) introduced the term *projective identification* to describe this mental mechanism for dealing with anxiety resulting from the interplay of the death and life instincts.

In the first half of the first year of life, the infant's mental state is in the *paranoid-schizoid position,* in which massive use of projective identification leads to splitting of the object into good and bad part-objects, hateful attacks on the bad object, and envious attacks on the good object, in comparison to which the self feels diminished. In the second half of the first year, the infant becomes aware that the mother identified with aggression and the mother identified with love and concern are the same person, an awareness that ushers in the *depressive position*. In this mental organization, the infant is capable of experiencing a whole object, tolerating ambivalence toward it, feeling concern for it, and responding to guilt for having mistreated it by making reparation.

We do not attribute death anxiety to the death instinct, as Klein did. We do recognize the occurrence of death anxiety, but we attribute it to a problem of containment: The object cannot contain the self. We attribute death anxiety to constitutional insufficiency of the self, overwhelming circumstances, inadequacy of the external object, or a mismatch between the needs of the self and the capabilities of the object.

Analysts who work in group and family therapy used the concept of projective identification to refer to a tendency in families to identify the adolescent with the part of the parent's self that was causing the most trouble (J. S. Scharff 1989, 1992b, Shapiro 1979, Zinner and Shapiro 1972). Other orientations have referred to this adolescent as the scapegoat, the one who is seen to embody all that is bad and destructive in the family's life. There is an attempt to isolate this quality, locate it in one person, and then expel that person from the family because of sickness or delinquency. We find that the same phenomenon of the projective identification of an individual as the host for a shared quality occurs in a small group.

We use projective identification as a concept that links the intrapsychic to the interpersonal. Projective identification gives us a way of conceptualizing how the ego relates to the internal object inside the self and how the self interacts consciously and communicates unconsciously with significant others, such as the mother, the spouse, or the therapist. Object relations are not finalized by the oedipal stage. Studies of adolescents show that the person continues to develop through processes of mutual projective identification from immature dependency to mature respect and love (Westen 1990). Object relationships continue to grow and change through adult life experience with work, friendships, relocation, marriage, and raising children. They also change in response to learning from experience in affective learning groups.

Winnicott

Winnicott (1960b, 1965) studied the mother–infant relationship extensively during his work as a pediatrican and child analyst. He noted two aspects of the mother: *the environmental mother* and the *object mother*. The environmental mother provides the arms-around holding that keeps her child safe and ensures going on *being*. The object mother is there for *doing*, for intimate direct relating, eye-to-eye relating in gaze interactions, vocal cooing, and loving touch. We extend this view of the infant's mother to conceptualize the role of the family in providing *emotional holding* and *intimate relating* for its members of any age. Winnicott (1951) described the potential space between the mother and the infant in which transitional objects can be found or invented. This space permits dreaming, creativity, and play.

We use Winnicott's concepts of the environmental mother and the object mother and the transitional space to inform the design of the program for teaching and affective learning. The institution that offers the affective learning program is like the environmental parent who provides the psychological holding environment for growth. The chair of the program and the session chairs are responsible for environmental comfort and satisfactory communication in the large group. Small-group leaders embody both aspects of the maternal function. In their environmental mother roles, they set the affective tone and the boundaries of the small groups. In their object mother roles, they are available for interaction. Winnicott gives us the metaphor of being and doing for our functioning as a faculty group, teaching and learning from the cognitive material, and providing meaningful core affective exchanges. The institution creates a transitional space in which the students and faculty can play with ideas.

Attachment Research

From his ethological research on attachment and loss, Bowlby (1969, 1973, 1980) found that the frustration of attachment needs leads to aggression and fear in animals, including humans. Like animal young, the human infant needs proximity to a trusted, caring figure. Bowlby's research supported the view that aggression was not derivative of the death instinct. Like the object relations theorists, he thought that aggression was a response to frustration in the environment. We think that the type, frequency, and intensity of this response affects the nature of the internal object relationships formed in response to the excitation, frustration, or satisfaction of needs. We value attachment mainly as a contextual necessity within which doing and being can then occur.

The contextual relationship that the adult offers the child may be categorized as secure or insecure. Slade (1996) viewed the gradations in quality of attachment patterns along a continuum of affect regulation and structure. Midway between the opposite poles are those adults in the autonomous/secure category, whose affects and structures exist in balance, and their secure children. Insecure categories are found at both poles of the continuum. At one end lies the category of avoidant/dismissive personalities, who have rigid structures for affect regulation, and their insecure/avoidant children. At the opposite end are the resistant/preoccupied personalities, with poorly made structures overwhelmed by affect, and their insecure/resistant children. Further out at the extreme tip of the resistant/preoccupied pole lie the disorganized/unresolved personalities, which show even less coherence of structure because of areas of dissociation, and their disorganized children.

As clinicians, we use attachment theory in assessment when we evaluate attachment strategies, strengths, and weaknesses in the patients' capacities for relating, and we alter our technique so as to engage them. We use it in treatment to guide us in adjusting the therapeutic relationship to suit each patient and in developing a focus for the therapeutic work. In affective learning groups, attachment theory helps the group leader be aware of the need to provide a secure base through regularity of attendance, attention to boundaries, and monitoring of personal reactions to keep a clear space for psychological work. Within that context, the small-group leader becomes an object of attachment. More than that, the leader becomes an object of attachment *and* detachment, of desire and disgust, of hate and denigration, of envy and admiration, and so on. Then the small-group leader actively interprets the experience of being used as this necessary object with whom to replay in dynamic interaction the internal object relationships that come to light in the transference–countertransference as the group pursues the learning task. In addition, the group itself becomes both an attachment object and a transference object for the individual.

Bion

Long before neuroscience could demonstrate the links between relatedness, affect, and cognition, Bion (1967) proposed a theory that dealt with the infant's learning to think and tolerate affect from experiencing the mother's mental processing of her infant's experience. Bion's theory of *container/contained* proposes that the infant's primitive anxieties are put into the mother through projective identification. She in turn treats them unconsciously, through her *reverie*. She comes to know them, tolerate and shape them, modify and structure them in the image of her own mind, organize them in the form of understanding, and then feed them back to the infant in a more tolerable, less toxic, more structured state. She gives meaning to her child's experience, and the child builds psychic structure from that experience of being understood.

Bion's theory refers to the way a mind capable of thinking is constructed out of prethinking processes that, when they meet events, result in thoughts. Equally and simultaneously, it refers to emotional experience as part and parcel of cognitive experience. Intellectual cognition itself can be conceived of as a container for raw emotion, and emotion can be conceived of as a container for purely intellectual conceptions. Bion's model emphasizes the reciprocity of container and contained. We cannot pick an actual starting point in one mind for a continuing cycle of influence between two people, nor can we privilege either affect or intellect in the mind's search for knowledge.

In affective learning, the group is a container. The group reviews and processes difficult cognitive information and emotional responses. The group accepts unthinkable anxieties and gives them back as manageable thoughts to the individual. The individual identifies with the metabolizing and detoxifying function of the group discussion and so develops an augmented containing capacity for learning theory and working clinically.

Affect Regulation and Brain Research

The concepts of object relations theory are being increasingly supported by the findings of neuroscience. Bion's contention that mind is interpersonally and intersubjectively constructed is fully supported by Schore (1994, 2000), who sees the parents' mind as the culture medium for the growth of the child's cognitive ability and affect regulation. Brain research has now established that the affective mode of experience, which is processed by the right brain and stimulates its orbitofrontal development, takes precedence in early life, when affectively toned interactions between infants and their primary objects predominate. Positively toned learning sets up the situation of optimal learning in the affective regions of the right frontal cortex, and negatively toned emotions of fear and anger dampen down the growth processes there. Cognitive development is grafted on this foundation later as the left hemisphere becomes dominant (Schore 1994, 2000). Most significant, Schore contends that the young child's mental processes and physical brain development are organized by being influenced by the brain (especially the affectively dominated right brain) of the parents. This is not conscious teaching but rather the continuous unconscious *entrainment* of two brains in communication using all available channels of sight, sound, and physical contact. Later, left-brain processes accelerate and dominate the parent–child communication.

In the affective learning format, stimulation across multiple channels is delivered by presentations, readings, videos, and large-group discussions to the small group in which the group becomes the agent of entrainment for the development of the individual's learning process.

Chaos Theory

Deterministic chaos theory (Briggs 1992, Gleick 1987) describes the dynamics of self-organizing systems. It offers a new way of thinking about individual development, group interaction, and therapeutic action in individual and group psychoanalytic treatments (Palombo 1999, D. Scharff 1998, 2000, D. E. Scharff and J. S. Scharff 1999, 2000, J. S. Scharff and D. E. Scharff 1998a,b, van Eenwyck 1977). Arising at the interface of mathematics and physics, chaos theory explores the nonlinear aspects of natural phenomena and the unpredictable movement between states from stability to instability. Nonlinear dynamic systems are multifaceted, interdependent, and unpredictably changeable, moving from chaos to order and back again. They receive positive feedback from the environment, and they respond and adapt. They are sensitive to minor variations in the environment, especially at the moment of starting out and during transitions.

We have arrived at the position of thinking that the models of deterministic chaos theory offer a paradigm shift for psychoanalysis as they do in the sciences and social sciences. The potential magnitude of the shift is comparable to the shift from classical drive/structure theories to object relations theory that the theory of relativity inspired in Fairbairn. Briefly, Fairbairn pointed out that Freud had used the principles of science drawn from the nineteenth-century Helmholtzian physics and the laws of thermodynamics as his model. In this model, both matter and energy were conserved, and the one was separate from the other.

Fairbairn found a better paradigm in Einstein's twentieth-century theory of relativity. In this model using the equation $e = mc^2$, it was understood that matter could become energy and that energy could become matter. According to this model, psychic structure and drive contents, which Freud had thought to be separate, were not separate at all. Fairbairn viewed all psychic energy for relating and experiencing as becoming the substance of psychic structure. Each basic unit is an ego structure joined to an object by the affective tone of the psychic energy connecting them.

The Heisenberg principle holds that it is impossible for the scientist to observe phenomena without influencing them by the act of observation. This contribution from physics raised awareness of the analyst's influence on the patient and the phenomena he observes. So, in addition to viewing the personality as a system of parts, we now work with the awareness that the analyst is interacting with and contributing to the system.

Taking in the implications of the theory of relativity, Fairbairn moved psychoanalysis from Freud's dualistic and Platonic philosophy of man divided in himself and opposed by social forces to an Aristotelian and Hegelian philosophy of man as an intrinsically social being embedded in his social context (Scharff and Birtles 1994, 1997). Fairbairn's view of energy and structure applies at all stages, from early development, when the baby is born in the matrix of the relationship with mother and family, to later development, when each individual is embedded in primary relationships, in groups, and in the wider social context.

Chaos theory carries the paradigm shift further. It provides new mathematically inspired models and analogies that are better for describing the complex phenomena of human experience than either old mathematics, which dealt only with solvable, linear equations, or Euclidean geometry, which dealt with stable forms and finite solutions. In the chaos theory of dynamical systems, the focus is on unsolvable equations, the areas beyond the known, the edge of chaos, the fold upon folds. The mathematician attempts a solution to the equation. This is not regarded as a final solution. It provides a value for the start of the next equation to be solved: $x + y^2 = z$ is solved, and then z becomes the new value for x in the next equation. This is called iterating the equation, turning it back into itself over and over. The equation is not solvable. The answers are random and unpredictable.

When such an equation is iterated millions of times—an exercise that has become practical only in the era of computers—these random numbers are found to form a pattern that is recognizable. This iteration technique can be applied to equations concerning weather, population growth, economics, wave dynamics, the rate of water dripping from a spout, and the movement of celestial bodies. Iterated equations describe all systems in which there is a continually new starting point from the point the system has arrived at, and they can be used to provide models for systems of continual feedback, such as biological and psychological systems.

Fractals, Fractal Scaling, and Self-Similarity

When such infinitely iterated equations are plotted in three dimensions, the image shows recognizable patterns that are repeated throughout the image at vastly different levels of scale. Mandelbrot (1982) invented this mathematical approach, and he called the image that it produced a *fractal*. Fractals found in nature include the tracery of the veins of a leaf being similar to the branching of the tree on which the leaf grows or the contour of a single rock resembling the shoreline where it lies. Mandelbrot called his area of mathematics *fractal geometry* to refer to its measurement of the irregular fractured, fractional, fragmentary, fractionated, and refractory areas of experience resulting from dynamic forces in self-organizing systems. A fractal is the footprint of a dynamic system (Briggs 1992, Gleick 1987).

We can now see that human life itself is an iterated equation: It always starts at the point it has reached so far and repeats certain patterns, although never in *exactly* the same way. Psychic structure is similar to structures found across different orders of scale, from intrapsychic to interpersonal, from consciousness to unconsciousness. Moment-to-moment interactions resemble the form of longer-term relational patterns. External events or third parties may disturb the pattern of a moment ever so slightly, and yet its effect may be seen years later (J. S. Scharff and D. E. Scharff 1998a,b). Therapy proceeds by patterns repeated at slightly different starting points, and so does affective education.

Sensitive Dependence on Initial Conditions

The principle of *sensitive dependence on initial conditions* was originally discovered in the field of the computer simulation of weather forecasting (Lorenz 1963). This principle is often illustrated by a phenomenon called the butterfly effect. Theoretically, the flutter of a butterfly's wings in Brazil could be so magnified and modified by other factors that it could result in a hurricane in Texas (Gleick 1987). Small, almost unmeasurable differences in the conditions at the beginning of a process can be magnified so that the results are unpredictably vastly different in one situation compared with another situation that initially seemed quite similar.

For examples, in the human embryo, when the organism is starting out, there are critical periods of rapid growth and differentiation of cells when a stage-appropriate stimulus leads to a response that sets the course of development forward. If that moment passes without the necessary feedback, the opportunity for developing in the new direction is irretrievably lost, and the embryo continues its growth around a deficit. Thus, small deficits at critical periods can make an enormous difference. Similarly, small differences at many periods of physical and psychological growth cause different patterns of development whose course can be understood in retrospect but cannot be predicted ahead of time because of the interaction of other complex factors. Dynamic systems are particularly sensitive to the conditions prevailing in the environmental niche in which they find themselves at the time of their origin, so that certain factors are far more influential than others.

Applying chaos theory to neuronal development, we find that the human brain is highly sensitive to its starting conditions of the infant's constitutional readiness and the mother's affective attunement. Born without sufficient cortical inhibition, the immature brain depends on the mother to be a regulating, calming, transforming object. Operationally, the mother's adult brain programs the immature brain through pathways developed during arousal sequences of high affect. But it is not a one-way programming. The two brains, and especially their right frontal lobes, are in a state of entrainment, a continuous feedback loop of mutual communication and influence. The growth medium for the infant's brain is the positively toned affective exchange with the mother's brain (Schore 1994).

The first months of life are defining. Like the human embryo, the infant brain continues to build order out of chaos at specific moments of transition into increasingly complex areas of development. Social and emotional encounters with the environment through the agency of the parents stimulate and fine-tune the neuronal circuits that mushroom at some critical periods and then require pruning when their function becomes obsolete at the next critical period. Brain structure in the infant organizes, disorganizes, and reorganizes in the light of environmental influence at critical periods. The shaping of ongoing neural structure and function occurs according to a series of timed sequences in interaction with the environment.

In summary, the appropriate sequence of interaction with the care and concern of the caregiver is critical for pulling infant neural development out of chaos and into a stable state of order through the selective establishment of further neuronal development (Schore 1994). In this process, small differences in these initial processes make large and unpredictable differences in the later sequences of development.

Understanding the impact of sensitive dependence on initial conditions, scientists admit that they cannot reliably predict outcomes in regard to complex nonlinear systems, although they can understand them looking back. Likewise, psychoanalysts cannot expect to predict, although we can use our knowledge of patterns to understand in retrospect how a result has come to be.

Sensitivity to Transition at the Edge of Chaos

Iteration may lead to either stability, periodicity, or chaos. These outcome states may change, depending on small changes in conditions and the time of observation. Structure emerges out of chaos in one part of the system, followed by the return to chaos before a new level of order is achieved in another area. The system of structure and process in a rhythm of chaos, transition, and order may appear to be simple or complex at different times. In order to understand this process, we need to understand the language of *attractors*.

Attractors

Simply defined, an attractor is a system represented by a point. The single point contains information regarding every variable that affects the system. All knowledge of a particular dynamical system at a single instant in time is collapsed to a point. The point *is* the system at that moment.

A Fixed-Point (Steady-State) Attractor

For example, a pendulum powered by gravity will tend to swing back and forth in movements of decreasing amplitude and eventually stop at a fixed point and reach a steady state. The action is governed by a *fixed-point*, or *steady-state, attractor*. Even while the pendulum is swinging, it appears to be pulled toward the steady-state attractor.

A Limit-Cycle (Oscillating) Attractor

A pendulum powered by electricity will proscribe an arc that is forced away from returning to a steady state. The pattern is repeated regularly in terms of time and distance. This is called a *limit-cycle*, or *oscillating, attractor*.

A Strange Attractor

A *strange attractor* is a dynamic system that does not seem to be predictable or to be organized in a consistent form. When the repeated solutions of the iterated equation for the strange attractor are plotted in the many dimensions of a mathematical construct called *phase space*, the resulting image shows the system as a point at a moment in time and at each later moment. With each iteration, the system changes slightly and the point moves, eventually tracing as it does so a multidimensional orbit.

The pattern formed by the strange attractor seems to be organizing the complex system when in fact it is the product of the organization of the system (Lorenz 1963). When the nonlinear equations needed for studying this unpredictable organizing force are iterated (the endpoint is taken as the new starting point repeatedly), the orbital pattern emerges. Order comes out of chaos through the action of the attractor. The attractor is the pattern that emerges from the plotting of the system, but its character has the paradoxical quality of seeming to be the thing that organizes the system.

Furthermore, the strange attractor seems to be drawing events in its proximity toward itself. This happens in the "basin of attraction," which resembles a river's watershed basin (Gleick 1987). The river appears to be creating the watershed, but really the watershed is creating the river. The system functions as though the attractor is pulling events toward itself, when really the cluster of events is creating the basin and the attractor itself. For example, the interaction between the infant's brain and the mother's brain at the cognitive and affective levels forms the system called the mother–infant relationship that creates the interactive sequences and that results from them.

Self-Similarity

Magnify a small portion of the inside of a strange attractor, and you find a pattern that is repeated at another place inside it. In chaos theory terminology, the strange attractor shows *fractal scaling* and *self-similarity:* The shapes seen at one scale of magnification are similar to the shapes seen in the detail at another scale (Briggs 1992). The deeper we look, the closer we attend to detail, and the more we find. Greater detail brings greater understanding, especially of areas that are immensely complicated.

Fractal geometry captures the obscure, the in-between, the folds, the world within a world, and the world between the known worlds. It shows the regions of chaos, the patterns of attractors, and the zones of transition at the edge of chaos. Fractals are useful in giving us confidence in predicting the shape of the whole from looking at a small part, though not of predicting the outcome of any change in the conditions.

The Application of Fractal Scaling and Strange Attractors to Transference and Therapeutic Action

Several psychoanalytic writings have applied the ideas of chaos theory to neural development, personality, parent–infant interaction, pathology, and the therapeutic process (Galatzer-Levy 1995, Lonie 1991, 1992, Palombo 1999, Piers 2000, Quinodoz 1997, D. E. Scharff 1998, D. E. Scharff and J. S. Scharff 1999, 2000, J. S. Scharff and D. E. Scharff 1998a,b). The continuity in form between the person, the body, the personality, the internal object relations set, and the transference is an example of fractal scaling. Transference is a fractal of the total personality. In keeping with the concept of fractal scaling, small shifts in the transference give rise to major changes at the level of the overall personality. The patient's internal object relationships refind their own form in the external world and in the person of the therapist. The chaotic dynamics of the unconscious flow between patient and therapist create a new relational formation that is a combined fractal of the transference and countertransference. Ogden (1994) has called this "the analytic third" (p. 76). Its unique pattern is a strange attractor with the potential to reorganize the personalities of both patient and therapist.

We have described the organizations of the internal object and the organized self as two strange attractors of personality that contribute to the pattern of the overarching self, which is the more complete strange attractor (J. S. Scharff and D. E. Scharff 1998a,b). Lonie (1991) thought of the mother's gaze as a strange attractor for the infant. We agree with her idea, but we feel that it is subordinate to the main strange attractor, which is located in the internal object relations set of the self. The self guides the personality system to fill a shape that is then expressed in external ways of relating to others, including the therapist in the transference. As Spruiell (1993) said, strange attractors move, shift, combine, and recombine and give rise to images and forms. The internal objects split, combine with parts of the ego, and recombine following modifying experience with the external object. In partnership with ego and affect, the internal object gives rise to an internal image or object relationship that governs the form of the personality and its interactions with others.

In keeping with the concept of sensitivity to initial conditions and transition points, tiny shifts in any realm of the internal object relations set produce changes in behavior toward the self and the other, both in development and in therapy. Unconscious internal object relations act as "basins of attraction," pulling events to fit the current organization of perception and expectation. Coming to chaos theory from an ego psychological bias, Palombo (1999) has described an "infantile attractor" that acts as a basin of attraction, tending to reduce a wide variety of events in adult life to a common denominator of similar, familiar experiences through limited understanding that leads to a narrow range of responses, no modification by experience, and thus no growth. In object relations terms, we think of the basin of attraction as the repressed internal object relationships that interfere with conscious communication and adult relating that could otherwise modify old, destructive patterns learned during infantile experience.

In therapy and psychoanalysis, the transference is the strange attractor that is the product of and the organizer of the therapeutic experience. It gives meaning to other pieces of experience. Interpretation breaches the limit-cycle attractor of the closed personality system and introduces the effect of the organizing potential of a neighboring system with its own strange attractor (the therapist's internal object relations set). This perturbation creates turbulence that leads to a new organization.

How systems disorganize—that is, leave the basin of one strange attractor to enter a region of chaos or to enter another region of influence—is of crucial importance to therapists and educators. When a system has been in the sway of a relatively fixed or limited attractor, such as a rigid personality characteristic or a fixed idea, it is relatively stable. In therapy and in education, persistent perturbations or disturbing influences progressively destabilize a fixed pattern so that it enters a chaotic region of disorganization. Systems that have moved out of one basin of attraction and exist at the edge of chaos are more susceptible to reorganization by a new strange attractor (Palombo 1999). This describes the effect of both psychotherapy and education—to move a person out of a preexisting pattern into a state of temporary disorganization comparable to a region of chaos and then into a new pattern of feeling, acting, and understanding.

In psychoanalysis or psychotherapy, the mind of the analyst is a strange attractor, as is the shared pattern of the analytic third cocreated by the analytic dyad. In group settings, the group transference is the strange attractor that introduces powerful perturbations into the emotional and cognitive organizations of its individual members. Group interpretation creates turbulence in the group system, which then moves itself first toward chaos and later toward reorganization. The individual minds of the leader and each member of a group are potentially strange attractors capable of pulling the system back toward basic assumption functioning or, if conditions are right, forward to new organizations. The group mind is the overarching system that each individual experiences as the most powerful attractor toward new systems of organization. The small-group experience in a weekend conference creates effects that reverberate in the periods between conferences and profoundly reorganizes the student's way of working.

Fractals and Object Relations Theory

Applying chaos theory and Mandelbrot's ideas on fractals to personality development, we note a correspondence between fractal geometry and object relations theory. The family is a tiny part of society. The person is part of a family. The personality is a part of the whole person. Each internal object is part of the total personality. The internal object relationships in dynamic relation are a fractal of the personality. Each internal object relations set is a fractal image of the family in which the person grew up. Each dream is a fractal of the personality, of the transference, and of the course of the analysis.

Psychic structure develops from a chaotic mix of neuronal profusion and destruction; hormonal shifts; sensations of hunger, thirst, deprivation, satisfaction, warmth, cold, pain, comfort, vibration, and position; new affective experiences; and recurring personal interactions with the caretakers. Some interactions are planned, predictable, and stable, as in good, reliable at-home parenting, while others are periodic and less expectable, such as the parent becoming ill or returning to work. Some parenting interactions create a low-intensity background of arms-around, good-enough environmental mothering that promotes going-on-being, while others involve eye-to-eye relating, sustained gaze interactions that dominate the foreground and challenge the infant to a state of intense arousal for new learning. Others are randomly fluctuating, such as the mother's mood in the short term, the size of the sibship, or the effects of divorce in the long term. Out of all this chaos, order, and the transition between them emerges a pattern of experience that gives a sense of personal meaning.

Object relations theory holds that experience with the external object in the chaos of early infantile experience is taken in to the personality to create a cybernetic system of parts, all in dynamic relation. According to Sutherland (1990), the infant ego is born already in the shape of a person. The infant ego seeks encounters with family members, whose loving expectations will encourage the child to grow into that shape and become a person. The individual is a system subject to continuing shaping by the caregivers, whose feedback not only helps conserve existing organization but also offers perturbations that lead to a continuing capacity for new and progressively higher levels of organization. Random, disorganized experiences do not necessarily ruin this development. They can require a strong repressive counterbalance that promotes reorganization, reintegration of parts, and growth, just as a period of confusion can stimulate a reorganization that gives new clarity.

Couple and family therapists have described the interaction between spousal partners as being similar to that between parent and child (Dicks 1967, D. E. Scharff and J. S. Scharff 1991). But the dynamics of individual therapy, the mother–infant relationship, or the marital dyad are insufficient to address the complexity of human interaction. Human behavior cannot be reduced to the study of the dialectic between two people because people are raised in the group context of the family the community of families, and society. As more members are added to the family, or again after divorce when two families are blended, the potential for interaction at the conscious level increases exponentially while at the unconscious level it approaches infinity. The firstborn enters a different dynamic system with more of an appearance of order than the third child, who enters later, when the family system is more chaotic and led by parents who have become less anxious about controlling their children's environment. The anxiety that the girl child experiences without visible genitals is more chaotic and diffuse than the anxiety that the boy faces with a penis as a ready focus for identity. This is why some girls focus on the sight of the penis in a nearby male as evidence of something missing in themselves. The penis becomes a strange attractor in proximity to which their attempts at comprehending their bodily and emotional condition are reorganized.

Interpersonal Expression of Internal Object Relationships in Teaching and Learning

Intrapsychic dynamic systems of internal object relationships are displayed in the interpersonal dimension as individuals recruit others to interact with them through projective and introjective identification processes—in marriage, in therapy, in family relationships, and in work groups (Dicks 1967, D. E. Scharff and J. S. Scharff 1987, J. S. Scharff and D. E. Scharff 1998d). The teaching setting that involves group interaction provides a situation designed to promote perturbations in existing patterns of ways of knowing and understanding. The system is designed to enable individuals and groups stuck in set patterns—determined by limit-cycle attractors and familiar basins of attraction to prejudged ideas and previous ways of understanding—to move into a transitional state approximating chaos in which they will be open to new organizations of thinking, feeling, relating, and working.

The affective learning model in the group setting offers a laboratory for here-and-now examination of the interrelatedness of self and object and the associated interaction between self and other as we work together in groups. Participants combine with others in subgroup formations that oscillate between supporting and subverting the work of the group and between chaos and stability, as they deal with what is already known, what has been experienced but is not understood, what is not yet known, and what is essentially unknowable.

Learning from Experience in Relationships

Even the well-functioning mother and child must be supported by a wider family and by social groups. Pairs in intimate contact exist within larger groups and are buoyed by the social order. Each infant, child, and adult lives and learns in the context of wider groups throughout the life cycle, some of them groups of which he or she becomes the leader. We learn how to be thoughtful, civilized human beings by living in relation to important individuals and groups. From that life experience, we build a system of internal object relationships. Similarly, we learn *about* relationships through being *in* relationships to study.

If we are trying to learn about self and other—about ego, affect, and object—we will learn most efficiently and thoroughly from studying the relation of self and other in depth over time as we experience it individually and in groups. The experience of *individuals studied in groups* and the experience of *groups studied by individuals* gives here-and-now evidence for the validity of concepts of self and other, ego and object. In the affective model, the group itself is a practical application of the theory to be taught. Like the strange attractor that creates the system and is at the same time a product of the system, the group process results from and stimulates the interaction of pooled internal object relationships systems. *This process is at the same time the subject to be studied and the medium for studying it.* This paradox introduces a powerful note of ambiguity into the heart of the study task, and this ambiguity promotes the oscillation between old attractors, the chaos of nonunderstanding, and reorganization through the influence of the new attractors offered by new ideas and new colleagues.

Most psychoanalytic theories address a context of growth and learning that is essentially dyadic. Object relations theory enables us to widen our focus beyond the psychoanalytic dyad to include the multiple dyads and triangles and the various larger groups of interacting, modifying influences in which the analytic dyad exists. We are then able to apply the concept of psychoanalysis not only to individuals but also to the functioning of small, medium, and large groups as they engage in studying the complexity of the human situation.

SUMMARY

Principles of affective learning derive from analytic theory of the individual and the group, recently illuminated by chaos theory. We hold that a person's current object relations influence the task of learning object relations theory and practice. If object relations theory is to be understood, our own internal object relationships need to be studied in action. Principles of complex self-organizing systems from chaos theory offer ways of understanding human personality development in normal interaction and in dysfunction. These are relevant to understanding how the brain develops in attunement with the caregiver, how personality forms from experience, how psychotherapy works by creating a shift in initial conditions, how transference is a part that represents the whole, how interpretations create turbulence and reorganization, and how learning from experience in a group enables the internalization of theoretical concepts at cognitive and emotional levels. Object relations theories of individual and group, research into brain development and affect regulation, and chaos theory provide the building blocks for the affective learning model.

4
The Rocky Road of
Affective Learning

INTRODUCTION

I have arrived at my thoughts on the affective learning experience from my experience in small groups first as a student and then as a woman faculty member attending many conferences on object relations. My ideas came together in their present form after leading a small group during a weekend conference devoted to studying separation anxiety from various theoretical points of view and to considering chaos theory as a new paradigm for thinking about human development and interaction. This chapter gives an account of the work of a single-weekend small group in approaching the learning task of that weekend conference.

MY THEORY BASE

Learning occurs within relationships. Objective and subjective inter-actions between those persons involved in the conference stir up the learner's relationships with internalized objects, just as their work with their patients brings their internal fantasies into the clinical situation, where they require work to make them usable for therapeutic action. When a trainee experiences fear or worry in the training process, learning is inhibited. The quest for knowledge can be interfered with, or blocked, by unconscious anxiety. Curiosity, for example, is curtailed by fears of disapproval or punishment. When the "teachers" who come to impart knowledge interact with the "students" who come to get knowledge, unconscious fantasies about getting and taking may, if not recognized, drive envy and lead to fears of retaliation. These mental operations make learning a problem. These kinds of deeper internal issues require a teaching–learning atmosphere in which the self of the learner is a primary focus.

The use of oneself as an instrument for therapeutic action requires a trainee psychotherapist to learn at deeper levels than can be achieved by reading or passively accepting the material of a lecture. Personal experience in the integrative small group, which meets following each major presentation and is a required activity during weekend conferences, is an extraordinary source of meaningful discovery about oneself as a person and a psychotherapist. On this particular weekend, the concepts of separation anxiety as a developmental challenge and chaos theory as a model and metaphor for human mental operations provided the springboard into these discoveries. At each weekend conference or institute, the focus on a different concept provides another platform from which to plunge into the learning process.

My concept of group process starts with Winnicott's theory of the *holding environment*. In this concept, Winnicott (1963a,b) considers the need of the infant for an environment that provides security. This allows the infant to depend on the reliable, consistent holding of the parenting presence that contains overwhelming anxiety coming from the environment and from the infant's interior. It helps the infant get through the anxious months of total dependency. In the process, the infant gradually develops object relatedness with a whole object for whom concern can be felt and to whom reparation for destructive actions can be made to keep the relationship viable and mutually satisfying.

Winnicott makes a distinction between two aspects of the mothering function: the *environmental mother* and the *object mother*. The environmental mother provides a predictable, safe setting; good, loving handling of the baby; and management of physical needs for food, air, warmth, stimulation, and rest. The object mother is the mother who excites or frustrates by arousing or satisfying the infant's needs. The object mother is in the foreground, being met head on in gaze and vocal interactions, while the environmental mother is a background presence. The integrative group can be conceptualized as an environmental mother supporting trainees as they struggle with the object mother in the form of the presenter and the concepts brought for study. Soon the group membership itself takes the center of attention as the object mother does.

THE GROUP AS A MATERNAL OBJECT

The group is an interpersonal situation in which psychotherapists can experience and examine the nature of their relationships in pursuit of learning the theory of the self and its object relationships and then applying their learning to their clinical work. The first obstacle to becoming a group rather than a pack of individuals arises from the difference between each individual level of desire to affiliate. We know from Bowlby (1969, 1973, 1977, 1980) that early patterns of interpersonal attachment have a critical effect on a person's later capacity to bond and that difficulties in bonding are connected with anxiety, frustration, depression, and aggression. The interpersonal power of the group must be viewed on a continuum with some trainees having high affiliative needs and others less so.

The next problem that the group faces is the image of the group as a maternal object created in the fused image of the maternal objects of the individuals in the group. There is an internal representation, unique to each person, of the group as a maternal object originating in the mother-and-baby experience. The infant's internal representation of the maternal object gets transferred to the family and then to peer, social, and work groups. This maternal representation in each group member's object relations will then influence the person's usual group behavior in terms of feeling excited or rejected, connected or disconnected, seeking pleasure or feeling pain, and expressing dependent needs or avoiding them. The relationship to the group as an object affects and then modifies the student's characteristic defenses of dependency and idealization against aggression and destructiveness.

THE SMALL GROUP AT WORK

This vignette describes my experiences as a woman leader working with a small group of five women whom I will call Terry, Laura, Margaret, Amy, and Linda, and a male coleader, whom I will call Joe. Joe and I met with the group for five sessions in the course of this single weekend. The small-group setting connects all the elements of the teaching and learning. Readings, lecture presentations, and large- and small-group discussions are integrated by each participant self interacting with others. In addition to the usual integrative task of the small group, my coleader, Joe, and I were particularly focused on examining the affective learning process in the small group that follows each didactic session.

Stranger Anxiety and Projective Identification

The First Presentation

The introductory lecture was a well-researched blend of Freud, Klein, and Bion that provided an object relations framework for thinking about separation anxiety in psychoanalysis from a predominantly Freudian base. It referred to primitive anxieties and defensive reactions, one form of separation anxiety being stranger anxiety. The presenter's style was scholarly, unassuming, low key, quiet, and at times tentative as he picked his way through complex ideas in English, not his first language. The first installment of the vignette describes the start-up of a new group, the ensuing group experience, and how it reflects the topic of separation anxiety. The group is dealing with its vulnerability as the members begin to trust one another and test the coleaders.

The First Small-Group Meeting

I began by stating our task: to relate what we had just heard in the lecture and large-group discussion to ourselves as therapists and to apply it to our work with patients. My statement was met with silence. At last, Margaret said, with a mixture of surprise and accusation, that she noticed the leader had started the group by stating the task. That was different from any other group she had been in. No other leader had done that. She was wondering whether Joe and I were competent to create a learning environment. No one responded.

Breaking the silence after a couple of minutes, I said to Margaret that she had a question about the leaders that she was not quite sure how to answer. I asked whether anyone else was also doubtful.

Laura replied that she had liked it when I stated the task. It helped her think about what the group is supposed to do. Uncertainly, she added, "But I guess I'm still not sure what to do." Her voice trailed off.

Terry said that she thought it was fine for me to behave differently. They had to get used to different styles in leaders and in group members. She explained, "I mean, I like all of you, but I find the group work hard. It stirs up some kind of worry I don't understand, and it makes me feel like I don't want to talk much."

I thought that Terry was struggling to make a link between herself, her own stranger anxiety, and the concepts of defensive reactions to primitive anxieties.

Linda picked up the theme: "So what do we do here? I've never been to one of these conferences before. Do we discuss the lecture, or what?"

Amy remembered that when she was there last year, she didn't like the requirements of attending the group, but by the end she got a lot out of it. She especially appreciated being able to talk about a case for which she needed supervision. It really made the weekend for her. "There was one other thing!" she remembered. "That speaker was warm and really human."

"I know who you mean, and I thought so too," said Margaret. "Today's presenter is a very intelligent, perceptive man but a little too quiet for me. Maybe he prepared his lecture thinking we were all analysts with an excellent knowledge of Freud and Klein. I'm still a beginner, and it scares me to think I should know all that stuff."

Amy disagreed: "No, his theory was fine. His whole book was great, basic separation anxiety theory. I think it's his style that's the problem for me. I felt sorry for him having to speak English. I got sleepy, and I still am sleepy—maybe jet lag or something."

Again the group fell silent. Laura commented that the group was having a hard time getting started. I wondered whether the silence was a protection against revealing critical responses to the presenter and his material. I asked, "Perhaps the same dynamic is contributing to the silences and to Amy's sleepiness. What might that be?"

Linda said to Amy, "I'm surprised to hear that you didn't like his style. I thought it was great. I don't know a whole lot about Freudian theory, but he was good for me."

Margaret said, "I just realized that he's not the problem. It's me. I'm just reluctant to get started in this group. I miss my old group from the two-year program. I don't know most of you. Now I have only three days rather than two years to get to know you."

Terry moved on to speak about the woman presenter she had met during the coffee break. She was looking forward to hearing her speak the next morning. Terry said enthusiastically, "She seemed very much alive and excited. I want to hear from her about vertigo and anxiety. I just remembered that I used to have vertigo around heights, and I have patients who complain of it, so separation anxiety must be an issue for me and them. I could really learn a lot from her." Terry's remarks were greeted with a round of nods and murmurs of agreement.

By the end of this first hour, the group was coalescing around the image of the exciting woman they longed for, found last weekend, and had now lost. The flight to this exciting object in its re-created form was an avoidance of their own stranger anxiety with the first speaker and with one another. They projected their stranger anxiety and their aggression toward one another into the speaker, whom they then identified as a "remote father" compared to the woman presenter, who was glorified in anticipation through a projective identification of her as a "warm, exciting mother" who stirred their desire for more of her.

As happens in group life, the anxious members were defending themselves by splitting into good and bad styles, unavailable father and gratifying mother, and dead and alive internal objects to deny their stranger anxiety and their aggressive attack on the whole needed-and-feared object.

> The group continued on the topic of unsatisfactory fathering. Most of the women commented about absence in their own fathering. Amy, in particular, spoke about her father, who was a silent presence in her home, except for occasional sporadic verbal gunfire with her mother. The absence of a live, participating father meant that Amy was paired off with a workaholic mother who never could be satisfied with Amy's efforts to manage the children in place of her. The grown-up Amy also worked long hours as a therapist and felt herself "go missing" in the process, just as she felt herself angrily "disappearing" when mother could never see her constructive efforts to manage the younger ones in the family.
>
> The night before coming to the weekend, Amy had had a dream in which body parts—arms, knees, torsos, and heads—littered the scene. Underneath these piles of human pieces, the words "object relations" moved like subtitles for a foreign movie. My association to her piles of body parts was that they might represent the group's experience of missing parts of their fathers, projected as a longing for the presenter to be a "father" who could enter their minds, enliven them, and give them theory in one piece and help them feel whole. But Amy was not thinking of the object. She was thinking of the self. This was a frightening dream for Amy. She connected it to worries that the participants would know how inadequately prepared and how incompetent she was. Now it was clear that she had projected her own frightened listening into the presenter and experienced it as his unconfident speaking. The effort of suppressing her worries about competence had made her sleepy, but now the insight made her chuckle. Amy decided this was not a "plain vanilla dream," but it was no longer persecutory. The group members agreed that all of us struggle to communicate and connect the parts of the "body" of theory in object relations.
>
> Amy went on to use "plain vanilla" to describe the quality of her feelings about the group so far. She thought the group's slow way of warming up was

contributing to her sleepiness, as if there was something everyone was holding back, and she was, too. I asked Amy what flavor "ice cream" she needed to keep herself alive in the group over the weekend.

Amy burst out, "Rocky road!" and everyone laughed. She added, "I have never eaten rocky road ice cream, but its lumps and bits seem better than sucking on plain vanilla." The group was coming alive in its laughter. Getting away from the bland vanilla flavor that was without trouble but devoid of interest, the group members concluded that they would have to "chew" on the material with one another and not just peacefully suck.

The early group process of members who feel vulnerable to anxiety about self-competence and self-exposure in the learning situation pushed the group to tackle important object relations theory, which refers to mental operations basic to development and human interaction. We use splitting and projecting as defenses to deny the aspects of the group we experience as bad, projecting them back into the speaker or even into historical reveries about internal mothers and fathers. There is a recurring tendency in groups to limit frustration with the group by assuming that hated attributes are in the individual: in the presenter (he is too quiet), in a group member (she is too quiet), or in the group leaders (they are too quiet). In this state of projective identification, the badness out there is perceived either as imposing on the individual so there is no freedom to be oneself (better be quiet) or as lacking in resonance, just as mother was when she was unavailable or too absorbed with another focus (might as well be quiet because no one is listening).

In this first session, the group had to locate the "missing father" in their individual historical experience, in their here-and-now-experience with the presenter, in their reactions to the concepts, and in the group's experience of me and the coleader, Joe, who was quiet compared to me. They had to find their own mother and father relationships as present, lively, and exciting or as absent, deadly, or quiet.

The presenter was cast as a frustrating image in which group aggression, anger, and hostility took refuge to protect the individuals who felt strange with one another. If the group as a whole had been allowed to continue without interpretation of its projective identification of the presenter as the "bad breast," the displaced negative transference to him as a weak father would have grown but would have remained unavailable for learning from one another in the group. Group members would continue with internal persecutory feelings about lack of competence connected to a false self. This is the "plain vanilla" that kills aliveness and creativity. The "rocky road" brings recognition of aggressive "lumps" and destructive "bits" in the material coming from the breast. The mature integration of good and bad aspects of objects is achieved by accepting and analyzing ambivalence and anger from the group toward the presenters, the faculty, the individual participants, and the group as a whole. Otherwise, the feelings get split, leading to idealization of the "good other out there," which reinforces the difficulty of finding the "good mother in here" in both the group and the self.

This work helped the group find itself as an object identified with the containing, nurturing function, which is also experienced as frustrating and painful. The frustrating bad object view of the group expressed in the beginning evoked schizoid anxieties about impoverishment. The group members adapted Amy's dream of littered body parts representing unintegrated part objects to express the longing to have a nurturant father and the fear that they were too impoverished, unprepared, and ill-equipped to attract his nurture. As they worked, the bones in Amy's dream pile began to structure themselves into a "mother" body that was not merely to be sucked like plain vanilla ice cream but more like a body that contained separateness and contrasts, much like the marshmallow, nuts, and chocolate chunks blended together in rocky road ice cream.

In this first session, my coleader, Joe, and I focused on the here-and-now process. The trainees gradually became more curious about the here-and-now process in themselves, relating to one another's comments and becoming more supportive. As coleaders, we applied our group therapy skills to relate to the group as a whole, to observe and listen empathically, to facilitate the members' interaction, and to reflect and clarify process. We applied our group teaching skills to link group process to the concepts of separation anxiety and chaos theory presented that weekend.

Following the Aggressive Affect

The Second Presentation

The second presentation was by an advanced woman student who gave a clinical case for discussion by the large group. The patient she described was needy, anxious, and demanding of extra attention outside the limits of the therapy frame. The student discussed her difficulties in responding to the patient's primitive anxieties and enactments.

The Second Small-Group Meeting

I will pick up the group in their second session after this presentation. The atmosphere of disappointment filled with longing, characterized as a flight from one another in the first meeting, was beginning to change.

Amy, Laura, Margaret, Linda, and the group's coleaders were in place, wait-ing quietly. Terry arrived, late, coffee in hand. She seated herself, smiled broadly, and said, "I didn't want to come back. I was having too much fun with some of my old group members, catching up." The group responded with a three-minute silence. I thought of Terry's need for something extra outside the group as a small dose of the same dynamic that the woman pre-senter faced with her patient.

Amy remembered another dream. Again this dream seemed to be her association both to the woman presenter's difficulties in responding to her patient's needs and to the small group's wishes for more. Amy said, "This time, it was about a patient I was terminating. It had been very tough work with her, and she had long been a pain in my neck. This dream was about a little creature, a kind of marsupial, who had made a pouch on my neck and had crawled into it." Amy rubbed her neck and went on. "When I was work-ing with her, I often had a lot of pain right here. Back to the dream: The creature gave me the same pain, but it was so comfortable in its pouch in my neck that I couldn't dislodge it. Then I woke up."

"Do you think your patient was also your marsupial, comfortable inside you but also a pain in the neck?" Laura asked.

"Well, yes," Amy agreed, "because she was a person with a bipolar prob-lem, rather like the patient we just discussed in the clinical presentation. She had a long therapy with me, full of anger and fragmentation. Her idea of get-ting close to me was to fuse with me, then be full of distorted anger when I didn't allow it. She couldn't tolerate the loss of me as a perfect therapist—mother."

Margaret said, "I think this group, so far, is a little marsupial. We want into the speaker's pocket, to be held without effort. But he doesn't invite it; he is too busy straining to speak English as well as he can. The sleepiness is back in me."

Laura agreed. "Yeah, right, I feel that way, too. I thought it was because I didn't understand the part in the presentation about that patient hating the genital mother and longing to idealize a more regressed kind of internal mother. Did anybody get that?"

"I frankly got more out of the large-group discussion again," Terry re-plied. "Maybe that's my way of being angry about our not talking much yet about our patients in the small group. Your dream, Amy, reminds me about working with patients who need me too much, and they just eat me up. How did you get that lady to the point of termination?"

Amy explained, "I had to work with her to express her emotional needs and dependency. Early on, she wanted to act them out. She learned she envied my separateness from her and then poured on the fusion when she was angry about that. But then we had to stop because she only got fifteen sessions from her HMO insurance."

My coleader, Joe, said, "Perhaps something like that is working in here in the group. Do we long to be effortlessly cared for like a marsupial in a pouch, and are we then angry at the presenter for not providing a continuous flow of nurture?"

Terry responded, "I am dealing with a reluctance in me to create a speaker I can use. I am splitting off from this group into the crowd at coffee time and getting my excitement out there. I really am annoyed with not getting more so far, but I'm also getting something from the group in here when we talk about real patients."

Joe continued, "Perhaps it was dangerous in the first group meeting to be so direct about angry feelings. Now that the anger in here has worn off a little, perhaps the disappointment can be acknowledged."

Terry said, "Maybe, but it makes me nervous to complain to you. My mother always complained about me needing too much attention. She always accused me of being overactive. She was petite and restrained. As you can see, I'm a big bouncy girl, and I like action. She made me leave the dinner table if I was too excited. So, yes, it is dangerous to tell you what I feel. I'm trying to keep myself excited and alive at coffee. Something in this group feels dead. Besides, I didn't trust you to accept the way I feel. I'm not an analyst, and I don't know all these analyst words."

"So, if you complain, you worry how we'll take it?" Laura asked.

Terry replied, "If I show you how excited I am, you'll think I have a problem or something. Amy talks so easily about her thoughts, her dreams, and then her experience with groups here. I guess I'm jealous of her fluency. It makes me want to shut up."

I said, "There's a group fantasy that if we long to have something, in this case fluency and expressiveness, something will spoil our efforts as a group and make the outcome too hard to take, and so it seems better to have some members hold in their thoughts and feelings."

Terry is learning that as she inhibits her expression of aggression, it gets displaced as envy of persons in the group, and the group grows more dangerous. She thinks that finding the words for displeasure is attention-getting and punishable. She is showing the remnants of her earlier struggles with authority. These kinds of struggles with separateness take the form of compliance or defiance, fight or flight. Characteristic defenses repeat, in the presence of the group, the roles learned in the past. Terry is one of the participants who is beginning the work of identifying the defensive function of keeping real affects out of the room. Things are not said because they hurt. It is dangerous to be separate enough to reveal these feelings.

Terry, for example, was not able to express her dependency needs. She split them off instead into two groups: an idealized group that met her needs out there during the coffee break, and a denigrated group inside the small group that she experienced as demanding that she be less excited and more analytic. She was experiencing depressive, angry, defiant reactions—an old struggle with the other—in the here and now of group life. Her struggle to come fully into the group was the result of feeling blameful, rebellious, and "sent away from the dinner" by the frequently quiet group as mother.

Projections into the group preclude Terry from using the participants to learn the analytic words she desires. It takes a "rocky road" in contrast to "plain vanilla" for a group to undo defenses and contain frustration so that more conflicts in experience can be experienced and explored. Group process gets these conflicts and fears expressed openly. Then Terry and others can be helped to apply their understanding of their fears in the group to those of their patients in therapy.

The Progression from Flight to Intimacy

The Fourth Small-Group Meeting

Picking up the group again in the fourth session, I will give a summary of the process to set the scene for the final piece of learning in the fifth session of the small group. From complaining that the original presenter was too quiet, the group has progressed to feeling assaulted by the liveliness of the next presenter, who talked about chaos theory. The group felt an unbelievable amount of anger toward the presenter on chaos theory for "dropping a think bomb" that was so full of excitement that they could not grasp much of it. The group felt painfully "pulled forward" into newer paradigms just as they had felt "pushed backward" into historical reviews and contemporary extensions of Freud, Klein, and Bion.

I focused on finding the destructive capability in the group. Where was it? We examined individual, pair, and subgroup responses to the didactic presentations. We discussed how stranger anxiety creates aggression hidden in compliance or openly expressed in defiance. Sleepiness, shyness, quietness, and reluctance were all experienced as emotional reactions to the turbulence of separation anxiety and the fear of exposure and shame that it may provoke. Frustration of needs led to aggressive reaction formations of idealization and then to envy of the idealized object and consequent diminution of the self. On the other hand, doubt and criticism were also expressed and contributed to a healthy differentiation of self from object.

After these interpretations of aggression were accepted, euphoria took over the group. It was as if everyone had found a mirror in someone else and that through these pairings the group had truly achieved a holding environment. Embarrassment and shyness lessened, accompanied by bursts of laughter and affection. Voices were quiet, reflecting an intimate level of communication that the main speaker had accomplished with his quietness. Glances were lengthened into sustained "visual holding" of one another. Throughout this session, the group expressed its longing for support of their psychotherapy work, which most of them did without colleagues and often without consistent supervision. The group members longed for full experiences with good feelings and were freshly aware of personal inhibitions that could prevent this. The magical delight of a "we-are-all-similar" feeling gripped the session. The group felt like a mirroring heaven.

The group was using the defense of fusion in response to my exploration of aggression and differentiation. The group fusion was also a defense against members' confusion as they struggled to integrate the concepts of chaos theory as metaphors for mental operation, useful for understanding the perturbations of separation anxieties in themselves, for example. Meeting an unfamiliar model of the mind contributed to the group's feelings of shame and embarrassment. Then the group discussed old models versus new models.

The Fifth Session

From this platform, we arrived at the fifth and final group session of the weekend. The group retained some of the warm, affective mirroring from the previous session, but there was also a hyper-responsible joylessness about the awareness that survival as a psychotherapist means tackling our own selves, fears of the new, aggression at what is strange to us, and tendencies to polarize desire for and denigration of the object.

The concluding excerpt illustrates the pain associated with conflict related to change. When expressed in the small group, we can learn from this conflict and move beyond it.

I said, "So, as we approach the end of this last session, we realize that as a group we have experienced chaos theory as both a thinkable and unthinkable experience. And that leaves us feeling both excited and depleted, as the theory is so complex and so draining of our energy. As a group, we have achieved connectedness in contrast to deadness at the beginning, but perhaps this closeness is covering over feelings we can't share and that could get in the way of the group reaching closure."

Amy admitted, "I have some stuff I've been keeping to myself. I'd been thinking of the references back to Freud as 'old fuddy stuff.' Then when chaos theory was explained, I thought, 'There is no way I can get this stuff. Why am I putting myself through this?' But I pretended it was as exciting as a moon walk and would 'kill' the 'old fuddy stuff.' That was dishonest. I was not figuring out that I had two feelings at the same time. One was about love of theory, and the other was about hate of it or the fear of it."

Joe asked, "And so what exactly did you hold back?"

Amy replied, "When I couldn't hold both things together, I had to make one of them into shit. That lasted in me for about a day. Now I can see how hard I was struggling to correlate the content in myself. It's so hard to hold together regression and progression."

Margaret said, "It took me a long time to want to be in this group this weekend. My previous experience had been so powerful and satisfying. I didn't want to lose that, so I almost didn't gain this."

I said, "Margaret and Amy are speaking for the need to recognize your conservative needs and your evolutionary needs, integrate them, hold them together, and so feel more whole."

Now the field of participation widened from the pair of Amy and Margaret to include Linda, Terry, and finally Laura.

Linda joined in to say, "Yes, and I have the same problem. All weekend I have been sitting with some kind of poison inside me. I am the only one here who has not been at one of these weekends until now. I have been struggling with whether to stay mature or to regress into chaos where creativity can begin. I have been loving and hating all of this weekend simultaneously and feeling that it is so dangerous I can't bear it."

Margaret agreed. "Me too! My heart is racing. I wanted all weekend, after my two year program, to have that feeling of competence and self-confidence. I'm so self-destructive when I desire competence. I have hated this group, and at the same time I felt lots of affection for each of you. I just want to be me with you without having to be so slick and cool. There, it's out. 'I love you' is out there—and 'I hate you' is out there. I'm getting better at feeling both."

Terry said, "Well, my stuff that I can't talk about is still envy and jealousy. I got close to one of the presenters at the coffee break, and I realized he reminds me of my grandfather. I wanted to be special to him, and I didn't want to have to come back in here. All right, I admit it; I wanted to dominate him, to have lots of excitement and attention for myself. I envy Amy, Margaret, and you, Linda."

Terry had omitted Laura in her review, but now Laura spoke up. "I've said the least of all this weekend, and that's my dishonest stuff. This is my first time, and I guess I just shut down a lot. No, what I really wanted was for someone to take me under their wing, and it didn't happen." Turning to me, she continued, "When you confronted me yesterday about the reality of my motivation and desire, it really sank in. Like a child in front of a toy store, I knew how much I wanted to come back and get more."

I asked her, "What was the cost of waiting so long with wanting?"

Laura countered with another question. "What's the cost of hanging on to a defense rather than facing the truth?" She got various responses from the group.

Amy: "Loneliness."

Terry: "Emptiness."

Laura: "Yeah."

Amy: "See? I told you. Rocky road is the flavor of choice! Vanilla is too painfully simple."

CONCLUSION

In previous sessions, the group members had worked through transitions from flight from one another, to fight with one another, to delight with mirroring, to loss as the weekend came to a close. There had been disappointment and defensive aggression in each transition. But they had taken advantage of the feelings of disappointment by owning some of the more difficult interpersonal feelings, such as jealousy and envy of the presenters and themselves. When these are defended against, they create distance. When these can be owned within the group process, reality-testing mechanisms come into play. There had been fury in response to the turbulence of new ideas and paradigm shifts introduced by chaos theory. By the end of the fifth session, the group, my coleader, Joe, and I had once more learned from the group process how aggression stimulated by stranger anxiety, separation anxiety, and new knowledge constructs, deconstructs, and reconstructs the internal object relations of the group members and the group as an entity.

5

Intensity, Brevity, and Focus

We aim to provide a teaching and learning environment in which participants can learn from experience and grow over time. To our teaching task, we bring a belief in the value of learning from experience. Writing about psychotherapy years ago, Freida Fromm-Reichmann (1950) said that our patients need experiences, not explanations. However, in the educational context, our students need both explanations and experiences.

Not all participants who want the integrated cognitive and affective approach to learning object relations theory are able or willing to commit long periods of time to their education in an area that is only one of the many theories they must know something about. So we have developed a particular way of leading the affective learning group that is adapted to the specific learning requirements of participants who choose to attend one weekend only, perhaps because they are interested only in the topic of that weekend or because they want a limited commitment like those in the group described in Chapter 4.

It seemed to us that the limited time frame of the single weekend called for a specialized application of the affective learning model. It calls for intensity, brevity, and focus, just like brief therapy. We have applied the principles of technique derived from object relations brief therapy to the short-term affective learning group (Stadter 1996, Stadter and D. Scharff 1999). In this chapter, we outline these principles of brief therapy and apply them to the use of the affective learning model for exploring object relations theory and practice with participants who commit to a single weekend.

In the five sessions of the single weekend small group over the course of a three-day conference, the faculty group leader keeps the focus on the specific learning tasks of that weekend rather than promote the wide-ranging discussion of various clinical and theoretical issues that can be encompassed over the course of a two-year program. The time limitation sharpens the focus and the empathic acuity of faculty and participants. By giving rapid access to more intense and fluid emotional states, the brief learning format promotes a greater affective intensity in relation to the learning task.

Once these principles were articulated with respect to the single weekend, we found that they applied to our work over each weekend with longer-term groups as well. The principles of intensity, brevity, and focus inform our approach to every module of our teaching programs. As in brief therapy, the brevity of the experience induces participants to expend greater effort. The power of each weekend conference comes in part from the time limits, augmented by respect for time boundaries shown throughout all the conferences. Attention is given to the meaning of time in terms of sharing resources and learning efficiently with others in a balanced way. The intensified affective level of the weekend reflects a combination of arousal and engagement that speeds and deepens the learning process. This promotes a type of learning that does not usually occur in longer conferences or weekly learning venues of equivalent hourly value.

BRIEF THERAPY AND THE GROUP AFFECTIVE MODEL: TECHNIQUES IN COMMON

Develop an Alliance

Like the brief therapist, the leader of the affective learning group needs to develop an alliance. In the learning group, however, developing the alliance refers to fostering a group alliance in which the members work with one another as well as with the leader. The alliance is created when the group leader adopts a nonjudgmental, empathic stance of attunement to the group as a whole and interacts with the members with respect, sensitivity, and compassion for their difficulties in mastering the material. This alliance must be developed rapidly—but not hastily. We cannot push the process faster than it can go, or there will be increased resistance or defensive idealization of the group leader and the process without real learning. We cannot achieve in a single weekend the depth of understanding possible for an ongoing group. But we can do useful work, often of remarkable depth, and we can at the least give the group a taste of what is possible.

When the group leader sets the focus on the problems in understanding the material, participants feel engaged in the learning task. The members build trust in the group. The leader directs interpretations at removing group blocks to an effective work mentality, and the group becomes able to address the integrative task. The small group's efforts at learning are also supported by the other settings in the institution: Plenary review sessions, large-group discussions of members' reactions to the presentations and challenging questions, and comments on the process in all group settings create a context in which participants can be adventurous experientially and curious conceptually. Small-group leaders, in concert with the aim of large groups in the institution, engage the group's curiosity about the inner world.

Set a Dual Focus: Didactic and Dynamic

The most important feature that distinguishes brief therapy from long-term dynamic therapy is the setting of a focus (Stadter 1996). In the object relations approach to brief therapy, we set a focus on two levels: symptomatic and dynamic. The symptomatic level typically addresses the psychological pain or functional impairment that brought the patient in, for example, a sexual problem, failing grades, or difficulty at work. The dynamic focus centers on aspects of the patient's underlying psychodynamic structure. Like the brief therapist, the group leader sets a dual focus—on the conference material (the didactic focus) and on problems and modes of comprehending it (the dynamic focus). Our goals are to educate the participants about the didactic material that is the subject of the conference and to help them experience and reflect on their attempts at learning from a dynamic perspective. The didactic and dynamic foci are usually closely related in the learning group, just as the symptom is linked to the underlying dynamics in therapy.

The following small-group vignette is taken from the process of a single-weekend small group during a weekend conference on hysteria in which the presenter emphasized hysterical mechanisms of denying and splitting off awareness of sexual phenomena and sexual parts of the self.

> During the third of five sessions, the group members were discussing how they had become so close so quickly. The atmosphere was one of great intimacy with rich and sometimes moving discussions of the material, relevant personal ex-

periences, and pertinent examples from their own clinical work. The group leader felt that the group was working effectively, perhaps too effectively to be authentic. He wondered silently as to what was not being said.

At that moment, a member said that she was engaged in the task and appreciative of the group, yet she felt that something was missing. The group leader asked the group to consider what that might be. There was a silence of about five seconds, and then two members simultaneously exclaimed, "Sex!" The group members then noticed that while apparently working together closely and intimately discussing other related topics, they had been relating as if there were no gender differences in the group and as if they had no sexual feelings. The group came to see this as a here-and-now example of hysterical phenomena.

The duality of focus in the learning task is emphasized when two coleaders lead the small group. At a given point in time, one leader may be actively working with the group on the didactic focus while the other leader is using her receptive capacity to attend to the dynamic focus and, at another point in time, each may move to the other level of focus. In this way, the coleaders embody the duality of focus, each working on both levels collaboratively and helping each other see both the surface and the depth. This is an advantage of coleadership that is particularly useful in faculty training.

Get Historical Material to Help with Focus Setting and Understanding Repetitive Patterns

In didactic presentations of theoretical and case material, the speaker emphasizes family and personal history, patterns of defense, and reenactments of old scripts. In the small group, participants may usefully associate to past influences on learning. The following are two cases of the use of historical material in the small- and large-group settings.

A man who did not speak at all in the large group offered a topic in the small group, but then said that there was no need to talk about it. When the group confronted him as to his intentions, he realized that this fit his usual pattern of passivity.

A Catholic woman who tuned out when the presenter raised the issue of dealing with patients' spiritual needs became able to engage in the large-group discussion after she recalled being taught that only Protestants questioned the word of God.

Invite the Group to Experience and Examine Relationships

The small group notices the behavior of the leader and comments on it. The leader tries to imagine what it is the group wants from him at the conscious level. He then tries to figure out what else is wanted for which this conscious wish is the cover. The small group joins him in examining the relationships that emerge and the subgroups that form and speculates as to what defensive or creative purpose these subgroupings serve for the group. Do they support or subvert the integrative learning task? In the plenary review meeting, all the small groups share aspects of their experiences and consider how the small groups relate to one another and to the institution. Large-group dynamics are subject to process and review to enlarge the learning platform.

Interpret Dynamics and Patterns When Appropriate

The small group notices the patterns, and the group leader paves the way for interpreting their defensive function and works to release the underlying anxiety, rage, and longing. Process comments in the plenary review and the large group contribute to this interpretive effort. Affective intensity, the use of self in the weekend's learning task, and the time limitations work together to heighten the impact of here-and-now group process interpretations even when there has not been time to gather the connection to historical material.

As in brief therapy, however, if we push too hard, we can damage the alliance and cause the group to fail in its learning task. Pushing too hard stems from being overeager to achieve in the time available, forgetting that the short time frame has been selected by these participants precisely because in part it imposes constraints. A solution for the group leader of the short-term affective learning group may be to interpret his own responses. He explores the here-and-now of the group process from the vantage point of his own affect. Leader-centered interventions are less traumatizing than participant-centered interventions, and they introduce the leader as a transitional object for group exploration. This learning about the "not-me" object can then be transferred to learning about the self if and when the group member chooses to do so.

Use Techniques Other than the Psychodynamic

In brief therapy, the dynamically oriented therapist may introduce pharmacological support or may suggest adjunctive cognitive exercises to widen the sphere of interventions. In the affective learning design, the group leader's dynamic orientation is the primary mode for reaching understanding, but it is by no means the only technique. It is only one aspect of addressing the task. The major nonpsychodynamic methods are the lectures and video presentations. There is a strong didactic element to which the affective element relates. Presenters give specific information, connect it to research findings, review the professional literature, and make recommendations on technique when consulting to case presentations and vignettes. Group leaders may provide short didactic comments so as to give the inexperienced group a bridge from the familiar tutored way of learning to our unfamiliar way of confronting the unknown. However, the group leaders limit their didactic contributions in the small group so as not to create or promote a dependency culture.

Just as brief therapists examine the unconscious responses to a nondynamic intervention, we invite participants to notice their own reactions to the content and mode of presentation of the didactic material. We encourage them to involve their subjectivity and learn from their sense of self so as to improve their capacity for dealing with the self of the patient in their clinical work.

Consider Serial Brief Courses

The brief therapist does what he can in the agreed time frame and accepts that he may never know how the current experience affects growth and development in the future when he is not there to take satisfaction in it. He also bears in mind that brief therapy is only part of the larger process of change, which may include the need for more brief therapy at a later date in response to new developmental challenges or life changes.

Similarly, the leader of the brief affective learning group does what he can in the time available. We accept the brief group as a limited but authentic experience with its own integrity. The effective single-weekend group also functions as a trial run for more intense involvement in the group affective model for learning psychotherapy (see Chapter 12). Some single-weekend participants return for multiple, single weekends. They prefer to learn in a series of single bursts, and they report that their learning builds from one conference to the next, even when the interval between each event has been more than a year. Their serial educational enrollment is analogous to the serial brief therapy described by J. S. Scharff and D. E. Scharff (1998d), Stadter (1996), and Stadter and D. Scharff (1999). This common phenomenon of periodic return to therapy after an extended absence has been described by a number of authors as a powerful use of limited resources of time and money (Bennett 1989, Budman and Gurman 1988, Hoyt 1990). As in the case with serial brief therapy, serial enrollment in our educational weekend conferences provide a whole that is greater than the sum of its parts.

Here is a vignette to illustrate the value of brevity, intensity, focus— and repetition—to a participant we will call Rudy.

> In the fifth of five sessions in a single-weekend small group, Rudy noted how much he had learned from the weekend conference and went on to present in detail some of the complicated theoretical concepts that he now understood more fully. The group members acknowledged Rudy's help in reaching greater understanding of these concepts, and yet they said that they never really got to know him despite his being quite active in the group discussions. He and the group discussed this impression, but he remained baffled by this feedback.
>
> In the next year, Rudy attended two more conferences as a single-weekend participant. In his second conference, one in which the topic was countertransference and so was highly personal, he was surprised to receive the same feedback from his new small group. In his third conference, he was in a new group with the small-group leader who had led the group he was in during his first conference. In the first meeting of that small group, the leader sensed that something was different about Rudy but couldn't be more specific about it. In the second meeting, Rudy told the group that this was his third conference and that he felt he had finally "gotten it." In the light of feedback from both previous groups, Rudy told this group, he had begun to observe his clinical work more closely. He said that he became aware that he was "deep into a conceptual understanding" of his patients but that his relationships with them were more distant than he had previously realized. He was troubled that this discrepancy had been diminishing the quality and effectiveness of his clinical work. He concluded by saying that he felt he was now able to connect with his patients emotionally and relationally and so was working in a more grounded way. Rudy was pleased when the small-group members in this conference gave him the feedback that they felt him to be quite connected with them during the weekend.
>
> One of the women reported a similar experience of needing repeated exposure for learning to occur. She said that it had taken her four weekend conferences to feel that she had really grasped the concept of projective identification (a slippery concept for many of us). She said that the combination of didactic and experiential learning, followed by time to explore and practice what she had learned in her own clinical setting, then reinforced by repeated contacts with the teaching institution, had been essential to her continuing education.

Provide the Potential for a New Ending to an Old Experience

The unique focus on the use of self in the learning process and the mix of experiential and conceptual learning used in the affective learning model leads to changes in learning behavior. Participants learn in ways they never learned before, and they see things about themselves that they never saw before. They see how their work with patients is complicated by their similarity to important figures who challenged, troubled, puzzled, or restricted them in the past. They learn how their own unconscious object relationships resonate in current relationships with group members as with patients. Gaining awareness of this through therapy, supervision, and case discussion lets them see their patients realistically, not through the prism of their own neuroses. The affective learning group offers another avenue for arriving at this crucial capacity to see the object more clearly. At the same time, therapists who participate in the learning group find out more about their own self. This enables them to be available in their clinical work as more than just a projection of elements in the patient's mind and instead to be fully present in their own reality as well, bringing "something *new* that the patient has not experienced before" (Guntrip 1969, p. 346). Similarly, the leader brings to the group a strong sense of self, a willingness to be used as an object, and something new: the opportunity for learning from experiencing the impact of the dual didactic and dynamic focus of the brief format.

APPROACHING THE LEARNING TASK WITH A NEW ATTITUDE

Here are some examples of changes in attitudes to learning as a result of participation in brief-format affective learning groups.

> A man whose father was never home had not been a good student and still had trouble paying attention, but in the group he was able to remain engaged in the work and learn the material. He said that he was more able to learn in this group not just because of the welcome male presence of two older men as group leaders but also because the group's feelings and fantasies about the men as leaders and authorities could be discussed and did not have to be held in and so block the energy needed for learning with these leaders.
>
> An inexperienced therapist who gave the small group lucid vignettes of her clinical work surprised the group when she said that she had not been able to describe her work in previous seminars or even in groups specifically for supervision. Building the group alliance and attending to the group process made the environment safe enough for her to try out a new capacity.

LEARNING THINGS ABOUT THEMSELVES
NOT SEEN BEFORE

Here is an example of some personal learning that occurred in response to the group.

> Group members were surprised and irritated when a brilliant, valued woman participant missed a session in a cavalier way with no regard to the impact of her absence. Even when she was present, she appeared and disappeared, one moment promising to talk in more detail about herself or her clinical work and the next moment deflecting any requests for information. At the end of the group, she said that the group had helped her see what an "exciting object" she was, in saying things of value, then missing a session, and then not following through on what she could talk about. She felt that her experience helped her understand the anger that she generated among colleagues and friends in her professional and personal life. She guessed that this behavior of giving and withholding, presenting and removing herself, could be upsetting to her patients, who might either quit in the face of it or stay unhealthily caught in the elusive object web. There was no attempt to explore the personal sources of this behavior, as would probably have happened if this were a therapy group.
>
> As she left the conference, the woman realized that she had gained an unanticipated bonus from the affective learning process. She said to her group leader, "I learned even more about myself this weekend than I did about the conference topics. I didn't get what I expected, but, thank you, I got more than I could have ever hoped for."

In this case, an individual characterological issue threatened to disrupt the group alliance, and the group objected. The group leader was not trying to change the woman's character or personality style. Interventions were directed at removing the block to the group's ability to get on with the task of learning together. Individual insight often comes as a by-product of the group process.

THE DUAL FOCUS IN INSTITUTE ADMINISTRATION

In our approach to administrative requests, we apply the same dual focus used in the brief-format affective learning small group. The requests are like presenting problems. They deserve direct attention in and of themselves, and we address them at the level of the didactic focus. At the same time, they point to underlying attitudes toward the learning process in the group setting, and we respond with the dynamic focus. Attention to the underlying attitudes helps us understand the nature of the request and informs our thinking in reaching an administrative decision. Requests for administrative changes usually arise from members in ongoing groups, but they do occasionally come from those who have enrolled for a single weekend, as the following example describes. I will call the participant Minna.

> Minna, who was enrolled for a single weekend, missed her first small-group session but attended the large-group sessions before and after the time for the small group. The dean sought her out and inquired about her absence. Minna said that she had come only to hear the presentations and had not intended to attend the small-group meetings. Working from the didactic focus, the dean reviewed with her the function of the small groups, empha-sized their importance, and urged her to attend them, as all participants are expected to do in order to contribute to the learning of others as well as for themselves. Turning to the dynamic focus, the dean then raised the question of whether there might be other factors affecting her decision to not attend. Minna acknowledged that she generally feels uncomfortable in discussion groups but denied that this was a major factor in her decision. She agreed to give the small group a try. Her small-group leader reported that although Minna was clearly anxious, she used the group well and found it to be a posi-tive experience.

More frequently, two-year program participants make requests for accommodation that they have not anticipated needing at the time of their en-rollment. We respond to these requests in the brief format. The request is made, a faculty discussion occurs, and the dean relays the decision.

For example, a two-year program participant might request a reduc-tion in tuition because of financial hardship. Another two-year program par-ticipant and mother of an infant might request that she bring her baby to the conference and breast-feed in the small group of which she is a member. First, we consider these requests in the light of the policies of the institute, prece-dents, and the individual practical needs of the participant. Second, we use the request as an opportunity for additional affective learning by the faculty and membership. Just as in therapy, the unique qualities of each individual and their relationship to the small group and the institution require that each request be considered on a case-by-case basis, with the dual focus in mind. First, let's con-sider the process of using the brief format of an administrative intervention to address the request of the new mother. I'll call her Leigh.

The faculty agreed that naturally a nursing mother would want to bring her infant with her for the weekend and that of course she would want to feed her child as necessary. At a deeper level, she might want to be appreciated in her role of mother and show off her wonderful baby. However, in Leigh's case the baby might act as a buffer to draw attention away from the group's feelings about Leigh, who had been absent from the group on previous weekends because of issues connected with her pregnancy.

Some of us thought that many members of a small group would support the idea of demand feeding, tolerate the baby's presence, or even enjoy having the baby in the group. Others felt that a positive outcome would depend on the members' life circumstances, the state of the group, the baby's competence or difficulty in feeding and quieting, and the mother's way of dealing with the exposure of her breast.

The year before, we had had a similar situation, and the mother found it impossible to give her child the attention he needed and still engage in the work of the group. The other group members found the distraction from the task, the mother's conflict, and the baby's distress all upsetting. The group leader reported an intense emotional reaction that interfered with holding the group in mind. We knew from experience that group members and leaders could be distracted from the learning task, and some of them could be upset, especially women who had not gotten over their inability to conceive.

As discussion continued on the current request from Leigh, the faculty realized that Leigh, as a new mother, or her baby might not be ready to separate for the duration of a small group, namely, for an hour at a time. If so, this might mean that it would be better for Leigh to delay her enrollment. The decision was made that the dean should reply to her that the faculty supported her wish to be with and feed her child and that the baby would be welcome at the large group, where the room was big enough to give her a measure of privacy, but not at the small group, where it would be too distracting. Leigh did not want to miss another weekend, so she arranged for a companion to take care of the baby for the hour of each group. She felt welcomed and supported by the conference and so was able to accept the limit regarding the small group without feeling rejected. The small-group members were able to deal with their leftover anger at Leigh, express their jealousy, share Leigh's joy, and integrate her back into the group.

Let's look more closely at the process of using the brief-format administrative intervention. In this example, we will address the situation of the two-

year participant midway through his first year in the program. We will call him
Sam and the group leader Mrs. Reid.

> In his small group, Sam had repeatedly referred to his difficulty of attending
> all the program events because of competing personal and professional com-
> mitments. Then he asked the faculty to consider a formal request to miss one
> of the summer institutes and part of one of the subsequent weekends so that
> he would not have to drop out of the program. Sam also suggested a number
> of accommodations that would allow him to "make up" the missed material.
> The dean talked with him, established the extent of the problem, and asked
> whether there were any other factors involved in the request.
>
> The dean subsequently met with a committee of the faculty to get a
> broader perspective. Together they discussed the issues from the dual focus
> before the dean would get back to the participant with possible options. The
> faculty group discussed the practical implications of such a request for the
> institute in terms of its impact on the budget, on the class if the man were to
> drop out, and also on his small group were he to miss many small-group
> meetings and large-group presentations. The faculty group discussed what
> Sam's request represented dynamically for the institution as a whole. Mrs.
> Reid began by referring to the small group's experience of Sam. She said that
> she had responded to his individual dynamics in relation to the small group
> with a countertransference of feeling controlled and worried about saying
> something that would result in his leaving. She said that his comments al-
> ways had an "I-have-to-have-it-my-way-or-else" quality. She was struck that
> his style of approaching the institution was like his way of participating in
> the group and that he had now made conscious the threat of quitting. Mrs.
> Reid said that Sam's characteristic way of dealing with these two situations
> suggested a sense of entitlement and an expectation of needs not being met.
> In terms of the small-group dynamics, Mrs. Reid noted Sam's repeating pat-
> tern of connecting with subgroups and pairs that form around issues of com-
> petition and specialness. She said that he seemed to have a personal valency
> for these issues and a capacity to pick them up in others.
>
> The faculty concluded that Sam's request for a special scheduling arrange-
> ment might, in part, unconsciously represent others' individual wishes to be
> special to this group leader. Through Sam, they might be vicariously raising
> the question of whether they would be missed. The faculty wanted to work
> with the participant rather than make unilateral decisions but without en-
> couraging individual special treatment that would take away from the over-
> all needs of the group.

We did not see Sam's request as simply an administrative issue that could be automatically resolved by checking the institute's policy guidelines. From the perspective of our dual focus, we reviewed his request on the administrative/practical issues and on the dynamic contributants. With our dynamic focus, we attended to the four levels in the educational system: the man's individual dynamics, those of his small group, the faculty, and the institution as a whole. The faculty decided that Sam's requested scheduling arrangement would unhelpfully single him out as the one with the wish to be special and the one to be gratified. The faculty also decided that it would be problematic both for his small group and for the institution as a whole.

The dean got back to Sam to say that the faculty appreciated his practical situation and offered a small degree of flexibility in his attendance. However, it would be the same level of flexibility that could be extended to other students in similar circumstances. The dean went on to discuss with the student the extent to which such flexibility might address some but not all of Sam's pragmatic concerns. The dean briefly explained the reasons for the decision from both an administrative standpoint and the standpoint of dynamics. The dean also indicated that the faculty hoped that this would work adequately for Sam and that he would be able to continue in the program. The dean also advised further discussion of the issue of specialness and worth in the small group. This limit, recommendation, and method of processing the request successfully secured the participants' commitment to the program and gave a boost to the learning of the entire small group.

The affective method teaches participants about object relations theory and practice by applying the principles and techniques of object relations to the methodology of the educational setting. The method is further enhanced by the application of principles drawn from object relations brief therapy. These principles of intensity, brevity, and focus are particularly relevant to the single-weekend group, but they are also useful for maximizing the effectiveness of each teaching module within an ongoing program. We have given examples of learning in the small group and learning from administrative decisions to illustrate our use of the dual focus on symptom and dynamic and to show the use of the countertransference to discover the dynamic elements in the here-and-now of the group process.

6
Therapeutic—but Not Therapy

AFFECTIVE LEARNING GROUPS
AND THERAPY GROUPS

Small groups using the affective learning model may have therapeutic side effects, but they are not therapy groups. This chapter explores the crucial difference between therapy groups and affective learning small groups. The therapy group has the primary task of promoting personal healing and relatedness. The affective learning group has the primary task of psychoanalytic education. Despite these differences in task, some of the interactions and verbalizations by participants and leaders in the affective learning small groups appear similar to those in therapy groups, leading to the false impression that the learning group is really just a therapy group in disguise. In view of the emphasis on affect as an important component of the model, this impression is understandable, but it is mistaken.

Admittedly, some small-group participants really do utilize the small-group experience as a personal therapeutic experience, openly or covertly. Nevertheless, the majority of participants are there to learn theory and apply it to clinical practice. However, having done just that, many participants, especially those in ongoing groups over one or two years, report the personal value of the group process. True, the affective learning group may be therapeutic, but it is not a therapy group.

If we were to examine a ten-minute segment of an affective learning group process and compare it to a ten-minute segment of an actual therapy group, it might not be clear at first which group was the affective learning group and which was the therapy group. This confusion can occur if only one segment of an ongoing group is observed. Over many segments, other dimensions emerge. The major difference is determined by the frame for the process, the goal, and the primary task.

First, the frame: The analytic therapy group usually meets once or twice weekly for an indefinite period of time. Members do not have contact outside the group. They are asked to keep group material confidential. In contrast, the affective learning group meets for a short series of sessions in a series of intensive modules over a weekend, a year, or two years. Members are fellow students who attend teaching events and socialize together. Discretion is preferred, but confidentiality is not promised. The affective learning group is part of a total learning matrix in which all group experience is processed and reviewed.

Second, the goal: In the therapy group, the goal is personal change. In the affective learning group, the goal is the acquisition of theoretical and technical knowledge, clinical skill, and an improved capacity for using the self as an instrument in clinical work.

Finally, the task: In the therapy groups, the task is to engage in a mutual healing process of sharing dreams, fantasies, and problems with personal relationships to arrive at insight and recovery. The task of the affective learning group is to integrate intellectual and emotional understanding by reviewing the didactic material and processing individual and group affective responses, to learn the concepts by experiencing them, and then to apply them to clinical practice.

In this chapter, we consider two questions regarding these two types of groups: What dynamics do they have in common? What are the points of difference?

Similarities

Group Functioning

Both therapy groups and affective learning groups utilize affect as a major focus of the experience. Both ask participants to be sensitive to inner images, affects, and physiology and to verbalize this inner experience. Both utilize principles of group dynamics to further learning about self and others. Both pay attention to boundaries and boundary violations. Both groups aim to provide a safe, consistent, nonjudgmental environment that allows the group participants freedom to explore their inner experiences of thinking, feeling, and relating to the group. In both settings, the ultimate goal is understanding.

Leadership

Both group therapist and the affective learning group leader maintain an attitude of neutrality and create a good psychological holding environment for the individuals in the group. Both are held ethically responsible for practicing with competence and respect. Both relate to the group as a whole entity. Both use the analytic theory of individuals, groups, and systems as their base. Both group psychotherapists who conduct therapy groups and group leaders who facilitate learning groups utilize techniques invented primarily by therapists. These techniques include interpretation, confrontation, containing the affect, and understanding individual and group defensive strategies against affect. It is the shared focus on affect that is most responsible for the resemblance between therapy groups and affective learning groups.

Individual Responsibility

Affective learning group participants choose whether to enroll in the program, to use the group, to address the issues from one perspective or another, or to commit tentatively or fully. Patients choose whether to enter group therapy, to work in therapy on issues of history or here-and-now transference, or to make personal changes. Responsibility rests with the course participant, just as it does with the patient in group therapy. The leaders exercise choice and responsibility as well. Like the group therapist, the group leader exercises choice over whether to lead a group, how to intervene, and how to maintain the group as a good environment.

Differences

Even though the affective learning group may look and sound like a therapy group at times, it is not a therapy group. The affective group is distinguished from the therapy group by the primary task, which is learning, not healing.

Primary Task

In the affective learning group, there is no contract between the group leader and the participant for therapeutic change. There is no agreement on the need to ameliorate psychological symptoms, to revise personality trait behaviors, or to alter characterological structure. Participants in the small affective learning group experience are responsible for their own experience and for how they choose to utilize the small-group experience for their learning. Some participants choose to focus mainly on academic material, others on group process, others on clinical cases, and others on personal issues. As a collection of individuals, they participate from their own vantage points to develop a group mind for dealing with all those aspects of learning. Individuals have unique points of entry into the group learning process, from which they emerge with a more integrated perspective on theory, practice, personal development, and group process.

Contract

A major difference is apparent when we compare the functions of the leader and the therapist in terms of how society views the contract for pursuing the task. In this respect, the responsibility of the group leader is quite different than the responsibility of the group therapist. The group leader of the affective group is not held responsible for the group participant's personal experience in the same way that a therapist is held legally responsible for work with a patient.

Confidentiality

Another major difference is apparent in terms of confidentiality. In the affective learning group, there is no privilege. Care is taken to deal with personal material in a discreet, sensitive, and respectful manner, but there is no promise to keep personal material confidential. On the contrary, sharing of experience is expected. Small groups convene once each weekend in a large-group plenary review meeting to share mutual concerns and to explore similarities and differences among the small groups. Group members are free to choose to what extent they reveal or discuss their small-group issues in the plenary. Sharing of group information also occurs in the faculty review meeting. There group leaders discuss how their groups are progressing, how they are dealing with the learning task, and how they relate to one another and to the institution. This discussion allows for institutional integration of the small groups' various interpretations of the shared learning task. The small-group boundary is intentionally porous to other levels of process in the educational system, so that the institution can profit from multiple perspectives on the learning process, maintain the integrity of the teaching, and so fulfill the mission of its primary task as an institution for teaching and learning.

Focus on the Group

Affective group leaders frame their interventions from the perspective of the group process and the reflection of the didactic material in the group and the individuals in it rather than from the perspective of individual dynamics. At times, however, a focus on the individual will be required temporarily to free the group to attend to its task. The focus should remain on the group for which the individual speaks. If this focus is repeatedly diverted to one individual so that the group cannot work, the individual is seen as being in need of personal therapy as well or the group leader is seen as needing consultation from the faculty group. Because of differences in their background training as therapists and teachers, affective group leaders vary in their ability to hold firm to the group learning task. By discussing their small-group issues in the faculty review meeting, they adapt to the culture of the institution and carry it back to the small group.

Some group therapists frame their interventions with the unique dynamics of the individual in mind and evaluate the effectiveness of their interventions by their impact on the individual as well as on the group as a whole. Other group therapists, however, comment mostly on group-as-a-whole themes or use these to make sense of the individual contributions to the group. The group conducted by the therapist who works from the group-as-a-whole framework might look more like the affective learning group at first glance. Still the work is different because the primary task is different. The affective learning group includes a didactic component and furthers individual professional learning, while the therapy group promotes individual personal healing.

Objectives and Evaluation

The affective group leader has three objectives: (1) to use affect to elaborate on cognitive comprehension, (2) to teach about the group dynamics that occur, and (3) to illustrate theory with reference to the group process. Unlike group therapists, affective group leaders do not focus on the therapeutic effects of their interventions. If they happen, they are by-products. Instead, the leaders focus on the group's ability to work and learn. They evaluate their effectiveness by observing the growth of the group's ability to learn from experience, understand the concepts, and apply them to clinical work. The participant evaluates the leader's effectiveness at the end of each module in a written evaluation form. When these are collated, the leaders get more information on how to improve their ability to facilitate the task of learning from experience.

The Didactic and Affective Components

Affective learning group leaders look for opportunities to use theoretical constructs that have been presented in the conference to inform their interpretive comments. Not that they distort the process by rigid adherence to a presenter's ideology; rather, they simply notice when the concepts are being illustrated by group process or individual development and then point them out to the group so that the group members can see the theory in action. During the weekend on separation anxiety, for example, interventions furthered understanding when they addressed the affective experience of loss and anxiety in terms of the absence of group members, the imminent end of the conference, and envy of couples whose individual insecurities were buffered by the partners' being together. A specific example from an actual small group illustrates this point.

A participant described the following dream to the other members in the small group.

> "Two people get in a car to begin a trip. I feel sad that they are leaving. I want to go with them, but that is not an option for me. It's hard to accept that relationships have to end."
>
> The group responded to the dream with various associations. One member connected the manifest content of the two getting into the car to the loss of the presenter and his wife, who would be departing the next day. A man linked the image of them as a couple to the parents that the child has to leave behind in order to go his own way. A woman thought of the couple as representing the group that she would be leaving. The group leader noted that the dream brought into focus the group members' awareness that they were to meet only five times over the weekend, that soon they would have to part whether or not they had made the trip into the areas to be explored, and that they had feelings of grief about the impending loss and separation.

This intervention relates the individual's dream to the frame of the group, to the group process, and to separation anxiety, which was the overall theme of the weekend conference. The leader's job is to relate the experience, including the inner life of the individual, to the theory base of the weekend conference, to other relevant aspects of theory, and to the group affective experience that embodies the theory. Always the goal is to understand the theoretical ideas intellectually and emotionally so as to apply them in clinical work.

Interpretations of the Integrative Task

Affective learning groups have many options for addressing the task. The group can deal with the presentation to the large group primarily in an academic and intellectual manner, discussing the theory and relating it to other theories. The group can relate to the presentation by responding to the style and personality of the presenter, the clinical case material presented, or the larger group's reactions and process. Small-group members can present material from their own cases and utilize the experience as a form of group consultation. They can generate issues for discussion directly from their own personal experiences in the present during the conference or indirectly from memories stirred by something that they felt that weekend. The small-group integrative task allows for flexibility of focus and depth of experience, depending on the needs and wishes of the particular participants. The interventions of the group leader follow the direction of the group, always within the orienting mandate to integrate the theoretical and affective components of the learning process.

Inevitably, some group members may experience the group as approximating a therapeutic experience from time to time. They experience it as a vehicle for their own individual growth as they work through personal issues while simultaneously achieving the group task of integrating the didactic material at both cognitive and affective levels.

An example from a different weekend when the topic was hysteria shows the group going back and forth between the concepts presented, their resonance with personal material, the group process that illustrates them, and their clinical application.

> The presenter had described his view of the hysteric's need to repress certain aspects of sexuality and sexual development. He said that the hysteric acts as if sexuality had been banished first from the family and second from the inner life of the individual, never to be thought or spoken again. In the third of its five sessions, the group had created a safe enough space to begin to share some personal reminiscences on sexual development, sometimes in support of the presenter's concept, sometimes refuting it.
>
> As the group discussion progressed, one female participant, whom I will call Alice, related how, during one of the coffee breaks earlier in the weekend, she had reached out and adjusted the male coleader's name tag, which was hanging upside down. She reported that she immediately felt both excited and shameful about making what she considered an intimate gesture. Alice defined her action as a boundary violation. From then on, she vowed to keep her distance from the male and female coleaders. She further said that she was afraid that the male coleader would tell the female coleader and that the female coleader would then be angry and become retaliatory toward her.
>
> The group worked with this in a variety of ways. The first response was from another female member. She described her own longings to be close to a male figure, but she couldn't express them because she was afraid that her

intentions would be misunderstood. Group members discussed feeling uncomfortable about sexual feelings in their personal lives, in work with patients, and in the small group. The female coleader connected the group's
anxiety and need for the group to not speak about sexual excitement as a group
reflection on the presenter's remarks on the hysteric's need to repress sexual
feelings for fear of retaliation. The group discussed the insight that therapists
who are unwilling to deal with their own sexual issues are likely to block
their patients' communications—and even their recall—of sexual experiences. The group members moved on to discuss their longing as children for
parents, both mother and father, who would be sensitive to sexual needs and
development.

The group works through its hysterical dissociation from the topic of
sexuality, confronts fears and longings, and so becomes a safe environment for
dealing with sexual issues.

Dealing with Sensitive Affective Material

In this atmosphere, another group member, whom I will call Bernadette, shared the following painful experience.

"This is difficult for me to say," Bernadette began hesitantly. "I've had a number of psychotherapists and never brought this topic up with any of them.
When I was an infant, my father abandoned the family. My mother and other
family members treated him as if he never existed. Nevertheless, he still
existed inside me in my feelings and fantasies. I always felt that things would
have been so different if he had been in my life. My longing for him never
subsided. As an adult I searched and searched for him, and I finally found him.
I was so thrilled to see him and to find that he was responsive to me. At the
same time, he felt like a stranger to me, and our reunion generated intense
sexual feelings that threatened to get out of control. I felt so ashamed of this,
I never told anyone before."

The group was supportive of Bernadette and compassionate toward her
longing and her shame. A few group members agreed that Bernadette had
taken a big step toward getting over this by speaking about it in the group,
but they expressed astonishment that this important topic had not surfaced
in any of her therapies. Bernadette replied that hearing the presentation,
participating in the group discussion, and most of all being in the group had
helped her see why it had been so difficult to share the material with her

individual therapists. She said that the group had assisted her in exploring an extremely difficult issue. She could now think about it instead of pushing it out of her mind.

At first, the discussion of crossing boundaries by touching the leader's name tag leads to an anxious response in each group participant that causes repression of sexual material, in parallel to the presenter's theory about the dynamics of the hysteric. But the validity of the concept, in conjunction with the group's holding power and safety in numbers, provides a context for Bernadette's revelation. Bernadette expresses the feeling that the group had a therapeutic effect on her, but this is a personal by-product of the group's attention to the primary task of learning about hysteria. The affective learning group addresses the content of the didactic material in a powerful learning paradigm.

CONCLUSION

Students are *incapable of feeling nothing about the material* they are learning (Salzberger-Wittenberg et al. 1983). They are also *incapable of feeling nothing about themselves* while they are learning. At a minimum, they "perceive either positive, neutral or negative feelings *about themselves with relation to the subject matter presented*" (Sonnier 1989, p. xi). How they feel about themselves influences what they learn and what they wish to learn in the future. All learning from others takes place in an affective matrix. Feelings may block or enhance our learning of any subject. When the subject under study is the self and the object, the feelings of ourselves and others can tell us what we need to know. Because the affective learning experience involves understanding and working with emotions as its central, organizing principle, it is easy to understand why there may be confusion regarding the difference between an affective learning group and a psychotherapy group. The key to unlocking the meaning of the concepts and integrating them in an enduring way is turned by our ability to resonate emotionally with the material being presented.

All effective learning must include an affective component. Affective learning may be therapeutic, but it is not psychotherapy. The goal remains the understanding of the theoretical ideas and the application of these ideas to clinical technique, including the use of the self in the therapeutic encounter.

7
The Group Unconscious and the Individual Dream

Cognitive learning alone is insufficient for the development of clinical competence at holding and containing primitive object relationship sets. As small-group leaders, we offer a training experience that elicits and examines the personal resonances that hinder comprehension. No written prescription is given to tell participants how to learn the concepts. Instead, we provide participants an over-the-counter accessibility to learning from experience using their own selves. Participants' free associations, incomplete thinking processes, transference, and countertransference generate an emotional appreciation of the concepts being taught.

Traditional training focuses on the intrapsychic dimension of the patient. Traditional supervision encourages the clinician to analyze the transference without involving the self of the analyst, as if the observing, emoting, and mentating functions could be hermetically sealed. The personal treatment component in the analytic dyad is kept totally separate from the training program. While we agree that confidentiality is required for treatment, we think that the divorce of emotionality from cognitive apperception leads to a split in the mind of the therapist. What is needed is a model that brings together the therapist's affect and cognition so as to lead to integrated understanding of the patient's experience and the therapeutic relationship. Those who are used to the traditional approach for acquiring knowledge find it disconcerting to engage in the process of learning about self and object that we are about to describe.

The innovative affective learning model consists of a unique, cohesive, psychoanalytic teaching–learning structure of gestalt proportions. This structure is systemic in scope rather than linear, emotional as well as intellectual, encompassing personal and professional aspects of the group members as they interact with peers and faculty in pursuit of the integrative task of the group affective learning model. The structure consists of a group matrix of various sizes from small to large in which to experience theory in action. It is to the small-group element of the total conference experience that we address our remarks, based on our experience as small-group leaders.

The small-group task is to integrate the concepts presented at the weekend conference with the group members' personal resonances and clinical experiences. In the course of carrying out the group learning task, participants experience feelings about and associations to aspects of the group leaders' personalities, the learning issues of other group members, the topic of the conference, and the administration. Associations might include ideas, recollections, fantasies, dreams, kinesthetic experiences, and so on. These are then subject to process and review. Themes emerge that further elaborate the concepts under discussion.

COMPOSITION AND THEMES OF THE SMALL GROUP

This example comes from our work as two male coleaders of a single-weekend small group. At the weekend conference in which this small group took place, the featured presenters, identified both as analysts and as husband and wife, provided material on separation anxiety, emotional vertigo, and the impact of dreams in psychoanalysis. With a panel, they discussed the application of chaos theory to psychoanalysis. Conference participants had read about vertigo and separation anxiety prior to the weekend (D. Quinodoz 1994, J.-M. Quinodoz 1991), but chaos theory was new to them (D. Scharff 1998, 2000).

The small group met for five one-hour sessions during this weekend conference only. The group consisted of five members—one man and four women—who had signed up for only this weekend and two faculty coleaders, both of us men, one of whom was senior in terms of experience with the institution. All of them had attended at least one other weekend event, and one of the women was quite experienced in using the affective learning model. Three professions were represented: clinical social work, clinical psychology, and mental health counseling.

We will call the male participant Steve and the women Evelyn, Molly, Paige, and Susan. We will refer to ourselves as Dr. Black (the experienced coleader) and Dr. White (an experienced participant but new to leading the group).

Dynamics typical of a family had emerged in our small group, including longings expressed for closeness to the parental and the marital couple and competition with siblings. These themes had been stirred by the presentations on separation anxiety and were heightened by the approach of the end of the weekend conference. Finally, one of the presenters gave a paper on dreams that accompany movement to a new phase in analysis. After this presentation, at the final group session, a woman reported a dream. This dream from an individual emerged as the final common pathway for understanding combined individual, group, and conference experiences and unconscious group themes and transferences. In this chapter, we hope to show a group dimensionality to Freud's concept of the dream as the royal road to the unconscious of the individual and Fairbairn's (1944) idea that dreams are "essentially 'shorts' [film clips] of inner reality (rather than wish-fulfillments)" (p. 105).

The topic of separation anxiety was particularly relevant in the last meeting of the group, when the dream to be described was introduced into the group. The group members attended to the regressive and progressive aspects of separation anxiety and applied their understanding to issues arising when patients end analysis. Dealing with this analytic topic highlighted the participants' separation anxiety about ending the small group, leaving the conference home, and feeling dead in their own environments that are less supportive to in-depth psychotherapy. Several important group transferences emerged and set the stage for the experience concerning the dream presented in the final meeting.

GROUP STRUCTURE AND THE CONTEXT FOR THE DREAM

At first, the group arranged itself in two subgroups: four women sitting together (all participants) and three men (one participant and the two coleaders). This seating pattern illustrated the group's use of the seating arrangements to defend against initial anxiety by developing comfort through gender affiliation, in contrast to the seating arrangement in the previous session, in which there was a more natural distribution of male–female seating following the accomplishment of comfort with heterosexual pairings.

From the first group meeting, unconscious and conscious group processes reflected personal and professional conference learning experiences. We helped uncover and amplify these processes. Our functioning in other roles during the weekend had further effects on the group process: Dr. White chaired the final presentation by the male analyst on dreams, and Dr. Black was in the chair for the woman analyst's presentation on the varieties of emotional vertigo that accompany separation anxiety. Dr. Black was also chairing the plenary session for all weekend-only participants. Working together in the group as coleaders and then separately in our conference chair roles, Dr. White being paired with the male presenter and Dr. Black with the female presenter, we provided differing models of couples that amplified the group's responses to the presenters as a couple. Later we will see these effects on the group's attempts at integrating cognitive data, individual affective responses, and conference experience.

The Group at Work

From the start, it was unusually difficult for the small group to coalesce in relation to the working task. Instead, the group was taken up with Paige and her negative attitude to Dr. Black. Paige harbored aggressive feelings toward him left over from a previous weekend conference group that he had led. He had noted then that she had found it difficult to use the group as a transitional space. Her vendetta against him persisted and set the stage for the group task over the present weekend. Disavowing of any impact the topic might have on her personally and disinterested in the leader's new role, Paige clung to the conviction that Dr. Black could not assist her toward a useful professional experience. At the same time, she was an emotional lightning rod for group affect. Her stance challenged the group members and the leader to show her the way to symbolic thinking and affective expressiveness. In this way, she both embodied and denied unmet longings for a caring holding environment and insensitivity to her impact on the group.

In contrast, Paige was comfortable with Dr. White and identified with him as a peer since she had enjoyed participating with him in a previous group before he was appointed to the faculty. She maintained a positive peer identification with him and created a split between "good" and "bad" men in the coleading couple. She knew from experience that Dr. Black was not attuned to her needs. She was outraged to be placed in his group once again, but oddly she had not requested a different group assignment ahead of time. She had grave reservations about the possibility of learning anything at all, even in other settings during the weekend, because the readings, particularly those on chaos theory by the codirectors of the institute, were "no good."

Paige complained that the presenter's clinical cases and the conference themes dredged up uncontained aspects of her dreaded issues that she preferred to deal with in therapy, except that her therapist was disappointing, too. Her attack on Dr. Black for being distant, uncaring, and intellectually over her head silenced the other members. At the same time, they were wanting to get on with the task, and instead they were struggling with the impact of conference themes on their own internal worlds and clinical work without the benefit of group participation.

Containment was not assured. Could Dr. Black bear being the "bad" coleader and manage to survive the attack on the conference, the leadership, and himself? Would he become defensive, giving reasons, apologies, or inauthentic reparative statements to soothe the offended member and protect the group from demoralization and the destruction of any good experience? We felt frustrated that this group was not getting down to business. We felt that the group would remain immune to our interventions and would persist in the group defense of substituting an individual's resistance for a group collaboration on understanding the issues of separation anxiety. Dr. Black said later to Dr. White that he felt like telling Paige that her rejection of what he had to offer was a projection of her fears of abandonment, but he did not because he did not want to single out Paige or act out his retaliatory feelings. Instead, he took up the deep silence that followed.

> Dr. Black broke the silence to say that he sensed anxiety about how the coleaders could remain effective containers under such an attack. Another member, Steve, who sat between the coleaders, responded by renewing the attack. Steve said that he had been listening to a tape of Otto Kernberg in his car on the drive to the conference that morning. After hearing the morning presentation, he also felt doubtful that the male copresenter would offer him much; his manner was so intellectual, so subdued, so less than phallic, so wimpy, and so unlike the erudite and ebullient Kernberg.

Interestingly, this member talked very little in the group sessions and was himself subdued. Perhaps he had joined with the initial attack on one of the leaders, the conference directors, and the conference male presenter, whom he described as "less than phallic," to contain his fears of Paige turning her humiliating attack on him and also to express his disdain for "wimpy" males, like himself, who perhaps could not well defend themselves openly. Silence was the childhood compromise.

Paige and Steve focused on their low expectations for being fed theoretically and affectively, in contrast to other members, who anticipated intellectual stimulation and attunement. Evelyn, Molly, and Susan expressed interest, hope, and curiosity in relation to the husband-and-wife team of presenters. The wife appeared to the group to be more nurturing and lively than the man. Perhaps in an attempt to repair the damage done by criticizing the male presenter's style, the group moved on to discuss his main theoretical points.

Before the discussion was fully under way, Evelyn remembered that as a child, at age 5, she was waiting for the bus to arrive to take her to her first day-camp experience. She held her father's hand tightly, and when the bus driver came to get her, she stuck her tongue out at her mother. Obviously, she spared her father, as though separation fears related only to her mother, and the anger she felt was unusual since she was satisfied with her good childhood. Silence once again ended the session.

Thinking about Paige, Dr. Black formed the hypothesis that she was hanging on to him so as to keep him and her connected, perhaps because in this one-weekend-only group she felt herself to be under the threat of premature separation. Thinking of Evelyn, he thought that her retelling of her spiteful nursery school separation from her mother "stuck" it to the woman whose complaints threatened to destroy the potential of her having a good group experience now by wishing to reunite in fantasy with her father in a "new" nursery school experience this weekend.

To understand the group dynamics fully, we have to take into consideration the group's behavior at lunches and coffee breaks. Members giggled about having excluded the two leaders from their group luncheon process. On occasion, they did invite either of us to join the group for lunch, but we declined, remaining in role as faculty. The group understood why the faculty could not attend their lunches and imagined that we envied the members' pleasure. Susan said that if they told us what happened at lunch, they would have to modify it to hide the truth from us. We worked together to show them that they were hiding from one another, too. Dr. Black said that the group members took flight from the working task by enjoying their social task and compartmentalizing these extra group experiences the moment they entered the group sessions with leaders present. Dr. White said that outside experience was being used to fragment the group's already compromised processing efforts.

In response to their comments, Molly admitted that she was identifying with her group therapy clients in fighting the analytic model and using lunch to avoid her vulnerability. She now felt that lunch was a place to digest food but not concepts. Keeping the leaders out of the erotic, dependency-gratifying lunch culture avoided having to deal in the group with longing for connection. These feelings were stimulated by thinking about the topic of separation and by being in a small group that held the promise of an intimate encounter from which they would soon have to separate. Their feelings of aloneness and longing were exacerbated by feelings of exclusion in relation to the faculty members who had the security of being part of a couple, not only us as a coleading couple, but also the husband-and-wife copresenters and the institute codirectors.

Dealing with the group's resistance to the working frame, Dr. Black said he thought that the group had a fantasy that men in authority cannot be counted on to be fully present in the group and are more likely to be there in a way that intrudes on and hurts the group. Therefore, the group had reconfigured itself as a family of siblings who can share, but this had not allowed a full experience in the group. At first, Steve, the man who preferred Kernberg, and Paige, who had agreed about expecting little from Dr. Black and the group, were united in feeling that Dr. Black's comment trivialized their experience. Dr. Black still appeared to be the "bad" object, while Dr. White was the "good" object, even though their capacity to collaborate had slightly improved.

Then a shift occurred. Paige differentiated herself from Steve. She now said that Dr. Black's comments about flight made her see that she had been monopolizing the group by talking too much. Dr. White, in keeping with being the good object, reassured her by saying that the group had required her to be the group's voice. She, however, countered that the group did not want that to occur as much as she did. Dr. White, the "good" leader, now made a move that led to his slipping from his pedestal. Some group members had not yet arrived, but to protect the privacy of the group, Dr. White decided to close the door. Since it could be opened only from inside, he told the group that he would be attentive to late knocks on the door. By keeping to the frame as a good leader protecting the group, he nevertheless seemed bad in Paige's view. When a tardy member had to knock for entry, she accused him of locking a member out, and his fall from grace was complete. Dr. Black showed her how she had been disappointed in the leaders as a couple from which she felt excluded and so had to make one of them bad and one of them good. Now that the projection had switched, perhaps she was ready to tolerate her ambivalence about them as a couple. Feeling that her perceptions had damaged the group, Paige now wept, overwhelmed with guilt. The "good" coleader became not so good, and the "bad" coleader became "good" enough.

We now move on to present the group integrative process at termination, illustrated by the dream.

The Moment Before the Dream

Molly, a veteran of many conferences, had not said much despite being an experienced group member. She now introduced a dream on the last day of this weekend conference. She had previously maintained in a half-serious tone that she had felt "jammed" by the group process and especially by our comments on it. She knew that when she pushed herself to work with her thoughts and emotions, the result was rewarding, professionally and personally. So she pushed herself over this block and worked with her experience, her anxieties about her competence, and her vulnerability about whether the group would accept her and her dream.

Molly had not wanted to dream, but she did anyway as she usually does on the final day of a conference. She had not wanted to report her dream, given how turbulent the group experience had been, but knowing that it might be of benefit to the group, she did anyway. She felt anxious and uncertain as to how it would be received. Everyone wanted to hear it, especially the member who was guilty for hurting Dr. Black and the group. Group boundaries and subgroupings had been difficult throughout the weekend but were worked through in the final session.

The Dream

Molly said, "The first part of the dream was short. I was going to a restaurant to meet some friends. When I arrived, they were not there yet, and two waiters did not want to serve me. I continued waiting for the others to arrive.

"The second part of the dream was longer. There were seven trees, at first bunched in two groups of four and three. Then they were all in a lineup of seven. One tree was different than the others. It had a bush growing out of it. A woman landscaper was gently trying to remove the bush so as to transplant it to a place nearby to make a lineup of eight. I was anxious that the little bush not be torn out by the woman tending it.

"As the little bush was transplanted, I saw underneath it a fissure with fire in it. This reminded me of the film *Journey to the Center of the Earth*. I rushed to the fissure and started to place earth over it, not because the fire was dangerous but because I had to smooth the surface out. I went on throwing more dirt over it and working with it to make it flat and eventually cover the fissure. I didn't fear the cauldron below: I just wanted to smoothe the earth on top to make the setting of the bush uniform with that of the seven trees. I really felt better for making the effort."

Analysis of a dream in a group setting is not focused on the individual unconscious that produces the dream. Dreams symbolize and refer to whole-group issues as well as to individual experiences. The group unconscious is displayed as the group members give their associations.

Surprisingly, Paige broke down and cried, saying that the group experience had transformed her. In this group, she had expected the two leaders to be as unresponsive as the waiters in Molly's dream, but she had found Dr. Black to be sturdy and kind, as was Dr. White. Both of them were able to contain the feelings of love and hate in the group as it tried to work on separation anxiety. She said that she had felt safely held in a loving and nurturing group experience. Evelyn suggested that the seven trees in the dream represented the group being lined up in a different manner than the clumping of four female members and three male members in the opening session. She pointed out the final seating arrangement with male–female equal distribution and regarded it as a sign that work had been accomplished in bringing alive the hope for a generative couple. Dr. White commented that dreams are a gift to the group and are elicited by the group process.

The theme of destroying and repairing loving feelings then emerged. Susan, who usually placed herself between Paige, the angry woman, and Dr. Black, the "bad" coleader, had chosen a different seat in the final session. Now she sat to the left side of Dr. Black, leaving him next to the formerly angry Paige. She went on to say that she had seen Dr. Black sitting at the conference with three seats vacant next to him. She wanted to sit next to him, but she was in the company of two other members, including Paige, who might be hurt if she indicated a desire for such closeness to him rather than her. She silenced her need and instead manipulated things so that she had the two other members, both female, sit next to him while she took the farthest seat. She now realized that choosing the group over her own desires played into her fears of abandonment, and so she gave up the protective function in relation to the warring couple.

Susan felt guilty for not revealing that she was angry at Dr. White for not coming to the aid of Dr. Black when he was being seen as a "bad" leader and so allowing himself to remain the "good" guy. This was her own issue, too! She laughed with pleasure at being able to admit to her warm feelings toward the coleaders. The "bad" (but gradually allowed to become good enough) coleader, Dr. Black, commented that for this member to deny her needs had not been respectful or beneficial to the other woman. Talking to Paige, who had been angry with him until now, he said that with so much passion for rage, the passion for loving must be very deep. Paige replied that his observation was accurate, but she felt unable to talk about the origins of this now.

To Evelyn, the number 8, composed of two perfectly intertwining circles, signified the generative state of the current group. Susan thought of the threat of destruction to the growing bush from deep within the earth as a metaphor for the anxiety of being separated from the mother–infant dyad. She noted that in this dream there was no man, which raised the anxious question of where the father was. Was he unconcerned, or was he dead? Mother Earth could be hateful and devouring or fertile and life affirming. The presence of the father could influence which she would be. Evelyn concluded that the group process had underscored hate and longing, limits and disappointments. Dr. White said that it had demonstrated male and female splits due to projections about the couple—female giving life, male representing loss of potency and death.

Then the group again addressed the portion of the dream set in the restaurant with the reluctant waiters. Molly associated to the social lunch times and thought that this part of the dream referred to the unconscious expectation that the two male coleaders would not serve the members' needs. Playing with concepts from chaos theory, Dr. Black said that he had been a strange attractor for fatally flawed parts of the self, while Dr. White had been a strange attractor for the good object, to keep alive the hope that the couple could survive, albeit in a "neutered" form.

A Coleading Problem

The group's use of the restaurant portion of the dream illuminated the split between the leaders and its effect on the group. A paralysis had occurred in the group because we did not manage to heal the split between us for some time, and so we could not maximize our collective process. We had the illusion that we were working together, even though our working alliance was under siege and we were polarized as the "good" and "bad" object. We felt that we were tolerating and containing the group process as long as we did not need each other's active assistance. We both wished to protect ourselves from the group's aggression in order not to join the group contagion. As individuals, our affective and conceptual impressions were colored by the group's valency for polarizing us. For some time, we could not get out of the clump of trees long enough to see the wood or tend the bush. We thought that attacks on the ability to think had occurred in order to prevent traumatic separation.

The dream helped us heal this split before the end of the group. At this final session, lively group discussion of the dream led to the culmination of the group's tensions and creative pursuits. The group conveyed gratitude, relief, understanding of fragmentation, and reparation as responses to the theme of powerful separation anxieties.

The Silent Male Group Member Speaks

With ten minutes remaining until the close of the five-session group, the only male weekend member spoke up. He was Steve, the one who idealized Otto Kernberg and anticipated dissatisfaction with the senior group leader. Having said little other than that, he now explained why he had remained silent. He had been holding on to an experience nine years ago with the codirector when she was leading a large-group discussion. After he made a comment at that time, she said something that he took as criticism, and he felt silenced. This unconscious memory returned to him when he encountered her again this weekend during the plenary that Dr. Black had chaired. He now recounted that his mother was always humiliating him. He expressed shame as he spoke of the transference from his mother to the female codirector and how protection from his father had been absent when he was growing up. He had not expected much of Dr. Black either, who, however, had shown that he could chair the plenary discussion effectively. At this late date, there was hardly time to work with these projections in the group, but there was some relief that he could give voice to them, if only at the close of the weekend.

Thinking back over Steve's previously silent rage and helplessness, we realized that his unexpressed wish for a male's protection and his negative expectation of the group and of the male group leader joined with a personal narrative. Steve had clung even more tenaciously than Paige to a bad object experience to avoid being alone, and he had therefore been unable to explore new object experiences until late in the life of the group. Steve and Paige had been paired in a destructive male–female couple, each of them bound to at least one other destructive male–female couple.

The question remains: For what aspect of the group unconscious was the woman speaking, and why was it given voice by the man so late? The group is over, the members have separated from the task and from one another, and the answer cannot now be found. But that realization takes us full circle to an appreciation of separation anxiety. It is not only about the fear of losing attachment to the secure and knowledgeable object. It is fundamentally about the fear of the unknown and the death of the self.

In our report of this final group session, we hope we have conveyed the group's use of a dream as the royal road to understanding the group unconscious. Learning is enhanced by immersion in theory and by the process and review of its impact on the student and the study group. As carriers and translators of this process and in keeping with our faith in unconscious communication and the value of countertransference, we emphasize the value of affect, ego, object, and the interpersonal field as essential to thinking. As a way of reaching all these areas, dream work is a useful component of the group affective learning model.

COLEADER REFLECTIONS

The male presenter featured at the weekend conference had brought a stark message for sober reflection. He said that in every beginning there is the shadow of an ending, that separation is an ever-present matter to be faced, and that we should come to accept the idea of our own deaths. This comment created considerable anxiety at first. The group responded in a primitive, paranoid–schizoid way of functioning with splitting into good and bad, substituting the individual for the couple and the group, and destroying the group leaders' interventions. Then the group moved into a more integrative, depressive mode with a capacity for concern, sharing, reparation, and tolerance of ambivalence. We think that our containment in the small group and in the plenary secured this effect. The group was enabled to develop a modified view of us as a couple after they saw us through the eyes of others in the plenary.

The plenary was attended by other weekend-only small groups like this one and by one- and two-year groups for more advanced participants who carry the culture. In his role as chair of the plenary, Dr. Black seemed sensitive and useful to plenary participants, including faculty members and an institute codirector. Dr. White was also seen as a reliable faculty member. In that setting, the "bad" small-group coleader was accepted as "good enough." Experience in the plenary expanded the small group's perception of the reliability and sensitivity of the coleading couple. The small group also learned when others spoke more freely in the open atmosphere of the larger group about anxieties aroused by separation anxiety, the topic of the weekend. Steve's ashamed silence and other small-group silences were humanized and normalized when other groups in the plenary more easily shared their experiences of nameless dread and death anxiety. This larger meeting carries a culture of process and review in the service of integration. It functioned as an alternative, less closed-in space for learning that then carried over into the small group. Its ameliorative effect, bolstered by the dream, was manifest later in our final session that followed the plenary.

A final example of splitting was seen when Dr. Black chaired the large-group session in which the wife of the presenting couple spoke on her topic: emotional vertigo. During discussion from the floor, comments on her presentation came from only her side of the room. Two halves of the field were split, as if one side represented life and the wife's engaging style and the other the absence of her husband, and therefore death. Although Dr. Black in his role as the Chair was aware of this intellectually, it was as though a state of paralysis occurred in him. The presenter's aliveness was being preserved in lively discussion, and he did not ask for comments from the silent ones, as though any mention of the "dead" audience would cause a trauma. He allowed the pattern of discussion to proceed as though it was better to let the dead remain so or to allow them to resurrect themselves on their own.

What emerged after the session was over was that Dr. Black had become "dead" to the conference dynamics. He was in a state of denial of his own oedipal rivalry for the alive and accessible mother, who was also the erotic, desirable wife, therefore his unwillingness to bring "alive" the deadness of half the audience. By not commenting on it, he could leave the husband out. Then again, he wanted to protect the husband from the unconscious attack that might have surfaced and offended him.

Returning to his group, Dr. Black found himself preoccupied with analyzing his recent chairing experience. He felt that he understood it sufficiently and now wanted to shut it out. That is the moment when Dr. White closed the door of the group, fell from grace as the "good" leader, and so contributed to the undoing of the splits that were undermining the small-group task.

POSTCONFERENCE WORKING THROUGH

Unresolved anxiety lingered and accompanied the "bad" leader home from the conference. As previously mentioned, as coleaders we had difficulty assisting each other. Our energies were caught up in containing group persecutory feelings bordering on trauma. We were too preoccupied with our individual functioning to think of ourselves as a team. Our energy was taken up with staying alive under attack by the group. We used the precious little time that we had—among attending conference events and faculty meetings, preparing for chairing responsibilities, catching lunch, and resting—to review our coleading. Several extragroup situations offered opportunities to process our coleading experiences, none of them successfully, because we were too overwhelmed to avail ourselves of limited time. This omission was both a response and a contributant to the group's substitution of an individual attack on one of us in place of joining as a group in the learning task.

Ours was not the only small group experiencing stress in relation to the material on separation anxiety, and we were not the only small-group leaders in need of consultation at the faculty review meeting. Twice we had to defer discussion of our group at times when we were relying on getting help. Anxious to make the best use of the limited time available to us for consultation from the faculty, we took notes after the group to prepare for giving a concise account at the faculty review meeting, but we each did so separately. This took away from time that we could have spent conferring with each other. We did not even make time to compare notes. The impact of the group's splitting processes in interaction with our own dynamics prevented us from adjusting as a pair to the relative lack of attention from the faculty group and the conference director.

There was an additional complication. Each of us was independently collecting material to contribute to the collaborative writing task that the faculty had agreed on in preparation for creating this book. Anxiety about this added task compounded the considerable anxiety generated by the conference themes. Faculty review meetings—a precious source of grounding, collegial thinking, and support for the work of the small groups—seemed less supportive than usual as the institution rose to the challenge of preparing for the publication as well. The faculty usually had plenty of time to discuss countertransference–transference phenomena reported by the small-group leaders, but now we also had to deal with the relevance of the material for publication, how to focus it, and whether we could meet the deadline. Anxiety arising from this complexity was acknowledged but not fully addressed within the conference boundary.

The customary discussion of the group process and review of countertransferences at and between faculty meetings focused mainly on the difficult task of tolerating and containing the splitting of us into "good" and "bad" objects. Given the circumstances and time constraints, we reviewed the salient points as well as we could. We relied on grace, goodwill, and friendship to manage our emotions and maintain our collaboration under threat until the next small-group session. The writing of this chapter provided us a further opportunity for collaboration, process, and review—a benefit of the writing task that offset the disadvantages we had experienced.

The experience of the group's issues remained troubling to Dr. Black, who had borne the brunt of the group's negative feeling. Having been separated from Dr. White and denied their preference for a supportive dyad by splitting in the group, by multitasking in the conference, and by geographical separation after the conference ended, Dr. Black felt a resurgence of abandonment anxiety on the long journey home. The writing of this chapter was an act of reunion (by fax and email) for Dr. Black and Dr. White with each other as coleaders (and now as writing colleagues) and with the codirectors (now as coauthors and editors). In this way, we could complete our task together. Having finished this chapter, we felt better connected to the weekend experience and better able to criticize the constraints that the institution imposed on our work. Typical of our participation as faculty using the affective learning model, we were encouraged to express the good and the bad in the panorama of experience.

II

Affective Learning in the Small Group

In Chapter 8, students describe learning theory, observing infants, presenting clinical cases, and processing their reactions in the small group, in the plenary, in the informal time, and in the large group. Their reflections on understanding concepts from personal exploration paves the way for Chapter 9, an elaboration of the theory of affective learning in the small group with many illustrative vignettes. In Chapters 10 and 11, small-group leaders describe their groups at work on concepts, group history, and current dynamics. In Chapter 12, an international student describes his experience of various affective learning groups in a style that is delightfully accessible even to the inexperienced or reluctant student. Written for the advanced student or potential group leader, Chapter 13 offers a complex, multi-level, sustained examination of a week-long small group as it responds to didactic material from many presenters on contemporary object relations theory and practice.

8

Reflections by Students

This chapter is opened by a first-year student and closed by a returning graduate. Both describe learning from their own object relations stirred in association to observing mother–infant relationships during a summer institute immersion in infant observation and attachment research. In the second piece, a reluctant graduate comments on her emotional constriction, analyzes her unexpected emotional response to graduation, and ends with hope for a better outcome. The third contribution is written by a student who supervises graduate students. It conceptualizes the institution's preparation of the student as teacher. Then a graduate looks back over the intellectual and emotional aspects of her learning experience. The last piece, written by a returning graduate on the mother–infant relationship, demonstrates the integration of cognition and affect in the learning process.

These accounts naturally reflect the writers' individuality and the nature of the small group in which they studied. The authors arrive at their own unique points of balance between learning from self and other, from intellect and emotion. Their reflections—affective, cognitive, and integrative—represent their unique positions along the continuum of learning from experience at this moment in their growth. In each account, affective and cognitive components can be found with varying degrees of subjectivity and objectivity.

THE MOTHER AS A DESIRED OBJECT

When I began the two-year program, my introductory experience was in the ten-day summer institute "Infant Observation, Containment and Countertransference." During each day, we moved back and forth, from a primarily didactic large-group experience to our small group of six women group members and a faculty leader. I was immediately struck by the rapid and gratifying bonding that occurred among the small-group members. I genuinely felt a kindred personal and professional spirit with these women. They were bright, articulate, and accomplished, and, after all, we had been brought together by similar clinical and theoretical interests. We all talked about the rich didactic material and ways in which it evoked an affective connection with the infant parts of ourselves. I began to feel anxious about the powerful affective focus of the group. I felt that we were using emotion to resist linking our didactic experience to clinical material. But I also knew that I often flee from uncomfortable feelings into intellectual areas. I began to feel hazy and unclear in my thinking. Were we off task? What was our task?

Over the first couple of days, I was aware of actively managing my competitive and envious wishes, particularly in the small group. We did speak of the wish to be thought of as smart or singled out in some way—but in measured tones. We were all careful to express mutual admiration. During one meeting, I was jolted and disturbed by the sudden and intrusive image of each of my small group members as a hungry wolf, each trying to elbow the others out as we tore and gnawed at the body of a dead deer, the group leader. Other times I had the experience of myself as an unfeeling rock, swept over by a powerful warm tide of loving, admiring, sisterly exchange. I was able to participate, but I also felt I had to work hard to conceal an internal experience of separateness.

The panel of presenters all offered rich, riveting material, which left us well fed and yet wanting more. I felt envious of their knowledge and experience. Several people commented that except for one appearance as a presenter, the female codirector of the institution had kept an uncharacteristically low profile. In addition, they noted that there was only one other female presenter. Questions were raised about the possible connection between there being a primarily male faculty and an entirely female student group. The questions seemed to indicate anxiety about whether the patriarchal institution could adequately meet the needs of its female youth and whether female faculty had been killed off along with the male students.

The woman presenter spoke about the impact of early trauma on attachment and its clinical implications. She talked about the interplay between dynamically internalized responses on the one hand and neurophysiological re-actions on the other. I was excited by the material and found myself working to integrate her ideas with older ones, such as repetition compulsion and identifi-cation with the aggressor. Her manner was soft, motherly, and self-effacing, particularly in contrast to the confident male presenters.

As she spoke, I began to have fantasies of engaging this presenter as a supervisor. I even got so far as to imagine that her schedule was full but that she would make an exception for me as a special case. I later learned that several of my colleagues had had similar fantasies; one of them actually did approach her to ask about supervision despite a 2,000-mile distance between their home cities. I felt that I got something special from her when she told me that the respon-siveness of my face had been helpful to her during one presentation. Then I felt anxious about my neediness for individual connection and recognition. Was it evident to all? I chastised myself for still, after many years of analysis, having to work so hard to manage regressive feelings of sibling competition.

Before this wonderful woman presenter began her final presentation, the chair, a man, announced that because of glitches in the presenter's flight arrangements, she would have to leave the conference without delay following her talk. This meant that she would not be part of discussions later in the day. We were all disappointed. The chair also announced that, in this her final talk, the presenter would show a series of drawings by traumatized children and dis-cuss them from her theoretical perspective on attachment. Instead of following her intentions as stated by the chair, the woman responded to our questions. We were gratified by her willingness to follow our line of interest at the ex-pense of her own agenda. With our encouragement, she got off on a fascinating sidetrack. I was lulled into forgetting that my interest as a child therapist was to see all the drawings and hear her discuss them in terms of understanding trauma.

Suddenly, the chair interrupted. It had become clear to him that be-cause of being delightfully engaged with us, the presenter was not getting to the drawings and that the presentation had lost its focus. He asked her to stay on task. There was a lightly humorous and teasing exchange between them about her "scattiness" and his "compulsiveness," but she cheerfully complied with his request in the time remaining. A child therapist myself, I felt glad that I got to see some of the drawings.

Later, in small group, I felt blindsided by one woman's rage at the chair. She perceived him as having "manhandled" the female presenter. Moreover, she suggested that he had done it out of envy or a neurotic need for control. The group had experienced her soft-edged style as maternal and responsive, while his was felt as hard-edged and paternalistic. The contrast between hard and soft, male and female objects, became a theme in subsequent group meetings. In the large group, this same woman gathered widespread support for the idea that the chair was refusing to accept personal responsibility for the damage he had done. The theme of his paternalistic attitude and the group's disillusionment resurfaced several times during subsequent small- and large-group meetings.

At the next large-group session, another woman faculty member showed a video clip of a family therapy session featuring an ambivalent and grieving mother of three small children. I found myself feeling irrationally angry at the mother on the video, whom I perceived as being unavailable, unfeeling, and self-involved. I even blurted out an impassioned comment: "She hates her children!" Clearly, this was going beyond the evidence on the video. It came from resonance with my personal experience, and it left me feeling exposed and embarrassed.

In the closing plenary, the woman student who raised the issue of her anger at the male chair now referred to a groupwide anger at him. She complained that he had interrupted a beautiful mirroring of the group's needs by the responsive woman presenter. She thought that he had behaved in an angry and competitive way toward her. She added that he had refused to recognize the need for an apology and that he had even prevented her from apologizing to the departing presenter for his rudeness by again being rude in insisting that the presenter be free to leave without delay to catch her plane. The student was furious at the way he behaved. Most of all, she was disappointed in his failure to own up to it and in his refusal to confirm her view of the damage he had done in his role as chair.

This student seemed to me to be acting as if the chair were the group's father, who had overwhelmed its mother, rendered her powerless, and made her unavailable to her children. He had further molested the children through his unwillingness to acknowledge the trauma and take responsibility for it. While I felt myself at times compelled by this transference idea, I was more aware of a feeling of relief at having been rescued from a mother—who did not set limits on our needs and who avoided our anger and disappointment—by a powerful father who contained rage in her stead.

The woman student and I had different transferential points of entry, both containing the idea of the loss of the mother as the desired object. Her group and mine had different experiences, but both focused on what each group did not receive in terms of mothering. There was no conscious experience of the institution as holding us at that time, and I did not appreciate it until I thought more about it later.

During the plenary discussion, it became clearer to me that the chair, representing the institution, had become the container for our paranoid–schizoid projections. Some saw him as frustrating, while I felt more idealizing toward him. I thought about my own vitriolic response to the mother in the video. The video of her, and indeed most of the mother–infant material, had been evocative for me of abandonment, which had been echoed by the suddenness of the departure of the wonderful woman. I thought about my experience in the small group—a setting that seems to me to be like a mother in its capacity to gaze intently on individuals and to contain affect. There I had felt adrift and vigilantly aware of destructive and competitive feelings, just as I had during the presentation on early trauma.

I emerged from the summer institute with a new understanding of the findings from infant observation of normal infants, infant attachment research, and studies of traumatized infants. More than that, I came away with an enhanced intellectual and affective awareness of the ways in which infantile experience drives later relating and determines the idiosyncratic transference reactions each patient—and each person—has to a given object. It became clear to me that the structure of teaching and learning, both in the large institutional group and in the small integrative group, evokes paranoid–schizoid responses and facilitates the move toward depressive concern for the object. I could also see how difficult it had been for me to make use of the small group as a place to integrate cognitive and affective experience because of my inclination to see the group and its male leader (the dead deer in my fantasy) as an ineffective, weak, and abandoning mother. I had come to this institute feeling well prepared to acknowledge and stay in charge of my transference vulnerabilities. I soon learned that blocks to my learning still operated out of my awareness. There will be time and occasion to work on them as the small group proceeds.

LETTING GO AND HOLDING ON

I've been in this group for two years, and it may be time for me to let go. The large group has been discussing separation anxiety, but our small group just feels it. How do I find the words to describe for you to read what I feel and think? My small group is filled with wounded souls, all asking that question, all bravely carrying on. We are all afraid of engagement, and we isolate ourselves from one another. Only the leader provides a touchstone, a boundary, and a connecting link to the larger faculty group. Time provides a frame for our small group, and our small group encircles us. In space, we become a circle within a circle, a tether holding us to the institution so we can't become lost. We know where we are.

I'm telling the group about losing my mother. My loss and the lack of space feel incredibly painful. The persona I use for presenting my issues is getting stripped away, and my interior psychic structure is slowly exposed. Enough.

As I said before, I'm not the only one. Another woman covers her wounds with a shell of harshness. Her shrill rebuke stings me. Her body shaking with rage terrifies me. I lose my center, and I feel only the shape of the chair against my body. So I push myself out of that place. I become Mrs. Mom; I know how to serve up the comfort food. Then my own rage breaks through at her for making me feel that way. I am shocked when I say I'd like to kill her. I'm not the only one. I'm not the only one who's frightened of rage.

Now I know it's my own rage that scares me. I am revealed both to myself and others. As I put it into words for the group, and now for you, I begin to acknowledge the loss I mentioned earlier. I can reflect, and later, often much later, perhaps weeks or months, I'll have turned the page.

Now it's the last weekend of the year, and we're studying the unconscious of the individual and the institution. After the lecture, during the coffee break, a phrase reverberates in my head: *autistic/contiguous position* (Ogden 1989). My associations start flying. I think of *Live Company* (Alvarez 1993). I think of bone chilling, a suck of air from the gut, my insides searing red-raw. I think of moves, too numerous to mention, all of them with little preface, little preparation. I think of the body disconnected from the head.

Suddenly, I'm drawn to the external world as the director greets me. He says, "Congratulations! Graduating tomorrow!" "What?" I say. "I can't. I haven't paid." "We talked about that," he said. "We know you're good for the money. You're graduating." I can't take it in. It's as if I didn't expect this. I'm not in a position to go.

My family always moved, never of choice, always saying good-bye. It's the leitmotif of my life. "We're moving, we've been transferred." Okay, keep the strongbox of valuable papers at hand! Ready to go on the Long March! To avoid a problem, seek an adventure!

Thus, "graduating tomorrow" resonates deep. I feel disconnected, aware of my new skin. I plunge from here into small-group process. I can barely speak. From the depths of fear, I say, "I am graduating." Their faces turn toward me. I want to disappear, not be seen. "Graduating? What's the problem with that?" At first they don't get it. But they stick with it. The voices of the other group members and the leader function as a container for my attempt to put words to feeling.

I'm not magnifying my experience out of proportion when I say that uprooting is my theme. My personal life included frequent moves of our entire household, usually with little notice. As the daughter of a naval officer and as a late child of the 1960s, I was always on the move. Staying put is new to me. So is belonging to a collegial group of people who work at allowing feelings to be processed and transformed. "You are graduating" equals "You are moving." I don't want to go.

We grappled together in the group, turn by turn, with associations and feeling states. What one couldn't do, the other could, as we jointly worked in group process. So, I learned, graduating was an unwanted repetition of the past in some respects, but it needn't mean the end. There's more to come, more group work to do, and more to learn. The connections are strong, the work goes on, the group contains, and integration is achieved.

POOR INDEED, IF ONLY SANE

It was the first day of my first summer institute at the beginning of the two-year program, and my small group began with zest. Within the first week, it came to a teeth-grinding halt when a woman I'll call Beth stopped participating in the small group. We found her, however, at large-group meetings, and we asked her why she was avoiding us. Beth reported feeling disliked, perplexed by the small-group process, and too threatened to join us. She withdrew from the two-year program before the first week was up. We were devastated and confounded. We searched grimly through the debris of our time with Beth, leaving nothing out, as if searching for something essential but unknown. It was like staring into a kaleidoscope; there was a pattern of something, but it would not stay fixed. The something that would not stay fixed was the effect of the severing of the connection. But we did not understand that yet. The course had only just begun; we had had only one lecture on Fairbairn's theory of human motivation based on the need for relationship.

In the large group, we began discussing Melanie Klein's theory of the most primitive anxiety of the paranoid–schizoid position as a fear of annihilation from within the personality (Klein 1975). In order to survive, she said, we project this psychotic fear into the external object as a defensive tactic. Through a combination of processes by which psychotic anxieties are held, digested, and modified, infants learn to integrate (Anderson 1992, Bion 1967). When this does not happen well, the ego makes excessive use of projective identification for its defense.

In small group, defense was in full array. We were fighting our monsters and fighting with each other! Without knowing much about Bion, we had changed from a task-oriented working group to an illusion-oriented basic assumption group. My personal illusion was of the pairing type: "If only I were with my truer mother as my group leader, I could be more my self." I had become strangely blank, stupid, sleepy, dopey, grumpy, and other gnomic states. What was happening? I will be positive, I decided, and just carry on. Small-group life was reminding me of the familiar fairy tale "The Three Little Pigs and the Big Bad Wolf." Except that in my story the characters were the seven small-group wolves, the big bad pig, and one lonely excluded pure white lamb (*moi*). Our group leader was frequently cast in the role of the big bad pig. I'll call her Louise.

Louise kept challenging us to explore the impact of the loss of our group member Beth. She probed the notion that we were missing something if we tried to control, get rid of, or short-circuit conflicts we were having over her departure. Beth left the group angry, we feared, and this worry continually emerged, ghostly and malevolent, in our group process.

Meanwhile, in the large group, we were being immersed in Kleinian theory. Klein emphasized the importance of envy and unconscious hatred in the psychotic mental organization. Then we turned to Freud. In his case histories, Freud wrote of a wounded self whose hate is withheld and rerouted. We learned how Dora's repressed rage had hardened into a chronic attitude of hatred that had deformed her character. We read of Freud's technique that required Dora to renounce her distorted perceptions in favor of his more objective scrutiny. Dora left Freud. Beth left us. Back in the small group, I was thinking that Louise was some kind of Mrs. Mac"Beth", neurotically obsessed with washing away every last speck of emotional dirt in us. She wondered constantly about split-off, repressed, and returning emotional baggage.

In the large group, we moved on to tackle Winnicott. We used his ideas to make a big shift in conceptualizing the self. Psychoanalysis, for Winnicott, is aimed at finding reality connected to desire rather than using a functional capacity to comply with and adapt to reality. Sanity alone is not enough. "The false self," says Winnicott, "however well set up, lacks something and that something is the essential central element of creative originality" (1960, p. 152). That called to me. I both shrank from its possibilities and rushed headlong into them.

I quit being so positive in the small group. I wanted to stop the focus on the fearful, hateful, and envious affects among us. I wanted to discuss lectures, papers, and clinical case material. Something in the small group was anesthetizing my mind. I wrote a note to myself: "I am losing my mind here; I am scared of something, and I feel like I'm going to pieces." Were these thoughts about madness bearing witness to some psychic damage in me?

A guest presenter arrived from London and led us in discussions of serious, criminal pathology. He told chilling clinical stories of how, in subtle and undetected ways, an underlying psychotic position can color everyday responses and even structure a whole life. He showed us that the power of Freud and Klein's vision had to be appreciated in work with psychosis. The psychotic often experiences himself as caught in a struggle with competing gods or demons. The only defensive solution is to put the pain of that elsewhere, or nowhere. An ideal reality is then made up as a substitute for real living. This is mental mutilation, diametrically opposed to making life truly full.

I heard this with a heavy heart. I wanted an idealized small group, a perfectly safe and sanitized one where people were attuned and reasonable, and I wanted an idealized group mother. Louise was always examining our affects, wondering whether an impulse had shifted direction and changed its valence, as when love is expressed as hate. Occasionally, the small group entered a state of perfect attunement. It was blissful. In a short while, that state of bliss became bland. Discomfort broke out again. The objectively preferred attunement with one another in a perfect reality—like the objective interpretation that was promoted as the curative agent in the world of classical theory—became an instrument that only led us back to the original problem. We needed our subjectivities, wrought in pleasure, pain, disagreement, and disgruntlement, for hatching as true selves in the group.

As a psychotherapist, I must hold dread and mental mutilation in mind while my patients struggle with those issues. To do that, I must risk being more subjective. Freud was suspicious of the imagination. He linked it with immaturity and infantilism. His classical analytic method was aimed toward the rational experience of the capacity to work and love. In our times, psychoanalytic thinkers write over and over again about the capacity to play, to be authentic, and to achieve creative personal expression. To do that, we have to take risks and explore the boundaries of the known world. That can make us feel frightened or even crazy. That means I must stop hanging on to rational discussion. I, too, will have to go a little crazy to get to a more authentic sense of my self.

Elizabeth Spillius (1988) said that in the modern use of transference–countertransference, the therapist is less concerned about making the right interpretation and more concerned about whether she has communicated understanding to the patient in a way that connects. Bion (1970) asked the therapist to open herself to the material without memory and desire. He made it clear to me that much hard work, patience, and revisualization of the therapist's sense of self is necessary in order to remain open. He encouraged therapists to enter a state of unintegration that the poet Keats called *negative capability*, a formless state of not reaching for the facts, so that we can tolerate the *unthought known* with our patients (Bollas 1987).

We have studied the work of Klein, Bion, and other Kleinians; Fairbairn, Winnicott, Bollas, and others from the British Independent Group; as well as Kohut, Grotstein, Searles, David and Jill Scharff, Mitchell, and Ogden from the United States. From this remarkable integration, we have learned that the essence of psychoanalysis has been reconceptualized. There has been a shift in emphasis from the analysis of instincts and conflict in the intrapsychic dimension to the analysis of the therapeutic relationship as the curative factor.

I try to remain open. I try to experience the subjective. I stay in touch with the kernels of psychosis in me (Milner 1987). I acknowledge and work on my holocaustic rage, insidious self-poisoning, ghastly emptiness, desperate inability to keep up with my sensitivities, giving of myself over to ghosts and spirits, crippling myself with shyness, hellish torment, and self-deadening. I have to work with the unintegration and reintegration of my self. Feeling cast out is the most dreadful anxiety for me; it can still make me mindless and blow my sense of self to bits. Paradoxically, I achieve connection by going deeper into that dread. This is also true for those patients who complain of an endless array of aloneness. In the face of being together in this aloneness, our shame for being left alone connects us to awareness in which we find meaning and intimacy.

On the day of my graduation from the two-year program, I wrote myself a message on the last white pad: "If I am crazy, I make myself more so by leaving it aside, or leaving the group like Beth chose to do. If I do not follow the craziness, I remain unborn. If I can have an attitude large enough and open enough to encompass it, I can learn from it and use it as my partner in personal evolution and in psychotherapeutic partnership with my patients. I can afford to be a little ill in order to learn, understand more, and help more. I am poor indeed, if only sane."

THE STUDENT AS TEACHER

I am an advanced student who at the same time teaches graduate students. In my view, one of the most important principles of affective learning is that students are also teachers. We all learn together from our experience. The experience of presenting as faculty or as student is another opportunity to explore the process of teaching and learning. When I was invited as a student to present a case at a conference, I felt valued by the institution. Participating actively as a teacher in the program gave me a more mature sense of identity and autonomy and at the same time strengthened my links to the institution. This led me to think more about the student presenter role.

To present well, the student has to organize the material of her patient's family and personal history, the history of the transference, and the process of a clinical session and integrate all that with theory. This is good practice for conceptualizing her work and for teaching object relations theory in the back-home environment. The time boundary puts pressure on her to convey enough information in the given time space so that the membership of the conference can understand the problems that patient and therapist are dealing with. This is good practice for making efficient use of each clinical or teaching session.

To maximize the value of the experience of presenting to the membership, the presenter is offered consultation from a member of the faculty before the case is presented. This professional mentoring interchange provides containment for the presenter's anxiety. For this to be helpful, the student presenter must have developed the necessary confidence in the good nature of the institution, similar to the good-enough experience that the infant requires from the mother (Winnicott 1960). When good containment is provided, the presenter also gets in touch with the limitations encountered in the consultant, in the institution, and in herself. At times the institution can function as a block if the presenter tries to fit some imagined ideal to please the object instead of presenting her work naturally to suit herself. The containing function of the faculty mentor who helps her prepare may be thwarted if presenter and mentor are unaware of projections that the presenter is carrying on behalf of the group.

Some presenters who are not yet experienced as therapists worry about what will happen. In disclosing the intimacies of the patient, they might feel uncomfortably exhibitionistic. They may feel protective of the patient and not realize that they are really protecting themselves. They worry that they will show that they, or their trusted supervisors, have the wrong idea. Then they might feel professionally naked or ashamed. During discussion after the formal presentation, other students and faculty members feel free to comment and disagree. If their work is criticized, presenters may feel incompetent. The task of presenting raises primitive fears of aggression and rejection, of failure, and of success.

Being conscious of affect as well as cognition allows learning to take place (Schore 1994). Being able to express their anxieties and think about them with the mentors gives student presenters the opportunity to contain their anxiety. The institute provides the psychological space for this metabolizing process to take place. It is only then that the themes of the clinical situation being presented can be fully thinkable (Bion 1967).

What is learned in the discussion is brought into future sessions with the patient. This permeability in the system nourishes the work. Back at work as therapists, presenters feel the support of the institution in their sessions. The institution provides space for growth and development using preparation for the case presentation and large-group discussion as another medium for the student's growth.

RESONANCE WITH SELF AND OBJECTS

I have graduated from the two-year program, and I keep coming back because I find the affective learning model useful. The focus on object relations and the framework used in the program helped me think about my own internal objects—my experiences of them, how I am shaped by them, and how I developed my internal world—as I was learning about the various theories. The large- and small-group work provided an excellent opportunity to experience my own internal objects at work. The topics of anxiety, primitive annihilation anxiety, and separation anxiety became fodder for learning as these concepts were studied and experienced in relationships with others in the program. Over time I was able to use the material to understand the internal world in myself as well as in my patients. Breaks in the continuity of the small group were opportunities to think about breaks in treatment. Time frames, parameters, and boundaries were explored from the point of view of the therapist and the patient. The attention to detail and to the unconscious helped integrate the experience through the thoughtfulness of the group both in the small- and the large-group process. My fantasies, feelings, thoughts, and dreams have all been a part of my learning process as much as the materials I have read, the lectures, the clinical supervision, and the case presentations.

Responses to Winnicott's Spatula Game

After seeing a video of an interviewer using Winnicott's spatula game with an infant, I found myself thinking about my use of the object and my use of the small group. In the small group, I found myself looking, checking others out, feeling my responses inside, and checking in with the group again. Like an infant picking up the spatula, I'd pick up my thought about the presentation or my experience in the group. I'd try to read the process of the group, perhaps experience fears of rejection and inadequacy, and check out my responses to the group leader. Then, like the infant throwing away the spatula, I'd get impatient with others and with myself. Fearful that my use of the group would be destructive, I'd withdraw momentarily, then pick up again. My attempts to use the group were awkward and tentative at first, but my confidence grew as time went on. The faculty made it clear that they realized all of us would be feeling such anxieties. They valued our experiences and provided us opportunities to have them and use them. This institutional philosophy facilitated our learning from the outside in and from the inside out.

Responses to Infant Observation

Gathering together the bits and pieces of the patient's self in a session and bundling them together to make a thought requires tolerance for the unknown. We want to hold the bits and pieces in mind without foreclosing, without pushing pieces in or out. To do this we construct a container within ourselves, capable of moving in and out and also of holding without contaminating the self, as we wait for the bits and pieces to be transformed into a thought that we can communicate.

Infant observation requires us to attend closely to the baby and the mother. We have to make observations without doing anything else. We have to delay our response until we are alone and free to write up the experience. This observational task asks us to tolerate anxiety. Gathering experience without premature discharge is practice for the therapist in building a container. Further thoughts about our observations occur when the large and small groups join in discussing our reports, rather like a therapist processing a clinical experience in a supervision or consultation.

In preparing for the infant observation, I began thinking about my own most primitive anxieties as I remembered them in the small group. I felt extremely anxious attending the group for the first time, like an infant joining her family—fragmented and unrelated to the others. Meeting faculty for the first time, I had to deal with anxieties about failing them, displeasing them, being inadequate, and feeling lost or abandoned. I thought about what it must have been like for me to be an infant and what my mother was dealing with. I thought about her attitudes toward me over the years, my feelings and thoughts about her, and the process of our relationship.

Just before waking one morning, the words *pas de deux* came to mind. This is a term for the dance of the leading man and the leading lady in which they both dance together, then each does a solo, and then they dance together again. The dream alluded to my mother because she loves ballet. I had been thinking about the infant observation as a duet, both mother and baby dancing together. As Winnicott said, there is no baby, only a mother and a baby. *Pas de deux* brings to mind a more complicated picture: Both mother and baby dance together with their shared anxieties and projections as well as each dancing solo with their private anxieties and fears. The mother dances her fears and bows to her fear of inadequacy as a mother alone as well as with her infant. The solo dance of the infant features his attempts to contain his own fears about survival. His fears of abandonment or inability to contain his mother's anxieties occur along with the dance with the mother. The week's discussion and lectures included recent infant research that indicates that babies read affective cues in their mother's faces, turning toward or away from what they see there. They dance together in visual and bodily exchanges.

I arranged to observe an infant boy and his mother. I had some idea of my own anxieties about their interaction based on my image of the dance of my internal mother and baby, together and alone. I wondered how I could tolerate them. I was still afraid that I might not be able to handle the anxiety of the infant I was observing. As it turned out, the baby was without the mother for the bulk of the time. The mother of my infant was busy and left him for an hour. I had thought for sure I would see more of the mother with her baby, but indeed she did not appear until the end of our time, which in fact I extended for ten minutes, not wanting to leave him alone until she came. I've done this with patients too, at times with the same thoughts, as if I were the mother and could not leave them in a vulnerable state.

Within the hour spent with this baby, I saw him experience need and discomfort. I saw him make attempts to soothe himself and delay his despair when it appeared to be mounting too high. I felt myself reaching out to him from inside, thinking about him, trying to help him in my imagination. I was relieved when the wave of his anxiety and displeasure subsided. Then there was a lull, and he had some moments of rest. He never was in such distress that I felt I had to get his mother to come for him because he could soothe himself. When his mother came, she stood before him in his rocking seat and spoke softly to him. The interaction was brief but connected and genuine. She gave him time to read her face. He seemed reassured, and without much fuss, he fell asleep.

This experience of observing—without rescuing or interpreting, just sitting with the emotions, thinking, and being available—helped me think about the function of containment in my role as a therapist. I thought about how I'd gone over the time limit with my infant, and I asked myself, "What motivates me to do that with patients?" Not only the fear that I would damage them but the anxiety that I would have to face their aggressive needs.

Containment

So, I learned that what I have to contain in a session may seem intolerable. Now I was in an environment where this could be discussed and processed by many minds together.

Further small-group work on containment produced a dream that included a garden with a fence around it, located down the road from my mother, in a place of envy. Again, I thought about my internal good and bad objects, the competition and envy with my sisters, and my experiences of rivalry in the small group. I thought of the ways in which I experienced myself in my family as containing without speaking or speaking and being devalued. I had been thinking of a container as a pot, a metal or clay pot, with a lid. Now here it was as a fence. A fence kept things out and also kept things in while allowing some exchange between inner and outer. The fence in my dream contained a garden. Now my image of my container allowed exchange and could grow things in it.

I had the opportunity to think about what stops me from containing. What prevents me from preserving the container is my anxiety that what is contained is too destructive for me or for the patient. My wish to discharge anxiety, to evacuate and expel it, or close myself off and jump away from it was identified, particularly in supervision. It was clear to me that I felt I could not stay with the containing process in a session. The more I could identify the pressures of my own internal process, the more I could use my countertransference experiences in sessions to build my capacity to contain. Applying Bion's concepts of thinking and reverie, I learned to hold the raw unintegrated beta elements and allow the alpha integrative function time to grow, time for me to give meaning to experience (Bion 1962, 1970).

Countertransference

I have continued to work on my conceptualization of the containment function—how it works, what it feels like, how to protect myself from toxic material contained for a patient, and how the experience of containment changes with different patients. This countertransference experience helps me think about and identify the transference process.

My mind now has a more reliable context into which my countertransference experiences fit. I'm building my awareness of patients' presentation of their internal worlds, what they put into me as the therapist, and perhaps what they refuse to take back. I'm still thinking about what it takes to contain the patient's experiences and give them back in a more manageable form.

Fleshing out Theoretical Concepts

The movement between experience and thought, between inner process and interaction with others, formed the basis for my conceptualization of Klein's (1946) paranoid/schizoid and depressive positions and Bion's beta and alpha function (1970). I learned how to nurture the construction of alpha function in myself. I could see in myself the process of picking up bits and fragments, holding them, bundling them together, and making sense of them. But I struggled with Bion's idea of *selected fact*. It feels as if I know the experience of it from my clinical work, but I still don't quite see how a selected fact occurs to us. I have a better understanding of Bion's complicated grid because a dream image came along to help me with that one (Bion 1965).

I dreamed of a group of therapists dancing at night around a bonfire, which was built of many upright logs bundled together. The dream said to me that holding together the bits and fragments of the self and its objects is like collecting sticks of many sizes and shapes, allowing the possibility for them to cohere as a thought and then perhaps as a realization that has the warmth and aliveness of fire.

9
The Affective Learning Small Group

THINKING ABOUT THE SMALL GROUP

The small group's central function is to be a *container* for the emotional and cognitive experiences of the members as they interact with the program being presented in the large group. The small group's containing function enables the processing and integration of those experiences by individual members. The small group is a smaller, more manageable venue within which members can deal adequately with inner and outer experience. As we lead a group, the framework for our orientation is Bion's (1962) theory of thought and thinking. Bion described the value of *learning from experience* and *notation*, in which an experience that occurs in the group is noted and described and becomes an object of group thinking.

The small group creates a paradoxical state of psychic reality in which the individual member works with three levels simultaneously: the individual as an individual, as a member of the small group, and as a component of the larger, institutional collective. Unraveling the overlap and displacement of issues is one of the most difficult tasks faced in the small group. This complexity gives the group several levels from which to exert its powerful impact on the learning process. Group members' individual statements may represent not only what any individual thinks at a particular moment but also, through the processes of projective and introjective identification, ideas, desires, and fantasies encountered by or generated in the small group, the large group, or the institution as a whole.

We value the small group's potential for access to deep levels of psychic experience that the group itself can learn to see and understand. The institutional culture promotes *free discussion*, which fosters a degree of regression and disinhibition, comparable to what we think of in analysis as "regression in the service of the ego." Members are encouraged to say what comes into their minds—thoughts, sensations, emotions, and daydreams. Thus, there is sanction for studying in a state of reduced resistance. The presence of others provides objects for the projection of unconscious fantasy. At the same time, the presence of others provides a reality check. Members place into the fabric or narrative of the group their unconscious hopes and fears. The group has the ability to suspend external aspects of reality testing and to substitute group agreement as the measure of what is real. This promotes the visualization and notation of the unconscious processes that power the group's experience. In allowing this metabolizing of individual fantasies, the group acts as a *container*, a detoxifying and metabolizing function that gives new meaning to experience.

We work with the premise that the central theme of each conference will be manifested in the totality of the small-group experience. This creates a continuous subtext that is available for study throughout the weekend. The didactic theme of the conference is only one element addressed in the small group. It quickly becomes evident that the emotional and fantasy elaboration of the theme, evoked in and through each individual, compels the deepest learning. This is emphasized when the small group is ongoing. Then the group's history and momentum transcend the theme of any one weekend conference.

When in role as small-group leaders, we use two approaches for dealing with the group experience: *group-as-a-whole observations* and *individual responses*. First, we make group-as-a-whole observations to identify fantasies and patterns, to engage the group in the review of its dynamic process, and to track unconscious themes that reflect the basic assumptions of the group (Bion 1961). These comments reflect the way the group acts "as if" it were a single, psychic entity. Fornari (1966) refers to this property of the group as a *fictive entity* and a *mystical body*.

For example, an individual may express fear and weakness. If the group coalesces to deal with that person's fear and weakness to the exclusion of discussing the concepts to be studied, the group is ignoring other individuals' fears and feelings of weakness. As a whole, the group is denying these qualities in itself, as if they belonged only to the individual who speaks of them. In that case, the group is using splitting, repression, and projective identification of one individual as weak to defend against shared anxiety about the group's adequacy to deal with its complex task. The leader comments on this behavior in terms of the group as a whole to relieve the individual of this role burden and to return the group to its task.

In addition, we respond directly to individual members. Individual responses are made either by group members or by the leader. These resemble responses made in a therapy group. Conflicted impulses, memories, fantasies, or inner object systems may be identified when they are displayed in the individual member's style of dealing with the small and large groups. These are transference phenomena and they may call for an individual interpretation not for the purpose of creating personality change but to illustrate a concept. For example, a leader might point out to an individual member, "Your rage and anger at the presenter's authoritarian style reminds me of the feelings of hate you felt toward your father for the way he treated you when he received your report card. This is an illustration of how transference affects the learning process."

To *widen the field of participation*, the group leader might then ask whether others in the group have similar and different responses to the presenter's style. In therapy, these responses to a person could be understood in terms of the group members' individual transferences. In the learning group, they are used to make clear the group's previous use of the individual to represent group conflict or desire. If the feeling is not shared, the group may simply move beyond this idiosyncratic response. To take it a step further, the leader may feel that what is needed is a group-as-a-whole interpretation of the group's use of this individual to speak for group discontent with the small-group leader himself—an example of displacement of the group transference to him onto the presenter. The combining of group-as-a-whole with individual interpretation provides multiple vertices from which to study the psychic continuum. The group observes the ways in which the individual and the collective group become objects for each other. Individual and group as a whole collaborate to *use each other as objects* with which to encounter and work out the basic issues and themes of human existence. At the same time, the group focuses on the key issue of the forces that favor learning and those that oppose it.

Bion (1961) called these the group's *basic assumption states*, or subgroup formations that coalesce around members' shared valencies to deal with the anxiety of working together in a group with a task leader. These take three main forms—each shaped by (1) dependent needs, (2) wishes to fight against authority or slip away from the job at hand, or (3) preferences to create an exciting couple relationship with the hope of creating a savior because the sub-group formation seems better than the current reality of a multiperson group. These basic assumption states both support and subvert the group's ability to do its work. In the case of the affective learning small group, these subgroupings are both interferences with the integrative task and objects of study that provide material for the integrative work task.

Structurally, the group has multiple work egos with which to approach the task of the group. Fantasies, emotions, and ideas that might be terrifying for a single individual to articulate seem to emerge more easily in the group. The presence of the other members enables the group to note and describe a phenomenon encountered in the group. The phenomenon itself becomes an object of thinking. When a group member denies the meaning of a communication, the commonsense perception of meaning by the other members leads to a state of shared understanding that can be persuasive. Even if the evident meaning is denied by the speaker, it is noted by the others and can then be held in a state of potential availability, waiting for the speaking member to claim it from the container of the group. Although we know that affect can spread through contagion, as it often does in groups and organizations, the presence of *multiple self-observing work egos* helps establish a strong container, which in turn leads to greater potential for group learning and growth.

The concept of developmental stages is another lens through which to view the group. For example, a group is sometimes preoccupied with feeling full or empty. This awareness of internal contents refers to having been able to take in the group experience or not. At the narcissistic stage of development, feeling full or empty may define who is complete and thus good and who is partial and thus bad. At the preoedipal level, we usually think that this question reflects concerns over attachment: who has or does not have the breast or the conditions for life itself. At the oedipal level, it signifies who has won and who has lost, who is powerful and productive, or who is insignificant and wormlike. The *full-empty paradigm* subsumes minimal existence on the one hand and the expansion of the self on the other.

Hatred of vulnerability and neediness feeds the resistance to taking in experience and knowledge, but it also provides the spur for continuing learning. As students and teachers, we need to accept that vulnerability (and some measure of shame associated with it) in order to work with our anxieties if we are to be able to learn. Said differently, the group struggles with dependency issues versus defensive and envious fantasies of a false independence based on spurious, magical knowledge. This is an expression of the pain of *separation anxiety* due to separation from an idealized but defensive state of being "in the know." This degree of separation is required in order to learn. The more we know about ourselves, the more separate, distinct, and vulnerable we become. When we experience desire to learn and to become knowedgeable, we face the fear of oedipal triumph or exclusion from those who are in the know. The group often creates a pairing and magnifies its value to gratify and displace this longing and fear and to project into the rest of the group the painful feeling of smallness and *oedipal exclusion.*

We see Fairbairn's idea of the *individual endopsychic situation displayed in the group process.* The group members may project the antilibidinal ego outside themselves into a leader whom they perceive as attacking the needy-hungry-ignorant infant/student aspect of themselves. We see Klein's idea of envious idealization of the good object. False idealization of the faculty leads to a corresponding denigration of those in the student role. The group may project that ignorant part of themselves into an individual group member and attack it there. Applying Klein's terms for individual psychology to the group, we note that when splitting of good and bad experience, projection of good and bad objects, and envious attacks abound, the group is functioning in a *paranoid-schizoid position.* When good and bad aspects can be appreciated as aspects of the whole group object about which ambivalence and concern can be felt, we find the group operating in *the depressive position.* Shame predominates in the struggle with the sense of failure and vulnerability in the paranoid-schizoid position, while guilt and wishes to make up for failures characterize the depressive position.

The group as a whole mirrors the feelings and fantasies of the members and gives them back to the members without inducing the experience of shock, shame, or guilt. The extrusion of one member's internal persecutor has the consequence of making the institution itself seem saturated with aggressors who wish that a needy member would take her neediness elsewhere. There is no growth without dependency, but there is no dependency without injury. This point highlights the narcissistic injury implicit in acknowledging one's need to learn.

The group works within two realities. It is a fictive presence, in essence a re-creation of the body of the mother that enables each member to enter a *transitional space* in which to refind the missing part-object mother through the object of the group. Simultaneously, it is an actual, external event that provides each member with an opportunity for experience, competence, and mastery of the social environment. The group also studies the elements that interfere with play, imagination, and creativity in the transitional space embodied by the group.

Examples of Small Groups at Work

With this theory as a background to which each of us brings our own variations, we approach our small groups. By the time we start work with the group, we have to let go of the theory. Following Bion's advice, we let go of our memory of how a group has been and our desire for how it should be. We let go of our wish for it to fulfill our expectations. We open ourselves to what is there. We learn anew from each unique small-group experience.

A few of us will now present examples from our work—as group leader in an institute on object relations family therapy, as cochair of an institute on object relations couple therapy, and as small-group leaders in conferences on object relations theory and practice. We show how a group gets going, deals with its hatred of vulnerability, tries to get dependency needs met, and hopes to become a transitional space. We then present a group dealing with envy and idealization of the male and reparation to the female. This group moves between the paranoid-schizoid position to the depressive position. We demonstrate the importance of boundaries in emphasizing the entity of the group as the place for reflection. Our next examples show how an individual defends against envy or expresses it on behalf of the group to allow the group to avoid recognition of hatred of vulnerability and how two groups deal with envy of the couple relationship and oedipal exclusion. Finally, one of us presents three sessions that show a group's struggle to study the concept of separation anxiety, which requires facing members' actual separation anxiety as they try to separate from old ideas and from the end of the group.

GROUP FORMATION AND HATRED OF VULNERABILITY

I was one of two small-group leaders in an institute on family therapy. An opening lecture introduced the topics of object relations theory and family therapy technique. The presenter showed a video of a cotherapy team working with a military family with female children. The video illustrated projective identification in a marriage, the substitution of the individual for the group, and the transmission of sexual trauma to the next generation. It also illustrated therapeutic technique for establishing a holding environment in which the family could feel safe to enter the psychological space, interpreting their repetitive defensive patterns, and following the affect so that the family could share their pain. Questions and comments followed. The small group then met to address its integrative task.

> The group had six members: Jeanne-Marie, Lillian, Rose, Klaus, and Irv. Lynette was enrolled but had to be absent for at least the first meeting. Her chair was left empty. I announced that Lynette could not attend because of a medical emergency. The group appeared to ignore this information and went

on to respond to the presentation. Some members agreed that they couldn't stand the weak, emotional, inhibited behavior of the mother in the video. Referring to the family therapy videotape, Jeanne-Marie expressed irritation at the behavior of the male cotherapist, whom she experienced as insistent and intruding on the young girl.

I felt that the same might be felt about me if I pushed too hard. The group seemed like a female body into which I would be intruding.

Lillian observed that the therapist had waited for quite some time to see whether the girl could find the words for her distress. I thought that if I continued to wait, the group might then experience my eventual intervention as more intrusive. As I was thinking this, the group members wondered how long a therapist should sit with painful feelings. Then they fell silent, as if to see how long I would sit and wait. There was agreement that the group felt worried and pushed by the time frame, and there was some worry about further absences or disappearances. A long silence followed.

I said that the group could not proceed because the members were not sure what they would get from the group and from me. They responded by raising questions. Should they present cases, or should they use the group any way they wanted? If they shared of themselves, would they receive criticism? Would they experience shame if they strayed too far from reality? Could they play with ideas in this group?

Jeanne-Marie recognized that her own military family background had caused her to project too much of herself into her perceptions of the family on the videotape. Klaus claimed that his poor English made it hard to communicate. I acknowledged that Klaus's English made it harder for him but that he was not the only one having difficulty speaking what was on his mind. Irv said that he was afraid of being too cognitive, and he realized that he was trying to sit on his anxiety. His comments stimulated an intellectual discussion on types of leadership. There was then a long pause.

The group focused on the empty chair. My explanation of the illness of an enrolled member had done nothing to alleviate anxiety about who or what the chair represented. The group developed a fantasy about the absent member as a woman who is articulate and who would have been able to lead the group. I said that it was easier for the group to find a leader outside the group than to think of taking individual responsibility for their own learning in the group, including learning about the impact on a group of an individual's absence. Lillian wondered whether the group would run past the time barrier, as if hoping that more time would mean more learning. On realizing that the time would not be extended, the group fell silent again. Rose said wistfully that she had been thinking of how this group might compare to other groups.

   I thought about the people in the other small group and wondered how my colleague was doing. I said that this woman's comment pointed to a groupwide fantasy that some other small group would be able to do the job that they were finding difficult and that some other small-group leader than I might teach them how to learn instead of waiting for them to learn from experience.

This process is typical of a group in its first session. The members sound both anxious and excited as they explore whether the group can become a transitional space for play with ideas and experience to enrich their learning, much as a family might feel in the opening session of therapy. A subgroup formation attempts to discuss the videotape but runs aground when questions of therapeutic technique reflect the group contextual transference to the small-group leader as intrusive into the body of the group. The members test out the frame, the expectations, and the role of the leader. They develop a fantasy about the missing member as a savior. They hint at a fantasy about another group, another leader—a flight to a new object. The group has shown pairing and flight basic assumption functioning. The group leader uses his countertransference to interpret the invocation of a savior and the flight to a new object as defenses against the fear of the unknown and the unstructured experience.

PARANOID-SCHIZOID AND DEPRESSIVE POSITIONS

   I was a small-group leader beginning a two-year group during an institute on object relations theory and practice. Each of the small-group leaders took a turn presenting theory to the large group. Just before the small-group meeting to be described, I presented a lecture on Klein's concepts of the paranoid-schizoid and depressive positions and the death instinct as the driving force of projective identification and on Bion's concepts of linking and containment.

   The small group consisted of five women and a male leader, me. The group complimented me on my skill as a presenter. They found my examples helpful in understanding the concepts, and they proved it by sharing many examples of splitting, linking, and containing from their own clinical work. Only one critical comment on a small point was made and quickly dropped. In general, it was a wildly positive response, totally divorced from the tense atmosphere the day before, when a huge altercation had occurred. I commented that the group was idealizing me so as to keep at bay the possibility of a resurgence of aggression and hurt that might not be contained. I said that this was a group demonstration of idealization as a defense against the paranoid-schizoid position.

The group members then dealt with the remaining anger and hurt left over from the previous meeting, in which two of the women had been in furious disagreement. One of the two women said that she felt that her intense feelings were not wanted by the group. The other said that she felt cut dead whenever she disagreed with an idea that the other woman expressed. The emotional tenor of the group was tense. The two women entered into a debate about which was more valuable—thinking independently or expressing feelings. They were becoming emotionally heated and miscuing on what the other said.

Provisionally, I read this debate between the women as a battle for control as to who would set the tone and who would adjust to whom. But I had not yet understood what was happening sufficiently so that the group could move on. After a silence, I understood it on a different plane. I said that the group response to learning about object relations theory and the mother–infant relationship had been to repeat an aggressive, poorly modulated female pairing.

One of the women whose emotionality often moved the group discussion from the intellectual to the emotional level noted that as the group became emotional, she felt unusually numb or dead. This felt odd to her. Listening to the intense disagreement in the group about how things should be, she found herself thinking mostly about the force of the death instinct in the mother–infant relationship. She commented that she too had an intense need for control ever since she had been unable to control the illness that led to her mother's death. She worried that her thoughtlessness as a young girl had contributed to her mother's pain. She wished that she had been able to be more fully present to deal with their shared distress at the end of her mother's life. She wished that she could have done more for her. Having experienced her own deadness, this woman concluded by speaking from a depressive position of concern for damage done to the maternal object and wishes to make reparation.

Her comment defused the tension. The two women who had been arguing turned to the two group members who had been silent, and attempted to get them to join in. This was their plea to the group to broaden the field of participation and relieve them of the burden of enacting a projective identification about the nature of a female-female relationship. One of the silent women spoke. She said that she was listening and thinking about illness and death in her family. The other began to cry and eventually explained that she did not ever want to feel pressured to talk. These two women set clear boundaries on their participation at this time and did not join in the fray.

The first two women lead the group in the paranoid-schizoid ways of relating that are full of aggression and misunderstanding. I am being idealized as a defense against competition, anger, and rage among the women for what I have. I point out the women's envy of me for my capacity to integrate intellect and emotion in my admired examples and in my group leading. The third woman expresses defenses against death anxiety and damage to the object. She also demonstrates reparation. She embodies the depressive position for the group. The other two women are identified as elusive objects about whom anxiety is felt. In not participating, the relatively silent women take part in driving the group process that is filled with anxiety about the mother–infant relationship stirred by the concepts. Their silence promotes the creation and maintenance of the angry female-female pairing to cover over the women's longings to possess the mother.

By the close of the group, I began to wonder if the all-female competition was for possession of me, the only male, and that the women's envy was of my uncontested position as the only desirable member of my desired gender in the group.

BOUNDARIES AND THE GROUP AS AN ENTITY

I was leading a small group of one-weekend-only participants. We were in the second of five sessions of the small group. In the first session, the group members felt that I had paired with a particular student to teach about a concept. Now, in the second session, they complained about that pairing and said that they envied it. At the end of the second session, a woman member attempted to give me a hug. I declined. In the third meeting, the group explored how envy of the pair is driven by the loss of self-esteem when one does not feel acknowledged or affirmed or cannot make a pairing oneself.

My maintaining the boundary in not offering a hug leaves the woman with a feeling of loss, and this deprivation motivates her to speak about her experience. Not accepting the hug is necessary to maintain the group as an entity identified with reflection, not action. This allows the individual members to learn about envy of the couple.

INDIVIDUAL AND GROUP DEFENSES AGAINST ENVY

I was leading a small group in its second year of meetings. In the previous academic year, a presenter had used the word *worm* to describe the underbelly of the narcissist whose grandiosity masks a deep and abiding sense of unworthiness. This year, a man I will call Winton said to the small group, "I have such a tough time learning, maybe I have a learning disorder. I feel like such a worm."

At the individual level, Winton might be using his previous learning to express a current dilemma about his ability and his sense of self. He might be retreating to an old mechanism of self-denigration. He might be invoking a memory of an earlier conference experience to fend off the pressures of envy and competition in the present.

At the group level, Winton might be speaking for a groupwide learning disorder evoked in response to envy of the imagined brilliance or real perceptivity of the small-group leader.

How can the group face the defensive idealization that protects the membership from its hatred of vulnerability, and its rage and anxiety over feeling so needy and helpless in the face of complex psychological experience? Letting a flawed but "good enough" object provide sustenance offers the opportunity of finding one's true self, but this requires acknowledgment of ambivalence toward a whole object. This difficult work must be paid for by bearing the loneliness of separateness and the fear of abandonment by, and destruction of, the object. In Klein's terms, autonomy and independence are achieved by integrating split-off objects and moving into the depressive position, where one takes ownership of the self and becomes responsible for all psychic acts, both aggressive and creative. Reparation makes responsibility bearable by reconstituting the damaged object and mitigating guilt and shame.

COUPLES AND OEDIPAL EXCLUSION

I was the chair of an institute on couple therapy, a weeklong module that uses a multichannel, cognitive-affective model. It consists of readings, lectures on psychoanalytic concepts and family dynamics, clinical illustration using video and process notes, a median discussion group, small groups, and plenary review meetings. As the chair of this institute, I was in a position to study the work of a couple of small groups without having the responsibility of leading either group.

The small-group task is an integrative cognitive–affective one in which the participant reviews the concepts of intimacy, unconscious communication, and sexuality presented in readings and lectures; discusses dynamics and clinical issues shown on videotape; and examines the emotional response to the material presented. As each participant takes up the integrative task of the group, a group process develops in which the concepts that are being discussed emerge in the interpersonal dimension, where they can be viewed and examined in vivo. The group leader provides a safe psychological space, interprets defenses against learning, uses the group process to illustrate the didactic material, and encourages group members to apply their learning to their own clinical experience. I will draw examples from the process of the two small groups that met to discuss various presentations during this institute on couple therapy. I will call them Small Group 1 and Small Group 2.

The first presentation was on the use of transference and countertransference in assessment for couple therapy. The woman presenter used a video showing a couple working with her and a male cotherapist. The video showed a woman who was overfunctioning and overburdened. She was angry and contemptuous of the man, who, according to her, was underfunctioning. She was afraid that she would get trapped in a boring marriage with him. He simply adored her, no matter what.

Small Group 1

Group 1 produced a pairing between the leader and the only other male member of the group. Competitive yet fruitful, their exchange led to a lively discussion about segments of the tape. A woman group member talked of feeling overwhelmed by the level of the woman's aggression toward her partner and the therapists. She related her difficulty in dealing with this aggression to her difficulty in moving from the ease of doing individual therapy to the strain of couple therapy. The group then struggled with the impact of seeing the cotherapists working together on the video.

The group members asked the leader to do some teaching about the use of cotherapy. They claimed that, if the presenter were present, she would teach the group. From this, he detected that the group members were anxious about whether a couple can be vital and productive—the patient couple on the video, the cotherapy couple on the video, the couples that might form in the group, and the couple created between the group leader and me, the chair of the institute. The group leader acceded to the group's request, and he went on to teach about the internal couple. In response to his taking care of their dependent needs and creating a couple in his discussion, the group became entirely silent.

Group 1 behaves independently in intellectual discussion and then emotionally becomes like a dependent child needing to have the couple relationship explained.

Small Group 2

In group 2, there was no discussion of the presentation at all, according to the group leader, but there was a pairing. A woman group member presented her own clinical experience of feeling hopeless when dealing with a couple where the wife is afraid of being buried alive. Here was an interesting association to the couple on the video, in which the woman was afraid of being trapped in a boring marriage. (The presentation was being referred to after all!)

The leader broadened the field of participation by asking whether the rest of the group wanted to leave the feeling of hopelessness as her issue or whether others also felt that way. The individual helplessness and hopelessness began to be shared by others in the group. Another group member said she would feel less anxious if it was possible to do cotherapy in private practice. Of all the group members, she seemed to be the one to wrestle with the concept of transference and countertransference.

The leader noted that the first woman had enacted the group feeling of being overwhelmed by the presentation, while the other seemed to be asking whether the more private "practice" area of the small-group room could allow for the group to co-work on the issues. He said that the group had created a nervous couple to stand for its ambivalence and anxiety about beginning to study the couple relationship.

The second presentation featured a child-focused couple.

The Next Meeting of Small Group 2

The group discussed the case for fifteen minutes. A woman member then said that loyalty to her family of origin and her country interfered with her being a good couple with her husband. Her family had a transgenerational history of women being accused of leaving the native land, so she found it hard to deal professionally with an accused mother or with a depressed father who was accusing his daughters of leaving him. She could not separate being a professional from being a wife and mother.

Another woman said that her issues resonated with that theme. She thought that she had a couple inside her that was full of anger about sacrifice. Other women complained that they have too much to do and too many obligations to their children. They asked how can it ever be understood that they have to make their choices. Some of these women had been powerful contributors to the large-group discussion of the didactic material, but then in the small group they came across as secondary and vulnerable to sacrifice.

Others in the group were crying. The group seemed to experience itself as the oedipal child being abandoned. The leader himself felt bored, distracted, and frustrated. He commented that he might be picking up the frustration of the maternal role. The women did not accept that interpretation. It seemed more likely that he was filled with the discomfort of the excluded oedipal child.

These three group sessions were chosen to show how, when the couple relationship is being studied, the group may identify with the couple or with the child who does not have access to the couple relationship. This phenomenon is amplified in the small groups. Group 1 created a male-male couple, had a lively intellectual discussion, related to the difficulty of dealing with a couple, and then listened like a mute child to the leader's description of the internal couple. Group 2 felt overwhelmed by the didactic material, like a child, and went on in the next session to talk about the child-centered couple relationship and to experience grief about the abandonment of family members by women who form new couples with husbands and children.

To be effective as couple therapists, we have to confront our own exclusion from the pair and our anxiety about intruding on their relationship. We have to confront in ourselves the unresolved anxiety of the curious child who should not be privy to parental intimacy. The group can help us resolve this conflict by giving us a space in which to externalize the conflict, rework it with the help of the group, and then reinternalize it.

STUDYING AND DEALING
WITH SEPARATION ANXIETY

I was the small-group leader of an ongoing group. The three group meetings that I will describe occurred during a weekend conference on separation anxiety that included lectures on chaos theory and dreams. After the presentation on chaos theory, a woman spoke in an excited, pleased fashion about fractals and strange attractors. Another woman who had told the group already that her father was a know-it-all was furious about the pleasure expressed because she believed it covered over the ignorance and uncertainty that most members of the conference felt about the new concepts of chaos theory and their application to psychoanalysis. She felt that people actually were in the dark and were too afraid to admit it.

The woman's reaction usefully widens awareness of the range of responses and the level of misunderstanding. At the same time, her reaction expresses rage against the intellectual challenge of a new paradigm that upsets the group's equilibrium. Each large-group presentation seems to "crack up" the internal balance, exposing the members to new anxieties. The threat of confusing new suggestions pushes the group backward over the edge into a paranoid-schizoid mode of thinking and relating.

A highly trained woman small-group member used the past tense to talk about her problems in dealing with group emotional issues. She said, "I used to feel so confused about the process." A less senior student confronted her about the way she was distancing herself from current difficulties in understanding complex material. The first woman defended herself, and an argument ensued.

Differences in training, experience, and professional status between these two members leads to an argument that sharpens the group's awareness of the polarity between authenticity and false-self relating.

The group members spoke about the confusion between need and aggression. They discussed how this confusion leads to fantasies of destruction of the object. They developed the hypothesis that if the object that they want to annihilate is also needed, that object is felt to be treacherous. I showed the group that it had quickly moved into this intellectual mode of discussing destroying the object as a defense against the dawning awareness that the object was about to disappear by its own agency—there was only one more small-group session in the weekend. The members became more aware of their feelings that there was so much to learn and so little time.

Separation anxiety saturates the group and now becomes not just the intellectual topic for study but also an affect with impact beyond the group's ability to fend it off. Now it gains power to infuse the study of separation and chaos with the collective sense of loss experienced when new theories impinge on old ideas and when known people and places have to be left behind.

After a presentation on dreams as a signal of an imminent turn for the better in treatment, the group continued.

> A man was first confronted and then protected by the group. He talked about how injured he had felt when the group felt that he had to be protected from anticipated hurt. He remembered the trauma of being protected as a child from knowing that his mother was sick and in the hospital. He was not told the facts and remained deeply distressed by the continual uncertainty about the seriousness of mother's condition. The group was supportive and empathic.
>
> I saw a parallel process. I thought that this man's personal memory might be speaking for group-level concerns. He might be asking in effect, "Is the group sick or well? Has it been injured or helped? What has been my role in its fate? Is the group an ill or ineffective mother?" I could think this, but I could not say it. I was captured within my own feelings of upset about the uncertain outcome of the currently terminal illness of a family member, and so I was vulnerable to resonating with the group's feelings of loss at its impending end. I could not contain my sadness and think with the group at the same time.

There are times like this when a group leader contains anxiety in silent reflection in parallel to the manifest content of the group without usurping its path. Perhaps this is one of them. I cannot be certain. At that moment I became the "disabled, sick" mother—sick with the shared illness of anticipated separation. I wish I could have spoken of it directly at the time, but in embodying it and surviving for the next weekend and the next group, I became able to contain the message, even without expressing it verbally.

It takes enormous energy and courage to deal with the manifestations of separation anxiety. During this conference on separation anxiety, the group seems to have made headway in evolving a containing structure that allows for the emergence of unusually powerful, infantile and childhood dynamics. Split-off, repressed, and projected aspects of the membership are identified, contained, and reintegrated. The group's emotional vocabulary enlarges with the help of the large-group presentations. The group's enhanced capacity to deal with a variety of anxieties facilitates its efforts to feel, think, and integrate.

> A woman talked about her competence as if it were a false-self attribute. She continued to view her level of wisdom as childish. Other group members confronted her with the nastiness of her self-deprecating remarks against herself.

The group confronts this woman with her submission to the power of her inner bad object. Her critical superego (the "internal saboteur" in Fairbairn's terms) is a harsh, persecuting inner object. The part of her self that is attached to this internal saboteur suppresses her attempts to be more real, direct, relaxed, and alive and punishes her. In other words, it is hard for her to be separate and distinct from the self-object merger that characterizes such internal confusion. Again, the compelling nature of the group's connection to her remarks leads to a personal insight.

> The support of the group was crucial as it witnessed and commented on the way the woman deprecated herself. Speaking for a moment at the individual level, I remarked, "You seem to be getting close to putting aside some of the limitations you've been taught in favor of more spontaneous and true aspects of yourself."
>
> A man broke into her moment of insight, saying that he hadn't had such benefit from the group. He was envious of her moment with the group. He said he now realized that he had disguised his hungry and aggressive aspects. He hadn't owned them and reintegrated them, as the woman was being helped to do.
>
> He said, "I've not been able to find my potency. It's been hidden behind my mask of being a loser."
>
> The group was kind to him, and we all sensed the generative power of this moment.

At the individual level, I see that this man's ego ideal insisted on repressing these unacceptable parts of the self. At the group level, I see him speaking for the group's tendency to denigrate its own potency as a defense against the dangers of too much assertiveness and autonomy and especially against the threat of too much separation from the good object. The group works to find a way to hold on to the "group object" that sustains them together and individually while making space for the new aspects of the self they discover in the course of the group experience.

I notice a steadier capacity for sharing from a vulnerable place, more willing admission of envy, and at the same time the construction of an enhanced transitional space within which to play with the emerging ideas and fantasies. There is more trust, more regression, and more resilience than before. I trust the members to do more of the work, and that allows me more latitude for my countertransference and reverie. At this stage in the evolution of the group, the boundaries around the roles that the group members adopted soften enough to allow for more participation and shared taking of initiative. The group allows me to be slightly less "knowing" and the group members are proportionately more competent and assertive.

The theme of separation catalyzes deeper elements in the group that, because of the group's history and momentum, also transcend the theme. The group members participate in an intense group experience of emotion and anxiety. This kind of experience in the small group is continually contained, transformed, metabolized, understood, and reintrojected. The group members discover newfound individual capabilities to identify and understand fears, projections, and unconscious behaviors.

CONCLUSION

It always amazes us how much material is dealt with in one weekend and how the activity of the learning group may bring out issues that it takes years to reach in therapy. The design amplifies and transforms affective material. The small group, however, is only one of the various learning group settings in the total conference, and any single weekend conference theme is only one aspect of object relations theory. The multigroup, multichannel teaching design releases the participant from the grip of affect and resistance, which then become the focus of study and the way toward learning. The matrix of small- and large-group events, conferences, and institutes allows the unconscious to come up for process and review in many configurations and manifestations.

10

The Individual and the Couple as Objects in the Group Dynamic

This chapter gives an account of my learning in role of a woman small-group leader of an ongoing group in the third weekend of a four-weekend group of advanced students. It demonstrates the interplay between the established process of the group, the impact of the didactic presentation on the group, and my interventions based on the concepts that had been presented in order to further the group's ability to learn those concepts. It shows my working to respect the frame of the group and to maintain my equilibrium as group leader in the face of unexpected challenges. This sets the context for the main focus of the chapter, which is to illustrate what can be learned when the group focus shifts to an individual. Finally, I show the process of my integration of the concepts as I learn from the group process and from my countertransference.

In this group, attention focused on individuals in a few ways. The group concerned itself serially, first with one individual and then another, in order to defuse the impact of the aggressive coupling of the two of them. Another individual was shut out of the group by the leader's boundary keeping, and the group was shut out by an individual who rejected the group's wish to understand by insisting on individual autonomy in making decisions. When a group repeatedly focuses on one individual persistently, this usually implies that there is a treatment issue for that person to address elsewhere (see Chapter 6). But this group focused on two individuals on this occasion, which was exceptional. At this phase of its development, the group used these individuals in turn to house projective identifications of disavowed or cherished aspects of the group in hope of dealing with them in one person because, when they suffused the entire group, they seemed impossible to manage.

I will call the group members Matt, Claire, Lizzie, Maureen, and Dorothy. Matt and Claire had been engaged in a debate full of anger and hurt the previous weekend, and the group had ended without resolution. The memory of their aggressive pairing seemed to be inhibiting the group out of fear of a repetition. Group discussion revealed that the battle for control in their pairing was a displacement from competition and envy of my leadership role. Therefore, this was not the only altercation to be feared. I responded to the events of the group with comments drawn from concepts that had been presented that weekend. These gave the group a common language for thinking about experience that was generated in response to both the didactic material and the ongoing dynamics of the group itself. The concepts helped me understand what was happening and gave me a fresh way to formulate my interventions.

Before the first small-group meeting of this third weekend conference in the series, Matt warned me that he would not be attending the fifth small-group meeting on Sunday, the last session of the weekend. He had agreed to get home early to care for his children so that his wife could take a business trip. As a veteran of the program, Matt knew the importance of attending the full series of sessions. He also knew that any announcement of unavoidable absence should be made in the group so that its meaning to the group could be discussed. His telling me, the leader, outside the group seemed to me to be another in a series of actions that he had been taking to challenge my functioning as group leader and to draw attention away from the distinction in roles between us. I also felt that his action reflected his wish to have an extragroup contact with me. In previous weekends, he had frequently been rejecting of my formulations and controlling of my behavior in role as the group leader. In seeking me out, he was now attempting to control any comments I might make to the group about his decision. In telling his announcement only to me, he was also being rejecting of the group. At this moment, I sensed that his rejecting and controlling behavior was covering over a longing to feel connected to me as the leader and to matter directly to me as a substitute for the group.

The First Presentation on Acknowledging the Object

During the morning lecture before the first small group, the topic had been the sense of solitude expressed in the dynamics of the transference and countertransference in patients who have difficulty acknowledging the presence of the object and the loss of it. Those who are most affected by the object and its loss are the ones who deny it the most. Patients who make excessive use of projective identification cannot recognize themselves and develop problems in the management of narcissism. Their frustrations provoke hatred, and their actions reflect their unacknowledged separation anxiety.

To illustrate these ideas elaborated in the morning lecture and discussion, the presenter described a case of a patient who complained of loneliness. I will call the patient Andrew. As soon as he felt himself committed to a relationship, Andrew did something to make people reject him. His strong feelings of separation anxiety were acted out instead of verbalized. Andrew had no idea that there might be a link between his anxieties about being abandoned and the feeling of aloneness that he experienced in the transference. On one occasion, Andrew had reacted to a separation by being unable to find his keys after he left his house. There he was, "alone in the street, in front of his home's closed door."

The First Small Group

Without any prompting from me, at the group's first meeting right after this presentation, Matt did inform the group of his intended absence. He did so, however, in a way that left the members unable to express their feelings. He couched his decision to miss the fifth and last meeting of the weekend in terms of the importance of meeting his wife's needs and as a reflection of his commitment to his marital relationship. He said that most men have difficulty working on relationships, and he was sorry that his wish to do so was taking him away from the group. He put forward the theory that that was why so few men participate in the affective learning. Matt's expression of regret to the group was experienced as gratuitous. Referring to the scandal concerning President Clinton's widely discussed affair, Matt went on to say that there are men who prefer a blow job to a real relationship.

Dorothy responded, "This feels dangerous to say, but I think you're doing a blow job on the group. You're saying that your wife is the real relationship and the group is not."

Matt vigorously denied her contention. He insisted that his motives were altruistic and related only to his wife's needs. He assured the members that he intended no disrespect toward the group. I was unconvinced. The group members pretty much gave up and left Matt alone.

Another member of the group, Claire, announced that she too would be missing a group meeting and vaguely suggested that her absence would most likely occur the next afternoon. She eventually spoke of her dilemma over whether to reveal the reason for her decision to miss the meeting. She felt that to do so would make her vulnerable but that to withhold the information would mean that she could not really be present in the group emotionally. Claire decided to tell the group that a close woman friend whose home was near Washington had recently committed suicide. Claire wanted to join other friends in helping the bereaved husband take care of some of her friend's personal effects. Claire also shared a dream she had had the night before in which she and other friends were frolicking in her friend's closet and trying on her clothing.

The group expressed compassion for Claire, helped her explore her feelings about her friend's suicide, and worked with her to understand the meaning of the dream as a manic response to the loss of her dear friend and as a way of staying close to her.

I linked the proposed absences of these two group members to unresolved feelings from their intense fight the previous weekend. I noted that Matt, Claire, and the other group members all ignored my remark and did not explore the meaning of the impending absences any further.

The two announcements of impending separations were made as if an individual's feelings and needs had nothing to do with the group and could be treated simply by action, and yet they had taken up the entire group time. There had been little discussion of the theoretical or clinical material.

The Second Presentation on Clinical Work

In the afternoon, an advanced student presented to the large group a clinical case featuring her work with a patient who functions on a primitive level (See Chapter 15). To avoid separation, this patient wants to get inside her therapist, stay there, and possess her. The student went on to describe the difficulty of working with her patient because of the fragmentation of her own thinking, which occurred in parallel to her patient's communications. As cochair for the weekend program, I had been assigned the mentoring task of helping her prepare this presentation. I was pleased at how well she did in conveying the facts of the case and the attacks on linking that made it hard to keep her thoughts together without letting that process invade the coherence of her presentation. She stayed relaxed and responsive to comments from the consultant and from fellow students.

The Second Small Group

At the start of the small-group meeting in the afternoon following the case presentation, I closed the door to the room at the correct time for starting the group. Lizzie had not yet arrived. Matt asked me whether I was aware that the door locked itself when shut so that it could be opened only from inside. When he heard that I was aware of that fact, Matt accused me of being sadistic by locking the door and making the late group member have to knock to get in.

I said that Matt seemed unable to consider that my closing the door was an action to protect the frame of the group. In response to her knocking on the door, I opened the door for Lizzie, who apologized for being late, saying that she had gotten lost in a conversation.

When she heard that Matt had considered my action a sadistic one, Lizzie disagreed. She said that she felt relieved that the door was shut. She would have felt anxious if it had still been open when she arrived late. She would not have felt safe if I had been unable to maintain the boundary of the group.

When the group discussed Matt's reaction to me, he explained that he was sensitive to this issue because he himself had been shut out. He told us that he had arrived for the group early and then left the room temporarily, closing the door behind him. When he tried to get back in, he realized that he had locked himself out of the room. He had to seek out a hotel maid to let him back in.

Matt had made an unconscious affective link with the material about separation anxiety. Unknown to him, he had enacted his anxieties about separation incredibly like Andrew, the patient who had been presented that morning. It was as if, like Andrew, he was "alone on the street." Matt's accidentally locking himself out of the room in the literal sense mirrored the way that he sometimes locked himself out of the group in an emotional sense. His intense reaction to my locking Lizzie out seemed to be a displacement of feelings of separation anxiety, for which he was speaking in the group at that moment. Not until this enactment occurred was the group able to take up the clinical issues in the case of Andrew. Having unlocked the door to Matt's participation, the group went on to discuss the afternoon clinical presentation as well, mainly expressing empathy for the student presenter's difficulty in dealing with primitive levels of functioning, with which as a group they too had been struggling.

The small group's consensus was that the presenter and the consultant had not fully acknowledged the difficulty of working with this patient's level of anxiety and her way of expressing it. I thought that the large group had not dealt with the patient's anxiety about separation, which she suffered every time her therapist (the presenter) traveled to attend the conferences. The small group's sense of the presentation and my own impression of it reflected our responses to the material and also to the group events that resonated with the topic of separation anxiety—the effects of separation by suicide and the temporary loss of a person who is important to the group.

The Lecture on Emotional Vertigo

The next morning, the lecture was on emotional vertigo as an expression of separation anxiety. The woman presenter outlined several forms of vertigo and identified the different types of anxieties that are contained in each form. She noted a developmental progression from a fusion-related vertigo that is symptomatic of anxiety about annihilation, to a suction-related vertigo that is related to fear of falling into the void, and to a competition-related vertigo that results from oedipal anxiety. She emphasized the value of the analyst's reverie for dealing with unconscious projections and the importance of paying attention to inner feelings and bodily sensations as countertransference clues that signal the existence of the patient's unconscious anxieties. She described one of her own countertransference responses of vertigo as so intense that it drove her to cling to the arms of her chair. She understood her action as a reflection of the intense projection of the patient's transference into her.

The Third Small Group

In the group meeting that followed, the group had an experience of vertigo, and I did, too.

Maureen opened the session by expressing concern that the group had not been helpful enough to enable Claire to stay and deal with the trauma of her friend's suicide. Claire talked about her upset feelings and shared a frightening dream.

In the dream, Claire, her husband, and her adolescent son were staying at a hotel. Claire could not find her son, who was last seen near the hotel pool. She knew how to swim, but she called to her husband for help. He dove into the pool and found the son caught near a piece of drainage equipment at the bottom of the pool.

Working on the dream, the group explored what Claire's anxiety represented for her and for the group. The idea that Claire was guilty for thriving and having a productive life was most helpful to her. Claire's helplessness and inability to jump in the pool herself, even though she knew how to swim, reflected the group members' holding back as well.

Claire spoke about feeling guilty for having held back from her depressed friend and also about feeling angry in response to the aggression her friend showed in her act of suicide, which the group now learned took the form of setting herself on fire. Claire found the group helpful in showing her that she felt guilty for surviving. She spoke of her need to not be self-destructive and to own her own aggression. She concluded that she would not have to miss the afternoon group session after all.

I tried again to say that Claire's previously planned absence might be a way of avoiding the aggression that she had expressed but had not resolved in the final session of the previous weekend.

This time, Claire and some other group members agreed that they were anxious to avoid another possible conflagration in the group this weekend. Claire acknowledged that there had been aggression in her now-discarded plan to miss a session this weekend.

Intending to shift the focus from the averted loss of Claire to include the impending absence of Matt and hoping to support the group members to address whatever could not so far be said, I pointed out that they were avoiding the meaning of Matt's absence for the group by accepting his persistent refusal to discuss it.

Matt said that he was furious at me for "being so mean as to point this out." I was surprised that he was upset. I would have thought that he would feel that I was righting the balance of attention and inquiry. But Matt was outraged. He felt that I was envious of the way he had been interpreting Claire's dream. Because of envy, he thought, I was shifting the focus away from Claire. The other members disagreed with his view. They experienced my intervention as an attempt at balance, but their opinion had no impact on him.

Matt persisted in his conviction. He accused me of hiding behind my role as leader to deny my sadism, envy, and aggression. Matt's attack was so intense and the projection of his hurt into me so powerful that I felt breathless and needed to hold on to my chair. I was not the only one to lose my equilibrium. Other group members felt unable to think. We were in a shared state of emotional vertigo. Matt's confrontation had successfully attacked me, the group, and my link to the group. The group was thrown off balance. It was Dorothy who gave voice to the shared sense that the group no longer felt safe.

With Dorothy's validation, I recovered sufficiently to address the process to some extent. I said that I had made my comment from my position of authority as group leader, which Matt had difficulty tolerating. In doing so, I was demonstrating the differentiation and separation between our roles. I pointed out that this competition between leader and member was an example of the conflagration that the group feared might erupt among themselves because of their competition, envy, and competitiveness.

Now as I write this, I realize that my position as cochair of the weekend may have augmented my specialness and inflated my authority to envy-producing levels.

Learning in the Faculty Meeting

In the faculty review meeting that followed, I got further help in regaining my equilibrium by thinking more about Claire's dream and the meaning of my own vertigo for understanding the group experience. I understood that in my countertransference to Matt's perception of me, I was experiencing emotional vertigo in relation to him in the group at that moment, in the same way the presenter had experienced it in receiving the projections of her patient. I also got help with the group's response to Claire's dream. Although Claire, Matt, and the group had worked well with her dream, we had not recognized its full meaning. One of the faculty said that Claire's dream about needing a man to save a boy who was stuck in a pool near the drainage equipment may have represented conflict over her aggressive wish to hold Matt under the water. This helped me see that I too may have wished for help from a man to help me with the conflict over helping Matt or dunking him in water to keep him from lighting an emotional fire.

After working on my countertransference response with the faculty, I felt on more solid footing. I returned to the group more able to deal with the theme of suction-related vertigo that was referred to in the dream, tragically enacted by Claire's suicidal friend, induced in the group, and symbolically invoked by Matt. Having metabolized this experience, I was able to face the possibility of more intense projections with confidence.

Presentation on Chaos Theory

The next didactic event was a presentation on chaos theory and self-organizing systems. The presenter and discussants explained basic concepts of chaos theory and used them as new metaphors for thinking about human relationships and the therapeutic process. They referred to vertigo as a reflection of chaos in the psychic world. They imagined life as an *iterated equation* in which the end point of one experience is also the beginning of the next. They explained the concept of *sensitivity to initial conditions*, in which slight differences in the initial conditions to which a system is exposed lead to widely diverging patterns and outcomes. They applied this concept to illuminate how the quality of the early mother–infant relationship determines brain development and affective correlates. They described the concept of the *strange attractor*, the pattern of complex dynamics that seems to organize the system but that is actually a product of the system. They applied this concept to the reciprocity of the mother–infant interaction. Gaze and bodily interactions between mother and infant form a system that organizes the experience like a strange attractor.

The presenter then proposed the idea that the frustration the infant inevitably experiences is like the *friction* that breaks up an organized system. If the amount of frustration is intolerable, the mother–infant organization has more difficulty reorganizing, and the infant may respond with anger or even hatred. Once there has been a series of these frustration–response cycles, the personality arrives at a basic organization that persists over time and yet will have the flexibility to change and develop as the years go by. A person remains the same person although always changing to some extent in response to circumstances, relationships, and the passage of time. If one part of you is lost, you are still the same person, but it throws off your equilibrium. This last concept seemed particularly applicable to my experience of myself in the following group.

The Fourth Small Group

At the start of the next small group, the members attempted to address the complex material presented on chaos theory. Then they cautiously tried again to engage Matt in a discussion about the meaning and impact of his coming absence. Matt led the group into a dead end by dismissing efforts to understand, refusing to be forthcoming, and not accepting the group's need to understand his absence. Maureen expressed her fear that the group would spend all its time the next day trying in vain to understand Matt's absence when he would not be there to work with them.

No longer in the grip of my own emotional vertigo, I said that the vertiginous experience I had felt in the group yesterday helped me understand the group's fear that expressing feelings about Matt's absence in his presence would result in chaos. I linked Matt's behavior in this weekend to his previous rejections of the group's attempts to understand his communications. Using the language from the chaos theory lecture, I said this was an iteration of his behavior in the group on prior weekends when he had occasionally been sucked into a vortex of fury and rejection. When that happened, he threatened to destroy the group's thinking capacity and his own reasonable, positive, thinking self. I said that a strange attractor drew him repeatedly to this position. The power of the strange attractor was partly determined by an old view of himself built up at a time when a powerful defense must have been necessary (none of the group's business unless he chose to work at this personal level) and partly as a projection from the group that assigned to him the role of the internal saboteur so that the others could identify with more ideal objects. I said that the group could choose not to engage in this iteration of frustration. After this, I noted that the group was able to disengage from their perseverating attempts at involving Matt in discussion and to deal with other aspects of the group experience.

Maureen began to address her competition-related vertigo in relation to a friend who was in role as a faculty member for the first time that weekend. While proud of the accomplishment of her friend's appointment, she also felt as if the ground were no longer solid beneath her. She found herself withdrawing and feeling resentful that the woman had intruded on her learning space. She said she knew that she needed to address this issue because it reminded her of other times when she felt ousted. With the group's input, she connected her vertiginous experience to her own earlier history of becoming self-destructive rather than facing her rage at being displaced.

In response to Maureen's opening up, Dorothy, who has a long-standing fear of heights, shared her experience of coping with physical vertigo. Her friend had invited her to view an interesting sight from the balcony of an apartment in a high-rise building. The friend offered to secure Dorothy in a body hold, but Dorothy asked her friend simply to hold her hand. Dorothy felt pleased at being able to feel secure on the balcony simply by having her friend's hand to hold. Maureen's telling of her vertigo led Dorothy to share hers.

I said that the hands that Maureen and Dorothy extended to each other offered a sense of safety for the group.

The Fifth Small Group

At the fifth group session, one chair was left empty by Matt's absence. I sat in a different seat than the one I had occupied in the previous session. The group members talked briefly about Matt's absence and then let go of their preoccupation with him.

Claire brought in another dream, this time featuring a friend and colleague of hers called Madge, who had stolen a patient from Claire. I noted the similarity between the names "Madge" and "Matt."

I remembered that when I met Madge through Claire at a previous conference, she had made a connection with me through her mother's name being like mine. This association, which I did not share, led me to think that the dream represented me as a repository for competition and aggressiveness. I was sensitive to the theme of stealing as a veiled reference to the wish to have my chair. Remembering my feelings as a student before being invited on the faculty, I suspected that these advanced students might be feeling envious of my added responsibility and visibility as cochair. I might be avoiding envy, for example, by taking a different seat than I usually chose in the small group. But I did not have to say any of this.

Claire and the other women agreed that they had been trying to locate all the aggression in Matt in an effort to protect themselves from the competition and aggressiveness that they feared could develop among the women, including competition with me as the leader. Claire went on to say that the patient's name in the dream was the same as one of the women in the group, Maureen.

The group agreed that this reflected anxiety about whether the difficulty they had to deal with in Matt would be located in some other group member when Matt was not there. With growing awareness of projection into Matt (for which he certainly had a valency) or into a substitute such as Maureen, the group ended a bit closer to a depressive position.

Because of the way Matt departed without participating in metabolizing the group's reactions, the chaos of uncertainty stimulated further separation anxiety in me and in the group. Because the conflict in his relationship to the group task was not resolved, I felt anxious about what I would have to deal with at the next conference. For a moment, I wondered whether he would return. From our experience with him over time, we knew that Matt is capable of working well in the group and that he pulls—and the group pushes—the focus toward him at times, as he did on this occasion. I reminded myself that another internal organizing system in conjunction with the group process pulls the individual out of the vortex in time to return to the group, willing to engage and able to learn from experience.

11

On Being Open to a New Object

W riting of my experiences first as the substitute leader for one weekend of an ongoing group and second as a single-weekend group leader, I explore a central process in the assimilation of concepts in a relational setting. I show how the process of a group was compromised by its inability to be open to experience with me as a new object, in contrast to another group that accepted me. First, I describe how I think about the group affective learning model. That thinking is the basis for how I approach my group-leading task and determines the type of object I offer for the group's use.

In the affective learning group, therapists engage in studying the theory and practice of object relations. They cannot learn either of them without internalizing the concepts, meaning that they have to let themselves be affected by what they are learning. Then they proceed to identify and work on emotional impediments to thinking. To think about themselves, their thoughts, feelings, and responses to others, they have to feel safe in the learning institution. We build a safe psychological holding environment for them and for us by eliminating critical judgmental responses from faculty and by encouraging student questions, comments, and criticisms. This frees the group to address the content in intellectual terms and then to work on the integrative task.

After thinking about what makes this possible for a group of participants, I've come to the conclusion that a key factor is the ability to make use of new objects. Modification by new experience with a new object happens at intellectual and affective levels. To the extent that new objects are experienced as nurturing, helpful, and thoughtful, the individual internal landscape manifests positive changes. The challenge to respond to a new object occurs within the environment of the affective learning culture in the large and small groups.

The group is faced with taking in new thoughts and sharing feelings about the experience of taking them in. As individuals, the group members are responsible for their own learning, but the group mind exists as a whole. The group as a whole relates to the new object—the concept, the presenter, and the emotional state invoked by the task of learning the concept from the presenter—in the setting of a group. Individuals take in and digest this experience in many ways unique to each individual and at many levels within the individual, the small group, and the large group. At the individual and group level, members can learn by taking in and being modified by new objects. If individuals or groups are closed off to new objects, they are less able to assimilate new learning.

Here I look at the extent to which a group, which I will call the "old group," was unable to be open to me personally as a new external object. I describe that group at length. Then, for contrast, I briefly describe another group, "the new group," to show a different level of openness to using me as a new object.

BEING A NEW OBJECT IN THE OLD GROUP

I had the opportunity to study the group's use of a new object when leading the old group under unusual conditions. The unexpected circumstance of a group leader's having to be absent for an important family event meant that I was assigned to his group as a substitute leader for one weekend. In preparation for the leader's absence, I joined him and the group for one small-group session at the conference the weekend before he had to be away. During his weekend absence, I replaced him for the five sessions of the group. This gave me the opportunity to notice how the group related to a new object.

I explore why this group was pulled more to therapy than to the learning task and especially what it was that disconnected it from discussing separation anxiety, the topic of the weekend conference. I think that the group members were suffering from separation anxiety instead of studying it. That was why they acted as if the task was to treat themselves (and thereby mistreat me) instead of to learn with me. They became a group of patients suffering from separation and loss instead of staying in role as a group of students studying separation and loss. They realized that, if they joined with me, they would have to separate from me anyway. So I became an unsatisfactory, superfluous object.

The History of the Group

The group was an ongoing, two-year group of five women whom I'll call Dominique, Karen, Lucinda, Joan, and Nancy. The group was reconvening after an interval of two months following the summer institute on the mother–infant relationship, containment, and countertransference. Issues of loss and anger left over from the stress of dealing with primitive anxieties raised by the material presented that summer were still prominent and were reawakened by the imminent absence of their group leader. This is the point at which I joined the regular leader and the group for one session during the weekend conference before the weekend of his planned absence.

Coleading the Single Session the Previous Weekend

Nancy was being judgmental about Dominique's attempts to address the issues. Dominique felt rejected without being able to understand what was happening to her. She did not understand that rage was being displaced onto her to protect the leader. Joan and Lucinda seemed less affected by the loss of the leader that the group was about to take, but Karen was talking about leaving this program for one that she would value more highly—perhaps an aggressive identification with the departing leader who had more important things to do the following weekend. The group did not yet seem to be in a place where those experiences could be worked through.

Adding to stress on the group, the format of the present weekend conference program was unfamiliar. Usually there was one main speaker and perhaps one or two other presenters. But this weekend had a special showcase design and featured classical and other contemporary psychoanalytic theories in addition to object relations. Rich in content and replete with presenters, it offered multiple objects to learn from. I felt that there was too much to be properly digested by a group that was facing a transition. It seemed to me that this experience on top of the previous one had left the group in a fragmented state.

Substitute Leading the Series of
Five Sessions the Next Weekend

The First Session

The next time I met with the group was seven weeks later. This time I was the only leader. The group seemed more organized and less chaotic than the previous weekend, but I felt that the organization was defensive. I thought that was occurring in response to my presence as well as to the absence of the regular leader. I felt this because, although the group did mention the absence of its usual leader, it did not deal with my being a replacement and did not *directly* recognize my presence at all. One of the members did address me, but she did so in a way that took my presence for granted, as if I might have been another group member.

The group talked about loss in their lives but not in the group. Led by Lucinda, the members spelled out in great detail all they had left to come to the weekend—leaving children and spouses behind. They agreed that their coming together again was important to each of them, unlike the missing leader, who had not given the group that much importance and was attending an event with family members whom he had not left behind. I thought the group members were uniting against the leader rather than making a place for their feelings about him in his absence, and I felt that they did not want to make a place for me. My fantasy was that these group members did not make a place for the usual group leader either. I began to think, "They don't really work on issues. They just *act* like they work on issues because they think that is what they are here for."

The Second Session

Nancy told the group that she had felt rage at me the previous weekend because she felt criticized when I had told her she was being judgmental about an older woman. Nancy then criticized me. She said that my comment was itself a judgment and not an interpretation of group process, as one would expect of anyone leading a group. I could feel myself wanting to pick up the challenge as to who was the real substitute group leader—me or her. I held the tension, and the group went back to talking about losses. Nancy then formed a pair with Karen that aggressively blocked out Dominique. I found myself resonating with Dominique's feeling of exclusion and unacceptability.

The Third Session

In the next group, Karen and Nancy arrived late to the group with an excuse that I took to be spurious. Nancy had been dealing with her stepmother, a personal issue that couldn't wait. Nancy and Karen continued to pair up in complaining about Dominique. I intervened and interpreted their angry pairing and aggression against Dominique as a way of registering a wish to keep me out. Dominique looked much calmer and said that she felt supported. Karen acknowledged her aggression. Nancy said that she felt criticized by me as usual. I felt that she dismissed me as inept or irrelevant. Joan and Lucinda remained silent.

What I dismissed as a spurious excuse was quite significant when I thought about it afterward. The excuse that Nancy gave had to do with her step-mother, and since it did not concern anyone else, she took care of it outside the group. I was aware of a feeling of aggression directed at me, but I didn't realize that she was also drawing attention to the group's having to deal with the stepmother role I was taking. Both she and I had misperceived her explanation as being only about her personal situation rather than about having to deal with the wrong mother, who, connected to the missing father, was standing in for him in the group right then.

The Fourth Session

As the group began, people brought in dreams. Dominique told a dream of a child being sucked into a vortex. This clearly reflected the topic of vertigo, which had been presented in the large group earlier in the day, but the dream was not worked with, nor was the topic. Karen and Nancy, the women who had paired up, reported a pair of dreams. Nancy dreamed of a mad, sick child getting her hair cut by her father. Karen dreamed of getting her hair done by a woman who was fixing her up. Karen then spoke openly about her competitive feelings with women colleagues and especially with a woman pre-senter. After she had finished, she became more accepting of my being the group leader. Dominique, who had been shut out, was then able to own her own ways of closing people out. Nancy, who dreamed of the child's hair being cut by a father and who had challenged me, was now able to listen to me without feeling criticized. I said that she was having to struggle to find her identity in the group and was holding onto being the father for the group instead of acknowledging her feelings about his not being there. This was a way of avoiding separation by the use of identity formation.

The Fifth Session

The group had made some movement on some of the issues of aggression, competition, and emotional relatedness. Although it hurt at the time, Nancy's and Karen's open admission of aggression was refreshing, and it cleared a path for growth. Dominique said that the group had now become safe for her. Karen said that she had gotten insight into how her competitiveness blocked her ability to learn. Nancy, who had challenged me, could not say she gained anything. I thought that she still did not want to accept me as the group leader, which would mean having to displace herself from the position that she envied. If she did accept me, she might fear losing her identification with the missing leader. If she did, she would then feel the loss of him and his valued image. Joan and Lucinda were less vocal. I sensed that Joan's silence was full of anger at the focus on Nancy, Karen, and Dominique, while Lucinda's participation was inhibited by anxiety about their aggressiveness and its consequences.

The group felt to me as if it did not have enough space to address the themes of the conference directly—neither intellectually nor emotionally. One dream had picked up the theme of emotional vertigo, but it was not elaborated. As she was leaving, Karen, who had worked on her competitiveness with the presenter, used a phrase that she had heard one of the presenters use in referring to dreams that marked progress in analysis. She said that she had "turned a page" in the group. I was glad to see the integration of some of the intellectual material with the group process, even though the intellectual work had happened mostly outside the group.

REFLECTING ON THE SUBSTITUTE NEW OBJECT

In review of my experience as a substitute leader, I realized that this group did not feel like a group at all. Loss had fragmented it into a series of individuals bunched together, two of whom (Nancy and Karen) occasionally paired to exclude a third (Dominique). Two other women (Joan and Lucinda) more or less stayed out of it. I kept thinking of what each individual woman needed. Dominique needed me to make the group safe for her by being a male presence. Karen needed an aggressive give-and-take to help her withstand the force of her competitive feelings. Nancy needed to have her wish to be the leader challenged. Joan, who said to me, "I am not present the way you think I should be," continued to puzzle me. I would need to know her better to understand her way of learning. Lucinda could express herself only around issues of loss apart from direct group experiences. I would need more time than I had with the group to find out how to include her in the group process. I thought of Jung's idea of individuation, and it seemed to me that I was reaching back to a concept from another theoretical base to help me deal with the impact of the group's experience of me.

Compared to other groups I have led, personal issues took over far too much. This made the group work seem more like therapy, perhaps because of the unique combination of personalities in this group, but more likely, because the group was traumatized by inconsistency in the leadership. Even more process work will have to be done for the personal development of the members,

for the development of a group mind, and for its connection to the leader before there will be enough space in this group for dealing with the didactic material in a thoughtful way. To stay emotionally connected to our work, we certainly need to keep growing and learning more about ourselves, but we also
need to benefit from the wisdom of the presentations on theory and technique.

I thought that the members in this group had trouble using me as a new
object because they could not face the loss of the usual object and because I was
a substitute object who would be gone as soon as the regular leader returned.
They were preoccupied with denying his absence by ignoring me, actively keeping me out, challenging me, criticizing me, and finally dealing with me. Because
of this, they gave too much attention to the leadership of the small group and
not enough to the subject matter of the presentations. As a substitute, I felt that
I lacked a secure base of authority from which to interpret their defensive use
of me as thoroughly as I do in other groups.

In short, the group was overloaded with emotional issues, and I was
overloaded with the group. This emotionality pre-dated my entry into the group,
but it was provoked by my being there, and it influenced how I was with the
group and how the group experienced me. The group had strongly affectively
charged objects that interfered with thinking about the ideas that were presented
for discussion in the small group. At the same time, some of the ideas came
through in the emotional content of the group. For example, the idea of emotional vertigo had been presented and was then unconsciously enacted within
the small group; it was then represented in the dream of the child falling into a
vortex. However, the dream was ignored, and the concept was not really worked
on. Individual emotional issues blocked the functioning of higher-order menta-
tion. I found that the group needed to work first on a more affective level before a higher level of thinking could emerge.

BEING A NEW OBJECT FOR THE NEW GROUP

In contrast, the small group that I co-led the next weekend was able to
integrate the concepts presented on hysteria within the group experience. The
presenter had referred to his theory concerning the shift in development that
takes place when the child separates from the maternal world of images to the
world of language represented by the father. Group members spoke of experiences with me, a male leader, that reminded them of experiences of separating
from their engulfing mothers and forming relationships with their fathers. This
group was well aware of difficulties stirred by the material on hysteria, but it
did not enact the mind–body split, as I imagine the previous group would have

done. This group worked with their experience toward understanding the concepts.

In this case, the group mind was not dominated by affectively charged objects, at least in relation to this material. It was also a single-weekend group, and so the deeper levels of experience had not yet emerged. The experiences in the group, the associations to affective and intellectual experiences of childhood, the memories stimulated by the material, and the group transference to the leader as a new object with whom to do this work combined in the course of group discussion to allow an integrative process to take place. The group worked smoothly with me as an object onto which they could project early experience and current group transference and at the same time use me as a new object for learning and modification.

COMPARING THE TWO GROUPS' USES OF ME AS A NEW OBJECT

In the two-year group, the first group that I described in detail, emotional issues blocked the thinking processes. Projection and regression dominated, with the result that the group appeared to be in need of therapy and acted as if getting treatment was the goal. After the group addressed its therapeutic needs, these were resolved to a sufficient extent that more thinking could then take place. In the second group, the single-weekend group, the emotionality was neither exaggerated nor repressed because of the combination of personalities and leader, because the group had not persisted over time, or because the group was not traumatized by working with a substitute for a lost leader. In the first group, psychological development proceeded stepwise from affect to intellect to a small degree of integration, whereas in the second group the integrative task was accomplished more seamlessly.

I don't mean to suggest that the second group was working better than the first. I just mean to say that it was easier. The first group was an ongoing group that was interrupted in the middle of its process by its leader's absence. It was experiencing a temporary regression in the service of doing profound work on the experience of aggression, competition, separation from the object, and object refusal. The second group would not last long enough for the going to get tough. Its members would not have time to invest as thoroughly in studying and experiencing the concepts in their full complexity. The ease I felt with the second group compared to the first is analogous to the clarity and objectivity that therapists experience during evaluation compared to the intensity and subjectivity of the midphase of therapy.

The affective learning model harnesses individual and group regressive forces whenever they occur to support the task of learning about developmental processes and pathological formations. Identifying with the positive parts of the affective learning experience, the individual builds new internal objects that promote significant psychological changes along with the acquisition of knowledge. Moving between levels of difficulty, balancing the emphasis on affect and cognition, and dealing with the group and the individual contributions to it, the group leader facilitates a complex integrative process that is the source of learning for students and faculty.

12

One Student's Experience
in Many Small Groups

After a yearlong seminar on object relations in my own country in Central America, I embarked on a challenging course of eight consecutive weekends in object relations theory and practice and a one-week institute on couple therapy. I had been told earlier of the opportunity in Washington, DC, for intensive study of the theory and practice of object relations. The idea was tantalizing, but my duties as a psychoanalytically oriented psychotherapist, as a university professor, and as a father—as much as my apprehension for working in groups—made me postpone the enterprise for two years. A colleague paved the way for me, and I took the plunge. For the next two years, I was traveling to immerse myself in object relations theory. This is the narrative of my experience as a student of object relations in the affective learning model that I found in the United States.

THE FIRST WEEKEND

In the first weekend, the first small group and its accepting, empathetic leader found me apologizing for my bad English. There were three men and five women, but there was an empty chair off and on because one of the women had previous engagements that made her miss the third and the fifth session. She didn't seem to realize that this would make the group process difficult and sometimes painful for the rest of us. Some members of the group, especially the men, expressed their wish to get something special, something not obtained before—an expectation that, in part, was not fulfilled. After ending the first session and getting out of the group, I kept speaking in English, even to a Spanish-speaking colleague, for which I apologized but that indicated to me that I was getting involved in the whole weekend process.

Every time I came in to the sessions, I felt tense, attentive to the passing of the time, and wanting the session to go fast so my suffering ended soon. Many times, I went out almost in a rush, running away from the place, from the group, to seek refuge in my room at the hotel where the seminars are held, shopping, walking, or having lunch by myself alone.

Since the first session, I felt compelled to play the leader's role, feeling myself responsible for the group. It's not easy to be 48 years old, thinking of myself as an experienced clinical psychologist and having to be in a student role. With such an attitude, I was not respecting the well-deserved role of the leader. I was competing intellectually, finding myself not attuned, out of phase, not accepting my reality as a participant member who was inexperienced in this area. At the same time, I was devaluing the leader's capacity. Guilty, I began searching for how to act in a reparative way.

The topic for this first weekend was love and hate in the therapeutic setting. In the large group where the lectures and workshops were given, I wanted to ask the presenter to talk more about the minor, frequent, semi-automatic boundary violations many of us get into during sessions rather than the less common, gross transgressions he had been describing. I rehearsed mentally my grammar construction and intonation, waiting for the right moment to perform. The day of his last lecture, I arrived in the lecture room fifteen minutes earlier as I always do in order to get the best place, not to miss even one word. To my surprise, he was already there alone. So I went to introduce myself, and for five or six minutes we had an interesting interchange of ideas about doing psychotherapy in a small city where contamination of treatments is like the daily bread. It was amazing to me to learn that Topeka, the famous city where he lives and works, is an even smaller city than mine! We discussed Nietzsche's phrase, quoted by Fromm-Reichmann, "that the idea of suicide has saved many lives," it being applicable to the case we discussed in the large group the day before. The last lecture over, the large group began its discussion, but I still didn't dare to talk.

Despite uncomfortable feelings prevailing in the small group and the fragmenting effect of the woman's absence, we managed to face some of the love and sexual attraction that had risen to the surface of the group consciousness and to think of the effects of these emotions when we are working with our patients.

As I left, the director of the program asked me how was I doing in the groups, and I answered "Struggling." He replied unhesitatingly, "Then you're enjoying it!"

THE SECOND WEEKEND

There were changes for the next weekend conference: a different lecturer and a new topic: adolescence.

In the small group, there were five male and two female participants and a different leader. My difficulties with the English language continued, so I withdrew again. But I soon learned that I appreciated the value of remaining silent. I could reflect on some of my deepest motivations and my behavior and its consequences on other people as well as the effect of the others' behavior on mine. I thought my silence indicative of maturity, a sign that I was coming back to my own internal life. I felt I was able to "be there" with my presence, if not with my voice. Nevertheless, there was a moment in the small group in which I was trapped in my silence, and I couldn't get back to the talking position. Somehow the leader understood this and invited me to participate, for which I thanked him.

The possibility of my foreign status affecting my behavior was discussed. A member of the group lowered my anxieties when he said that he considered me a very thoughtful person and that he was waiting for me to speak in the large group. I told him that I had felt many times prone to talk as if to prove to the others and myself that I was there. In the group, I felt it was not necessary to talk and that the group members could contain me and my anxieties. I felt that talking could be a sign of trying to calm down my own and other people's anxieties. Talking could be a way of avoiding the self and camouflaging the self with other people's selves. I said that we can speak to others in order to forget ourselves, and I was glad I hadn't done that.

We witnessed the debut of a different leader, a man who was leading a group for the first time. I studied his performance closely and looked out for any sign of anxiety on his part. He seemed to me a brilliant man who made audacious interpretations full of paradox. When he entered the room on time for the first session, the group members had already been introduced to one another. I thought that he might have felt excluded when the group didn't start with the usual personal introductions (which, I later learned, is not obligatory in this teaching and learning method). The way we excluded him was not faced until the fourth session, when it eased.

In the third session when I said that I was feeling fine, he looked at me in a way that seemed to say, "Let's not talk nonsense!" He asked me to explain my feeling. Then I said that to make short a long story, I have always had to go in front because of the predominance of women in my family and that in this group I felt relaxed being with so many men to share the task. Then his look changed, as if to say, "Oh, you're not speaking silly things."

In the plenary session attended by all the small groups, the leaders explained that the main purpose of the plenary is for the small groups to get together so they can gather information, comments, complaints; pick up whatever loose ends there are; and in general work together to review their learning that weekend and come to understand the whole experience. During that plenary, the lights twinkled twice, and a member's guts roared. Both events made people laugh and contributed to lessening tensions. It was the consensus of the plenary that up to this point the main lecturer hadn't fulfilled the expectations. Perhaps this was true only in comparison to the spectacular success of the previous weekend presenter. Would it always be this way with a second child, or with a stepfather, or with a surrogate teacher? Does it have to be true that the second person never makes it? If so, what about me since I am not the first from my country to be here?

I thought that the attitude of this lecturer on this, my second weekend, showed more commitment to internal life. Perhaps this style works better for being a therapist than for being a successful teacher? Others said that the lecture on brief object relations psychotherapy (which was given not by the invited guest but by one of the faculty) was as competent as anything by the great names of Malan and Balint. However, the plenary group members felt that the objectives of the weekend conference were unfulfilled because they did not get a full explanation of the Kleinian point of view and its relevance in brief psychotherapy.

We had learned that the codirector of the institution had been seriously ill since the last weekend and that she was now recovered. The group expressed shared fears and thoughts about her illness, and we were glad to hear that prompt attention had controlled the problem. Many group members wished they had been informed about it while she was ill. Her husband, also codirector of the institution, said that he had been too preoccupied with his wife's illness to be able to think of informing all of us, although he now appreciated that members would have liked to know. I felt relieved that it was alright to talk about it and also that it was over.

Again during most of this conference, I rehearsed the things I would say in front of the audience. I liked the lecturer's concepts of adolescent pregnancy. He spoke of having a baby as a shield against the wish to be a baby, as an envious destructive attack on the parents as the ones to give life, as a motive to go on living, and as painful evidence of the loss of the adolescent's infantile body.

Therapists have to consider all of these elements because if we can deal with them, then so can the adolescents. But I still didn't say all these thoughts.

THE THIRD WEEKEND

The third weekend was an unusual, special event featuring two parts. The first part of two days was the typical program with in-depth discussion of one major speaker's ideas, and the second featured many distinguished guest speakers in a showcase type of program. The topic for the first two days was the connection between individual development, psychotherapy, and organizations. Many participants came to hear the presenter because they wanted to think about the organizational aspect of their work. The large group discussed with him the influence of schedules, administrative services, location, distance, and fees—many factors that influence us as well as affecting our patients.

For the first two days, ten of us were enrolled in the small group I was in. For the third day, the group enrollment was smaller, and we were reduced to three men and a male leader.

The small group had a number of interesting experiences. The leader was the one I met the first time I attended a weekend conference. The first two days of the present weekend's small group, there were nine members I didn't know and only one that I did know. The speaker's topic definitely shifted our focus of discussion to the workplace. We discussed losing jobs, whether because we wanted to leave or because we were fired. One of the participants was a very young professional who brought out paternal feelings in men in the group. The two foreigners (a Japanese man and I) attracted the group's attention to us and the cultural influences on our work, which made us feel accepted. My English didn't improve, but on the contrary, it seemed to get worse. Perhaps it was just that the learning process was making me more conscious of my mistakes and limitations when speaking.

During one of the coffee breaks, someone said that even though the seminars are so enjoyable for us, it's not so good for our patients, who have to miss their sessions because of what we are having. I said that the patients are the beneficiaries of what we learn. I also said that the treatments of the patients who are mental health practitioners like us are the most troubled because of our intellectualizing mechanisms and the professional contamination we suffer, and so we need more of these brainstorming conference discussions to help us in our roles as therapists and patients.

The second event of the weekend was enlightened with the presence of great figures of the psychoanalytical field, such as John Steiner, James Grotstein,

Jeffrey Seinfeld, Edward Shapiro, and others who highly contributed to the excitement of this weekend. There was no doubt that this event was special. Held in celebration of the Tavistock's seventy-fifth anniversary, the program included a reception and a ball, where we had fun and pleasure.

Next day in the plenary, a participant gave a dream to which all were invited to associate. The large group responded spontaneously, associating to the elements of her dream. I had always thought of dreams as private matters for individual introspection. I was so astonished that I don't remember a thing about this one, except that it seemed to be useful for our learning at the time. With curiosity and interest, the group reflected on the vanishing of the boundaries between teachers and students felt during the celebration. We discussed the power of the group and its encompassing force over its members. Perhaps this fact is vividly known by some who, me included, resist participating in many group activities.

A female participant didn't attend the last session of the small-group weekend, and the group was quite emotional about losing her. Nevertheless, the fact that the group was reduced to three male members and a leader—all over 40 and married with children and all of us in mental health professions—gave the opportunity to open up more personal topics and discuss them freely. The leader commented sadly on his sense of aging, which, however, is letting him do better as a psychotherapist. I told him it is a good achievement to become a good therapist. It's a precious part of our time on this earth that we share with our patients. The relationship we settle into with them is more emotionally intense than many other relationships.

THE FOURTH WEEKEND

This was the fourth and last weekend conference of the first year of my participation. Our small group of four men and four women had coleaders: a man and a woman. The first session we spent making clear gender distinctions. I noted that the total group had the perfect number and composition for forming exactly five couples. When one of the female participants showed her apprehension about the task, I tried to comfort her, telling her that no matter how experienced one is, one never knows where the group will lead—I, who was so afraid myself! My second intervention was to tell the group about an insight that related to something that happened to me twenty years ago. All I said about it was that it related to the experience Guntrip narrates in his paper about his analysis with Fairbairn and then with Winnicott. I asked them to forgive my not sharing with them because I wanted to share it with my wife first since she was the object of the feeling. The group felt manipulated. I soon realized that I was behaving in an immature way to get attention from the group.

In the second session, the members related to one another in such a way that the mixture produced the five couples I had imagined earlier. Perhaps it was in imitation of the couple of leaders who were in charge of the group. Or perhaps it was a comfortable response to the material presented. We agreed that we liked the phrase "a hidden self with a secret hope," and we spent some time discussing that idea. We also discussed the presenter's idea of the constant readjustment we experience in our own selves all through our lives.

In the next session, we discussed something we hadn't liked in the lecture we had just attended in the large group. We didn't like hearing from one of the presenters about the details of one of his children's deliveries. I'm not sure whether he was talking about the birth of his own daughter or the delivery of his daughter's child. Either way, the description was too vivid, and we felt upset at being taken in to such a private place. It seemed to us like a transgression against her or against us. In the third session, I noted that the couples broke up and the group reorganized along lines of gender difference again. I thought that this might be a response to the unconscious command of intellectual defenses that arose because of feeling guilty about the transgressions that were involved in listening to the presenter's personal story.

The facilitator's role being shared by a couple was a new experience for me, and I embraced it with pleasure. It was comfortable to feel emotionally held by a good nonconflictual couple, like good parents who contain the group process and whose neutrality lets the participants have room to grow. We discussed the two lecturers' personalities (one being totally extroverted and acting as sure of himself in his choice of words as in his dress and the other quite low-key), the differences in their psychoanalytic points of view, and their impact on the group. It seemed to me that the female coleader of our group was searching for approval from the male coleader. I said that I wished to transmit to her that she didn't need his approval since she got mine. She asked me whether she looked as needy as that. Her question helped me realize that my perception of her was primarily a gross projection from myself to satisfy my oedipal impulses.

The members of the group played consciously and unconsciously at sitting between the coleaders, and we each got to do it at least once. And then we were caught in a dynamic of becoming couples. We would fight one another, apologize, love and get along, reproducing and mastering a couple's life. A sexual four-letter word was both used and rejected repeatedly through the sessions, its meaning obviously intended and denied at the same time.

The fourth session showed a more relaxed integration, but in the fifth session, the last of the weekend, one "couple" was missing, and the group mourned the loss felt at the couple's early departure. It was my turn to have the experience of sitting between the members of a couple when I sat alone with an empty chair on either side of me, the two chairs left empty by the missing "couple," who had left early. It could have been a matter of chance, or I could have been myself staging an oedipal theme. In fantasy and in my feelings, I had the opportunity to act my wish to be equidistant between the leaders as a couple as if they were parents, perhaps trying to control them, to get reassured that they cared for each other, and to not feel excluded. At the same time, I was competing with my siblings and dispossessing them of the paternal attention and reaching a privileged place in the family, both in the paternal system and in the fraternal one. The empty chairs at both sides dramatized the multiple losses of beloved ones I had actually experienced during the last two years, losses that also could push me to search for a sheltering paternal couple. In a progressive way, it could have represented that now, far from the storm of the oedipal phase, I could relive those feelings of longing in a secure context. From a regressive standpoint, it could symbolize my feeling of being a foreigner to the group and that therefore I was more prone to search for the comforting parents in a pair that was actually missing.

When I was handing my evaluation of the weekend to one of the coleaders, he told me that he had appreciated my sense of humor. I was grateful and thought to myself that if that was true, it meant that I was feeling more at ease and being more myself in the group because I have always wanted to see myself as someone who tries to take out of life as much pleasure as possible.

My comfort with group work enabled me to join two of the women in this group in making a greater commitment. I signed up with them to be the core of an ongoing group with the same leader for four weekends starting the next academic year. Unfortunately, there weren't enough of us to fill a whole group, so we could expect to have new members each weekend. But we would be together as the core of the group, and we were promised the same small-group leader for four weekends. I had got up the courage to make more of a commitment to my learning, but I still hadn't found the courage to speak up in the large group, even though I rehearsed mentally lots of ideas and listened carefully to how others said their thoughts.

THE FIFTH WEEKEND

The next weekend, my fifth at these conferences, was at the same time a new experience for me, being the first of the four-weekend group I had signed up for beginning in my second year. The presenter was a truly revered theoretician. We were all thrilled, but I have to admit I was so enthralled with his brilliance, I don't recall the elegant theories he presented most of that weekend.

My small group had three foreigners (a Mexican, a Korean, and me), three Americans I didn't know, and the two women with whom I formed the ongoing core of the group: in sum, five women and three men. It turned out that some of them had signed up for more than one weekend. We looked at one another knowing we could be working together for this and the next three weekends. The three foreigners sat together facing the American group as if that made us feel stronger, maybe because of feeling rejected. Nevertheless, I felt much more integrated, as much with the natives as with the foreigners, because this was my fifth time coming.

My feelings of being responsible for the group and my competitiveness with the leader continued. I was starting to realize that these feelings came from my own dependency on my father and my wish to deny it through the drive of competitiveness. I was still formulating my insight according to Freudian principles that I already knew. But the underlying preoedipal internal object relations were beginning to be revealed to me by the group process. I found myself realizing that sometimes I had intended to say something different from what I finally achieved and that the act of speaking developed my ideas. I was starting to accept my role as a member of the group, leaving aside my other roles as psychologist, teacher, and father. I was pleased when the leader recognized my preference not to be obvious or repetitive, which I have always taken as a valuable trait of my personality.

The weekenders' plenary review session, which included all of us who came to this weekend but were not in the two-year program, began with a long silence. I, who couldn't remember what the presenter had been saying, was the one to interpret that the group might be bowing in silence before the unreachable status of the idealized lecturer as a kind of Greek god before whom our work could look so uninteresting and devalued.

In stark contrast to its idealization of the lecturer, the plenary group made many criticisms of the hotel—not the familiar hotel the program had used the year before. Participants who were staying there said they hated its smelly, noisy rooms. We even complained about the lack of a motherly housekeeper to console us in the face of the hopelessness and envy that we felt during this weekend. I then referred to the split between good and bad objects that was being expressed by the negative idealization of the environmental mother who took care of us so badly while we worshiped the wise man.

Some of the participants tried to apply the presenter's concepts and terminology to the clinical cases presented. This had the effect of excluding the potential value of various perspectives on mental functioning by following only his ideas. The presenter himself stated that he thought this was not the best way to approach any clinical situation. It was better to do so through our own understanding of the uniqueness of the individual patient. Reaching our own point of view is what we hope to arrive at through the use of the group.

THE SIXTH WEEKEND

In the small group at the sixth weekend, the second in the four-weekend series, the same five women and three men were present as the previous weekend. But oddly there was an empty chair. It seemed to suggest loss and mourning to me, even though I thought that no one was missing. Then I learned that someone else had signed up for the remaining weekends but then had to cancel this weekend's participation because of a death in the family. She expected to return for the balance of the previously committed weekends. There were empty spots in the group discussion, when premature comments led the group to sustain long periods of silence. The persons who kept silent for the longest periods were idealized almost to a saintly level. They finally explained that they could speak but that they preferred to listen and that they didn't feel bad in the group.

My own silence was filled with sorrow. I confessed that I had just left my two elder daughters in Mexico at college and that it was so emotive to me that I cried before my wife. When she started to console me, I realized that I was just feeling sorry for myself. The girls were feeling fine, as I did when I left my country to go to study, so it was not nice to be crying for myself and not for them. The group joined in my feelings of sadness about separation, and this moment created a capacity for group cohesion. This was furthered when the group members talked freely with one another during coffee breaks, and at lunchtime as well, in a way that was continuous with the group.

In the next group session, we talked mainly about the learning model. We wondered whether creating an affective bond was necessary in order to facilitate learning. Some members talked with disgust about the idea of using other people for their learning, but it was recognized that we are always using other people as much as they use us. We have a right to hope for a positive interchange and not a unilateral abuse.

The leader now demanded more from me and asked me to look at my English slips. He pointed out that I had said "perking" instead of "percolating," which meant to him that something was about to pop up. He suggested that behind this slip and my using the word *retribution* to mean "giving back," there must have been some burden of aggression. Some group members accepted my intention of simply meaning "to give back," but his questioning gave us the opportunity to examine the aggressive element against the leader. I finally agreed that I had tried to repress my aggression against him and nonetheless it had popped up through using technically inaccurate words that conveyed my unconscious meaning.

I appreciated that the presenter, though a consummate Kleinian therapist, approached the case presentations more from a sharp clinical perspective rather than from a preconceived theoretical standpoint. Once she sat at my side during a video presentation to the large group. She thanked me for helping her remember the name of the Italian movie director Pasolini when she quoted his film *Teorema*. So, an Italian name was the first word I dared to pronounce in the large group! The name of this Italian poet-director is associated to my college days, when I partly filled my hours and longing for my family in a foreign country with films and books as well as admiring works of art. I studied Italian as a second language, which I link to the fact that some people said my father looked like an Italian. Perhaps I would have liked to speak in English with the fluency I managed in Italian, or it could have been a way of telling the large group that I shared with the presenter (also a foreigner) something that they could not. It meant a great deal to me that she sat with me and let me help her with her words.

At first I had no specific idea about the meaning of this to me, but I just thought it was great that she validated a not-so-repressed part of myself that is responsible for my attendance in the conferences. I now realize that it has to do with a valued mentor, a parental figure for me, who presented a brilliant conference on Pasolini's *Teorema* in the year of my marriage. As my affection for the English language comes from my father's love for it, too, I'm quite sure now that her sitting beside me represents a validation and acceptance from my father to the fact that I'm studying object relations theory in the United States.

THE SEVENTH WEEKEND

This was the third of the four weekends for the four-weekend group. There were now six women, five men, and an empty chair because the absence of one member continued. All that was manageable, but who were these two other guys? The man who had been our small-group leader for the two previous conferences had to cancel at the last minute because of illness. He was replaced for this one weekend by two male coleaders. One of the coleaders' names was similar to that of our missing leader. This made me feel uncomfortable, and the new leader pointed out my discomfort at hearing his name. I was surprised at the tone of my own voice when I replied that this name or the other name, this leader or that, it would all be the same to me. My tone was disdainful and reproaching.

I was indeed angry and disappointed with the substitutes (though trying unsuccessfully not to externalize it) because I considered the original leader to be a fabulous one, because like me he was a Ph.D. clinical psychologist—an obvious narcissistic identification that prevented me from accepting at an equal level other leaders who were mental health practitioners coming from other fields—and because the many times I had seen one of the new leaders in the other conferences, I had said to myself, "This man depresses me; I don't like to see him." Actually, I simply did not like substitutes.

In the first spontaneous seating arrangement, the coleaders sat with members divided on each side into old and new members, as if to protect the new ones from the old. Wishes and fantasies about taking away the empty chair were discussed. The members of the group agreed finally that the chair should not be moved because doing so would not erase the history of loss of the opportunity to know the person who should have sat there. The new members inherit the trauma as much as they inherit new leaders. We said to one another how terrible it is for younger children to inherit a trauma previous to their birth.

The group complained about male predominance in the weekend: Presenter, chairs, and even the clinical case were of the male gender. The complaints seemed to be a clear reference to dissatisfaction with having to have the male coleading couple, even though their paired presence and their combined personalities produced a secure holding for the group process. When the third session of the group ended, I found one of the leaders in the hallway and began to talk to him. He recommended instead of seeking him outside the group that I participate during the sessions. The right place to talk was in the group and not outside of it.

By the end of this weekend, I had a very different image of the above-mentioned coleader to whom in the beginning I didn't want to say a nice "Hello." At first, I had no respect for him. He was not a psychologist, he was not my type, he made me feel depressed, and he seemed totally unlike me. "Why does this man try to be nice to me each time we meet?" I asked myself. "Why does he make me feel depressed?" Then I realized that I had projected onto him my own otherwise hidden depression following six or more losses during the last year and a half. I took back my own sadness and recognized my feelings of inadequacy that I had put into this man, who represents another profession that I was prejudiced against. Following this experience with him and with other mental health professionals in the United States, where there is more respect for nonpsychologists than in my own country, fortunately my prejudices against other professions have now almost disappeared.

I started to think that not participating in the large group but only in the small group was a way of repeating my strong idealization of my original family in order to keep my small-group "family" unreachable for the rest of the "families." With this insight, I was able to free myself of inhibition. For the first time, I asked for the microphone and participated in the large group. Again I used a foreign-sounding word, *desperado*, which is really a condensation of Spanish and English, bringing Spanish-speaking me closer to the rest of the English-speaking group of mostly Americans. I didn't make a major intervention, but I said enough to be sure that I had tamed my fear of being ridiculous in front of the audience. One of the faculty told me she was glad I dared to talk and that she considered my point relevant, for which I was thankful.

THE EIGHTH WEEKEND

The next weekend, in the last of the four-weekend small group, we enjoyed meeting the woman who had been absent, and we were reunited with the first appointed leader. This time there was also a coleader, a woman of high empathic capacity and fine, sensitive intelligence. I ought to admit that I neglected her as a leader during the first meeting of the group, and it was only during the next coffee break, when I was browsing through the program and saw her name beside the habitual leader, that I realized that she was not just another participant. I confessed this in the group, and she invited me to examine my feelings.

I associated my overlooking the new woman coleader with my wish for the first leader to come back and with my difficulty in accepting a substitute figure, like a substitute teacher in elementary school. The issue was alive for me because of the absence of the leader from the small-group experience the weekend before and because the guest presenter who was supposed to have been featured for this weekend had to cancel suddenly because of illness, and it aggravated my sense of loss. The directors of the host institution filled in for him by presenting material from their own soon-to-be published book. They produced a full curriculum on transference, countertransference, chaos theory, and object construction at the last minute—all interesting topics, but not what I had been prepared for. I felt let down.

Various group members commented and others cried about losing the idealized parental figure and having to accept these substitutes. Some group members who had worked with the presenters in another program complained about their behavior toward them in previous groups. "Mother, you are not the angel you think you are," I said to myself, like an angry child who won't accept consolation. Eventually, we faced our authority figures from a more adult point of view.

One session ended with a member crying. When this happened, one coleader left on time as usual, and the other stayed to console the affected person. I didn't know what to do, feeling that if I left, I'd be a traitor to the group, and if I remained, I'd be unfaithful to the other coleader, who I knew had acted the way the faculty were supposed to act by leaving on time. This was one of the most difficult moments of my life in the small group. I even talked about this outside the group with two faculty members. I decided to skip the evening lecture and go for a walk to put my thoughts in order—or to distract me from them? With such an attitude, I put distance from the whole weekend process that was producing my intolerable anxiety about taking a side in a disagreement between two beloved parts—the two leaders. Fortunately, the next day I was reinvigorated. I thought back over that evening and realized that we keep coming to these groups because we are searching for something and because we are getting something, including the opportunity to cry about our longings, lackings, and resentments left over from former groups and not yet overcome.

I talked about my aggressive fantasy in response to the absence of the lecturer who had canceled his appearance at the last minute. I thought that maybe he had had the same destiny as the main character of *Misery*, the novel by Stephen King that he recommended for reading prior to his weekend teaching us about creativity and destruction. I think it's a ghastly novel. The main character, a great writer, gets captured and tortured endlessly. When I saw the film of that book, featuring James Caan and Kathy Bates, I told everyone not to see it because it was too aggressive. I said that I could not imagine how the presenter could recommend it and then not be present to deal with the murderous themes. Now everyone knew that I wanted to torture the man who tortured and abandoned us. I felt relieved by displaying my aggressive fantasy, and it let me feel more sense of belonging to the group.

After this, there was a direct reference to the small-group leader's previous absence. He gave us the information that he had caught a childhood illness from his child and that he was simply too ill to get on the train. Our disappointment was acknowledged and was matched by his regret. I was able to forgive him for his absence when he said that he had to cancel his patients as well. I learned that he was really in trouble and that we group members had not been abandoned for being less important than the rest of his life.

Besides being frustrated by the absence of the distinguished lecturer on this particular weekend, I was especially upset because it was his weekend topic on creativity and destructiveness that most attracted me and led me to sign up earlier for the ongoing group through all the other weekends. And then this special weekend didn't happen! In addition, I was also upset because this was the last weekend that the two groups of the graduating two-year program would attend, people I'd been with during eight weekends for almost two years. I would never see some of them again, and things would never be the same. I was also ending my four-week commitment with this group.

Some other participants adjusted more easily than I did to the substitute presentations. They really enjoyed the topic of chaos theory, and, as in many a seminar, one or two words captured the attention of the group. One word becomes the fashion of the moment, perhaps because it summarizes the basic idea of the weekend or because it brings new meaning to our work. This time, *fractal* was the elected one, taken from a lecture on chaos theory titled "Fractals of the Unconscious: Play and Dreams." This weekend you could see many participants smile when they could include this word in their speech. Their learning process resembled a child mastering a new word. Participants had found a new shared code that expedites and guarantees acceptance in the group. I learned that *fractal* is a concept derived from geometry to describe the footprint of a dynamic system. I thought that the behavior of enjoying the use of new words in our small groups is a fractal of the whole teaching–learning process.

I was able to think and to enjoy the creativity that was in the air following the chaos theory lecture. But I had not quite recovered my equilibrium. During the graduation ceremony, I took pictures, only to find that one film was ruined because the camera's button was not in the correct position. I could say it was because of my inexperience as a photographer with a sophisticated camera, but I really think this lost image might have come from my envious feelings because the graduates were getting a certificate and I was not. Of course, in addition to the eight weekend seminars, they had had two summer courses that I didn't attend.

After recognizing my feelings, I stated this situation to the director and asked for requirements to fulfill in order to obtain the necessary credits and get the certificate. The answer was negative because a full two-year commitment to the same small group had to have been made. Only the full experience earned the certificate. Anyway, I was really satisfied, and I planned to keep coming as long as I could, as I said in the plenary review meeting. I planned to come back for a different, slightly longer event a few months later, and to that I would bring my wife, partly to share this unusual learning experience with her and partly to get away together to Washington.

MY NEXT EXPERIENCE:
THE COUPLE THERAPY INSTITUTE

Now I am enrolled in something with a different focus. This is a six-day institute on couple therapy, Monday to Saturday, beautiful days in June. The group consists of about twenty people, and that's what's called a median group. Then there are two small groups. I have brought my wife, also a psychologist, with me as I promised. She is in the other small group.

In my small group, the leader is an older man. He and I are the two men of the group, together with five women participants. Sitting beside him brings me feelings of being close to my father. The group feels like a family to me because its composition is akin to both my family of origin and my present family of many women. The pleasure I derive is enormous and so is the comfort with which I interact in the group. The group holds me, and I take the role of the brother who may help the father enable sisters then, or daughters now, to solve conflicts. The topic of the six days is couples, but families are on my mind. I experience the group the way I experienced my parents as a couple— that I am the boy in their family.

The group works through a member's mourning of her father's death and her experience of his last words. It is an emotive moment for all present and for me, who also remembers (though I don't express it) that some of the last words of my father were directed to myself. The topic of family is on her mind, too. In fact, we all seem to be thinking that way. There is a continual sibling fight for the biggest chairs in search of a comfortable one, but as a matter of fact they are all comfortable. Perhaps what we seek is to have a bigger share in the group, to be close to the leader, or to take his place. Little changes of territory occur.

I learn that multiple couples are mentally formed from experiences with a neighbor, a teacher, a relative, a friend, and so on, relationships that will complement or fulfill the internalized parental couple. I learn that these internal couples influence the choice of a mate—or indeed the selection of a group member to interact with closely. I form a series of temporary working couples with various members of the group. I learn from a video of a couple in assessment that some couples are formed when one of the partners is attracted to the weak part of the other. That can make for a stable but compromised relationship, and it falters if the strong one gets sick.

Each small-group leader gave one presentation in the median group. The lecture our small-group leader gave was severely criticized by our group, perhaps as a result of our anger at sharing him with the other small group or because he could have looked weak, inadequate, or imperfect to the other group, which included my wife and a friend of mine. Each of the two groups is curious to know how things are in the other group. The two small groups form another couple.

The members of our group interact with one another during recesses, lunchtime, meetings. Even if we are left with a longing for knowing one another better yet, still the exercise has been quite satisfactory. Two foreigners arouse the curiosity of my small group—me and a Korean psychologist. I am now less of a novelty, and so she gets the interest of everybody. She illustrates the problems of communication and the advantages of coming from another culture.

I look at the codirectors of the host institution who are there together for the closing plenary. I know that one of them is American and the other is a foreigner, from Scotland. I also know that Fairbairn, whose theories they appreciate, comes from Scotland. Then I move more internally and think that I have always loved Mexico (still toying with the idea of moving to live there) and that my wife is Mexican. I went to Mexico to get a profession and renew my self—a new birth directed by myself. The codirectors have been taken several times as a model of a couple and as a parental couple about whom there are fantasies typical of how we feel about couples. Free discussion of this permits our understanding of this area. We reveal the fantasy that they have sent their children to spend vacations somewhere so that they can devote their time to us. From this standpoint, we can imagine ourselves their children, the accepted children to learn and identify with them. At this moment, I am staring at a bureau in the conference room. I start wondering what there could be inside. I think of my parents as a couple. I feel glad that I'm taking a couple therapy seminar where a part of my self is able to make contact with old and new objects.

The group shows interest in knowing more from me. I say that I am not as extroverted as I might look and that perhaps it is quite the contrary. I am still not sure of myself, the foreigner. One of the participants understands my embarrassment when I mistake the name of the patient on the video. He is called Green, but I think his name is *grief*, which is not related to the word I heard. She says that her husband is European and that after many years of living here, in the United States, he once misheard *chain* instead of *shame*. He became very ashamed and self-disappointed, as if he would never master this language. I think that he and I are making severe demands on ourselves. Even the mother tongue is not completely mastered to a point of perfection! Experiences of failure in English may be associated to guilty feelings about our loss, abandonment, or betrayal of our mother tongue.

My adventures in speaking English have made me enjoy more fully certain subtleties of this culture, a different vision of the world not easy to convey by means of a translation. It has been a playful adventure, a continuous-discovering one, a finding myself in domains I would not dare in my native language. Of course, I have also used this matter of language for many defensive purposes, especially to avoid my fears of getting involved in a given moment or even to avoid the linking of some thoughts.

As the last plenary review meeting begins, I realize that in the room there are only four people present on time: the codirectors, my wife, and myself. My wife and I comment gleefully that we four are the only two couples, one from the faculty and one from the membership, and I joke about waiting for the "kids" to enter the room. Soon the rest of the students and faculty arrive. I comment to the plenary group that being at the couple therapy institute in Washington was an excellent opportunity for my wife and me to share as a couple during the whole week, leaving our younger daughter at home. After this, I am very happy. I feel fulfillment. For me, being able to use humor with my wife says that I have finally been able to relax and enjoy the things I was learning.

By the end of this ninth event at this institute, I realize that I have attended more than fifty small groups and more than twelve plenaries; so my sense of security is justified. Nonetheless, I am surprised when, before saying goodbye, the director communicates to me in private that the faculty will invite me to join, which certainly makes me happy. I regard his invitation as one of the top achievements in my professional and academic life, but at the same time it scares me as much for the high level of training of the faculty members as for my deficient English and especially for the level of personal development this new role would require. I ask him to give me time for thinking it over.

A FINAL COMMENT ON MY LEARNING EXPERIENCES

Prior to my group experiences, I had already been through two intensive psychoanalytic treatments encompassing about nine years. Having a personal, individual, analytic treatment is quite unlike learning in a group. In the group, the focus is on the group, and the purpose is to study the concepts and learn from experience in the group. In analysis, all the attention came to me, and the purpose was healing. I had to say everything that was on my mind. No part of me escaped. The close and intensive relationship in psychoanalysis demands a dedicated effort for just one person, amounting almost to an identification with the patient as a special person. Not so in the group where we have to share.

Despite a less continuous process in weekend-only small groups, there is a richness in learning from the many perspectives and continually changing dynamics. Although sometimes my individual unconscious processes pass unnoticed more easily in a group than they would in analysis, other times it is quite the opposite. Several pairs of eyes staring at you push you to think and say something that might never come up in the protected space of the analytic couch. The pressure of the group can be hard to bear as much as the support can be comforting, but either way it generates learning. Personal analysis and affective learning groups, small and large, helped me as a man and as a psychologist in different ways. Though quite unlike my analysis in setting, focus, and technique, I have always considered my participation in these groups an equally valuable opportunity for learning about the unconscious and for helping the self to grow. Together, analysis and the affective learning group gave me what Bion recommended: a bifocal knowledge of oneself through individual and group experiences.

Evaluation of learning is a highly individual matter, so others might disagree with my impressions. Speaking for myself, I held the contributions of my group leaders throughout the eight weekends and the June institute in the highest regard. For sure, one weekend might have been better than the others, depending on personal factors, the setting, the membership, and the lectures, but all the group leaders were first-rate in my estimation. I admire their commitment to the task, their intelligence, their caring for the group, their good manners, and their education. I feel very lucky for having had this opportunity to learn and grow beside so many distinguished participants in such a safe and challenging holding environment. There I go idealizing again! I must be trying to stop myself from feeling sad that this phase is over for now. Let's simply say that I'm grateful that it was good enough—and that I'm good enough for them.

I will end with an anecdote from a patient of mine who had to bear my frequent absences. On the verge of my fourth trip, she told me, "I used to suffer a lot when you went to Washington and left me. . . . Now I don't care too much because when you're back, you know more."

13

The Course of a Small Group in a Five-Day Conference

In this chapter, we write as a faculty group, recalling and discussing the small-group leaders' reports on the course of a seven-session small-group meeting held during a five-day conference on object relations theory and practice. Designed to showcase contemporary British object relations thinking, the conference was hosted at the Tavistock Clinic in London. American participants traveled to study ideas at the leading edge of British object relations theory, attachment theory, and group theory. Each day, British analysts and psychotherapists gave lectures and joined in the large-group discussion. Our faculty introduced the topics of study, chaired the discussions, conducted plenary review of the learning experience, and led small discussion groups. For the purpose of this chapter, we zoom in on the course of just one of the series of small groups discussed at the faculty meeting.

THE DESIGN OF THE CONFERENCE

The design featured the usual combination of learning formats, but there were many more guest speakers than usual. An overview and a review by the two directors of the conference set the frame for the ten didactic presentations by invited British faculty (see Table 13–1). These included theoretical papers, clinical case illustrations of technique, research, applied psychoanalysis, and consultation to clinical material provided by a conference participant. All events included discussion in the large group. Discussion continued in small-group meetings throughout the week in a seven-session sequence. The small group experience is the cornerstone of the learning process and the subject of this chapter.

THE SMALL-GROUP TASK

The small-group task is to integrate discussion of concepts at the intellectual level with emotional responses stirred by the material and to study the group dynamic that reflects the students' struggle to grasp the concepts under discussion. The leaders of the small groups share their experiences with one another and with the director of the conference at a faculty review meeting. This meeting gives small-group leaders a small group of their own in which to process their work and receive consultation. At the same time, it enables the director to develop a broad perspective on the issues arising across the spectrum of all the groups. We find that each small group strikes the balance in focus somewhat differently but that all approximate the integrative task.

The small group that we selected for this chapter was led by two women faculty members. This was their first time as small-group coleaders, but they had worked together before, were friends, and were comfortable with each other as colleagues. We chose their group for our study because they presented detailed accounts of each group session along with their countertransference responses, their interpretations of group dynamics, and their between-group observations relevant to the learning objectives of the weeklong conference. We recognize that their views and memories of what happened may differ in some measure from our account of what they reported and that each participant has a unique view of the group experience. So we are not pretending that ours is a perfect record. This chapter simply presents the faculty's view of the learning process of the selected small group as it approached the learning task during the seven sessions so as to illustrate the way that the affective learning model works in the small-group setting.

Prior to giving the accounts of each group session reported by the two group leaders in the faculty meeting, we summarize the didactic presentations that preceded each group. This hardly does justice to the excellence of the presenters, but it shows each small-group session in relation to the conceptual material the group was trying to understand, internalize, and apply to the clinical situation.

In the group that we have chosen to describe, the integrative task is accomplished with more focus on the group process work than on the intellectual review. We do not intend to focus on or judge the participation of any participant or group leader; rather, we simply want to show how each individual contribution combines to create a group learning environment. The identity of all small-group participants has been changed not to deny their individuality but to protect their identity outside the conference institution. We have called the participants Sue, Lucy, Andrea, Julio, and Philip. We have called the group leaders Dr. Hernandez and Mrs. Dupree.

TABLE 13-1. Conference Schedule: Presentations and Small Groups

First Day
    "Overview of British Object Relations," by David Scharff
    "Subjectivity and Objectivity in Borderline States," by Ron Britton
    Small Group 1
    "Bion and the Reality Principle," by Martha Papadakis

Second Day
    "Traumatic Experience in Groups: A Fourth Basic Assumption," by Earl Hopper
    "Creativity and Destructiveness in the Life of *The Singing Detective*," by David Bell
    (replacing his scheduled paper "Work with Psychotic Patients")
    Small Group 2
    "Othello's Demand – Seeking Truth and Being True," by James Fisher

Third Day
    "Latent Murderousness," by Arthur Hyatt Williams
    Small Group 3
    "Clinical Seminar," by Robin Anderson and Christine Berwind-Viney
    Small Group 4
    "What Have We Learned – a Review," by Jill Savege Scharff

Fourth Day
    "The Experience of Psychic Reality in Normal and Atypical Children, Adolescents, and
        Adults," by Mary Target
    Small Group 5
    "Attachment Research – Mentalizing Functions," by Peter Fonagy
    Small Group 6

Fifth and Final Day
    "When Do Sessions Start and When Do They Finish?," by Dennis Duncan
    Small Group 7

FIRST DAY

Presentation 1

David Scharff, in his role as director of the conference, introduced the learning task with a breezy talk: "Overview of British Object Relations." He covered the contributions of Fairbairn, Winnicott, Balint, Bowlby, Sutherland, Klein, and Bion. He introduced the concepts of projective and introjective identification, transference and countertransference, the holding environment, containment, repression, dissociation, and group analytic theory.

Presentation 2

Ron Britton, co-author of *The Oedipus Complex Today* (Britton et al. 1989), read a complex paper: "Subjectivity and Objectivity in Borderline States." He described patients' borderline attributes as either thin-skinned (in which case the positive maternal transference is paramount, the fundamental anxiety is fear of destruction, and the analyst overfunctions and then feels shame and guilt) or thick-skinned (in which the positive paternal transference predominates, the fear is of the void, and the analyst feels futile).

Objectivity (by which Britton means the capacity to appreciate a third-person point of view) arises from the resolution of the Oedipus complex, which can only occur if there is a secure maternal object from which to enter the oedipal triangle and face the primal scene. This object gives the capacity to tolerate the third position, to explore interactions from that position, and so to develop the internal space of the mental triangle. If patients lack the third position, they cannot stand the union of the analyst with his thoughts. Empathic understanding (viewed as maternal) and intellectual understanding (viewed as male) coming together in independent analytic thinking is dreaded because it represents consummation in the analyst's mind and then intrudes as an envied coupling into the patient's mind and leads to destruction.

Small Group 1

Dr. Hernandez introduced the task of the small group. She said that the group has an integrative task based on attending to the material and learning from experience. She said that she and Mrs. Dupree would facilitate the group's attempt to review the material that the speakers had presented, discuss the concepts, apply them to clinical work, and examine individual emotional responses and group dynamic reactions as the group struggled to learn. In this way, the group would provide an environment in which to integrate and internalize the information. She waited in silence for a minute before the group took up its task.

A female group member emerged as an alternative leader and broke the silence by proposing a naming procedure in which all group participants and leaders had to introduce themselves. The woman took the lead in implementing the naming procedure and introduced herself as Andrea.

Dr. Hernandez reported later that she immediately felt a subtle attack against her role as the leader, as if she should have recognized the group's need for structure and individual recognition, even though she knew that she and Mrs. Dupree preferred to let the group manage its start-up anxieties in its own way.

Andrea declared that she did not value groups, and neither did her roommate, Margie, who was attending the conference with her. Andrea said that Margie wasn't hopeful about her small group, and she, Andrea, wasn't expecting much of this group. Andrea asked for other names.

Lucy introduced herself as a person who did value groups, and so she was anxious about whether this group would be all she knew that it could be.

Sue, who valued groups but was scared of them, noticed her relief about the naming procedure because it gave the illusion of providing structure to her many questions about how the week would proceed.

Philip introduced himself as not knowing much about groups.

Julio introduced himself as quite experienced in groups.

Whether positively or negatively disposed toward the group, all the members acknowledged, expressed, and shared their anxiety about being in this group process. They asked many questions. They made repeated requests for copies of the paper that had just been presented, as if the ideas existed only on paper rather than in their minds, after they had just heard them presented.

Mrs. Dupree said that there was a need to use names to defend against anxiety about the lack of structure, and Dr. Hernandez added that the group was asking for information to get help with anxiety about the unknown regarding the theory and the group process.

Andrea insisted on wanting the paper and said that Margie wanted it, too. Others in the group agreed with her request and said that not getting it left them with the feeling of not being cared for by the institute. This was particularly hard for them to take when they had felt so uncared for by the hotel where they were staying. Another member, Sue, who had come late, spoke of her fear of isolation, and this led to others worrying about being included or excluded in the group process that might occur.

Dr. Hernandez and Mrs. Dupree said that the group was approaching the learning task by looking for an alternative leader in Andrea and for a way of organizing to meet the members' dependency needs, which are exaggerated by anxiety about lack of familiarity with both the city of London and the unstructured group with the ambiguous task. From being a dependency leader, Andrea progresses to being a fight/flight leader and is joined by the group in hopes of protecting against the perceived failure of the leaders. The pairing subgroup formation is represented in displacement to Andrea and her roommate, Margie, who seems almost to become a member of the group. This pairing fantasy is accepted and enjoyed by the group because it validates the alternative leader's perceptions and augments her authority. Already in the opening moments of its work, the group has illustrated Bion's concepts of basic assumption group life in dependency, fight/flight subgroup formations, and pairing, although that pairing existed outside the group. The pairing fantasy about a couple outside the group comes next in a form that is quickly condemned.

During the naming procedure, the group discovered the presence among them of a person whose analyst was also in the conference in another group. The group members were uniformly surprisingly judgmental toward the analyst for participating but not toward the group member who was his analysand. This so-called elicit pairing became an object of attack, and this dynamic reminded Mrs. Dupree of Dr. Britton's remarks about the avoidance of anxiety concerning the primal scene leading to destruction.

Mrs. Dupree said that the patient—analyst couple was being experienced as an internal couple whose activity and destructive potential was feared. This couple provided in the group imagination an image of the primal scene couple that could not be thought about but only condemned. Obscured by the number of group members and defended against by the naming procedure that emphasized individuality, this internal couple was now emerging, but it was a cover for a more immediately threatening couple. She said that the internal couple the group feared fundamentally was the coupling of empathy and intellectual understanding, represented by the pairing of Mrs. Dupree and Dr. Hernandez, because of fear of the destructive potential of such knowledge.

The group seemed stunned by this and quickly reconstituted in a subgroup formation to criticize the hotel where many of them were staying. They were so upset that they had been thinking of shopping for other hotels. They complained about the coffee, the price, the bathrooms, and particularly the "battle-ax" of a woman who guards the food and the products there. This dependency subgroup wanted to get it out of the old battle-ax, and they were resorting to all kinds of ruses or aggressive maneuvers to get her to give in to their requests.

Mrs. Dupree said that the group members were afraid they would have to get it out of the battle-ax because they couldn't get "it" out of Dr. Hernandez and her, as if each member didn't have the intellectual and emotional resources within and in creative interaction with other group members to find the understanding and objectivity to which the paper points. Dr. Hernandez added that she thought they wanted the paper as a substitute for this real learning. The group denied this possibility. They said they needed the paper because they wanted to work with one another to cull the inspirational points from the paper.

A dissenting voice remarked, however, that reading was not always the answer anyway. Sue said that, for example, she had been unable to "sit reflectively at the edge of the shore while the waters of inspiration flowed over her"—an approach to reading Bion mentioned in David's introductory overview. She had felt more like throwing the book in the water.

Aggression is now back in the room, splitting the leaders and making Dr. Hernandez the unsatisfying one.

Julio said that the paper was wonderful. He said he was going to discuss the paper right now and say what he got from it. He explained at length that he had learned that Oedipus is more about knowledge and the denial of knowledge than it is about sexuality and aggression.

Andrea said that the paper was wonderful. She had learned that the analyst may think of an interpretation but need not say it and that instead the shift would somehow be communicated nonverbally.

Dr. Hernandez said that the group was looking for knowledge in the object instead of finding it in the self and its relationships.

Julio's comments usefully lead the group toward the intellectual aspect of its task, but then the group uses his leadership initiative to organize itself around intellectualization to get away from emotional knowledge.

Faculty Discussion

In this opening group, we see the common defenses of individualization to defend against the fear of loss of the self in the object represented by the group and fear of chaos due to lack of structure. We also see the group's valuing of cognition over emotional intelligence. Both Dr. Hernandez and

Mrs. Dupree reported to us a sense of Margie as an absent, unassigned, unseen, but important group member who is being used to pair with for support when dependency needs are not being met. The group is in a paranoid–schizoid position in relation to the group leaders whose capacity to provide a good environment for learning is doubted and attacked. The group members use the defenses of being thick-skinned or thin-skinned to get rid of anxiety but then feel scared and abandoned by the consequences. Mrs. Dupree reported to us she sensed that she had been overfunctioning, and Dr. Hernandez said that she felt her work had been viewed as futile. In these countertransferences, Mrs. Dupree is responding to the paternal and Dr. Hernandez to the maternal transferences, corresponding to thick- and thin-skinned defenses, respectively.

The group transference views Dr. Hernandez and Mrs. Dupree not as a differentiated couple but as a single battle-ax who is withholding and uncaring. The group's fears of the primal scene couple and of the integration of empathic and intellectual understanding are addressed early because the pairing of two group leaders draws out this fantasy and the didactic presentation provides a concept through which to address it. The group's stunned response indicates that the interpretation may have been premature, a result of Mrs. Dupree overfunctioning in response to thick-skinned defensiveness. Dr. Hernandez and Mrs. Dupree will look out for further resistance or forward movement in response to this interpretation in the next group.

Presentation 3

Martha Papadakis read "Bion and the Reality Principle," a paper presenting various concepts of Bion, including symbol formation and the contact barrier, and illustrated her points with case vignettes showing the difference in the dynamic process between subject and object in the dreams of those who had suffered oedipal loss and those who had suffered trauma. She explained that the unconscious surge under the influence of the pleasure principle provides a better reality than actual reality until symbolization becomes possible. Symbol formation leads to a capacity to adapt to reality and a greater distance from part–object relating. The symbol is a compromise between giving up and retaining objects, and it ushers in choices instead of compulsions, a realistic view of the world, and a potential for work. If a powerful impulse meets external reality and fuses with it so that there is no difference between fantasy and reality, as happens in sexual abuse, mourning of the loss of fantasy cannot occur, and therefore a new object cannot be found.

SECOND DAY

Presentation 4

Earl Hopper talked about his Foulkes lecture "Traumatic Experience in Groups: A Fourth Basic Assumption" (Hopper 1997). He began by adding to the oedipal situation a fourth angle concerning the influence of social circumstances, culture, and group experience on one's perceptions. He called this *squaring the therapeutic triangle*. He went on to refer to Bion's (1962) theory of subgroup formations of dependency, fight-flight, and pairing, and to Turquet's concepts of primitive large-group behavior: *fusion* and *disarroy* [sic]. Dissaroy (a cunning neologism that alludes to the unconscious attack on the king inherent in the primal horde) describes a group where there is chaos, isolated bizarre bits of functioning, and no leadership. Fusion characterizes the group where identity derives from belonging, where there is no role authority, and where the group blindly follows a charismatic leader. Hopper suggested that this type of fusion may result from piercing interpretations of envy that traumatize rather than help the group. He proposed a fourth basic assumption arising from a helpless response to trauma. This assumption is one that oscillates between fission/fragmentation (which is like disarroy) and fusion/confusion (which is an amplification of fusion), and this oscillation is defended against by encapsulation.

Personification of the fourth assumption leads to corruption and perversion. Drawing on his background in sociology, Hopper also applied the terms *aggregation* (the formation of a group based on primitive socialization led by a crustaceous, contact-shunning personality) and *massification* (the creation of a horde through fusion and confusion led by an amoeboid, merger-hungry personality) to group life. Hopper referred to the fourth assumption by the acronym I:AM, standing for the oscillation between incohesion (I) and aggregation/massification (AM).

Presentation 5

David Bell was slated to give his talk "Work with Psychotic Patients," but he preferred to read another paper, "Creativity and Destructiveness in the Life of *The Singing Detective*," a study of the psychological television drama by Dennis Potter from which Bell showed selected clips. The central character of the story is a successful writer of detective stories who is arrogant and dismissive of attachments. The drama's multilayered, nonlinear narrative moves back and forth between the protagonist's present reality as a writer, a hospital patient, and the husband of a cynical wife who may be betraying him; his past reality as a child who witnessed the terrible scene of his mother with her lover and who was traumatized by her subsequent suicide; and his alternative fantasy self as a singing detective, the subject of his stories, who turns out to be linked to his musical father. At the end of the video, the man becomes able to accept the sight of the copulating couple and the suicide in his mind's eye, and then his recovery can begin. Bell showed how the back-and-forth of the narrative and the dissolving film technique combined to convey objects not as static but, rather, as changing within a range of expression and developing over time.

Small Group 2

Following the lecture from Hopper, Andrea led the small group in understanding difficult concepts that he had presented. Soon the group coalesced to focus on the fourth assumption, the I:AM acronym, the definitions of the unfamiliar terms *aggregation* and *massification*, and culture shifts illustrated by the differences between Irish and American culture. The group moved to a discussion of how these differences were illustrated by Mrs. Dupree and Dr. Hernandez, who are from different cultures.

As discussion proceeded, it became clear that the main distinction between the leaders was being provided by the group's projections: The group shared a fantasy of Mrs. Dupree as an explosive and possibly charming leader with masculine qualities and Dr. Hernandez as a remote and insignificant female. Sue, who had previously been in a group led by Dr. Hernandez and a male coleader, had seen her as insignificant compared to him, who had been like the explosive man on the video. The group substituted and aggrandized Mrs. Dupree in place of Dr. Hernandez's prior coleader.

Mrs. Dupree pointed out that the group had projected enhanced competence into her and insecurity into Dr. Hernandez and had tried to change the coleaders' female-female couple into a preferred male-female destructive couple in fantasy.

Lucy focused on the trauma that is the ultimate trauma of loss of the self, and Julio focused on the trauma of loss of one's country. Dr. Hernandez pointed to an underlying theme concerning a preoccupation with loss, damage, and dead mothers. The group members looked sad.

Faculty Discussion

Here we see a shift from the intellectual level to the emotional level of group functioning. How does Dr. Hernandez arrive at her interpretation? She reported to us that she had felt attacked by the group, which then seemed to be afraid of dealing with her, the woman they had damaged. She thought that the group members felt alone with their anger while Mrs. Dupree was making her intellectual comment, and she wanted to speak to their anger, loneliness, fear of damage, and the resulting loss. The following group association tends to confirm that she is in touch with the group unconscious.

> Sue associated to a family she had seen in the plane on the way to the conference. Two parents were managing five children, one of whom was not their own, and doing quite well under difficult circumstances. It made her think about how the family would manage with only a mother. There was an uncomfortable silence.
>
> Dr. Hernandez then asked the group whether they might be worried about being in a group with two mothers. The group completely ignored her comment as if she were crazy.

Dr. Hernandez and Mrs. Dupree reported on how they used their countertransference experiences. Mrs. Dupree felt uncomfortable in the silence, which was of a type that she could not figure out. It reminded her of other silences when something portentous is being withheld. Looking back on this moment with hindsight, the group leaders thought that this was the first clue of the group's unconscious reception of the activity of a trauma that would not emerge until the final session. At the time, Dr. Hernandez knew only that she felt dropped by the group. She examined her countertransference and concluded that the group had needed her to hold and contain anxiety about abandonment, confusion, and devaluation provoked by the group's being exposed to the knowledge and expertise of the presenters. Having thought this through, she was then able to make her interpretation—and get dropped again.

> Mrs. Dupree came back to Dr. Hernandez's question about being in a group with two mothers, saying, "The group is being led by a female-female pair, and what is that like for you?"
>
> Group members protested they did not see Mrs. Dupree and Dr. Hernandez as two mothers, or a female-female pair, or a homosexual couple. They saw them as a mother–infant couple. Mrs. Dupree asked the group to consider whether seeing Dr. Hernandez and her as a mother and an infant might be a defense against the earlier view of herself as a male and Dr. Hernandez as a female because the creativity of a male-female couple might ultimately end in group destruction because of envy of the couple in the primal scene. The group began to talk with dismay about not having a male coleader. At first, they were not really able to deal with what the female-female pair meant to them.

Julio referred to the evocative video of *The Singing Detective*, in which he saw a powerful woman with a nice man, and it reminded him of his childhood fantasies as a little boy, based on his experience of being raised by a powerful mother and her sisters. He seemed to be telling this story mainly to Mrs. Dupree, as if Dr. Hernandez were not there. The rest of the group responded to him with various comments on the content of Bell's paper, including disappointment that Bell had not discussed psychotic patients as promised. Nevertheless, he had given them plenty to think about concerning reality, fantasy, and the trauma of the primal scene. Mrs. Dupree commented that the scene in the video, when the man had become able to bear the memory of having seen his mother with her lover, had illustrated the value of the third position for expanding mental space, the concept referred to earlier by Britton.

Dr. Hernandez and Mrs. Dupree presented their observations and hypotheses at this stage. They noted that the group tended to kill off Dr. Hernandez at this stage and also ignored Martha Papadakis's paper, perhaps because one of the dreams she presented was painful and remained opaque to the group's attempts to understand and because Papadakis, like the group leaders, was a woman and apparently not to be given authority. The group paid more attention to male presenters. The leaders agreed that the group seemed to be preferring the possibility of a single leader, whom they imagined as male, not two females paired together, so as to avoid both the fear of an augmented image of woman as authority and the oedipal-level rage at the image of the absent male-female couple. In fantasy, the couple has been killed by the group's ambivalent attachment to it.

Faculty Discussion

This second group does return to the subject of Mrs. Dupree's interpretation of its fears of the pairing of Mrs. Dupree and Dr. Hernandez. At first, however, the group remains in the cognitive dimension. The members work on Hopper's concepts of incohesion and its oscillation to aggregation and massification as helpless group responses to trauma, but they do not extend themselves toward a more fully developed cognitive review of the complex concept of the fourth basic assumption. They do not discuss Papadakis's presentation of the impact of trauma on dream life and personality development.

One of Hopper's concepts is seized on to provide a segue into useful work on the issue of the group's coleading pair because the group is ready to respond to the interpretation about their avoidance of the primal scene couple.

The members develop their ability to differentiate between the two individuals of the coleading team, but their views are dominated by their projections, which are defenses against their fears of the destructive actions of, or ambivalent and envious responses to, the couple. The two-female pair is problematic for them. They wrestle with two preferred alternatives: the male-female couple or the single-mother noncouple (both of which also carry problems and neither of which is a satisfactory substitute for reducing anxiety). They then work on fear of loss of self and other in such a group. The group seems to be both galvanized and traumatized by the interpretation of the effect of the primal scene fantasy. The concepts of responses to trauma are explored in action more than in reflection.

Presentation 6

James Fisher presented a literature-inspired clinical paper called "Othello's Demand—Seeking Truth and Being True." It began with a long recitation and discussed Othello's inability to bear his sense that Desdemona had changed. Shakespeare's play shows objects linked together cruelly and made bad by the inability to reflect on experience. In a clinical vein, the paper moved on to describe countertransference responses to three vivid transference dreams that brought to attention the pain of a patient whose vitality was seriously compromised and who gave no sign of the impact of interpretation and yet continued to attend analysis faithfully. Fisher discussed his work with the countertransference of feeling his analytic confidence being deadened.

THIRD DAY

Presentation 7

Arthur Hyatt Williams presented his paper, "Latent Murderousness," the topic of which was movingly illustrated by vignettes of powerful therapeutic interventions with murderers and other violent prisoners. Some criminals are unaware of harboring murderous feelings, whereas others know of their murderousness and keep it under control. Fragmentation occurs when one is in a state of dreadful illness or mourning for a lost love object. Then the murderous constellation invades the personality, and all strength goes into completing the murder instead of into keeping it from happening. Other precipitants include retraumatization by agents that are similar to the original traumatizing agent, and inadequate therapy that leaves weak patches in the ego, or therapy that has produced a negative reaction. Once murder occurs, equilibrium can be restored only if mourning is done every day for the rest of one's life.

Small Group 3

One of the two male members of the group, Philip, announced that he had previously arranged a nonrefundable follow-on trip to Europe and would miss the last two groups. He said he regretted having made this irrevocable decision earlier at a time when he didn't realize the value of a group, and he could now see that he would be missing something. There were mixed reactions to his announcement. Some were gratified that he had been persuaded of their value to him. Some envied his ability to ignore the schedule and flee away from the task, and some admired his independence in sticking to his plan. The group expressed sadness at losing him, guilt over feeling rageful at him for abandoning them, and irritation that he might actually be taking sadistic pleasure in getting away from the group and dumping the others with the task. Dr. Hernandez mentioned that the group had many different ways of dealing with loss. Like Philip, but in different ways that were not as irrevocable, other group members had intended to avoid attachment by not connecting with the group in their minds ahead of time. This way they could imagine that they could avoid the ultimate loss. Silence followed.

Dr. Hernandez described a powerful countertransference that she had been containing. She felt full of the group members' projections of abandonment and sadness. She felt that they needed to get away from her and the bad objects she was carrying for them. As in Shakespeare's character Othello, objects are made bad by the inability to reflect on experience and get projected into the other, which they then spoil. The group members did not respond directly to her comment but connected as a group and returned like repentant children to continue the task, but they did so only in the cognitive realm and did not maintain that direction either because of unresolved issues at the emotional level interfering with their learning.

There were three abortive attempts to talk about the presentations and the concepts of trauma and murder in each of them, and there was a total avoidance of dealing with the anxiety evoked by Dr. Hernandez's comments on attachment. Philip associated to his need to look good. He did not want to express his vulnerability.

Mrs. Dupree remarked on the interruption to the flow of the group process and made a number of comments asking the group to examine why they had ignored Dr. Hernandez's comment and had avoided dealing thoroughly with the future loss of Philip. She did not seem to be getting through to the group until she spelled it out more clearly: Without proper mourning, she said, this loss could become a trauma for the group and might then lead to fourth-basic-assumption problems of oscillation between incohesion and aggregation/massification and eventually to a threatening encapsulation.

This comment seemed to have been helpful because there was now a good discussion of Hyatt Williams's comments on fear of attachment, fear of attachment shown by patients, fear of being killed by patients, murderous rage, hatred, death, and deadliness. The group was almost at the time boundary, and Mrs. Dupree said that she had just become aware of an avoidance of Fisher's presentation of the therapeutic relationship between a sensitive therapist and a fascinating male patient with whom he felt unsure of the impact of his analytic efforts. The group responded by remarking on the patient's feeling emotionally dead. Instead of discussing how the therapist's confidence was deadened, they imagined that the therapist was killing off parts of the patient and causing his immobilization. The responsive part of the group to that material had been killed, until Mrs. Dupree and Dr. Hernandez brought the oversight to the group's attention. Mrs. Dupree said that the group had wanted to avoid the problem of emotional deadness and the therapist's resulting insecurity about the value of analysis because it was associated with Philip's imminent absence and the group's uncertain reaction of their meaning to him. The pain of both situations had to be fused and repressed.

Faculty Discussion

The third small-group process provides an illustration of the use of a countertransference analysis. In discussion after the group, Mrs. Dupree told us that she had not been able to commit herself to being a coleader until the last moment before the conference. Therefore, she personally felt helped and understood by Dr. Hernandez's remark about defenses against involvement in the group but she did not share this with the group, because she wanted to hide her reluctance to commit.

Mrs. Dupree told us that when she noticed how many times she tried to get the group to look at why they were constrained in dealing with Dr. Hernandez's comment about attachment, she realized that she was trying to get the group to work on it instead of doing so herself. When she analyzed her own response, she realized that she felt ashamed of her indecision regarding accepting assignment as a group leader and of her need for help from Dr. Hernandez.

She realized that her suppressed response had contributed to the group's inhibited response following Dr. Hernandez's comment.

Once Mrs. Dupree has analyzed this in herself, she is able to speak more directly to the group's defenses and tie her comment to the presentation. After her countertransference-informed intervention, the group is able to move into the subject of attachment and its loving and hateful aspects.

Presentation 8

At the next event, called the Clinical Seminar, a student presented a clinical case report using process notes and showing a drawing the client had made in the session. The client was a highly intelligent but socially inept, fragmented man who ignored his physical health. His main companion had been his ailing pet, which had just died, and so he was alone. He was surprised to feel relieved, not sad, because he no longer had the burden of staying home to care for the animal. His new freedom (and his improvement due to therapy) enabled him to accept a social invitation from a neighbor who may become a friend. Vandalism had occurred at his home, but, as with the loss of the pet, he felt relieved, this time because he would be handsomely reimbursed for his loss. His mother had died that year, but it was not loss that bothered him. What got him depressed was the feeling of being trapped in a relationship such as with the clinging, dependent pet and trapped in an unfavorable view of himself that his late mother had held in her frozen, unchangeable way. Thinking of her, he felt hopeless and drawn toward death. He drew a picture of a man who looked like he was dying. He would like to die as a free spirit the way his mother chose to die—properly medicated but not in a hospital and not in pain.

Without trying to list the man's stream of associations, this brief account pulls together the thread of two sessions and unfortunately may give an impression of clarity that was not there. It hardly does justice to the client's idiosyncratic thought process and the therapist's sensitive attempt to puzzle her way through it without intruding on his personal style. As the consultant to the clinical process, Robin Anderson worked with the presenter to encourage a free-ranging large-group discussion of comments, hypotheses, connections to theory, and some free associations to the material. Many of the comments were attempts to read the client's unconscious from looking at the drawing and responding to the narrative by using intuition to divine the theme that could connect his disparate thoughts.

Small Group 4

Only Dr. Hernandez and Mrs. Dupree were present at the beginning. Soon they were joined by Julio and Philip, who talked about the camera that Julio was putting away. Julio was late because he had been taking a photo of Abbey Road, which reminded him of his nostalgia for the good-old bad-old days of the Beatles. Julio had enjoyed *The Singing Detective* video. He said he would recommend trying to get that video (another use of film to keep experience alive). The women arrived one by one as the men were talking.

The group then went on to talk about the clinical case presentation and the consultant's style of leading the large-group discussion. The student had presented a lot of intricate verbal and visual material, and the consultant had been facilitating of insightful comments from the audience. They were, however, disappointed. They wanted all the consultant's opinions and clinical wisdom. Andrea filled the gap by discussing the dynamics of the case authoritatively. When she went on and on to the exclusion of others, Mrs. Dupree worked with her on seeing that she, Andrea, was doing this as if to embody the missed consultant. The group listened to Andrea and must have wanted her to fulfill this function, and yet no one cared enough about her observations and ideas to talk with her about them.

Dr. Hernandez said that the group was making an attack on the linking that had occurred in the large group and on the couple of Mrs. Dupree and Dr. Hernandez because of fears of sibling rivalry and fears of competing, as if there were only one way to teach and only one person to teach it. Mrs. Dupree was puzzled and had to ask Dr. Hernandez what she meant. Dr. Hernandez felt that the group members were disavowing their own knowledge and its impact. She said that when Mrs. Dupree worked with Andrea to show her how she was engaged in a dynamic of re-creating the lost object, Mrs. Dupree created a substitute pair with Andrea that attacked the couple of Mrs. Dupree and Dr. Hernandez. Mrs. Dupree nodded in agreement and said that she now realized that her puzzlement earlier had been in concert with the general attack on linking, in this case herself attacking her capacity to think.

As Andrea continued to dominate despite this intervention and as other women joined her, Mrs. Dupree noticed that Julio was becoming silent and was practically asleep. She later told the group that she was thinking of him as a child sleeping with women all around him. But she simply asked him what was going on. He said he had been frozen.

Julio told the group that he had been lost in thought about the topic of murderousness. Julio had been applying Hyatt Williams's ideas to working with a potentially murderous patient whom he was currently treating. Julio spoke in depth about his crushing fear that this man's wish to strangle women might someday lead to a murder. He described the man's family history of growing up with sisters and gave a few vignettes from anxiety-filled parts of the treatment process. Admiring the specific technical interventions of great sensitivity and humanity that Hyatt Williams had made to good effect with a murderer in treatment, Julio thought that surely Hyatt Williams would be able to contain the terrible anxiety that Julio's patient evoked. Julio said that he would love to call for supervision and wondered whether he would be accepted as a supervisee. By the time he said all this, he clearly had roused himself from sleepiness and seemed quite alert.

Mrs. Dupree said to Julio that in his silence he had attached to a man from the past, namely the patient, and to a man in his future, namely Hyatt Williams, rather than join the discussion by the women of the group and Dr. Hernandez and herself, as he was now able to do. Julio looked hit. He remained silent and thoughtful.

Lucy said, "I just remembered. Philip will be leaving, and when he does, there will be no other man here besides Julio in this group."

Andrea said, "How will the women feel to hear from Julio about his patient who likes to strangle women if there is no other man than Julio in this group?"

There was a gasp of astonishment, and the question was quickly dropped.

Turning anxiety back on the man, Sue said, "It will be like being with your mother and her friends, Julio."

Julio still looked quite bemused. He said, "I don't know what you're saying. I can't take it in. I'm still thinking about Hyatt Williams and the good session he had with his murderous patient."

Philip spoke of Hyatt Williams and of Hopper as well in idealizing terms. He said he really loved them both.

Dr. Hernandez said the group was needing to leave behind the aggression of the two men and cover it with love. She challenged the group members to question how to use the men's aggression and how to work with their own aggression.

Julio was embarrassed because he could not take in the comments from either of the women. He said that he had kept thinking it was not an issue of fear of aggression because he had "dealt with that" in his own analysis. However, he then associated to a time when as a little boy he found a photograph of his mother. With glee, he showed how he had used a pencil to poke that photo, and then got in trouble. As he said this, he seemed thoroughly engaged in the material.

Sue complimented him on coming alive but said that she couldn't go along with this idealization of him or anyone else as "the fully analyzed therapist."

Julio protested that truly he had dealt with that in his analysis.

Dr. Hernandez explained that objects are not static, as Bell had shown.

Mrs. Dupree said that she felt that the women did not want to explore their worry about sex and murder if left alone with Julio, without another man present to be like a father who could contain Julio's sexuality and aggression.

Before they could respond, Julio assured them there was nothing to worry about.

Faculty Discussion

The group is now in the midphase of its existence. This session shows the group working on the educational context and its effect on learning. Disavowing the knowledge displayed by all participants of the large group (including themselves in the large-group setting), the small-group members complain that they have not been given enough from the consultant. They revert to a dependency subgroup formation and create a substitute gratifying dependency leader but fail to engage with her and learn from her. The group process deepens. We see a member's recovery from silent preoccupation, competition, attacks on linking, using the individual to substitute for the group, disavowal of the self's knowledge because of idealization of the object's wisdom, and recreating the lost object.

Mrs. Dupree creates an enactment of pairing with a group member and responds to Dr. Hernandez's interpretation of her attack on their pairing by reestablishing her capacity to make links and to understand what has been confusing for her before. We note that the coleaders' ability to question and help each other is improving. Julio entrusts the group with his deeply disturbing clinical experience, and the group responds respectfully and helpfully. Julio and other group members bring in material concerning aggressive attacks on women and express their fear of them, but this theme is not fully explored at this stage of the group. When Philip's imminent absence is thought about as exposing the group to sexual and aggressive anxieties, the group ends in a confusion of fear, conflict, and false reassurance that will need further exploration in subsequent sessions.

At the faculty meeting Dr. Hernandez mentioned her observation that Julio had re-created the group in fantasy as all male, four Beatles in the photograph he remembered, and four men now: the supervisor he longed for and his murderous patient, and Julio and his own murderous patient. In this way, Julio avoided the reality of the present group of women and one man who would be leaving him alone with the women. This is an example of a group defense expressed by an individual who creates in fantasy an alternative group to avoid the anxiety that male-female collaboration and creative understanding in the group will lead to sexual arousal or other forms of aggression that must be strangled and so may lead to personal destruction or destruction of the group. Julio's illustration of the pencil poking the photograph and the women's fear of a single male alluded to a conflict over male-female aggression, but it was not resolved.

Like the patient in the clinical presentation who had relational difficulties, the group shows difficulty in being responsible for the well-being of both self and objects if sexual and aggressive feelings are acknowledged. The group uses imagined and remembered attachments to distant figures partly to avoid and partly to support its contact with present ones. In general, the group's capacity for affective engagement and intellectual reflection is growing.

Presentation 9

In a review session chaired by David Scharff, Jill Scharff presented her review of what she was learning. Although she was clearly the presenter, the main image before the group was not of her as an individual but of her and him as a couple. Jill Scharff applied Britton's concept of the mental space of the triangle to the conference. Learning from others develops the ability to fill a position at any of the three points on the triangle, giving access to internal space for thinking and feeling—and more learning from others. The learner can see herself as the object of the presenter who is the subject, she can see herself as the subject of the learning experience related to a succession of objects who present material for consideration, or she can create a couple with a speaker, a faculty person, or a group member as both of them try to understand, to teach, and to learn together. This role flexibility re-creates the parental couple inside the self, where it allows the union of empathy and intellectual understanding. This is good for the development of the self's capacities and is hated only if it represents consummation from which the self is excluded.

Jill Scharff gave two examples, one from a published self-analysis in which the internal couple was repaired and one from a couple therapy in which the man was ultimately unable to marry the woman he loved and longed for because he remained wedded to the child position in the triangle in relation to a warring parental couple that he hated. He was afraid that if he took his place as the husband in the new couple, he would feel like his childhood self—remote, afraid, helpless, and excluded from the couple he could have created with the woman he loved.

Jill Scharff reviewed Hopper's concept of squaring the therapeutic triangle to include the social influence outside the family and his concept of encapsulation. She referred to Papadakis's paper on dreams of people with neurosis and those with encapsulated trauma. She said that teaching and learning about trauma stimulates countertransference feelings of exposure and betrayal. We have to confront and analyze these if we are to free ourselves to learn about trauma.

FOURTH DAY

Presentation 10

Mary Target gave a lecture and slide show called "The Experience of Psychic Reality in Normal and Atypical Children, Adolescents, and Adults." After reviewing analysts' assumptions about psychic structure and defenses, Target referred to her study of 750 case records of child psychotherapy at the Anna Freud Centre. She found that psychotherapy is 80 percent effective if the child has a single diagnosis of some type of emotional disorder and a high level of adaptation. In that case, interpretation, especially of transference, is useful, but nonintensive therapy is as effective as intensive therapy for those cases. The severe cases with mixed cognitive deficits and affective disorder, attachment disorders, poor adaptation, and multiple diagnoses did not respond to interpretation and paradoxically benefited most from intensive therapy if modified by developmental help. Children with autistic features were the least improved, even with developmental help. Her follow-up reports on two traumatized children, now adult, showed how they had benefited from a warm therapeutic relationship, combined with specific developmental help geared to improving communication that was probably of more help than interpretation. She recommended integrating various techniques into the classical model: explanation; labeling and narrativization of experience; breaking down experience into manageable bits; working on recognizing affects, what triggers them, and how they impact others; and providing a supportive therapeutic relationship. Developing imagination of other people's thoughts and feelings enables the child eventually to arrive at an increasingly complex view of self and others.

Target continued with a description of the maturation of the core self through two basic mental stages: (1) *psychic equivalence*, in which thought or feeling is real and inner experience is identical to outer experience, and (2) *pretend mode*, in which a thought or a feeling is only an idea, disconnected from outer reality. The persistence of psychic equivalence in adult life leads to preoccupied attachments, while pretend mode leads to dismissing attachments. An integrated attitude permits mentalization and gives the child's communication meaning. This then leads to a capacity for reflection and mentalization that gives continuity and meaning to one's own and others' experience.

Small Group 5

The men were not present.

Sue said wistfully, "I'm thinking about Philip, who is leaving today, and Julio isn't here either."

Emotionally dismissive of her attachment concern (while associating to it intellectually), Andrea began to speak about Target's presentation. Her mental attention was connected to the findings and their implications for child analysis, but her affect was connected to how wonderful Target had been. She was so glad to have a face to put on the work of the author whom she had been reading. Lucy also thought the content of her lecture had been great, but she could not recall the specifics of it because she was too preoccupied with Philip's leaving.

Sue looked relieved when Philip entered, and said she was glad to see him. Philip explained that he and Julio had been looking at photographs of conference events. Lucy talked to him sympathetically about his lateness and his impending absence, and created a dyad with him. He seemed appreciative that she would miss him. Julio entered and sat slumped with his head down. The group members thought that they knew why he was late and no one questioned him, as Lucy had done Philip. He remained silent and seemed withdrawn.

Lucy created a dyad with Andrea, both of them jumping into further discussion of the findings from the study mentioned in Target's presentation. They agreed that her lecture was excellent. The format was familiar, the material was full and rich, and the overheads were terrific, even though they really hadn't understood them.

Dr. Hernandez said that they didn't want to work: They wanted to simply enjoy what they had experienced as a good feed from a woman. Dr. Hernandez's remarks were followed by a long silence.

Mrs. Dupree pointed out that after Dr. Hernandez had mentioned that a good feed from a woman had been obtained in the large group, this present group seemed to be hallucinating a lost mother–infant dyad by re-creating pairs rather than returning to the threat that was experienced in yesterday's group. She said she thought the threat had been referred to obliquely by Sue's mentioning the loss of Philip, the absence of Julio at the beginning of the group, and Julio's silence since he had arrived. She said the threat that the group was avoiding was the situation of being without another man to protect the women from the remaining man, who was filled with concern about a possible murder, and to protect him from the counterattack of the anxious women.

The two men, Philip and Julio, now created a reassuring, placating pair. Philip asked Julio what he thought of the photographs that made them both late. Julio said that he was late but he would have been only a little late from looking at the photographs. He explained that he was late mostly because he had been looking for his folder, which had important papers in it. Mrs. Dupree said that she heard him say a "ca-" sound in front of the word *folder* and asked whether he had been about to say a different word before he selected the word *folder*, perhaps in Spanish, his mother tongue. Puzzled by her request, he had to think it over. She explained that she was asking because she guessed that the word he eliminated had the function of a lost object. He remembered that the word he had been thinking of was *carpeta*, which simply means "briefcase" or "folder" and that his slip into Spanish occurred perhaps because the folder was something he wanted to keep close to him.

The group returned to a discussion of the presentations. As they reviewed the preceding events of the last day and a half, they recalled three presentations, of which two were wonderful and one was not. On the contrary, Dr. Hernandez said, since the last group there had in fact been four presenters, one of whom was Dr. Jill Scharff, the institute's codirector, whose review had not been mentioned. She wondered in what way the group had experienced her, so that they were not remembering her as a presenter or commenting on what she had said. Andrea said she didn't think of her as a presenter because she was usually sitting in the membership of the large group. In fact, she often sat there with Dr. Hernandez, and so she had thought of her almost as one of the group. When she left the audience to go up front and present, it was a big shift. Lucy said she had felt a loss that Jill was no longer one of them. Worse than that, Sue said, she had been the sole presenter in a session chaired by Dr. David Scharff, and Sue found the image of her being a couple with her husband upsetting because it disturbed her enjoyment in seeing her together with Dr. Hernandez. Sue said that this was a loss to her because she liked to imagine herself as being close to Dr. Hernandez, like Jill was. Seeing Jill leave Dr. Hernandez to be with her husband had interrupted her fantasy.

The image of the Scharffs as a couple leading the conference institution was preoccupying and obliterated the content of Jill Scharff's review. One group member saw them as a weak man together with a strong woman and felt annoyed at a couple like that. One saw a facilitating man with a competent woman and admired that. One saw a powerful couple and envied that. One saw a respectful couple worth emulating. Whatever their valency for perceiving the nature of the couple relationship before them, they all remained preoccupied with that male-female, married couple, which some viewed as a threat to the couple of Dr. Hernandez and Mrs. Dupree.

The group members then turned their attention to the couple leading the small group. Their earlier projective identifications surfaced, and they again experienced Dr. Hernandez as female and Mrs. Dupree as male and idealized. Dr. Hernandez and Mrs. Dupree talked together respectfully about each other as coleaders and about the group's problem in integrating these two aspects of women. By doing so, they probably reassured the group that their coleading couple was still intact and functional.

As the group drew to a close, Julio said that having these two aspects of woman integrated in Dr. Hernandez and Mrs. Dupree was helpful to him. Then he said good-bye to Philip, and others followed suit. Mrs. Dupree summarized what Philip had been carrying for the group: freedom to engage in flight, autonomy of decision making, underestimation of the value of the group, and balancing and limiting the female attack on Julio.

Dr. Hernandez and Mrs. Dupree concluded their account with a summary of their observations. The mention of the absence of the men created group anxiety about the lost object. Then the group acted in pretend mode, in which thoughts and feelings were ideas disconnected from the actual reality of the group. Anxiety about the lost object persisted with the theme of Julio's lost *carpeta*, the missed good feed, and Philip's planned absence.

Faculty Discussion

Bion's description of the use of pairing as the third-basic-assumption process for defending against anxiety in group life helps us understand the group process at this point. The two men are paired in their absence. Then a veritable cascade of pairs occurs in the group. This is interpreted as a pairing defense that occurs to re-create the lost mother–infant couple that enjoys a wonderful feed. At this stage in the group's experience, it might seem that the pairing persists because this interpretation is incomplete by Bion's standards. The underlying wish for a messiah and its location in Philip who will be leaving is not adequately interpreted.

As the group progresses, it emerges that the group is reacting strongly to the emotional impact of dealing with a couple in authority. Wishes to be close to a partner are being expressed in the sequence of pairings and eventually are expressed in words. The destructive, envious feelings that are stimulated are defended against by idealization and admiration of the male-female couple (the Scharffs) and then lead to a destructive attack on the actual couple leading the small group (Dr. Hernandez and Mrs. Dupree).

Presentation 11

Peter Fonagy presented his attachment research, which provides a developmental framework for clinical work with severe personality disorders. He reviewed Ainsworth's categories of attachment styles—secure, anxious-avoidant, and anxious-resistant (all normal variants) and disorganized-disoriented (a pathological variant) attachment styles—and discussed their genetic and environmental determinants. He went on to describe adult attachment categories: autonomous secure, dismissing (or avoidant), preoccupied (or resistant), and unresolved in respect to trauma. These tend to produce corresponding attachment behaviors in the offspring. High reflective functioning in a parent tends to be associated in that person's child with the development of an autonomous secure attachment to that parent. Work with severely personality disordered people in the disorganized category goes best if the therapist recognizes the person's lack of adequate representation of internal states. Then the therapist knows to use simple interpretive sentences focused on the here-and-now to convey an authentic reflection of the patient's experience from which the patient can develop a true reflective function.

Small Group 6

None of the participants was present at the start of the group. Mrs. Dupree and Dr. Hernandez began the group alone and talked by themselves about their experience for quite some time. They discussed how rejected and abandoned they felt and reflected on how the group might be feeling similarly. They developed the hypothesis that the group was passing on the trauma of Philip's leaving, identifying with it, and making them suffer for it.

The women then arrived in a giggly mood. They admitted to taking sadistic pleasure in their lateness, imagining that they would be leaving Julio to suffer with Mrs. Dupree and Dr. Hernandez alone. By being even later, he had foiled their intentions. Then, when Julio finally arrived, they were relentless in criticizing him for being late, until he protested that he felt "dumped in shit." Andrea laughed at this expression, and Lucy admitted that they had been planning for him to suffer. At another level, they had also been thinking that they would relieve Mrs. Dupree and Dr. Hernandez of having to work with them in the group, thinking that the coleaders had found them tiresome. Moving into a state of concern, they realized that the absence of all of them would be hard for Mrs. Dupree and Dr. Hernandez.

Dr. Hernandez asked for their fantasy of what she and Mrs. Dupree would do without them, and this led to a discussion of their fantasies about their meaning to the coleaders. It emerged that they thought that they were a narcissistic extension of Mrs. Dupree and Dr. Hernandez's ambition. Their lateness was their way of removing any narcissistic pleasure the coleaders might be getting from them. Working together and building on each other's ideas, Mrs. Dupree and Dr. Hernandez gradually conveyed their sense that having sustained the loss of a group member and having heard Fonagy's review of adult attachment styles and their influence on children, the group members were defending against their own longing for attachment and love. These longings had become complicated because of anxiety about women being alone in a group with one man who was concerned with issues of male aggression in his patient and by inference also in himself.

The group members spoke of their feelings of various experiences of loss as the group ending approached. They were sad because the group had been so much better than any of them had expected. With attachment, naturally, comes loss. Julio talked about experiencing the critical women in the group as critical sisters. Like his patient, he had found that it was not easy to be a man with five sisters. He regretted that this was just a learning group instead of a therapy group. If this had been group therapy, he could have attacked these women with his interpretations. The women expressed outrage at the idea of using therapy to justify making women suffer, but their outrage was short-lived, and they quickly went on to express how they do, in fact, suffer.

The group members then joined to focus on their suffering in therapy, in families, in training programs, in conferences, and in this group especially. Dr. Hernandez said she thought that this emphasis on suffering was a defense against acknowledging the pleasure they had had in working together on concepts and their elaboration in the group.

In response to her comment, Julio began to talk to Dr. Hernandez with pleasure about the murderous patient with whom he had suffered so much. He used this topic as his entry point to be charming, thoughtful, and entertaining but addressed himself only to her. Here he was investing her with wisdom and authority, which was a welcome development, and it showed that he had integrated competence and femininity in one image and also that he had removed his previous idealized attachment to Dr. Williams. On the other hand, he seemed to be creating a couple with Dr. Hernandez to exclude others. Mrs. Dupree revealed that she had had a fantasy of Dr. Hernandez and Julio as a Latin internal couple and that she had become quite preoccupied by the seductiveness of this image, so much so that she could not make sense of it. She asked Dr. Hernandez to help her.

Dr. Hernandez said she thought that the group was allowing Julio to make a couple with her in order to devalue the group. As they neared the end of it, they did not want it to be something worth missing. The group was trying to focus on suffering, when they were also here for the pleasure of learning together, because they did not want to face loss. It was that disavowed fantasy of pleasure that was being expressed in the manic creation of the Latin couple.

Faculty Discussion

Fonagy's material is explored in the here and now of the group process more than in terms of discussion of his content. It appears that the group has to do it this way to allow mourning as the end of the experience approaches. For example, there is no discussion of Fonagy's concept of mentalization, but the two group leaders are left alone to embody the reflective function for the group. The group's preoccupation with suffering is pointed out as a defense against acknowledging pleasure and the imminent loss of it. Meanwhile, the group shows the formation of an intriguing fantasy couple whose purpose is being questioned and provisionally explained but not fully understood because not all the information is accessible.

At its next meeting, the group will learn of a repressed attachment-and-loss trauma that is being contained within the group, referred to obliquely by the persistence of the theme of suffering, manically repaired covertly in the dyad of Julio and Dr. Hernandez, and silently inhibiting the discussion of Fonagy's material.

FIFTH AND FINAL DAY

Presentation 12

Dennis Duncan gave the closing lecture, "When Do Sessions Start and When Do They Finish?," in which he presented a case to illustrate the point that the clinical session often starts before or ends after the actual period of time assigned to it. He said that we can often detect this and learn from it if we look out for it. The beginning and the end of the session are notional milestones for therapists, but the process is going on all the time—in the cab, while at work, or during dreaming. For example, prior to the session, the social exchange of greeting and the relation to the waiting room furniture have meaning that can be understood once the unconscious material begins to flow in the therapeutic space. Theory is another notional system that is not as complete as therapists wish, and yet without it they cannot make contact. Theory operates most effectively as a signpost to where the conflict is. Any interpretation can only address one point along a continuum. The analytic narrative has to be complex, confused, and nonlinear, reflecting that untidy passion that is life.

Small Group 7

At the start of this last small group of the sequence, Andrea started by expressing her gratitude for the week's conference. She said that she and Margie came to London expecting a few good presentations but that both of them had been surprised to find that all of them were very good. She had expected nothing of the small group but had found it extremely enlightening after all. Margie, on the other hand, still thought that her group was a waste of time. Andrea had tried to persuade Margie to get more involved in her own group, but Margie was not convinced. Andrea felt guilty that she was getting something that her friend was not. Feeling more engaged with the experience, Andrea also felt tension with Margie because she was being pulled away from activities for which she might have left the conference to enjoy with her friend. In a way, she was letting Margie down, and this left her feeling bad about the effect of her good experience on Margie.

Sue said that this had been a meaningful week for her. She already appreciated the value of group work even though she was often scared and isolated in groups, but this group had been inclusive of her ideas, and she had felt unusually safe to express herself. Even though she was sad the group was ending, she also knew that she had gotten what she needed, a whole experience to take away and mull over.

Lucy said that she was appreciative of the conference and of the small group but that she couldn't help feeling angry because it was ending. She heard Sue saying that she would take the experience with her but that that didn't change the fact that it was ending.

Julio said that this was a meaningful experience for him. His experience with the other women in the group helped him understand the situation his male patient was in: living in a house with a lot of sisters. He was able to understand a little bit more of his relations with women because of having two female leaders and relating in different ways to each one of them.

Following up on his earlier near slip into Spanish, Julio said that he had thought more about his almost saying *carpeta* instead of *folder*. In his *carpeta*, he carries a letter faxed to him from the new woman in his life who is important to him. The Spanish for *letter* is *carta*, and so there may have been a compression of sounds and meanings pulling him toward his mother tongue to express the possible loss of something close to his heart. Julio said that this woman is offering him a new way of relating in a loving way, and he feels profoundly grateful to her. He also felt grateful for the chance to work on his relationship to the women in the group and wished the group could continue so that he could learn more, but on the other hand he was also excited that the group was ending so that he could go on vacation with the woman he loves. This remark was followed by silence.

Dr. Hernandez said that there had been mostly positive remarks, and she asked for any negative comments.

Andrea said that groups weren't all good. Margie still didn't like having to be in the group, and Andrea hadn't been able to convince her that it was worth it. For example, she said that she had been shown how she projected some things into Mrs. Dupree and others into Dr. Hernandez. From being in the group she had learned how she must project into patients, colleagues, and family. But she was still confused as to how it was that the group of women ended up acting toward Julio in the same way that he feared would happen. They went on reviewing what happened again, trying to understand the playful aspect of their actions toward him as well as the aggressive one. One of them mentioned that Julio was acting as if the women were the only ones who were aggressive. Where was his own aggression against women? Julio did not respond.

With difficulty, Sue narrated how her relationship with Julio started before the first small group. She met him in the bookstore. She approached him and started a conversation. Soon he was telling her of his experience as a child being sent to Los Angeles, away from his family because of the trouble in Nicaragua. By an amazing coincidence, she had been a hostess on an airline that carried Nicaraguan children to the United States. As he learned about her role, Julio was eager to know which airline she had flown, trying to find out whether she had been on his plane.

Sue was filled with emotion. She said she felt awful and prayed that he wasn't on one of her flights. She felt so guilty about these children. They were very afraid, crying, and lonely, and she would be the one to soothe them. By this time, Sue was in tears. She said that the awful part was arriving in Los Angeles. Sometimes there would be no one to pick them up. Her shift would be over, but she couldn't bear to leave. Waiting and hoping that relatives would show up, she would stay the whole night with the children at the airport until she was forced to call the police to take them away. She was surprised and upset when, after having this intimate interaction, Julio pulled away from her.

Julio's affect was not in the same place as the rest of the group. Other group members were moved by Sue's account, but Julio was surprised at the intensity of the group's empathic reaction. He could not identify with pain that was felt on behalf of him and the other children. Mrs. Dupree referred to the depth of Sue's pain and the strain of containing this important piece of information during the entire week. This shared history of early failure to meet dependent needs might have been functioning as an encapsulated trauma of abandonment, affecting the group dynamics. Mrs. Dupree worked with Julio's reaction and tried to help him make a link with his early experience, but he said he just could not get in touch with it. He was more in touch with resentment than with sadness and longing.

Dr. Hernandez said she realized that Julio wasn't ready to deal with this issue now from the group's point of view. She went on to say that an interpretation of unconscious issues may feel so alien from our experience that we reject it as not being true for us but that it may resonate with different meanings for others in the group or for ourselves at another time. Learning what others make of what is said helps us develop the mental space of the third position.

This, the last group of the week, would be over in a few minutes. Dr. Hernandez gave a closing statement. She referred to the small-group task of mastering the concepts through learning from experience during the week. She highlighted a few of the ways in which the group members reenacted in the sessions the content of the lectures in order to integrate theory and experience, for example, as had happened following Fonagy's presentation on attachment. She concluded by saying that, like the person in the session that

Duncan presented, this group had started with a trauma long before the first session and it was revealed only at the end. Mrs. Dupree added that it was revealed *because* it was the end, brought out by the separation theme inherent in the trauma and in the end of the group. Dr. Hernandez expressed her appreciation for the experience of working with the group and with Mrs. Dupree. Mrs. Dupree said that she appreciated the sense of gratitude being expressed and that she too had valued the experience of being in a small group after not working as a leader at the last conference and that she had also enjoyed coleading with Dr. Hernandez for the first time. Dr. Hernandez said that she learned from everyone's different approaches to the various subjects and from the group's struggle with finding meaning in experience.

Faculty Discussion

In the first third of the group session, appreciative remarks, evaluative comments, and statements of what has been learned make it sound as if the group is already over. This premature closure is a resistance to experiencing the group in the present right up to the moment of ending and serves to avoid acknowledging difficult feelings at the point of separation. Dr. Hernandez asks about negative experience. First, the group replies through the feelings of Andrea's unconvinced friend, Margie, who carries a split-off, skeptical part of the group. The group does not seem to notice how Margie is referred to again as if she belongs in the group. They do not address the way in which she is used as an object for the projection of paranoid-schizoid functioning. They keep this aspect of their negativity in the displacement.

As the session proceeds, after the request for negative comments, the group responds at the core of its experience. The leaders' willingness to hear about negativity encourages the person who is holding at bay a negative experience of interaction to bring it to the group for resolution. The group catapults itself into an affective engagement in a final piece of learning to understand the complex interaction of intersecting individual life histories, present ways of relating, and group process.

Like the flow of the clinical session and its context described in the final presentation of the conference, the process of the group session is seen to begin outside the hour of the session. Looking back over the sequence of group meetings, we can see that earlier group sessions dealt with this issue when members discussed their fantasies prior to being late for the group meeting. This final group of the sequence detonates an encapsulated trauma of recent interpersonal longing and rejection that revives trauma from years ago and re-creates it in the group. The trauma was present years before the group. It will continue to reverberate after the conference institution is over. The small group concludes with this final piece of learning about self and object, the encapsulation of trauma, the difficulties of communicating empathy, developing insight, and achieving the third position.

This account of a small-group meeting for seven sessions illustrates the way the small group deals with the didactic presentations cognitively and emotionally. It shows how the small-group process reflects the concepts that are presented to it as the members learn from experience and work toward understanding. It provides a full account from which to assess the advantages and limitations of the use of the group to enlarge the mental space of the individual and to secure the integration of intellectual and empathic understanding. The faculty discussion of the group process shows how the small-group experience is supported in the learning matrix.

III

The Shared
Experience of
Teaching and Learning

In Chapters 14, 15, and 16, David Scharff, the program director and weekend conference chair, describes the student-as-teacher event in which a student presents a clinical case to the large group with the support of the conference cochair. Into his narrative he weaves first-person accounts from the main participants to create a tapestry of experiences concerning the student in role as teacher and the impact of this role shift on the institution-wide learning process. In Chapter 14, he describes his selection of the student. Then, the conference cochair and the student give their accounts of working together to prepare for the presentation. The small-group leader tells how the other group members reacted before and after this presentation by one of its members. In Chapter 15, the student presenter summarizes her presentation and what she learned while doing it. In Chapter 16, David Scharff summarizes the other small groups' learning processes in response to the presentation, and the student presenter reflects on her teaching and learning experience.

To protect the identity of the main participants other than himself, David Scharff refers to the student presenter as Ruth, and she calls her client Helen. Ms. Susan Ford is the name chosen for the weekend conference cochair and Dr. Michael Thomas for the faculty member who was both the leader of Ruth's small group and the chair of the session in which she was the presenter.

14
Preparing for a Presentation

SELECTING THE PRESENTER

In most weekend conferences and for a number of clinical presentations in the summer institute, students volunteer or are selected to present their
work as a clinical text for group supervision and for the study of theory. We
ask for volunteers, and someone who feels ready for the public nature of the
presentation may offer. Or we may become aware that a certain student has a
case that is particularly apt for illustrating a specific theoretical topic or clinical
focus, and we will ask that person to present. As program director, I consult
with faculty, especially with the cochair of the conference, in deciding which
student will be ready to present clinical material to the large group. We choose
a student who has had enough experience in the program to know what we are
looking for, who has the self-confidence to present without feeling unduly at
risk, and whose clinical skills are sufficiently developed that student and discussant will be comfortable working together. Usually, this means that we wait
until at least the second year of the program before we select a student to present
formally. By that time, the student will have had other informal opportunities
to review cases in the program—in their small groups and study groups as well
as in supervision. We rely on feedback from faculty, small-group leaders, and
any supervisors in making the selection.

For making a presentation during a weekend on separation anxiety,
emotional vertigo, and chaos theory applied to psychoanalysis, I thought of asking Ruth, a graduate who is returning for further study. I had worked with Ruth

in paired supervision for a year and again more recently in a supervision group of four advanced participants. In both settings, she had presented a patient she called Helen. A severely disturbed and traumatized woman, Helen had given Ruth a tough time until, in supervision, Ruth had learned to set limits. Only then had the issues around separation anxiety become understandable and workable. It seemed to me that this case could provide a good learning experience for the large group and for Ruth.

Ruth had made great progress in supervision. She came to the two-year program while in the latter stages of certification as a marriage and family therapist. Her training had been almost exclusively in systemic family systems theory and therapy, and her first significant exposure to psychodynamic theory and practice came from attending our two-year program in object relations theory. In the beginning, she had no theoretical or clinical understanding of how to work with a borderline patient such as Helen. Ruth was a receptive, eager supervisee who learned quickly. The other clinician who shared the paired supervision with her was further along in the process of learning, but he, too, was presenting a patient who tested limits and boundaries regularly. So, the discussion about how to set limits on Helen's many demands and intrusions was of interest to both of them. They shared the process of study as Ruth worked to translate Helen's nonstop enactments into words. As Ruth did so, she stopped giving the ready reassurance that Helen demanded and instead used language to describe what was going on between them and then gradually progressed to making dynamic interpretations. Ruth had a good intuitive sense of Helen and soon turned this into a capacity for detecting the transference. She made steady progress toward direct interpretations based on her countertransference—even when she was referring to Helen's experience outside therapy.

In the next year, when Ruth presented Helen's material in group supervision, I could see that Ruth's gains had persisted and that Helen's therapy had continued to progress. Ruth was having an easier time with Helen, was more able to conceptualize Helen's intrapsychic dynamics and the processes in which they were engaged, and had developed considerable perspective on the chaos of the early treatment phase. In the group supervision, Ruth could now participate as a peer with students who had considerably more experience and theoretical training than she, and she was able to comment helpfully on the other supervisees' struggles with patients who pressed at therapeutic limits.

With this progress in mind, I suggested that Ruth present her work with Helen to illustrate the theme of separation anxiety. Like all students whom we invite to present, Ruth was offered help aimed at learning to construct a good teaching presentation. I hoped this would put her at less risk for feeling exposed or embarrassed and would give her confidence to present in the expanded setting of the large group of peers and teachers. I asked the cochair of the weekend, Susan Ford, an experienced supervisor who herself presents competently, to help Ruth prepare the case for presentation. I thought back over Ms. Ford's own previous development from the time she was one of our students. Although she was then already a senior faculty member in a university psychiatry department, she was unsure of her teaching and presentation skills, and so she was reluctant to present in public forums. Over a number of years, with mentoring by several faculty members, she had developed not only her considerable clinical skills but also her confidence in clinical and theoretical presentation. Her previous vulnerability had become a strength in her capacity to support and teach others to present. I did not expect that Ms. Ford would need routine help, but, as I always do, I offered to be on standby to support her mentoring task in case an unexpected problem came up. I think of my role here as facilitating the faculty's growth as they perform a parallel facilitative function for students.

Now we turn to Ms. Ford's experience in helping Ruth prepare the case. For this chapter, I asked her to comment on the process of facilitating Ruth's work and growth and for any brief reflections on what she learned in the process of doing this particular task, which she has done on several previous occasions with other students.

MENTORING THE PRESENTER

I (Susan Ford) felt that my work with Ruth flowed easily. She had approached me three months earlier about her upcoming presentation. I told her that she ought to prepare a brief history of the patient and have two sessions of process notes to present. It was agreed that she would contact me after she had put together some ideas and that we would then go over it together, which is what we did. The three-hour time difference that separated us did not prove to be an obstacle. On all occasions, we connected on the first try, so that we did not have the repeated experience of failed attempts to reach each other. I mention this because I found it reassuring that Ruth was not using such potential obstacles in the service of any reluctance or anxiety she might be feeling.

Ruth was nondefensive, eager for help, and willing to rework material that I thought seemed unclear. Though she spoke of being anxious about the case and of needing the consultation on it, she seemed more concerned about wanting to make her presentation clear so that it would be a good experience for others. When she said this, I clarified that my role was to be her consultant for the task of presenting the material, not a supervisor for the case. I made this statement as much for myself as for Ruth because I realized that I was tempted to make general supervisory comments and had to remind myself that that was not my function.

As I worked with Ruth, I found her to be receptive to my input and especially interested in clarifying the confusing areas of her report. As I helped her with anxiety about presenting and organizing her material, I was reminded of the way I had been helped by the program chair when I had faced the task of presenting cases to the program when I was first on the faculty. I recalled the way his availability and steadiness provided the holding and containing I needed. I felt that I was now in the position to provide that for someone else. I recalled how uncertain I was that I could help someone in this way when I was first asked three years ago. Recognizing the greater sense of confidence I felt while helping Ruth, I realized how much I had grown. Yet I felt close enough to those anxieties to feel quite in tune with her.

During the weekend, as I sat through her presentation, I felt Ruth's interest in making this a good learning experience for others. I was surprised, however, by the way the group took a more optimistic view of this patient's pathology than I had felt. I thought that had to do with the way in which Ruth had presented as well as the supportive and holding dynamic between her and the weekend's principal guest presenter. That experience said something to me about the anxiety I had adsorbed in the process of helping Ruth and perhaps about my own sense of worry about patients such as Helen who produce so much anxiety in the therapist. The optimistic group response to this "difficult" patient seemed to be a product of the containment experienced in Ruth's supervision, my help to her, and the presenter's work with her.

Working with Ruth was mutually satisfying and growth producing. As I helped her face a developmental challenge, so I continued my own professional growth.

PREPARING THE CLINICAL PRESENTATION

I (Ruth) anticipated the preparation for this presentation with a mixture of hope for stretching myself personally and professionally—and fear of what I would find out about myself. As I contemplated the topics of separation anxiety, chaos theory, and emotional vertigo, it became clear that my work with Helen certainly fit the themes. Helen struggled with intense separation anxiety in her transference with me. In addition, we both struggled to find order in her chaotic internal world and in our therapeutic relationship. And at times, when the work was intense, we each struggled with an emotional vertigo. As chaos theory, emotional vertigo, and separation anxiety were the topics for the weekend, I thought her case would fit in perfectly.

By now I know how it works: The assigned readings are typically brought to life in each conference weekend by the integrative experience of weaving back and forth between the intellectual–cognitive exploration of material in the large discussion groups and the more emotional–personal exploration of the same material in the small groups. This time, the readings had more impact on me because I knew I would be significantly more active in illustrating the concepts in the readings.

For example, I read and pondered a quote from Freud: "The final transformation which the fear of the super-ego undergoes is, it seems to me, the fear of death (or the fear for life), which is a fear of the super-ego projected on to the powers of destiny" (1926, p. 140). As I read, I began to relate Freud's idea to my own personal anxieties related to presenting this case. Thinking about my performance anxiety, I realized that some of my fear had to do with my projection of my own critical, rejecting self onto faculty and fellow students. My anxiety had annihilated who I believed them to be, just as I had so many times felt annihilated by the intense negative projections of Helen and also of important caregivers in my personal life. I had also killed off an integrated sense of myself with my version of the splitting and projection mechanisms that I readily recognized in Helen's material. Here was an important interface between my patient and me. It was so much easier to see and think about these intense projections in her than in me, but now I had to see my own projection of my rejecting object relations. And so my reading went: thinking about the ideas in the material, identifying them in my work with Helen and other patients, and experiencing and identifying them in my personal self.

Trusting the frame held by faculty for conference participants and by myself for my patients, I knew that the dreaded and longed-for aspects of myself would not be left lodged in my patient. Agreeing to present represented an internal agreement to work more intensely on identifying and reuniting with split-off aspects of myself. My anxiety diminished and was replaced by a sense of manageable loss and then hope. The reincorporation of this lost piece of myself was clearly reinforced as I gradually felt able to think and feel more clearly about this presentation.

I prepared the first draft of my presentation, which included a brief history and material from two sessions, in an overconfident and harried way. My therapy practice had been particularly busy at this time. As prearranged, I faxed it to Susan Ford. Her feedback made it abundantly clear that I had communicated the chaos, vertigo, and separation anxiety induced by the case through the vagueness of that first draft. The vagueness both obscured and revealed the overwhelming feelings of craziness and lack of differentiation I often experienced with Helen. She tried desperately over the years to get into my psyche and into my life, as if that would reduce her feelings of aloneness and sense of rejection. At times, I experienced a loss of my own ability to think and separate her experience from my own. Here it was again, re-created in this first draft. With diplomacy and compassion, Susan made suggestions to clear up the ambiguities.

For a couple of days, I sat with the experience of bad objects stirred up within me by this first draft. Was some primitive aspect of myself confused with my patient? As I thought about it, I felt devastated by the realization of the chaos communicated in the write-up. I struggled to keep perspective, observe my reactions, and find some balance as I experienced my own primitive, regressed feelings. On the third day, clarity and integration began to return. I could see how much more comfortable I had been with working on these regressed, primitive aspects, as if Helen were the only one in the relationship to possess such discomfort. Now I became more aware of these difficult and painful objects in myself. Differentiation from Helen now returned slowly, but this time I felt an increase in empathy and compassion for her as well as a significantly increased capacity for containment. I was more able to *feel* her overwhelming and chaotic feelings in a personal way without having to *be* overwhelmed and chaotic.

I was interested to find that I experienced a decrease in another pattern, one I had recognized before but had certainly not fully tamed: I commonly project out some of my own good qualities of clarity, competency, and integration onto others—specifically, onto more seasoned therapists and faculty. During this exercise, I had an increased experience of clarity and competence in myself and a more realistic experience of the abilities of others, having removed some of my more idealized projections from them. I now felt capable of preparing a useful presentation. The second draft was remarkably clearer—communicating the feelings of chaos, anxiety, and vertigo, but now in a more contained, understandable form.

I had presented Helen's therapy in paired supervision. Then I joined a group supervision where I continued to get help in working with her. Supervision in this group format was particularly helpful, and that accounts for my being able to present such a difficult case. Discussing and exploring many of Helen's primitive longings and acting-out behaviors in the group increased my ability to stay emotionally available to Helen while increasingly being able to contain her difficult material. On many occasions, my own fears, anxieties, and wishes for narcissistic gratification were stirred by Helen. For example, Helen had many sadistic sexual fantasies in which she killed off my husband, kidnapped me, and subjected me to various forms of sexual torture until I had lost everything of value materially and emotionally. These fantasies stirred up a host of overwhelming feelings within me and led me to feel numb.

Group supervision provided me a safe space for exploring her painful longings and projections and for integrating my experience of her with my theoretical understanding. This support allowed me to observe and contain my responses to Helen and her communications to me through projection and projective identification. This increased ability to stay with her emotionally and cognitively was essential to her developing more of an ability to understand herself and to move away from enactments toward thinking about her internal experience. Helen's unmetabolized material was located in me and in the relationship with her. With the group's help, I continued to grow in my ability to understand, put my new understanding into thoughts and words, and feed back interpretations she could tolerate and use in her development of a more cohesive sense of herself. It was the growth from working with the material in the group supervision that provided enough understanding to give me the sense that the case could be a helpful one to present at the weekend conference.

With the final draft complete, I faxed a copy to the discussant a week or so before the conference. Although our contact before the conference was brief, I had already developed a sense of trust in him based on the authenticity of his writing. His response was warm and supportive, albeit short and via facsimile. But it was enough to let me feel open and ready for what would come.

On the morning of the first day of the three-day conference, he had given a lecture on separation anxiety in the large-group session preceding the one where I would present. I found myself feeling relaxed by his style. He conveyed an understanding and compassion for his clients that I imagined he would extend toward me. I still felt anxious, but it was tempered by the comfort I felt with him.

My case presentation was planned for later that day. This was a relief to me since it followed one small group in which I could prepare, and it preceded many other small groups in which I could process any unmanageable experiences elicited by my presentation. There were also coffee breaks and enjoyable dinners where I could relax or vent my distress with colleagues.

Following the guest speaker's presentation, there was lively discussion in the large group. Suddenly, I found myself feeling anxious about my turn to present to this large group later in the day. I felt painfully aware of my newness to the field of psychotherapy. However, these anxieties were somewhat tempered when I looked around the audience and saw, one by one, how many well-meaning colleagues were there sitting with me. Again and again, I found myself relying on my consistent experience of support and well-intended feedback in these large groups to keep me anchored in reality.

During the first break, I was introduced to the presenter by Susan Ford and by the chairperson for my presentation, who also happened to be my small-group leader, Dr. Michael Thomas. We discussed my presentation and how best to use the material I had provided. I knew that the faculty preferred presenters to give the background summary by talking informally instead of reading a written statement, but I expected to read mine anyway. I felt a pang of anxiety when Dr. Thomas asked me not to read the history but to briefly describe and discuss the case from what I knew of it. Keeping in mind the discussant's relaxed demeanor and the clear support of the faculty, I gathered myself together and agreed to make the changes. I did feel cut off—a form of separation anxiety, I thought—from my well-thought-out write-up, which I believed presented Helen's chaotic world better than I could do spontaneously. I wondered whether I would feel the chaos, fragment, and fail to put my understanding into words. Would I, with my performance anxiety returning, be able to hold a sense of clarity and competency, or would I feel the way Helen does at times—overwhelmed, fragmented, crazy? Although these feelings had intensity, my anxiety was made manageable by the work I had done over the years to try to understand Helen and to separate her material from my own. But I felt pretty anxious about having to speak spontaneously in front of the large group, no matter what I told myself.

A few minutes after this change in plan for the presentation, my ongoing small group commenced. This was the first of five groups for this weekend. By this time, we as a small group—with the assistance of Dr. Thomas, the group leader—had created a relatively safe holding environment in which to explore a wide range of thoughts, feelings, and experiences. I usually entered the small group with a twinge of excitement about what I might learn about myself and others. I noticed immediately that this time was different. I went into the group defensively, hoping not to stir up any repressed, bad object relations within myself before presenting in the afternoon. The members noticed this and invited me to use the group to think about what was happening with me, what I might be holding for the small group, and what I might represent for the students in general. I said I did not want to regress. I was afraid that if I dropped into my feelings in this group, I would not be able to think and feel simultaneously during the presentation. With ample psychological space provided by the group, fears of inadequacy and rejection came rushing in. I became aware that these were not founded so much in the present but were more an aspect of my own internal object relations being projected onto others.

The compassion and resonance of the group members for this kind of internalization and projection helped me see this fragile aspect of myself in a more realistic way. I became grateful that I was talking about this rather than using energy to keep this material split off and projected. Others shared their own experiences of presenting and spoke to their feelings of inadequacy evoked by the process of preparing their presentations. We used the small group for understanding these aspects of ourselves that we held in common. What I had imagined to be a separate idiosyncratic issue was, to my surprise, shared to some extent by each member of the group. I felt a tremendous relief.

I had felt every insecurity and every fear of rejection ever experienced by any therapist presenting a case. I feared that others would judge me as harshly as I can sometimes judge myself. With the help of the group, I realized that a critical voice that was really my own had been projected onto others, and I was beginning to think and act as if it were true—exactly what had happened to me with Helen. Now I was left with only my own individual introjects and projections. Realizing this, I was able to grieve for some of the origins of this internalization, moving away from the anxiety I felt to be associated with my splitting and moving toward a depressive position. My clarity returned once again, and I felt relaxed and open to providing the best presentation I could—for my patient, for the members of the large group with their own difficult cases and aspects of themselves, for the discussant, and for myself.

Separation anxiety was clearly an issue throughout the process of preparing to present. Over and over during the preparation, I experienced separation from a familiar attachment to an old, distorted view of myself and a familiar way of being in the world. Pushing myself to learn and to risk in various ways that used different aspects of the program's holding environment allowed me to separate from some familiar distortions—to make room for something more reality based, more relaxed.

Now we will hear a report on Ruth's small group from the group's leader, Dr. Thomas. This report focuses on the group meeting immediately before her presentation.

THE EFFECT ON THE PRECEDING SMALL GROUP

In addition to being Ruth's small group leader, I (Michael Thomas) am assigned to chair the session in which she will make her presentation. In this small group, all the members are graduates and therefore familiar with the general emotional and cognitive norms and expectations of the institution. The

group's anticipation of Ruth's presentation will no doubt challenge the narcissistic illusion that the group exists as a unity where all members are precisely
equal: I know from experience that one member's emergence out of the undif-
ferentiated matrix of the group liberates competitive energies associated with
object relational striving as members are forced to acknowledge differences in
status, place, and dominance. The "happy family" of the group unity disappears
in the atmosphere of competition. Envy, jealousy, and resentment emerge,
whether or not the group acknowledges its plight.

> Ruth began this first group with the statement, "I won't be able to use the small
> group because Dr. Thomas is both the chair of my clinical presentation in the
> large-group setting as well as my small-group leader. I won't be able to regress
> here because I'll have to deal with him as chair of the session this afternoon."
>   Other group members tried to identify why she made this assumption. They
> asked, "What is there about Dr. Thomas that will act as a block to Ruth's regres-
> sion? And why do you feel you have to regress just because you're anxious?"
> Though empathizing with Ruth's feelings, the group did not join with her to see
> me as the problem. They wanted to know what made me such a threat to her.

The projection of a punishing, internal bad object (a sadistic superego
in Freudian terms, an antilibidinal ego in Fairbairn's theory) onto my image
seemed to account for Ruth's transformation of the group from a safe into a
dangerous place. Because of the gentle way the group questioned her assumptions, Ruth's paranoid–schizoid sense of the group was modified, splitting was
reduced, and integration of experience was accomplished, for the moment.
Through empathy and care, the group provided a detoxifying effect for Ruth
individually. The group then helped Ruth see and reflect on this process of container and contained. Being able to accomplish this for one of their own solidi-
fied the integrative potential of the group as a whole for all its members.

In discussion of this small group at the faculty meeting, another faculty
member suggested that Ruth's reaction might be understood to reflect separation anxiety caused by having to share her idealized object–leader in both small-
and large-group contexts. When she lost me as her individually owned object,
I then became a rejecting object, full of her split-off anxiety and rage. The group
helped her experience the group as a whole as an environmental object powerfully capable of neutralizing intense anxiety and fear. It enabled her to refind
me as a good-enough leader and restore me as an integrated object.

> The focus on Ruth led our only male member, Dan, to feel invisible. He
> introduced his wish to be seen by pointing out an article he had written. I

thought he was ignoring Ruth's concerns because he was jealous of her turn in the spotlight, and in so doing he confirmed her fear of rejection. On the other hand, Ruth's worry about whether I could provide safety in the small group may have reflected her hope to deflect just such a competitive attack by pleading vulnerability.

With these thoughts in mind, I said, "Maybe the question before the group is 'Who contributes and who doesn't?'"

Referring to a pregnant group member, another women said jokingly, "Jenny's going to make a huge contribution." Others went on to speak about the envy and pity that they feel toward Jenny.

The hope associated with the unborn child is a literal expression of the *pairing basic assumption group* (Bion 1961) in which the group's unconscious fantasy forms around the idea that a couple (in this case, Jenny paired with an un-named other who in fantasy is me, the leader) will give birth to a savior who will solve the group's problems, thus sparing the group from doing actual work. The discussion of Jenny's pregnancy is a displaced expression of envy of Ruth, who at that moment was pregnant in anticipation of her delivery of the case presentation. So, the group is taking inventory and exploring various versions of its envy of members.

Theresa said that she felt that there was a pejorative and judgmental feeling about people who meet their needs by coming back to conferences for more learning. The group seemed split by this. One part of the group agreed that our "culture" is against neediness and vulnerability (the bad internal object "hating" the empty child). Yet another member challenged Theresa to consider whether she's afraid of not being able to think for herself.

I said that the group's reaction to Theresa's comment suggested to me that the group was having an envious response concerning Ruth's inexperience, her justified anxiety, and her right to learn in contrast to Theresa's unconscious assumption that she should no longer have such needs. I pointed out that if need for repeated learning is bad, the faculty must be the worst and neediest of all since they form a group of learners that come back more than any other group in the institution. In saying this, I meant to challenge the split that leads to the false idealization of the faculty and a corresponding denigration of those in the student role.

Theresa seems, at this point, to be the spokesperson for the tendency to project the antilibidinal ego outside, where it then attacks the needy-hungry-ignorant infant–student aspect of themselves. Shame, more than guilt, dominates in the struggle with the sense of failure and vulnerability. This projective extrusion of one member's internal persecutor has the consequence of making the institution itself seem saturated with aggressors who wish that a needy member would take her neediness elsewhere. The group is all too ready to let Theresa take the heat for her leadership in examining the vulnerability that others also feel.

Several themes emerged during this discussion: There is no growth without dependency, but there is no dependency without injury. There is narcissistic injury in acknowledging one's needs and anxieties—for which Ruth spoke initially, followed by Dan, Jenny, and Theresa.

> Frustration was palpable in the group, generally marked by silence.
>
> I observed, "No wonder they call people who don't know things 'boobs.' It's a way of attacking the object that frustrates us as well as attacking the self." I needed to use humor to put forward my idea that the vulnerable learner is identified with the bad breast. Another member picked up the burden of understanding and integrating the task, and the group continued its struggle.
>
> Ruth, moving into the role of task leader, brought the group back to the topic of the weekend. She said, "Look how the topic of separation scared us. The more we know about ourselves, the more we are separate, distinct, and vulnerable."
>
> Lila answered that this discussion about dependency brought up "deep feelings of sadness and yearning." She related a piece of her personal experience to exemplify her sense of the group's struggle, thereby personalizing and humanizing what was in danger of becoming an abstract and therefore defended idea. When Lila shared herself with the group, the group members said that they felt more connected, real, and safe.

Separation anxiety was overcome by the shared work done by Ruth and Lila. On this occasion, Ruth asked the question, and Lila connected the group in a meaningful affective moment. Their dialogue provided the group with a moment of shared learning that integrated affect and cognition and reduced the tension between hatred of vulnerability and acceptance of need for knowledge to permit learning. Said differently, the group struggles with dependency issues and shame versus defensive and envious fantasies of a false independence based on spurious, magical knowledge. This, too, is an expression of the pain of separation anxiety—the separation from an idealized but defensive state of being "in the know." Separating from this defense is required in order to learn.

15
The Presentation

THE PROGRAM DIRECTOR'S ACCOUNT OF RUTH'S PRESENTATION TO THE LARGE GROUP

As program director, I wanted to choose Dr. Thomas as the chair for this session because of his skill in facilitating the dialogue among student, invited guest, and audience. He was, however, Ruth's small-group leader. Small-group leaders and group members do interact in various roles in other settings of our program, and so this would not be an unusual overlap. Nevertheless, I wondered whether it would have been easier for Ruth if Dr. Thomas were not also her small-group leader. On the other hand, I thought that this relationship might also feel protective to her, and so he was assigned as the chair of the session.

Dr. Thomas introduced the event and its purpose and then introduced Ruth with the same formality with which chairs introduce faculty and guest presenters. He cited her participation in the program, where she came from, the nature of her practice, and her other major endeavors and accomplishments. He noted that she had been asked to say a few words about the patient's history, then give one session briefly and, later, a second session in more detail. He then turned to Ruth and asked her to begin.

Ruth gave her case presentation in a relaxed, chatty, narrative form, giving the patient's background first. I noticed that she did not indicate that this had been a case in supervision or that I had been the supervisor—until the large-group discussion after she presented the second session.

Ruth began with the history. She had written a succinct two-page summary of Helen's family history and the history of her therapy with Helen leading up to the two sessions she had selected to present in detail. As requested, Ruth spoke spontaneously for approximately five minutes about the patient. We prefer a spontaneous narrative to reading the write-up because the material is much more accessible to the audience. It is more effective to simply tell the story. The disadvantage is that it confronts the presenter—and therefore the group— with the full force of anxiety about presenting. Since we prefer to learn from working with this anxiety and its effects—on the presenter, the discussant, and the group—the atmosphere is more hospitable than might be imagined. Nevertheless, not everyone can face this challenge, and we never insist that they do.

Here I am quoting what Ruth shared spontaneously with the large group. She had prepared more, but this is what was available to everyone in the large group at the session. Her relaxed, competent, narrative form conveyed the impression of a patient who, while presenting considerable challenges, was engaging and likable.

The Patient's History

Ruth began, "Appropriately, I am feeling a little bit of separation anxiety from my seat over there in the audience. Instead of reading the history that I have written, I am going to tell you a few things about Helen, the patient I will be presenting today. She's a 49-year-old woman, divorced, and has now been in a lesbian relationship for the last eighteen years. She has been in face-to-face psychotherapy with me initially for five sessions a week, decreasing until, in the last year, we have been seeing each other two, sometimes three, times a week. She's seen many previous therapists, even one she charged with unethical termination. She was institutionalized at the age of 19 for psychotic behavior, attempted suicides, and acting out. She was referred to me by outpatient county mental health. I was new—I was an intern at the time— and was prelicensed when I took her on. I had a sliding-fee scale, so part of the reason she was referred was that I was inexpensive. They imagined that this would be intensive long-term therapy, which it has been.

"Just a little bit of history. Helen's mother was psychotic. In all likelihood, she also had bipolar disorder. Before she was referred to me, Helen was diagnosed as having rapid cycling bipolar disorder. She had a severely abused childhood—sexually, physically, and emotionally. When I began working with her in therapy, she was often suicidal. She spoke about it constantly and acted out a lot. She had great difficulty managing separations, which is why I thought her situation would be relevant to this weekend's focus.

"I also want to mention that she has done a lot to try to get inside me. She's had difficulty with the breaks between sessions. She has come by and sat outside my office many, many times. I live in a small rural community. For instance, she found out where I lived and drove by my house and followed my husband home one night from an art opening when I was here in DC. If I say I'm out of the office for a day, she will park outside the office to see if I'm seeing other patients after all. So, I came to call her affectionately my 'What about Bob?' client. Thinking about her in this way is also an attempt at managing anxiety about her trying to get into me so intensely.

"I have experienced Helen as exhausting, interesting, demanding, witty, overwhelming, sadistic, and frustrating—as well as gratifying to work with. Over the course of the work, she struggled with a marked inability to organize her experience and with lots of fragmentation which has gotten into the therapy. It's been difficult for me to sort out my thinking about this case because as the therapy progressed and as I used my defenses less, she has gotten into me more. I've gradually come more to know what it is like for her to be so fragmented. On the positive side, there's been progressively less acting out over the last four years—a lot of which I attribute to good supervision. I have learned how to hold the container better for her, to contribute to her increasing ability to move into symbolizing, and to talk about her feelings instead of acting them out with me.

"Helen is currently taking Lithium and Zyprexa.

"So, maybe what I'll do is just begin with the first session, and then we'll go on to the next one?"

The chair nodded in answer to her question, and Ruth began to read from her notes.

"This session was on Tuesday, after a week of intense acting out. In that week, Helen had been extremely angry with me. She had gone to the public library, where she had seen my husband—actually his car—and she had imagined that he would say hello. She had run into him before in our community. She was angry with me because, she said afterwards, what she wanted me to do was to tell him to acknowledge her and say hi to her when he saw her in public. When I did not say I would go home and tell him to say hi to her, this brought a lot of anger toward me. We spent that week working on that."

The First Session

Ruth continued, "I'm just going to abbreviate a lot of this first session I'll present now. Helen came in talking about not doing the self-regulatory behaviors that she had been learning. When we first started work, she wouldn't take her medication regularly, didn't eat, didn't take care of herself in most ways. She had been beginning to do so, but after her lesbian partner, who lives out of the area, went back home, and after I had been gone on a long weekend break, she had regressed. She wasn't doing the things to care for herself that she had been doing previously and was quite upset about it. We also talked about a number of other losses in this session. Then she talked a little bit about how she was managing feelings of abandonment and isolation and how her ambivalence about letting go of those feelings was in the way of her desire to live in a new way. She has been handling her feelings of abandonment by driving her car sometimes hundreds of miles a day, eating enormous amounts of what she calls junk food, and other behaviors.

"As the session progressed, I brought back in her anger toward me from the previous week. I said, 'A lot of what you are talking about reminds me of last Friday's session, when you felt frustration and disappointment with me.'

"Helen said, 'Yes, I have to put all these feelings somewhere. Sometimes at night I get extremely emotional. It's like the death of a loved one.' She began to tear up at this point. 'A need comes to go where I want in terms of being kind to myself rather than do things in the old self-destructive way. But the loss is so intense, the loss is worse than the self-destructive feelings and behaviors.'

"I said, 'The good brings feelings of loss for you.'

"Helen said, 'The good feelings inside me lead me to feel that I don't belong. The loss comes from nowhere. I can be just reading, and it comes on me. I'll feel good about me, and then I'll think, 'He he he, ha ha ha, you fool, you can't do this!'

"And I said, 'When you begin to take care of yourself, to follow through and do things that are good for you, you feel a loss of something bad you've held on to tightly most of your life.'

"She responded, 'It must be. The urgency is so intense—to stop, get candy, soda, chips, to drive endlessly, to do anything to get this feeling in me to stop. If it gets really bad, I will go to a motel.'

"I found myself connecting this to our previous work. Helen has had many sadistic sexual fantasies about me. They have changed recently in that they are much less frequent and much less sadistic toward my family and me. So I said to her, 'And then the sexual fantasies come.'

"She said, 'These fantasies come up at home, too. But these are much more intense.' She paused and then went on. 'The sexual fantasies give me a sense of connection because they make me feel whole. They contain anger, too. I want my parents to get off and away.'"

After reporting Helen's feelings about her parents, Ruth remembered the discussant's presence. She asked him whether she should stop there, and he told her to finish that session.

Ruth continued, "I'll summarize here. Helen went on to talk about the frequent battle inside her. And then she began to talk about the fears of real loss on the outside. For example, her parents are aging and dying, and she didn't want to have things end the way they get along now. Then she brought it back to my husband and began to talk about what he symbolizes for her. She tried to make sense of what she believes to be his protecting me and also of her need to make some connection with him. She began to associate to how knowing him would make her feel accepted and connected, the way she wanted to be in her family. Now, I'll go back to reading from the process notes.

"I said, 'You wanted your father to accept you as a member of your family.'

"Helen, now very upset and angry, said, 'He would kick me and tell me how awful I was. I said back to him, "Someday I'll be as big as you, and you'll see."' Helen became subdued at this point. She went on. 'But that day I was walking down the street, and I waved and called to my dad. He wouldn't even acknowledge me. I melted on the sidewalk. That was the beginning of my running away behavior that I've done 'til now.'

"I said, 'All that played out with us. My husband is the father who would not respond acceptingly, and I'm the mother who won't confront his behavior and make him treat you the way you need.'

"Helen said, 'My mom was numb. I've had so much rage at my father. I couldn't rage with my mom. Most of my rage is still at my dad, even though I know something is really wrong with that. I couldn't yell at my mom because she was so sick. The strong can fight back and yell. She lived in her own world, and I protected that.'

"And I said, 'So Donny [this is her lesbian lover] left and went back home. And when I left and was out of my office for a few days, you got mad at my husband."

"Helen said, '*I* feel protective of *you*.'

"I said, 'Now you want to protect me from yourself, not from the father.' I was thinking about how she would protect her mother from her father, possibly unconsciously from even her own rage.

"Helen said, 'Yes, but sometimes I still want you to do something so I can feel that you get it, even though I don't feel that so much anymore.' She noticed the time was up. She pulled herself up, ready to go, and asked, 'I can

do this work, huh? I mean, I'm doing this, but . . . ?' She paused. 'I sometimes have a hard time seeing that it will be different.'

"There had been a long history of asking and trying to get me to reas-
sure her, so I said, 'I wonder if asking for reassurance is a way of saying that
it's hard to end a session when you wish I could give you something to take
away the pain. Sometimes you feel like doing something to try to force that
out of me, even though you're able to not act on that feeling.'

"Helen, visibly relieved and smiling, said, 'I guess so. It's always hard
to go, so I'll see you on Thursday.'"

First Dialogue with the Audience and the Discussant

The discussant began by congratulating Ruth on dealing with a bipolar
patient with a borderline personality who is, in many ways, more difficult than
a fully psychotic patient. He picked out for praise several things that Ruth had
done. He emphasized her rapport with a patient who had begun treatment with
a negative transference, perversity, and conflict between love and hate. He
praised Ruth's capacity to set limits, and he gave a summary of the progress in
the treatment and in the session. In this way, he set the tone for a positive and
appreciative way of understanding Ruth's work. Finally, he said that the patient
had a central conflict between a homosexual and a heterosexual orientation,
which expressed her wish not only to possess the mother but also to be accepted
by the parents as a member of the family.

Dr. Thomas now turned to the large group, which requested more
information from Ruth, beginning with the threat of unethical termination
against a previous therapist. Ruth said that she began Helen's treatment with a
dread that she did not process or even acknowledge. As she became more experienced, she came to understand the forces brought to bear on the previous
therapist. Ruth said that her feeling threatened had underscored the difficulty
of dealing with Helen, before she had begun supervision.

The next questioner asked about Ruth's motivation for working with
this patient, when she was a green therapist without analytic supervision or ideas.

"I didn't know even how to think about her," Ruth said. "My previous supervisor told me to support her, take her phone calls, and be like a kind
mother holding her child. This plan backfired: It only made things worse.
Helen began to stalk me. I didn't understand the problem until I got into
supervision here. My supervisor helped me understand the actual holding
power of setting limits. Once I got the hang of the idea that my limits
let me be a better container for her aggression, I found she didn't get

under my skin so much, and I wasn't thinking about her so much between sessions."

Ruth talked about her unconscious wish to fix up her own disabled and impossible mother—which she had since decided was impossible—either in actuality or in the displacement of her work with Helen. She now thought this was both her own issue and an introjective identification of aspects of Helen. Ruth said that as she became more realistic and less identified with the position of savior—a projection of Helen's desperate wish—the treatment became more tractable.

"It's funny," Ruth mused. "As I'm thinking about this right here in the presentation, I'm dropping back a little into that fragmented state and finding it harder to think. It's the way I can feel in sessions. But now that the therapy has progressed, the aggression comes and goes. More of it is verbalized, so it is a little bit easier to tolerate." She concluded, "My empathy for Helen matured in the process of understanding her needs and their meaning."

In the discussion, there was a notable absence of critical comment, a tone set by the response of the guest discussant, by the high quality of the presentation, and by Ruth's nondefensive, relaxed style. A number of comments linked Helen's struggles to issues of separation anxiety, which, as the topic most in focus for the weekend, was therefore on people's minds. A faculty member asked about Ruth's way of dealing with the aggression intrinsic to Helen's perverse transference sexual fantasies. These fantasies, he thought, carried the unspoken threat to destroy and humiliate Ruth and to transform her into a version of the patient's degraded self. Ruth replied that the fantasies were ones that Helen might have been willing to enact at the beginning of treatment, but Ruth never felt threatened by that, perhaps because she did not get the elaboration of the fantasy material earlier in sessions, when Helen's acting out had been so massive. What Ruth did feel threatened by were the concerted, seductive, verbal attempts to get under her skin. Now, because of transformation in therapy, these fantasies were represented by smaller aggressive enactments that could be safely delivered into the therapeutic space, where they could be contained and understood.

In response to a request for elaboration, Ruth described Helen's perverse sexual fantasies. The fantasies involved a homosexual relationship in which Helen got in the middle between Ruth and her husband, humiliated him, killed him, and gained sole and sadistic possession of Ruth. In actuality, Helen had recently given up homosexual activity and had begun to date her ex-husband, whom she had not seen for twenty years, and to fantasize less sadistically and more heterosexually.

The discussant then gave a more extended formulation of Helen's dynamics and of the oscillation in the session between homosexual possession of the mother and heterosexual acceptance. His hypothesis was that Helen was initially identified with the penis of the father, wanting to get rid of the person of the father and take phallic possession of the mother herself, not out of love but out of hate. Helen's sadistic fantasy is of getting inside Ruth and controlling her from inside her body and her mind. With progress in her therapy, he could see the emergence of Helen's wish for acceptance by the mother, who is heterosexual and in a couple relationship. Despite difficulty tolerating Ruth's tie to her husband, Helen also wants his acknowledgment. In the transference, Helen wishes for a father who offers membership in the family and longs for Ruth as a heterosexual mother. In this session, Helen oscillates between the two transferences: a homosexual wish to possess Ruth and a heterosexual wish to be included in her family.

The chair thanked the discussant and the large group for their comments and suggested that Ruth continue with the second session.

The Second Session

Ruth resumed, "That first session had taken place on Tuesday. The second session, which I will present now, took place on Thursday, two days later.

"Helen began talking about a public holiday coming up in two weeks' time. She said to me, 'I've been thinking about the week of Thanksgiving. I get so confused about my response to this. On the one hand, I want to see you, and on the other hand, I just want to quit. I am thinking about this in black and white.'

"I said, 'My being gone makes you anxious.'

"Helen said, 'I am thinking in the waiting room, "Why am I here?" I am aware of how dualistic this is, cling versus don't cling. I can't run anymore. Nothing curbs this feeling. Yet if I quit, I seal my fate. I'm angry that I don't feel more normal.'

"And I said, 'What is your best guess about what is going on here?' I was picking up on something else that was going on in the moment. It felt as though she was not saying something.

"And she said, 'Punishment! The nicer I am, the more pronounced the penance I have to pay for all the negative in my life. Then I say to myself, "This is as good as it gets, and this is where you are supposed to be, you fool!" Punishment I understand better than I ever have, and I feel more of a right for life, but there is this incessant belief that tells me I have to pay and that I can't have the good.'

"I said, 'My being out of the office for Thanksgiving week ties into this.'

"She said, 'Yeah, I need to get it together and leave you alone. I'm *doing* more than ever. Yet I'm thinking of quitting the gym where I just began working out. The trainers made a really good plan for me, but I cut an exercise set short when it gets too hard. I tell myself, I can quit if I want to, or I can go get junk food if it gets too hard. It's the same with my job. It's tedious, demeaning work. It's especially difficult when I'm capable of doing so much more. Yet I'm really not capable because I lack self-discipline and the ability to follow through.' Helen paused and went on. 'I don't belong anywhere. I tell myself that I'll stay and not run away. And then I can't stop myself from eating junk food. It's like a drug. I build this porcupine-needle wall outside myself. Junk food makes the needles retract. I eat until the shell is gone, and then I beat myself and tell myself that I'm a spineless wonder. I'm concerned about this dual picture. If I deny myself the junk food, I spiral deeper into the agony. So, the food always wins.'

"I said, 'My absence brings up painful memories and thoughts about how you'll be with yourself.'

"She said, 'The hardest part is keeping the sense of belonging. Your week away tramples on that.'

"I said, 'My vacation leaves you feeling like I'm leaving you for a week and leaving you feeling you don't belong.'

"Helen responded, 'Yeah, we lose contact with you for a whole week.'

"I felt at this point a sharp pain of hurt and loss, when Helen said 'we.' She uses 'we' when she is referring to an inner child and her adult self. I've never had the sense that she was a multiple personality, but this way that she deals with the needy, infantile part of herself seems so childish and desperate that I feel the pain in it. So, as I often do when she reverts to calling herself 'we,' I had a picture of a small child longing for a mother, pleading with her not to go. I then flashed on a scene from *A Christmas Carol* where Scrooge is looking from the cold dark into the warm family home of the Cratchets, never having known that feeling of belonging. And I said to her, 'And this hurts.' But the difference in saying it this time was that I was actually feeling her hurt rather than feeling I had to keep her from intruding on me.

"Helen responded, 'I don't know about that. I sleep a lot. I eat junk food. That's how I try to numb everything.'

"I asked, 'Is that what you did when your parents were unavailable?' I realized at that moment I was holding her sadness about this because she was fending it off. I wondered if there was any way to help her connect with it.

"She said, 'I used food and sleeping a lot to manage the trouble with my parents. I struggled with living and dying constantly. A glass of water when the pain was unbearable would bring so much comfort. At times nothing else brought comfort. It was the same in my 20s when I was living with an abusive husband.'

"I said, 'And now you see this abuse in how you treat yourself.'

"She said, 'I get sickened by this compelling need to tear myself apart. I eat. I have to do the ritual of eating and driving endlessly, or I plummet into the depths of despair.'

"I responded, 'Perhaps there is something else you would also like to tear apart.'

"She said, 'Well, my rational thinking says I would like to tear my parents apart. But I don't feel this.'

"I said, 'What do you make of this?'

"She said, 'I'm trying to keep the fantasy of the good parents intact. I am thinking about calling them again.'

"I said, 'You want to hold on to this fantasy of the all-good parents.'

"She said, 'Also, I blame myself for what happened.'

"I said, 'You eat to try to control the rage. You try to take it inside, where you can control it.'

"She said, 'When you go away . . .' She paused. Then she said, 'I am thinking that I would like to see you once in the week.'

"This time, instead of seeing her statement as a threat to act out by pursuing me, I saw it as an invitation to explore the feeling. I said, 'What is it like inside to know that won't happen?'

"She said, 'I think of my mom not being there. She was so crazy. Men wanted her. I would beg her not to go to them, but she couldn't be reached.'

"I was thinking at this point that Helen sees me off with a man and that she can't reach me.

"Helen went on. 'She was crueler than my father. She always blamed me for her purgatory. Hell! I worried that I was going to send her to hell! I have so much difficulty being angry with my mom, she's so sick. I tried to get what I needed as a kid. She would tell me how my father wanted to kill me. You and I know how volatile my rage is. I don't want to rage at my parents now. I want to know them as they are now. I don't want to discuss this stuff with them any more. My father is 81 years old, and he's suffered so much. He's carried so much guilt, and I don't want to rage at myself or at others anymore. You know, I don't snap so much anymore since seeing you. I may still do it, but I clean it up and I do it better. The hell I put on myself. I'm worried about wearing you out. It makes me feel ugly.' Helen began to cry, then went on softly, 'Sometimes at night I think about my mother and how much I want her to know that it's okay. But she won't get that. I wake up and I hear her calling me in my mind. For my mom, I carry sorrow and self-punishment for what's happened. She couldn't survive in this world. She chose to escape it.'

"I said, 'My being absent triggers the longing for a mom who couldn't come.'

"And Helen responded, 'With my mom, it was always, "Come!" then, "Get away!"'"

"I said, 'My being here and then leaving for a week reminds you of the old come-then-get-away feeling. And then you imagine yourself eating and pushing yourself away.'

"Helen asked, seductively, 'Can I do this differently?'

"I felt the pull of Helen's wish for me to do something, and instead I wanted her to talk about what she was pulling for. We've had many sessions in which we worked on understanding her assumption that if I truly understood her, I would do something that she wanted and that would solve her problem. I responded by paraphrasing her question: 'I wonder if I understood better, could I respond to you differently here?'

"Helen said, 'Maybe your understanding can help me change my behavior. I'm not wanting you to change. Your understanding will help me change. I get angry at myself, and I always go back to eating junk food and then punishing myself. My parents made us feel like garbage. The internal turmoil was so hard.'

"I said, 'The junk food is a seductive come-let-me-make-it-all-better-and-numb-out-all-the-bad promise. And it works for a fleeting moment, and then comes the away-you-disgusting-thing message, which you tell yourself later when you realize what you've done.'

"Helen responded, 'Yes, yes, the seductive, gutless wonder! I just thought about the nurse at the state hospital when I was 19 years old. She asked me my name, and I said, "Creep." She said, "Great, we're fresh out of creeps today, and we could use some more."'" Helen and I both laughed at this point.

"She continued, 'As much as I think about your leaving, I'm going to miss you for that week.' Seductively but jokingly at this point, she said, 'You're not going to be seeing anybody that week, are you?' She laughed.

'Well, I hope you choke on your turkey. But it's okay if someone performs the Heimlich maneuver on you. I want you to be okay and be able to come back.' She paused. 'I know the intense attachment I feel for you comes from the transference of my mother onto you. In this way the attachment makes sense to me. Even though I don't call you anymore, I have been driving by here more in the last few weeks. Becoming more disciplined scares me, and then I need to hold on more. Symbolically, I'm afraid of being disconnected from you at this point, even though I'm doing much better. I need you now more than ever. Well, time to go. I'll miss you over the weekend.'

"I found that last sentence very moving. I thought she was expressing her attachment and her love, and I felt she was more integrated and accepting hate and love at the same time. And she accepted being dependent. When she said that she needed me now more than ever, I felt glad she could verbalize that rather than acting it. When she said, 'I'll miss you over the weekend,' I could see that she can now verbalize many things she couldn't before.

"So, I'm waiting for questions. Discussion?"

Second Dialogue with the Audience and the Discussant

The discussion following the presentation moved quickly to a consideration of the problems in the transference and in interpretation. Two students began by commenting on the difference in the feel of this second session. They detected a move from enacting to discussing, from the paranoid-schizoid to the depressive position. This movement implied impressive progress but still posed the question of how much and which aspects of the transference should be interpreted.

Ruth answered, "My capacity to tolerate the difficult days in therapy, such as the first session, grew in supervision with David." (It was only here that Ruth mentioned, in passing, that I had been her supervisor.) "When I was tempted to rejoice at the healthier days, I remember him warning me, 'Yes, this is a good session, but there is more turbulence to come.' As someone in the audience said, there was movement back and forth between paranoid-schizoid and depressive positions and movement between splitting and integration in the transference. I felt that Helen was being authentic. She was clear how she felt about me—'I want you to choke, but I don't want you to die on me.' So, yes, I think now that it's okay to deal with the direct transference in the here and now. Before I had supervision, I tried to move out of it because it was like being blasted by a fire hose at two feet. It was very intense and I didn't have a way of organizing my own thoughts about it. I felt fragmented because I didn't know what to make of all this. It has been a gradual process of learning how to deal with Helen's assaults so I can make more interpretations in the here-and-now. The other thing is that as I'm able to tolerate more, and as the therapy is containing more, I am able to be more thoughtful about the direct transference and what it brings up."

The discussant described the back-and-forth flow between raw, unmetabolized elements and integrated thought and feeling characteristic of the patient's style. A faculty member noted Ruth's use of the "fire hose at two feet" metaphor and asked whether this was an indication of countertransference introjective identification with Helen's sexual abuse. Ruth responded that the content of Helen's descriptions of abuse had been vague although filled with emotion, so that Ruth was still unsure about the extent of abuse or whether it had happened at all. Ruth said, however, that she was clear that Helen had internalized an atmosphere of sexualization and emotional abuse. This led to a dialogue among faculty and students about the patient's use of junk food for self-soothing, which was her way of trying to manage her prickliness.

The large group now discussed the patient's wishes to enter and possess her therapist and the oscillations between "good" and "bad" object relating as features of the hysterical organization and of the transference. Applying Bion's theory of beta elements—unformed sense impressions that cannot be integrated or symbolized until they are transformed by the alpha function of maternal reverie—to Helen's case, a student suggested that Helen sprayed her impressions at Ruth in the unconscious hope that Ruth would be able to use her alpha function to give them meaning. Associating to the image of the patient's prickliness in relation to an empty interior, the student recalled Tustin's picture of one kind of autistic personality as a spiny porcupine with no backbone. Another faculty member commented on the countertransference being used as a metaphor for Helen's transference in which she was sometimes overwhelming and intrusive or, as at the end of this hour, more like a modulated stream that could be taken in without the sense of threat. The alternation of exciting and persecuting object relations in the transference—and in the audience's countertransference experience of Helen today—fit with Fairbairn's description of the cycles of rapid alternation of excitement and rejection that result in the hysterical personality and are repeated in the therapeutic relationship.

"Yes," said Ruth. "In the beginning, Helen would spew me relentlessly with material that seemed unmanageable and intolerable. What has changed the most is the way Helen now titrates this in alternation with integrated material. She even seems to be giving me a modulated dose according to what she feels I can tolerate."

In closing, the discussant said, "What is important is to link, for example, the head and the neck. You want to make Helen conscious that she can hate you explicitly without losing you in the transference. When she says 'Come and get away,' she can link both aspects of her affect. You have to keep the pieces that go together and link them."

> Ruth confirmed the validity of his comment: "Helen did say, 'Well, I hope you choke on your turkey. But it's okay if someone performs the Heimlich maneuver on you.' I see that as her way of bringing the two opposites together."

Dr. Thomas noted Helen's courage and generosity and adjourned the session at the time boundary.

DISCUSSION

This chapter shows how the dialogue unfolds in a large-group discussion and amplifies the learning. The chair facilitates a large-group process in which direct questions to the presenter or the discussant lead to dialogue that gradually gives way to multilogue. One member associates to the comments of another, and the presenter or discussant responds periodically to the theme rather than to each comment. These strands from the presentation and the discussion are woven into a tapestry of the patient and the therapeutic process, enriched by concepts of object relations theory. Referring to the theoretical contributions of Freud, Klein, Bion, Fairbairn, Tustin, and others, members link their thinking with the clinical discussion and join these familiar concepts with new ideas presented in this conference and illustrated by the case being studied. In these ways, different perspectives illuminate the case. The many facets of the discussion offer multiple entry points for joining in the learning process, each member coming to the experience from a unique position along the continuum of knowledge and experience.

The diversity of this exercise gives everyone the opportunity to speak or to remain silent. Many students learn better when their own thoughts are accepted into the multilogue. Absent this opportunity, they harbor their thoughts and find it more difficult to take in the thoughts of others. Furthermore, we all have the opportunity to learn from the contributions of students at all levels. Even an inexperienced student often has ideas that are fresh and valuable. In addition, from the participants' comments, we learn what they do and do not understand of what we are trying to teach. We assess the teaching and learning process through monitoring the in vivo exchanges of the group. Even in their silence, students constantly give faculty information that is essential to the integrity of the learning process and therefore to their progress. In this discussion, many students take in what faculty say, associate to it helpfully, and elaborate on it in ways that reflect both prior learning and their independent capacity for analysis and synthesis.

Further discussion then continues in the small-group setting. We now turn to Dr. Thomas's report of the small-group meetings that followed Ruth's presentation. Then we explore the impact of Ruth's presentation on the other small groups. In the small groups, both individually and together, the continued process of learning is displayed for us to study.

16
Reflections on the Presentation

THE IMPACT ON THE PRESENTER'S SUBSEQUENT SMALL GROUP

I (Dr. Thomas) was about to join the small group that Ruth was in and that I was leading. My mind was filled with the experience of having just been in role as chair of the session in which Ruth presented. I sensed that her presentation of the case of Helen had been experienced by the large group as lively and compelling. Ruth described vividly the burdens of treating this difficult, complex patient. She illustrated splitting, projective identification; attempts to control the therapist; episodes of massive regression; splintering of experience; confusional states; moments of compensation; and signs of integration. Ruth also demonstrated her empathy for Helen and Helen's feeling of trauma due to separations from Ruth. Helen's wide-ranging responses to these separations included regression, stalking, impinging on Ruth's life, and other forms of demandingness, all of which presented difficulties for Ruth in her efforts to provide psychological holding and containment.

I thought that Ruth's presentation was well done. It showed a competent, at times elegant handling of an extremely demanding individual. Her demeanor throughout the presentation was relaxed, and she seemed comfortable and in charge of the experience. I was impressed. I also felt a flutter of jealousy. I was jealous of Ruth's comfort and of the audience's easy listening to her. Unlike other participants, I could not simply relax and enjoy the presentation.

My role as chair of the meeting caused a division in me: I wished I could give myself over to a clinical reverie so as to access unconscious material related to the case. At the same time, I needed to maintain vigilance for the needs of the large group, presenter, and discussant during the event. Monitoring time boundaries, large-group process, and the flow of clinical material introduced a transient state of internal splitting of the kind that I'm used to when filling this role but that was somewhat exacerbated because of my additional role as Ruth's small-group leader. I managed, but the effort left me feeling saturated with affect and depleted of energy. I felt glad for Ruth and for myself that things went well. I wondered how it had been for our small group, and I was about to find out.

The First Small Group after Ruth's Presentation

The group congratulated Ruth on the success of her case presentation. I had the impression that the somewhat gushing positive feedback served to hold aggression, envy, and criticism in the shadows. I remembered my own experience of jealousy during the presentation. As I sat pondering the group's as-yet-unspoken mixture of feeling, I also experienced a dilemma about whether to speak for negative feelings: I knew that they were there, but if negativity were seen as coming from me, then the group would have a more difficult time finding it within its own experience.

Competition and envy, which are elements of the problem of difference, surfaced again. Ruth's success fed the narcissism of the group: One of its members had brought attention and esteem to the group, but at the same time the nonpresenting members felt lessened by the reality of Ruth's wonderfully competent presentation. The group sensed that we were not "all for one and one for all." The group recognized that some of us are different and have received less enthusiastic responses from the institution on similar occasions.

Competitive devaluation now came to life aggressively through a projection that spared the group its internal competition by externalizing the issue outside the group. Jenny, the physician member of the group, complained that she felt put down when one of the program directors, a woman psychiatrist like herself, had asked her a question about a psychiatric medication. The group thought that Jenny would have been pleased that her expertise was recognized, but Jenny felt put down by the codirector's lack of investment in Jenny's area of specialization. She was angry that both codirectors knew so much about object relations and so little about medication. Hidden in Jenny's complaint against the codirector was an attack against Ruth for her enhanced status in the large group. Her complaint against both the codirectors as a pair served to deflect intense envy—felt but denied—within the group. Jenny's attack on the couple outside the group protected the group from attacking the couple inside the group—Ruth (as a presenter) and myself (as chair of the session). Ruth and I had been perceived as a couple when we worked together successfully in the large group. Our fertile combination evoked primal scene envy and hatred. The codirector couple was a displacement to deflect the envy of Ruth and myself at this moment in the group. The intensity of the envy of us, however, was also derived from the group's feeling of exclusion from the codirector-couple.

In the next phase of the group, members referred to feeling excluded or diminished by Ruth's presentation. Lila, acting as the emotional task leader as she often does, brought back the feelings of abandonment and loss that she felt at the last weekend conference, when I declined her hug at the end of the group. This memory reminded me that envy of the pair is driven by the loss of self-esteem when one doesn't feel acknowledged or affirmed or can't make a pairing oneself. The group realized that my maintaining my boundary as group leader in not offering Lila a hug left her with the feeling of loss but maintained the group as a clear space for our work. The theme of being deprived by a leader linked up with Jenny's feeling put down by the codirector. I observed at the individual level that Jenny had a valency for feeling put down in relation to the success of Ruth's presentation and for leading the group in this basic assumption attack, and at the group level I noted she carried for the group an overall sense of narcissistic injury. My remark on the central group dynamic was not elaborated on by the group, presumably because they were not yet satisfied that their plight had been adequately given voice or because I had addressed myself too much to Jenny's personal contribution and not enough to the group's dynamics.

Now Theresa indirectly picked up the theme of not being acknowledged. She told the group that she would be leaving a supervision group after many years and no longer knew where she fit in. She implied that she may not fit in this small group either. Her need for status was frustrated by remaining only an equal in a peer setting where she is the most advanced participant.

At this point in the group, I felt somewhat confused by and saturated with the multiple layerings of the group's transference to me, to the directors, and to the institution. The burden of trying to make sense of the simultaneous layers felt unusually overwhelming. Reviewing the process after the group was over, I thought of my feelings as a countertransference to a group projective identification through which the group was trying to tell me how hard it is to do its work. I wish, in retrospect, I could have told the group that I felt their burden, but I could not or did not. If I had, we might have been able to understand the feeling that several of us—and therefore the group as a whole—had of being too burdened to work adequately. At the time, I was not sure why that was so.

My subsequent review of this paralyzing countertransference with the faculty led me to wonder whether the group was identified with Helen's painfully obvious intense neediness. The group members may have been making an unconscious plea to Ruth and me as a pair to take care of their need. This would explain the complaints voiced by Jenny, Theresa, and Lila about failed dependency and the anger against the pair, captured in the complaint against the codirectors. My own inability to give voice to feeling overwhelmed may have stemmed from my identification with Ruth, whom Helen so often overwhelmed in order to feel that she had communicated to Ruth the overwhelming nature of the internal burden with which she lived.

The Remaining Three Meetings of the Group

In the three groups that followed, I could still see traces of the impact of Ruth's role as the presenter. Ruth herself worked, with increased acuity, on issues of envy and admiration—the group's and her own. She paired with another woman to work on the issues of self-esteem that had been heightened by her star turn. As the weekend wore on, the spotlight on her faded. She returned to being the usual group member she is—creatively pairing, supporting others' work, and periodically moving forward in her thoughtful way. Her presentation continued to have a ripple effect, but not one that kept her in the center of focus. Group members took turns looking at their issues of envy, grandiosity, self-denigration, and need for support, but in general the group enjoyed the pleasure that one of our own had performed so admirably and so it entered a phase of solid collaborative work.

THE LEARNING PROCESS IN THE
OTHER SMALL GROUPS

So far, we have followed the discussion in the small group that included Ruth, the case presenter, and Dr. Thomas, the chair of the presentation. Now we turn to discussions of other small groups immediately following the presentation. The other small groups had no reason to focus on the case presentation beforehand, and attention to Ruth's presentation came only in the subsequent meetings.

The Small Group Led by Dr. Dole and Dr. Ransom

Dr. Dole and Dr. Ransom (a man and a woman) were the first to give an account of their small group of members registered only for this weekend. The group began with a mood of sleepy flatness that contrasted with its energetic discussion in the morning. Someone said petulantly that she identified with Ruth's patient. She regretted the tendency in case presentations to blame patients for their difficulties and to treat them with aggression rather than understanding. Another group member was reminded of a patient who had a dream of a being a marsupial on her therapist's shoulder. This patient's primitive fantasies led her to see herself as a baby in the therapist's pouch. The group noted its own quietness and flatness and gradually realized that group members were encountering an experience of loss and separation. In the morning workshop, they had felt that they got something from the guest presenter; however, during Ruth's case presentation, when, as the discussant, he was not in the forefront, they got less of him and his expertise at the same time that the group was confronting feelings of incompetence and hopelessness.

Dr. Ransom said to the group, "Here you can see separation anxiety and loss being felt in respect to the guest presenter. He is there for you functioning in a different role, but as a group you keep him as a figure of fantasy and perfection, and then you miss him compared to the idealized inner object you have made of him. You may feel that this is Ruth's fault. You don't want to attack him, and you don't want to attack Ruth. In that impasse, you are withdrawing, and the group seems flat and even sleepy." This comment relieved the sleepy atmosphere. The group realized that it had been holding back an envious attack on Ruth for being paired with the discussant.

A man said that this talk of idealization and envy reminded him of being idealized when he presented on a previous occasion. He had volunteered on an earlier occasion to present a different case to another previous speaker, but his offer had not been accepted that time because the clinical case slot had already been scheduled for presentation—by Dr. Dole, who was now coleading this group! The group could not recall Dr. Dole's clinical presentation. It was buried by the group's shared repression. The group members did, however, realize that they were using this as a defense against their experience of envy and loss and thereby finding it difficult to learn from the case just presented to them by Ruth.

The Small Group Led by
Mr. Malachi and Dr. Garcia

Mr. Malachi and Dr. Garcia (both men) reported next. Their small group also examined the impact of the case presentation. One woman group member noted that students and faculty were not distinguishable in the large-group discussion compared to her experience in a psychoanalytic institute where she said it was expected that "students listen and faculty teach." Following this comment on the process of the large-group discussion, another member reflected on her own work. Early in her career, she felt she had hurt vulnerable patients by taking aim on unconscious material too early. She appreciated the way Ruth had not attacked Helen and so had avoided eliciting retaliation. The group members then found that they missed the informality of lunchtime when they gathered free of leaders. They became indirectly critical of their leaders, one of whom was like the guest presenter in not being American. Partly this criticism seemed to derive from a feeling of wanting more of him, and partly it seemed to be a veiled envious attack on Ruth for being a competent presenter.

During the faculty discussion of this group's learning process, several dynamic reasons were suggested to account for envy of Ruth. Envy was aimed at her opportunity to pair with the guest presenter, her having an articulate patient who was doing well, which left participants feeling incompetent in comparison, and her gratitude to her supervisor. The supervisor being the program director increased the envy—which was enacted by members' attacks on their own group leaders and on the guest presenter. This idea, which was formulated through the work of several faculty members, is the kind of insight we expect small-group leaders to hold in mind in order to test its usefulness in future meetings of their groups where it might or might not be used directly.

The Small Group Led by Ms. Ford

Susan Ford, who had also cochaired the conference and had helped Ruth with her presentation, reported on her small group of students committed to the group for one year. Her small group had discussed the case presentation only briefly. Instead, the group lived out problems of separation and boundaries (see Chapter 10). The group members connected these enactments to their individual issues and to the struggle in the group between intimacy and separateness. This group began when Ms. Ford entered the room at the time scheduled for the group to begin and shut the door behind her. A member of the group objected on the grounds that another member had not yet come in, implying

Ms. Ford had been hurtful to exclude the missing group member. Without explicitly connecting this matter to the conference theme of separation anxiety that Ms. Ford assumed to be organizing some aspect of the discussion, the group explored the problem. All the group members knew that the door is always shut at the scheduled beginning of the group and that any members arriving late could gain entrance simply by knocking. Why, then, did this experienced group member object to Ms. Ford's locking the door? It turned out that the group member who had raised the objection had come early to the group, then had left the room, locking himself out of the group room a few minutes before the group began. Then he had to find a housekeeper to let him back in.

Group members developed the theme of locking themselves out of opportunities when the key was in the group and in themselves. The closed door, which in a paranoid-schizoid mode seemed to bar entry to the learning task, could be seen in the depressive position as a boundary that made learning and intimacy possible and safe. This was acknowledged by another group member who had come late but who had seen the closed door as reassurance that the group had kept its usual and reassuring boundaries.

Finally, the group explored why the closing of the door had been challenged and discussed at so much length when it was such a familiar procedure, but the group remained puzzled about it. In the faculty meeting, Ms. Ford joined other group leaders in considering this question. Discussion led to the suggestion that the group had joined in an enactment designed to get Ms. Ford to give them a familiar response that would have the effect of reassuring them. That is, they acted as though they were locked out of the learning task without her predictable answer and thereby tried to get her to do the work instead of identifying and working with their own separation anxieties engendered by the missing group member. In effect, the group made Ms. Ford the housekeeper from whom they had to get the key, acting out an unconscious group dependency instead of reaching inside the group's own "pocket" to find it through their own work.

In constructing this hypothesis about the group's dynamics, faculty members called on their shared experience of several of Ms. Ford's group members who, in small groups in earlier conferences, had tried to tempt them with small pieces of action unconsciously designed to get predictable responses. What seemed initially to have been an attack on Ms. Ford through splitting and projection could now be understood as an attempt to get a good, expectable, and reassuring response in which primitive anxieties both about separation and viability could be assuaged. Remembering that Ms. Ford had been Ruth's tutor in preparing the case presentation, the faculty could now see that Ms. Ford had unconsciously been recruited to fill a role in relation to the group similar to the one she had filled with Ruth in her role as weekend cochair: to show the group members how to do the work and even to do parts of it for them.

Throughout the discussion of this group, the faculty could see that the group was primarily in an experiencing mode that did not lead to verbalization and linking of the group process to the themes of the case presentation. Insisting on doing so would have been an artificial, rigid intervention, and Ms. Ford preferred to let the group pursue its own course.

The Small Group Led by Mr. Lang

Mr. Lang, the next faculty member to report, was leading an ongoing group of students in the two-year program. However, Mr. Lang was there as a substitute leader for only one weekend while the regular leader had a planned absence to attend an important family event (see Chapter 11). Therefore, the faculty group was alert to issues of abandonment or loss in Mr. Lang's group. Mr. Lang reported that two members began the group by discussing Ruth's case. They criticized two male analysts who they heard as expressing doubt about the veracity of reports of sexual abuse by patients. (In fact, it was Ruth herself who expressed uncertainty about the actuality of abuse in the case.) When Mr. Lang questioned the meaning of this discussion and the attack on the male analysts for their comments on the case, one of the group members said she felt dismissed and criticized by him. The group then turned their attention on feeling failed by fathers without connecting this theme to the absence of their regular male group leader. The attack on men threw them on a search for a mother within the group. This led once more to longing for fathers with an intensity that rivaled the hunger that Helen had expressed toward Ruth's husband.

This group experienced current separation and loss because of the absence of the regular leader, but this link was not fully made during this session. Faculty discussion made this link, but it was not until later that we developed the hypothesis that the group might be blaming the administration for the absence of its leader—the thematic "abuse" that needed to be understood in this group. The theme was being processed without specifically being named, in the same way that many sessions of psychotherapy may go by before a theme openly declares itself for explicit recognition and interpretation.

The Small Group Led by Dr. Richards

The last of the group reports came from Dr. Richards, a man whose two-year group began with several members discussing the case presentation substantively, thinking about how to work with psychotic patients, and considering whether Ruth's way of working was the best model for all cases. Dr. Richards thought that the discussion was the most sustained clinical discussion his group had carried on in the time they had been together. The group then turned their attention on an absent member who had earlier warned the group that she was not feeling well and might have to miss the afternoon session. Discussing their difficult, mixed feelings about her took them to a discussion of their previously inexpressible anger at others for being absent or for leaving them, including one valued member of their group who would be leaving them shortly. Members acknowledged the relative ease of speaking of their anger when the persons involved were not there. This led in turn to a discussion of how much the group members could square with one another over difficult feelings and how much they thought they could work together to plumb the depths of the unknown.

The specific links between the theoretical content of the weekend, the case presentation, and the here-and-now group themes were not spelled out in this session.

These group reports summarize a variety of ways that groups can pursue learning. All the groups present a blend of learning from the didactic presentation of theory, from clinical case study, and from their own experience. But some aspects of this blend are more prominent in one group, while others are emphasized in another. In some group sessions, there is direct clinical study in a didactic mode, while in another the process momentarily resembles therapeutic process. As leaders strive to help their groups pursue the integrative task, they are supported by the faculty group that works with the program director to clarify themes and links and to facilitate learning in each small group and in the program as a whole.

THE PRESENTER'S REFLECTIONS

I (Ruth) was surprised that my first words at the beginning of the presentation were about my feelings of separation from my seat in the audience, from the safety of sitting among my peers, and from my written history. Acknowledging this, I began the presentation with a feeling of honesty that carried me through the hour and a half. Within minutes, I felt relaxed, comfortable, and grateful that I had been advised against reading the history. Speaking spontaneously facilitated a connection with the case and with the group that felt invaluable for discussing my work with Helen, so that the experience felt rich and complex.

As I now look back, the experience of presenting my work with Helen let me reflect on the ways I had worked to create a secure holding environment for her in which she was able to develop a more cohesive sense of herself and decrease her experience of suffering. Likewise, the discussant and my peers in the group—who were not as shy in offering me feedback as I am when our positions are reversed—gave me insight into areas in which I colluded with her. And I still do. For example, there are times when Helen goes to great lengths to tell me what a great therapist I am and how much she has changed in therapy—which she has. After several sessions in which she attacks and attempts to annihilate me, I find some of these reassurances particularly pleasing. At times, I want very much to believe that I am helping her and that we have outgrown her attacks. The large group kindly pointed out that her insight into my excellence and her improvement might be ways of seducing me into not punishing or leaving her rather than evidence of the miraculous turning of a therapeutic corner. I was able to see how I tended to overlook how seductive she can be with me at times when she attempts to protect herself and preserve my availability. And I began to see my corresponding gratification of her covert seductiveness to feed my narcissism. Since the presentation, this insight has helped me keep more perspective when this occurs in our work, and, consequently, it has reduced Helen's splitting in this area and has increased her ability to understand her fear of my retaliation after her angry acting out.

I would like to add a few more general comments about the experience of presenting during this weekend. There was an exciting quality to the presentation—some of which was personal and some of which related to the type of case I was presenting. On the personal side, I brought a hope that this presentation would be helpful in my effort to overcome a pervasive shyness in large groups. Although one would previously have had to drag comments out of me, I have held a belief that I have some useful ideas to share in large-group settings, and I have longed to do so, and yet I've felt inhibited—even handicapped—by insecurity. Overcoming most of my fears and anxieties within the first few minutes of this presentation made way for a reconnection with some lost and longed-for aspects of myself, including a sense of competence, openness, vulnerability, and relatedness in a large group. This made way for an enlivened sense of myself that let me enjoy relating to the material with the group. Prior to this experience, I had been keeping some of this aliveness lodged in idealized others—for example, faculty and seasoned students—through projection. That is to say, during my presentation I found approval from an ideal object that was supportive and facilitating. I experienced this as a welcome surprise.

Another contribution to the exciting quality of the presentation was related to the case itself. The group's reaction to the intensity and fear that emerges when working with a patient who has so much pain and anger echoed the painfully exciting countertransference I experience with Helen. Additionally, some of the group members were reminded of some of their most difficult cases in which it is common to experience feelings of overwhelming and excessive excitement.

The large-group discussion provided layers of observation of myself in relationship to Helen and in my relationship to the large group. Many questions focused on my transference and countertransference in the therapeutic relationship with Helen. This has kept me asking questions since then. By and large, the questions and comments were supportive and helpful. The group's support made me realize how much I anticipated criticism. This holding environment provided another space in which to think about my work with Helen from many new and innovative perspectives, and it helped me to be more benignly critical myself.

Afterward, many group members spoke with me about their experiences, and some discussed individual cases. Some mentioned that they wanted to present a difficult case at some point in the future in hopes of obtaining similar containment and helpful ideas from the large group. Privately, some gave further insights into the work with Helen that have been extremely helpful in my work with her.

Shortly after the presentation, our small group reconvened. I received much support for the presentation. But I also got confronted with the self-devaluation that I have engaged in over the years by projecting out some of my own good objects. Both the support and the confrontation helped me know myself better and, consequently, helped me understand my work with patients. In addition, the group came back to the theme of separation anxiety by pointing out my own issues of separation, which had been contained in my projecting outside myself any competence and capacity for integration. The work in the group helped me reown aspects of these. As this happened, I could see that the group was using my experience to reown its own competence. Not only was this experience extremely useful in my growing understanding of myself and my patients, but my participation in the work of the group also enhanced the sense that I had something to contribute to my colleagues.

Since my presentation, I have observed continued changes in myself. My understanding of separation anxiety in my patients has been widened to include separation from old, familiar, damaging views of themselves in which they project out the longed-for aspects of themselves and identify them as residing only in others. My own emotional process of refinding and reclaiming some lost pieces of myself has created an experiential understanding of what patients may be experiencing as they struggle with these issues fearfully and painfully. Consequently, I feel a deeper compassion for the difficulty one often encounters in the separation from the familiar that comes with the effort to reconnect with a lost part of one's self.

Finally, the experience helped me realize that practicing therapy can be a defense in itself. Each loss experienced and explored with my patients has the potential to elicit my own losses, with their accompanying pain. When I keep the focus outside myself, I only see the primitive, painful, overly exciting aspects of myself that are lodged in my patients. I am beginning to see how that defense actually keeps reviving them in me. My awareness weaves back and forth between them and me as I see patterns that traverse both my patient's world and my own. This facilitates my increased understanding and empathy—for my patient and for the therapeutic process. As I acknowledge and identify these aspects of my patient, I increasingly see them more clearly in myself.

IV

Leading from Affective Experience

We begin Part IV by exploring the role of the leader in the learning process and conclude it with a large-group discussion of the leaders' presentation of the affective learning model. In Chapter 17, we outline our concept of the role of the chair. We delineate the functions of the chair and illustrate them with vignettes of problems typical of those that a chair must solve to maintain a good learning environment. In Chapter 18, a small-group leader who was also serving as cochair of a week-long institute discusses the impact of his multiple cochairing functions on his role as small-group leader and on the process of his small group. In Chapter 19, we describe the supervisory process that is embedded in the learning matrix, and we illustrate this with an example of a supervisor working in consultation with the faculty to help an advanced student confront and resolve a learning block. Chapter 20 deals with institutional reactions to the codirectors whose pairing is evocative of the internal couple in the group unconscious. Chapter 21 concludes Part IV with a discussion of risks, advantages, and applications of the affective learning model, featuring the two of us as presenters with Anton Obholzer as the discussant joined by the large group of faculty and students. In the epilogue, David Scharff as program director has the last word on the current evolution of the model. The Appendix harkens back to a precursor, and so brings us full circle.

17
The Role of the Chair

INTRODUCTION

As program directors, we have noticed that an effective, experienced chair for a psychoanalytic educational presentation in large-group settings enhances the teaching and learning environment for presenter, faculty member, and student. Few inexperienced chairs take to the role naturally. Some of them struggle to become competent, usually with little instruction, supervision, or literature to consult, and others are oblivious to what is required. Even though the designated chair may be a talented analyst, competence as a chair cannot be assumed.

In our experience, all chairs require a concept of the role, and most of them who want to fill the role competently will require training. On the basis of our study of the role of the chair at lectures during conferences of the International Institute of Object Relations Therapy, we have arrived at a concept of the role of the chair based on object relations theory (J. S. Scharff 1999).

In this chapter, we define the functions of the chair and give guidelines for preparing for the role and carrying the various chairing activities adequately. We recommend a self-assessment review process and illustrate various challenges encountered by experienced and inexperienced chairs. We aim to demonstrate the value of training for the role of the chair in the teaching environment that uses the affective model for teaching object relations theory. We are interested in whether this concept of the role of the chair is applicable in other psychoanalytic educational settings.

THE AUTHORITY OF THE CHAIR

Authority for managing the learning environment is delegated to the chair from the faculty and the director of the program. The chair keeps the derivation of this authority in mind and facilitates the learning task on their behalf. If difficulty arises, the chair is authorized to take a decision and expect that it will be supported. On the other hand, the chair may want that authority reinforced by checking a decision with the program director or may ask for assistance from the faculty to deal with an intruder, noise pollution, temperature control, technological support, or the speaker's unexpected needs.

THE FUNCTIONS OF THE CHAIR

The chair is responsible for creating a good learning environment and is supportive of the needs of the student body and facilitating of the aims of the presenter. The chair establishes a relationship with each presenter that supports the presenter when facing the unfamiliar audience and identifies the students' needs and represents them to the presenter. In short, the chair acts as a link from the faculty and the student body to the presenter. The chair is not the main actor in the teaching event but takes the role of the producer who presents the star and makes the event a success.

To prepare for the role, the chair may find it useful to conceptualize the role with reference to two object relations concepts. These are Winnicott's (1945) concept of the environmental mother and Bion's (1967) concept of containment. The environmental mother provides an arms-around relationship in which her infant can go on being and can grow (Winnicott 1945). In life the infant develops, in therapy the patient recovers, and in psychoanalytic and psychotherapy education the student learns best within this holding environment (D. E. and J. S. Scharff 1987). The containing mother takes in her infant's unthought anxieties, transforms them through her reverie, and gives them back to her infant as thinkable, manageable experience (Bion 1967). The chair enables the large group to perform this transformative containment for the presentation so that individual members of the group can find the concepts manageable and so take them in.

In a teaching event, the "infant" is neither tiny nor helpless, but a large group with students, faculty, and speakers. The caring, holding, and containing functions are done not by a "mother" but by a chair of either gender. To press home that point, from now on we will refer to the chair in the masculine gender. In any case, the chair's role in facilitating the interaction between audience and presenter is equally analogous to the father's role in providing a good context for the relationship between mother and infant.

Although the learners are not infants who need to be coddled, their own internal object relations based on infant experience are stirred as they attempt to master the concepts of early development and to do so in a large group whose dynamics generally include those driven by primitive anxiety. The learning environment has to create room for the expression and reintegration of primitive parts of the self. Although much of this work is done in small groups with a faculty leader, the large group has to be conducive to learning as well. If the concepts presented to the large group are to be thoroughly internalized and not merely grasped on an intellectual plane alone, the large group requires a chair with a good containing function that metabolizes the students' primitive anxieties and with which the students ultimately identify. Once a containing culture is built, it is easier for the chair to work successfully.

The chair exercises the *holding function* by managing the actual time and space and by creating a psychological space for the teaching and learning group. He monitors the noise level and the climate control of the room in which the session will occur. Respecting time boundaries and participants' rights to be heard, he provides an atmosphere of security for thinking aloud together. He contributes to the development of a psychological space for thinking and feeling that leads to understanding for the individual and the group.

Within the secure environment, the chair exercises the *containing function*. At the same time that he is attentive to the details of the environment, he is also drifting in a reverie in which he notes the pattern of the group's response, senses the atmosphere in the room, and monitors his own reactions. He observes and interprets the group dynamics as the group attends to the lecture or participates in the workshop. In this way, unthought action is made available for thinking about how it obstructs or informs the theory and practice being discussed. The chair contains the presenter's and the students' anxieties, metabolizes them, and gives them back to the large group in a more manageable form that advances the learning process.

THE ACTIVITIES OF THE CHAIR

The chair's holding and containing functions are in use before, during, and after the event.

Preparation before the Event

The chair arranges to talk with the presenter ahead of time. In the case of a panel presentation, he will seek out each presenter in turn or else connect with all of them as a group. He wants to learn a bit about the presenter, to find out how to make the introductions, and to establish the content and the teaching format. The chair takes notes on the teaching plan, writes down the introductions for accuracy, and copies the timing of the segments of presentation and discussion both for himself and for the presenters to follow. If video or slides are to be used, he should check that the equipment is provided and in working order.

If a paper is to be given, the chair will discuss with each presenter where the natural stopping places are so that the audience can engage with the material as it goes along. He prepares the presenters to think about the participants in the audience and how to interact with them. If there is any problem with this, he can ask for support from the faculty at the faculty meeting prior to the session. Whatever arrangment is agreed on, the chair will help presenters stick to it. He monitors the rhythm of presentation and discussion using a prearranged signal for stopping in time to make room for each component of the experience. He explains to presenters that this signal takes the form of notices of time remaining at the five-minute and one-minute marks and of announcements given to the audience when just one or two more questions will be taken before the break. Finally, the chair arranges to meet the presenters again ten minutes before the start of the session.

Management during the Session

The Environment

In keeping with the environmental aspect of the role, the chair gets there fifteen minutes early to check with the administrator that the equipment is in order, that there are enough chairs at the presenter's table, that it is set up with water and enough glasses, and that the correct number of seats is provided in a suitable format for the large group. The best seating arrangement for the presenter and chair is chosen to set off the presenter to advantage and yet give the chair full access to the audience. The chair checks the time, the sound system, and the temperature of the room and arranges with the administrator a way to signal the need for any changes as the session proceeds. Then the presenter arrives ten minutes before the event starts. This leaves time to place the microphone, check the sound levels, and settle in. If there is a panel of presenters, the natural relation of each person's presentation to the other; their ages, race, and gender; and the visual impact of how they come across are all taken into consideration in arranging where each one will sit.

So that each presenter and everyone else can hear when a member of the audience speaks, we pass a roving microphone to those who want to speak from the floor. The chair arranges ahead of time with a member of the faculty to pass the microphone for the duration of that session and keeps in eye contact to ensure that person receives communications from throughout the audience and does not overlook anyone. He also arranges for someone to shut the door and manage the lights, the video, and the overhead and slide projectors.

The Chair's Use of Time Boundaries

The chair ensures that events begin and end on time, as announced in the program. As in analysis and psychotherapy, a time boundary provides a secure frame for the work. We find it helpful to have a hard edge that demarcates each learning experience. Participants come up against the time boundary and learn from their reactions. Frame violations, slippages, and deviations can be subjected to examination, as in analysis or therapy. The time boundary serves to sharpen the focus and increase the intensity of the learning process. It is a reminder that our exploration of unconscious phenomena exists within the domain of consciousness and competing realities.

The Presenter or the Panel

The chair seats the presenter comfortably. If there is to be more than one presenter, he introduces them to each other and reminds them of the format, the program outlines, the time boundaries, and the warning system for staying within the allotted time. He puts the lapel mikes on in the proper place for each speaker and checks each microphone's sound level independently. He helps each speaker who is using a projector for slide, overhead, or video check the equipment and make contact with whoever may be monitoring the equipment. There is a lot to do to ensure that the program runs smoothly and that everyone can be heard equally.

Having covered all these points, the chair then has done all he can do in advance to make things go well. There is no expectation that he can or should control everything that happens. Distortions in the frame frequently occur thereafter because of mechanical failure, human anxiety, narcissism, and inability to trust authority. The chair is simply expected to use his holding function to prepare, create, and maintain a good environment that is fair to each speaker and that lets the students use what they are being given for their learning. He is expected to use his containing function to make learning from experience more likely. Whatever happens as the event proceeds is also a learning experience for him in his role as chair.

The chair begins the session on time. After asking for any announcements, he proceeds to make a brief introduction of the speaker and the teaching format, telling the audience when their comments will be sought. With the speaker now holding forth, the chair relaxes into the teaching-and-learning event. While listening to the presentation, he identifies with the learning role, but must not get lost in it because he has to stay alert to the audience's needs. He monitors the environment. Is the door shut so that confidentiality can be maintained? Can everyone hear? Is the light level good for watching the video, for viewing the slides, and for writing notes? He does not fuss over every detail, but if any of these provisions is clearly inadequate, he signals for a faculty member or the administrator to make the necessary adjustment. He continues to watch the time, keep the presenters moving on through the presentation, and make space for audience discussion.

The Audience

The chair welcomes the audience's questions, comments, and critical remarks; reminds them to use the microphone so that everyone can hear; and dissuades anyone from speaking without it while the next person being called on to speak is waiting for the microphone to arrive. The faculty member passing the microphone is an extension of the chair's authority. They work together as a team. The faculty member with the microphone helps the chair by actively looking for the next contributor to the discussion, checking with the chair, who may indicate that person or someone else; and getting there quickly.

The chair's containing function then comes into play. In the first instance, this takes the form of observation. He monitors the flow of the discussion. He aims to make plenty of room for the students to air their views and ask their questions. If the discussion is being dominated by faculty comments, he points that out. He checks on whether all constituencies are being represented. Has there been a run of men or of women speaking? Have minority members spoken? Have there been comments from new members as well as from returning members? Has one area of the room dominated—front or back, left or right side?

In the second instance, the chair's containing function takes the form of managing and reflecting on the anxieties of learning. He maintains the balance between presentation and audience participation. He moderates the tension experienced between differing opinions. He makes hypotheses as to how the emerging pattern of participation reflects the theme. He may present his hypotheses or may ask the group to consider why this pattern is happening. Always, he subjects his own experience to process and review, analyzing his countertransference feelings or fantasies in response to the material of the presentation, the personal style of the speaker, and the audience's reaction to the event that he is chairing.

As the time boundary approaches, the chair returns to his holding function. If the discussion is lively and a number of people are in line to speak, he will warn the group of the approaching end of the session by announcing that there is time for one or two final comments in the large-group setting but that of course participants may continue to explore the themes and their relevance in the ensuing small-group discussion. The chair thanks everyone and ends the event on time.

After the Session

The chair thanks the presenters and gives positive feedback. Any negative response should be mulled over. The chair can decide later whether the speaker wishes to learn from feedback. Even if feedback is sought, it is better to save negative commentary for later, when there is time to work it through. Participants who want a little bit extra from presenters one-on-one may approach the dais with an individual question instead of going outside with the other participants for refreshments. Some speakers welcome this, but may want to safeguard their privacy or their rest. Some of them want to move on with the large group that has adjourned to the coffee room and do not want to feel trapped by an individual. The chair protects the presenters by ushering them to where they can relax, and by bringing coffee to those who prefer to stay and chat at the dais.

Process and Review

The chair learns from the experience of chairing. While working toward an ideal, he will be faced with conditions that thwart his ability to stick to his plan. He will try to hold the line and yet be flexible enough to change when that is either called for or becomes inevitable. Inexperienced chairs need faculty support to prepare for the role. They are asked to read a set of practical notes (or this chapter) that spells out how to create a good holding environment. Process and review after each event develops the containing function.

For his private review of the performance of his holding and containing functions in the role, the chair may ask himself the following set of self-administered questions:

1. How did the session go? Did I observe the time boundaries at the start and end of the event, and did I maintain the agreed pace? If not, what were the forces that made it hard for me?
2. Were my provisions for comfort and clarity adequate?
3. Did the presenters accept my help, or were they too self-directed?
4. Did I feel that I had the authority that I needed? If not, why not? Was it vested in me by the faculty but not by the speaker? Or did I feel too insecure to accept the authority that was given to me? What would help me take it on next time?
5. Did the faculty in the audience support my role?
6. Did I stay in good communication with the faculty member passing the microphone?
7. Did I ensure a broad-based participation in the discussion?
8. Did I use an effective group interpretation to promote participation and focus the discussion?
9. Was I able to be myself, or did I get pushed into being a certain way that I did not want?
10. Did I get defensive? What made me anxious?
11. What good qualities did I bring to the presentation—good framing and boundary control, good containing, enlightening commentary, integrative remarks, humor, excitement, or relaxation?
12. What would I do differently next time if faced with a similar situation?

The chair may find this personal review sufficient. Inexperienced chairs need consultation from an experienced chair to help them review their performance in the role and learn from it. Any chair may ask for feedback and consultation from the faculty as to how he dealt with the challenges imposed by the event of which he was the chair.

CHALLENGES TO THE CHAIR

The following examples are taken from discussion at faculty meetings, from supervision of faculty members new to the chairing role, and from observation of the role of the chair when one of us was in the chair or in the audience.

The Easy-to-Chair Presentation

The room was ready, and the chair gave an easy introduction of a charming, informal type, including a personal recollection connecting him to the presenter. He established the format for presentation and discussion. During a presentation on the absent object, the speaker became anxious that he could not be heard or followed. The chair thought that the speaker might be identifying with his subject and worrying about his own absence, but he did not say so. He simply checked the sound level with faculty at the back of the room and reassured the speaker. The presenter went on to describe inner object disappearance due to aggression. At this point, the speaker asked the chair whether the room was cold. The chair told us later that he had not thought so himself and tended to think, as he had earlier, that the subject matter was having an impact on the anxious speaker. But he decided to check with the audience and signaled for the heat to be turned up a little. The speaker smiled appreciatively and finished the first part of his paper.

It was time for discussion, and a silence ensued. The chair waited patiently for the large group to find its voice. The speaker intervened to ask for a question. The one that emerged under the circumstance of obliging the speaker was rather poorly formulated, and the speaker could not make sense of it. The chair rephrased it in terms that the speaker could respond to and checked with the questioner whether he had captured her meaning, which he had. At another point, the chair helped the speaker understand a question by whispering a clarification to him while the questioner finished his sentence. This could be regarded as demeaning, but the speaker found it discreetly collaborative. In these ways the chair related both to the speaker and to the audience. To fill a silence in the discussion, the chair gave a clinical example of the concept of the absent object and tied it to previous comments from the audience. In this way, he exercised an illustrative and integrative function. When the chair ended the discussion period, the speaker resumed reading from his paper, and the chair checked on the number of pages remaining. The speaker asked how much more there was time for and used the chair to guide him to the end point of the session.

The session received a good evaluation. It was impossible to tell whether the chair's ease and competence was the crucial factor in securing the success of the event or whether this presenter was particularly easy to work with and learn from. Seamlessly working together, they facilitated the task.

When the Topic Reverberates in the Unconscious

The chair was there on time but found that the solo presenter was already there and had "miked" himself. This threw her off, and she forgot to check the sound. The room seemed comfortable, but the arrival of extra people after the session began made it get hot and hard to hear at the back. Her own voice was loud and strong as she welcomed members of the cosponsoring institution whose presence was highly valued. The lecture and discussion for which she was the chair was at the more formal end of our range. She gave an excellent formal introduction appropriate to the occasion and handed over to the speaker.

The speaker preferred not to use the formal podium and chose to sit at the table with the chair instead. She was agreeable to this, but she did not realize that his seating position would compromise the effectiveness of his lapel microphone. So, she had to interrupt to have him reposition the microphone, try to persuade him to use a microphone on a stand instead, swap microphones with him, and eventually settle for the sound as imperfect but good enough. She was right in her conclusion that the talk was audible, but she did not take into account the experience of the older members of the audience and those in the back, who had a hard time straining to follow his complex, tightly reasoned paper. Because of the interruptions, she let him run over the time for presentation by about five minutes, which might have been a good decision since the audience wanted to hear his complete paper, except that the audience was exhausted by listening to faint sound.

Each question and comment from the audience then led to another minipaper from the presenter rather than to a shared, spirited discussion. Near the time boundary, the chair took one last question, which was kept suitably brief, but the presenter responded with a long answer that she had not allowed for. The session was running over and the audience was tired, so she had to find a way to cut the presenter off without seeming rude. He happened to touch on the issue of separation, and she was able to say rather neatly that she would now have to introduce a note of separation to end the evening.

In review afterward, the chair said that she felt fine ahead of time but that as the session progressed she felt increasingly cut off from the presenter. She thought that the topic of absent, destroyed objects, as well as of loneliness and persecution was re-created in her experience of the speaker. She felt removed from him. The only evidence of linking was the connection between him and each individual questioner—dyadic interaction that each of them valued. She was so relieved at these links being made that she failed to comment on the large group's dynamic of using dyads to attack the linking possibilities in the large group. She, and the large group itself, became relatively absent objects. We expect the subject matter to stir the group dynamic, but on this occasion the chair could not interpret it. She did not get support from other faculty members to rescue the event because they were also resonating unconsciously with the internal object relationships. Despite being an experienced chair, she felt challenged by the speaker's style, the formality of the occasion, the formidable presence of members from the cosponsoring institution, and the unconscious reverberations of the topic.

The Chair as a Container for Projections

The distinguished guest presenter was a quiet, unassuming man who was well prepared. The experienced chair had everything ready. Water was available, the sound was good, and the room was comfortable. The teaching plan was stated and was held to. The presentation was of excellent quality, and the presenter left room for the audience. It looked so easy, as if there was no need for a chair. The chair artfully accepted a final comment and gave the participant a clear message as to how long she could take. He brought the session to a perfect end.

Unknown to the audience, the chair was having to manage internal anxieties stirred by the compliant, nonaggressive nature of the presenter. When he was reviewing his experience later with the faculty, the chair said that he had felt overstimulated by sadistic fantasies during this presentation until he felt on the verge of fragmenting. He imagined that the faculty would have to separate him from the speaker and humiliate him by locking him in a padded cell; or, more hopefully he had thought, the faculty might kill the speaker and have him watch her brutal demise.

These fantasies were ways in which the chair dealt with his rage at the speaker, imagined the faculty's response, developed and indulged his fantasies, analyzed them, and ensured that they did not erupt into reality. In this way, the chair metabolized his experience of having his own aggressive internal objects resonate with a degree of unconscious sadism that he projected into the apparently nonaggressive speaker, who, he thought, was unconsciously projecting aggression into others. Whether this thought was correct or not, the chair contained the experience so that aggression did not get projected into the participants, who could then continue their work free of the burden of this dynamic. Of course, another chair might prefer a compliant speaker and might not have these aggressive fantasies. This example is given not to validate the chair's perception of the roots of the speaker's unconscious process but to show the kind of internal work that the chair often has to do to make the session go well.

The Chair's Interpretive Role in Facilitating Discussion

The chair was a man, and the speaker was a man. The speaker introduced the terms *maternal order* and *paternal order* as new ways of talking about primary and secondary process thinking. He held that the maternal order referred to the world of the imaginary and the paternal order to the demands of reality. He said that the name of the father has the power to move the child from the maternal order of language as acoustic signifier and sensuous experience to the paternal order of language as thought. The chair opened the discussion.

Various comments were forthcoming, all of them in agreement with this original way of putting things. The chair noted that all these comments had come from men, and so he asked whether the women had been silenced by what they had heard. This intervention was successful in enabling one woman to find her voice. Another woman who did have something to say indicated to the chair her wish to speak. He acknowledged her and sent the person with the microphone to the back of the room where she was sitting. Another man on the way back to her also wanted to speak, and the chair took him out of turn. The discussion ended before the woman could speak.

The speaker then resumed the presentation. When the next discussion period came around, the chair ensured that the large group did hear from the woman who had lost her chance to speak. Speaking as a woman and a mother, she said she could not accept the validity of the speaker's use of the term *paternal* to signify thought as if *maternal* did not because mothers narrativize their infants' experience and require them to meet the demands of reality as much as fathers do. The speaker explained that he was thinking metaphorically, not concretely, using a time-honored division of attributes. Her point was not argued, and the discussion moved on. Another woman later reported that until this point was made, she had been unable to think and so had concluded earlier that the speaker must be right in attributing thought to the male. The chair's role in facilitating the voice of the silenced women was important in getting dissent out into the open and in freeing other women to think.

On another occasion, this speaker was talking about the public's unconscious perceptions of the maternal and paternal aspects of political philosophies. Although his professional attitude to his material was suitably impartial, it became clear that his personal sympathies were with the liberal point of view. Responding to a cluster of associated comments, the faculty member running the microphone got trapped in one part of the audience to the left of the speaker. The chair pointed out that all these comments were coming from the "left," and she asked for contributions from other parts of the room. The person with the microphone moved away from the cluster and actively sought opinions from other areas. The next comments included views from the right side of the room as well as the left, and a broader discussion of "right" and "left" views followed. The chair's intervention ensured that liberal opinions were not privileged just because they were close to the speaker's own.

The Impact of the Group Dynamic on the Role of the Chair

There was to be only one presenter (a distinguished international guest), the audience was a median group of twenty people, the setting was informal, and sound amplification was easy. The speaker was giving a talk on how institutional dynamics reverberate with serious pathology. There was an abundance of overwhelmingly upsetting clinical material of gripping intensity. The chair noticed that the large group was unduly silent and unresponsive to the speaker's earlier invitiation to interrupt him. He felt that the group was traumatized by the pathology and its devastating effects on the staff of the institution. He thought that he should interrupt the speaker and ask the group for comments so as to release accumulated tension by giving space for reflection, but by then the presenter was determined to tell the whole incredible story. The chair felt that the session was dragging and that everyone was waiting for a pause that never came, but he felt unable to create the space for discussion by interrupting the speaker.

At this point the program director interrupted to speak from the large group. This was a relief to the chair, until the director went on in the same way that the speaker had. The chair was again aware that the large group needed him to interrupt. He thought of saying, "We need to hear from others now," but he did not give voice to this thought. He realized that he was enjoying the director's comments for himself and so overlooked the responsibility of moderating the discussion in his role as chair. He did not want to risk interrupting, only to find that the group remained silent and unresponsive as before. He realized that he had been worried about a void and had been happy to let the speaker and the director fill it with their interaction, but at the same time he felt excluded by their pairing. Like a child, he was waiting for parents to make the hurt go away.

Having analyzed his submission as being due to his entrapment in an oedipal dynamic, he recovered his effectiveness as the chair. He found it easy to interrupt the director tactfully, and then made a lively intervention on behalf of the large group, which created a space for teaching and learning together in group dialogue. The group recovered from its stunned silence, enthusiastically related to the clinical and institutional material, and got excited by their discoveries. The chair ended the session on time, he thought. Caught up in the excitement, however, he had run over the time boundary by a couple of minutes, evidence to him of a rebound phenomenon in which he escaped from the triangle and appropriated the two extra minutes as a token of the lost space he wanted to recapture.

An Attack on Female Authority in the Role of the Chair

The following example comes from a conference cosponsored by two institutions that had shared interests, but had different cultures regarding teaching method, management of boundaries, and the value of group process.

The chair of the panel to be described was experienced and had prepared well. She was the only woman on the dais, chairing a group of male presenters who had been the featured speakers in the events of the conference that day. The panel was lively and excited a rush of responses from the audience, but only one of them came from a woman, who may have been able to speak because she had the authority of being a designated speaker the day before. Men on the panel and men from the floor all seemed to be trying to say as much as possible in the short time remaining. Toward the end of the event, yet another man indicated his wish to speak from the floor. The chair was hoping to find a female contribution that would bring balance to the discussion, but there was no woman waiting, and so she accepted his contribution.

The man's comments were complimentary, challenging, and excellent. But he did not stop. He went on at length to restate points from his paper the day before. He had had his turn as a speaker to present his views individually from the podium, and now he seemed to want to be on the panel this day as well. The chair was aware that this man had taken up more than his share of the time for audience participation and that his was the last in a long line of male comments that had received enthusiastic responses and rebuttals from the male members of the panel. Other men on the panel responded to his overtures and entered a heated debate, excluding other opportunities for audience participation.

The woman chair said that she felt that this was like a lemming rush-along toward the end of the panel event and that this dynamic might be silencing the female voice. She asked for another comment from a woman to add to the only other female comment. No woman was forthcoming, and so the chair planned to move on to the men who were waiting at the microphone. She announced that she would have time for two more comments from the floor, and she named the two men who were in line to speak.

Ignoring the authority of the chair, the voluble man insisted on his right to keep speaking from the audience. He talked over her as she made her observation, her request, and her announcement. As one of the designated speakers and as a member of the cosponsoring institution, he shared with faculty the responsibility of considering the needs of the whole group. She asked him to let her move on to hear from the two men in line, but he continued to speak about his ideas on the real object versus the split object.

The chair thought that he seemed to feel that his comments were more important than others he had not yet heard. She noted the content of his remarks on splitting and reality and thought that he was enacting the defensive process he was harping on. Her comment from the chair had been designed to reverse the splitting process that was occurring between men and women, between designated speakers and audience members, and between idealized objects and real objects rather than to allow him to enact and perpetuate the split. He made that difficult for her, but eventually she enabled the other two men to make their comments from the floor. Almost at the time boundary, the chair reasserted her role, thanked the participants, and brought the event to a close.

The chair later reported that she felt that the panel had become a runaway train fueled by male competition and envy of prominence and that she had had to accept defeat. She noted the men's difficulty in respecting her female authority, and she regretted her inability to make more space for comments from the floor, especially from women. She wondered whether her role as chair was being experienced negatively by the women and whether this was why they were not participating. Perhaps the women in the audience did not want to feel run over, as she did. Perhaps they did not get enough leadership and support from her. Perhaps they envied her position among the men and enjoyed watching her being beaten. Whatever the unconscious dynamic, without respect for the chair the panel resembled a competitive situation, such as a dysfunctional family dinner table, where the loudest, fastest talkers dominate, many of them men, and the female element is reduced to a silent audience. The chair did the best she could and accepted defeat gracefully, a position from which she and others could still learn.

Any of these factors may have been relevant. But faculty members from her own institution pointed out to her that lack of respect was not specific to this female chair. No chair in that conference had been fully vested with authority because of differences in the cultures of the cosponsoring institutions. Lack of consensus about the need for a firm frame with consistent chairing had surfaced during the preparation phase and could not be resolved. Some members of the panel from the cosponsoring institution were not in agreement with the need for speakers' sharing time with the audience or for attention to the time boundaries. Some gave lip service to it, while some held it in contempt. Others truly might have been in agreement theoretically but either could not make the personal commitment to preserving good boundaries or did not have the experience and training to follow through on supporting a firm frame.

Good chairing depends on a shared culture of acceptance regarding the basic principles of contextual boundaries and management of the self in the teaching-and-learning role. This agreement has to be continually reaffirmed in action by the support of the faculty during each event. In the absence of that support, there is no delegation of authority. Then good chairing is impossible.

Transformation by Support for the Chair

The distinguished guest presenter was to give a workshop on theory and practice. The chair had discussed the format with the presenter and learned that he planned to read straight through thirty pages of closely argued text. When the chair presented the plan of work at the preceding faculty meeting, the faculty responded with suggestions for improving the group's access to this material. We understood that the speaker needed to rely on the written word because he was not a native English speaker, but the faculty advised no more than seventeen pages for this ninety-minute workshop. They reviewed the thirty pages and gave alternatives for how to cut the paper. The chair agreed with their plan to edit the paper and to break it up into three sections, each to be followed by discussion, but when the presenter preferred to keep all thirty pages, the chair gave in again. The faculty asked the director to intervene. With his support, the chair explained the reasons for the change and insisted that the faculty's carefully argued plan be followed in order to improve the group's ability to take in the presenter's excellent material.

The chair had read the practical notes on the role of the chair issued to all inexperienced chairs, and he took the role seriously. He had spoken in advance with the presenter and arranged to meet him ten minutes in advance of the time of the presentation. The chair himself was there fifteen minutes ahead of time, and this gave him time to prepare the room. He tested the sound and ensured that the quality of amplification was excellent, an important point when the presenter is an older person with a small voice, especially if he is not a native English speaker. The chair began the session with a clear announcement of the plan of work, the presentation being in three stages with discussion between them. He invited the large group to join in debate at those times. The chair kept the presenter informed of time boundaries and moderated the discussion so that it did not invade the time allotted to the presenter.

In review afterward, the faculty agreed that the intervention by the chair described previously had transformed the effectiveness of the teaching. This example makes the point that the function of the chair is crucial for getting the most out of a presentation. In presenting a guest speaker, the host institution is not creating a space for a performance that bears no relation to students' needs. On the contrary, it is up to the chair to educate the presenter in the institution's methods and learning objectives. Then he must work to see how much accommodation can be made to the speaker's style and still get what the faculty wants for the students. If the speaker remains uncomfortable about the chair's expectations, the chair yields. Usually, however, the chair can help the presenter shift his style to allow for more discussion if he makes provisions that help with the anxieties that a free-form teaching and learning situation may provoke in some who are not used to it. In other words, the chair negotiates the relation between self and other in the teaching and learning context.

CONCLUSION: THE NEED FOR THE CHAIR

This chapter aims to draw attention to the value of the role of the chair and to demonstrate the effectiveness of training for functioning well as chair. The role of the chair is primarily one of creating a good psychological holding environment and containing anxiety for the presenter and the large group. Specifically, the chair is there to help presenters put forth their views clearly, to make a bridge between their teaching objectives and the goals of the host institution, and to reach the students. The chair also helps the students interact with the material and to argue, comment, and discuss the diverse views expressed in the large-group setting. The chair represents the faculty and the director in establishing the context and setting the focus on the educational objectives to be met. Through sensitive, clear management, the chair role embodies the institution's primary tasks of teaching and learning. To avoid feeling overburdened by this responsibility, the chair can get support and authority from remembering that he is there as a representative of the faculty's teaching and administrative role and of the students' learning role. An effective, experienced chair is invaluable in enhancing the teaching-and-learning environment for presenter, faculty member, and student.

18
The Small-Group Leader as Chair

INTRODUCTION

I was the male cochair of the six-day institute Family Therapy with Young Children. At the same time, I was one of the two small-group leaders. Like the other small-group leader, also a man, I presented a clinical case for consultation by the guest discussant in the median group attended by the members of both small groups. Unlike me, he was new to the role and did not have additional responsibilities of an administrative nature, except that he chaired one teaching session to learn the role of chair.

The other cochair of this institute on family therapy was Dr. Jill Scharff, who, with Dr. David Scharff, is also the codirector of the host institution. Jill Scharff was responsible for the family therapy curriculum, program design, and assigned readings. She taught once each day, but, unlike me, she was not present for every event, and she was not a small-group leader. She served as a consultant to the two small-group leaders and monitored the group process in relation to the learning objectives of the institute. She followed the progress of both groups and their relation to each other and to the faculty, a role essential to understanding the total impact of the institute.

This six-day institute was attended by sixteen students. The length of time allows for immersion, while the limits on time, size, and topic create intensity and focus, principles outlined in Chapter 5. The design makes for a powerful group experience. The members of the small group met together for eleven sessions, and for the rest of the time they joined with the other small groups in a median group setting. There they attended theory lectures, clinical case presentations, and video vignettes. They discussed theory and technique and gave examples of clinical applications. In two plenary sessions of the median group, they reviewed the quality of the learning experience.

For the purpose of this chapter, however, I will ignore the experience of the other small group in order to focus on the experience of the small group that I led. As cochair of the institute, I was managing time and space boundaries, chairing, teaching, and arranging social life as well. I was constantly aware of having many other responsibilities in addition to leading this one small group. In this chapter, I want to explore the effect that my multiple roles had on my effectiveness as group leader and on the functioning of my small group.

THE COCHAIR'S MULTIPLE ROLES

In my role as cochair, I had the following tasks. I participated as a session chair for several presentations by other faculty. I presented a family case for consultation by the guest speaker. I participated in an experiential play exercise led by Dr. Jill Scharff. I was discussant of a play-age family video presented by Dr. David Scharff. I also cochaired the plenaries, where members can discuss any aspect of the week's experience. I had evening social responsibilities for the participants in both small groups because many of them came from out of town. Along with my cochair, I hosted a potluck farewell party and arranged a theater and dinner outing to which we drove some members. I arranged a bookstore outing and drove a few members from both small groups to that and to the theater. I was glad to carry out these tasks, and they did not seem too much for me to do, but they stretched me beyond my comfortable, familiar role as small-group leader.

All these roles and activities outside the small group built up expectations, consciously and unconsciously, that became charged with affect in the small-group meetings, and this determined how I performed and how I was utilized. Members' experiences were more difficult for me to process when they and I also had to cope with my realities and behaviors in various roles as cochair. Reactions became blurred and distorted because of regressive pulls. Experiences were harder to formulate until this dynamic was fully recognized. When a small-group leader functions in multiple roles, his small group's experience of him in these other roles stimulates unconscious basic assumption functioning that both resists and illuminates the learning task.

As cochair, my wider institute participation had important learning consequences for the small group. My various roles were not incidental to the group experience; nor were they entirely central in a conscious sense. The group's reception of material presented in the institute teaching events blended with the group's experience of my multiple roles, and the two aspects merged in the group unconscious. At some points, the variety of my roles and institute tasks became a burden for my small group in that multiple transferences to me emerged in connection with the parts I played in the larger institute structure. The small group had to make a considerable effort to process my influence on their learning in addition to mastering material presented in the planned program.

Before considering further the impact of my multiple roles on the small group, I will describe the kind of personal reactions that the small group typically has to come to terms with during a weeklong institute.

PERSONAL ISSUES AND THE SMALL-GROUP LEARNING TASK

Intrapsychic and interpersonal issues can prevent learning. If they are not dealt with, distortions occur in the small group, as may fusion or fragmentation. When members become too preoccupied with internal issues, the group's capacity for integration shrinks. Then the small-group leader has to help the group resume its task. He may interpret the flight from the cognitive and draw the group back to discussion of the material that was presented. He may offer containment (Bion 1967), by which I mean that he will try to process the unthought anxieties and give them back to the group in a form that is thinkable. He keeps the balance between cognition and affect.

Group members may have had minimal exposure to an affective group process model. They attempt to change the group to one with a task that they know better, such as a therapy group, a reading seminar, or a case conference. The more sophisticated group members quickly decide that this new group must be what they remember as a Tavistock process group, and they attempt to get the leader to inhabit what they experienced as a withholding stance. Added to this general disorientation, their leader's ability to contain the initial anxieties of joining in the group task stirs members' concerns about how good they are at containing anxiety as clinicians in practice.

Facing the challenge to their clinical and theoretical knowledge, the demands of time-intensive learning, and the stress of leaving behind their personal lives and practices, small-group members feel exposed before their peers and small-group leader. They may feel unduly dependent on the leader for guidance and for teaching. Some of them may wish to have a special relationship with him apart from the rest of the group. Sometimes they deny their dependent feelings and fight against the leader as an authority figure instead of working with him in the learning task. They may wish to flee the task or to fight to change it into something more manageable.

In an institute where the topic is the family, anxieties about their own multiple roles—as mothers, fathers, sons, daughters, professionals, and students of family therapy—are compounded in a small-group setting. In addition to this, the members feel the powerful unconscious pulls of child and family traumata stimulated by the material in the clinical cases and by the size of the small group. They may feel helpless, incompetent, or too stupid to think their way through the experience. All this is relevant to the learning task, but at times such experiences can be used in the service of defeating it.

The integrative task is quite daunting, for it requires members to express and discuss all the elements of their experience as central to processing the learning experience.

Dynamics Altered by the Leader's Multiple Roles

Leading the small group and at the same time functioning as the cochair of the institute, I noticed that the usual small-group dynamics of fusion, dependency, fight/flight reactions, and pairing were complicated by the small group's preoccupations with how I functioned differently than the other group leader in being the cochair. The group's complex response to my multiple roles were not simply an interference with the smooth running of the group. It was an additional object for study and so became an integral part of the affective learning experience. All elements of a group's experience become objects of study. This element was particularly relevant to the study of parental administrative and educative roles when the topic being addressed was working with children in family therapy. Because of my small group's experience of me in diverse roles and my own response to increased responsibility and visibility in the median group, the members had to deal with increased intensity of affect and consequent pressures on them and me.

GENERAL REACTIONS TO THE
LEADER'S MULTIPLE ROLES

In my small group, the members focused on internal group matters as a defense against having to share me with the larger institute, where I cochaired, and where I did not behave as a constant object devoted only to my own small group (unlike the other small-group leader). The group experienced conflict over the wish to idealize me because of my importance and the fear of not having enough of me. The group members wondered whether I would be lost to them through my availability to the other participants. They competed for one-on-one attention and tried to get more time with me during the breaks. They experienced envy of the members of the other small group for having a devoted leader with a more circumscribed institutional role and yet pitied them for having the less senior leader. They were angry when the other small-group leader appeared to enjoy his participation in a large-group event that I was not chairing.

The tendency to try to possess me may have been driven by the clinical material being presented, in which several of the families being discussed were deprived of attention from fathers who were portrayed as troubled, distant, and not attuned to the family needs. The clinical cases described or presented on videotape showed families and therapists dealing with the unresolved grief that follows suicide, the horror of Munchausen by proxy syndrome, the puzzle of delayed development in an adult child, and the destruction of damaged parental and marital couples. In the median group discussion, members struggled with disillusionment and wondered aloud whether they could ever imagine themselves being therapeutic in the face of deeply scarred couples with disturbed young children. The more intimate level of discussion possible in the small group revealed the extent to which the group resonated emotionally with the affects of disturbed children, couples, and families and developed strong countertransferences to the clients and their therapists.

In the small group, conscious and unconscious issues created a group transference to me as a longed-for, depriving, and feared father. Group members consciously longed for a good pairing between father and child. Individuals repeatedly chose to sit in my seat moments before beginning group sessions, as if unconsciously climbing on my lap. At the same time, each individual dreaded the consequences of sitting in my place. Longings to pair with me and be my mate re-created a small-group version of the male and female pairings that they had seen me engage in with some of the other presenters and with my cochair.

The group suffered feelings of fragmentation in response to the sense of ambiguity surrounding my role as cochair. The members became regressed and hostile toward me. My natural aliveness split into two parts—hyperfunctioning on the one hand and deadness on the other. The group members idealized me and the group itself and then denigrated themselves and me, an attack on the idealization process itself. Annihilation anxieties manifested as destructiveness of playful interaction and its potential for creativity, sexual energy, and fertility.

From members' recollections of their own childhoods in comparison to those childhoods marked by abuse, neglect, and incest shown in the clinical case presentations, shared experiences of the absence of the father figure emerged. Indeed, fathers were variously viewed as major threats, as persecutory objects, and as longed-for exciting objects. Some husbands and some male clients were perceived similarly.

As these issues were discussed, the boundaries of the group were sorely taxed. The group container was flooded with anxieties needing to be processed. My ability to provide a good holding environment for my group was compromised by my being in my other role. Fear, distrust, and envy of any attempts at pairing with me were heightened. There was a destructive attack on any potential couple the group might produce because any fantasy about "couple" was regarded as being synonymous with family trauma. Safer pairings with group "siblings" were sought instead. But this kept me out of the sibling culture, creating a split in the group. Then the group was like a family without parents, and I began to think of myself as the institute cochair who was stuck in the small group rather than as the small-group leader who could function fully in both roles.

Individual members linking up with me created pairs that functioned like a sexual couple and like a couple with children. I interpreted these attempts to create ideal family types as defenses. I said that they were ways of keeping the institute cases from traumatizing members, repairing the damaged families, and keeping hope for a "sibling" family alive. Members then acknowledged their underlying fear of the destructive aspects of the pairing aims of men and women.

When members eventually experienced a constructive relationship with me, they feared that something destructive might occur and that rivalry would kill off any pairing. They worried that, if members felt cared about by me, longings for the good father would get out of control or become unbearably painful. Talking about the longing for good mothering was conspicuously absent in this group's discussions. Though all but one group member was female, discussion of the need for a good mother was sidetracked in favor of discussions about female independence, leaving their mothers and their homes, and regret over the fragile mother's inability to provide sufficiently for her children.

INSTITUTE SUPPORTS FOR THE COCHAIR

In my role as cochair and small-group leader, I thought carefully as to how I might influence and be influenced by all these factors. Would I be available, would I think ahead, or would I not be paying sufficient attention, being preoccupied with my wider responsibilities? What if I should become over-whelmed by the multiple tasks? Depending on my energy level, defensiveness, and anxieties about keeping my roles separate, might I tend to pathologize? Would I view the group as disturbed if it complained about the institute, for which I was partly responsible? Might I be tempted to label the group as a clinical problem rather than relate to it as a small group with normative issues whose task was to learn from experience?

I used the opportunity to process my experience in a daily meeting with my cochair, Dr. Jill Scharff, and the other group leader. Here anxieties and concerns could be vented, reviewed, and understood or at least tolerated until meaning emerged. During these discussions, it occurred to me that the mother figure, often absent in the discussion of the small group with its male leader, was present in the person of Dr. Jill Scharff, whose principal role was to consult with the two small-group leaders. Her presence behind the day-to-day struggles of the small groups and their male group leaders helped in the running of the institute, much as a traditional family runs when the mother engages in a work pairing with the father, who is carrying the burden of providing. The arrangement was also reminiscent of the best kind of divorce in which former spouses work diligently on behalf of the children's needs in cooperative co-parenting. It brought to mind a related family model, one in which the father or mother is frequently away from home on business and constantly communicates with and updates the other on the family's behalf.

The cochairing team of male and female working together and separately was effective in containing institutional anxieties, in stimulating transference experiences to parental couples, and therefore in facilitating the learning task posed by our group affective model for teaching and learning psychotherapy with families.

TWO SPECIFIC RESPONSES TO THE LEADER'S MULTIPLE ROLES

Here are two illustrations of the effects of my multiple roles on the small group. The first example features the use of my small-group leader's chair and the seat next to it to express group dynamics in response to my role as co-chair of the institute. The second example shows how the group's deadening of my containment capacities was positively influenced by my presentation of a family case to the median group, an event that introduced me in yet another role.

The Use of the Small-Group Leader's Chair

The median group had listened to a presentation by Dr. David Scharff, the other codirector of the host institution, who was a guest teacher in this institute on family therapy. He showed a video of his consultation with a family—consisting of a mother, father, three young girls, and a baby girl—who sought his help because of one girl's premature sexual activity, shameful silence, and depression. The girls shared a hunger for a more active fathering presence and experienced their mother as unavailable and somewhat paralyzed. Most institute participants were also female and tended to view the family through identification with the girls. They were most concerned with the father, whom they experienced as stiff, dead, unavailable, and likely to foster sexual preoccupations in his daughter.

> In the small group that followed this presentation, a female member had taken the chair that I usually preferred for myself. She became embarrassed at her position and got up as soon as I entered. Attempts to discuss this initially brought blank stares and a few giggles. The members went on to describe their own clinical cases of families like the one on the video, and they shared personal vignettes of life with overbearing fathers or of moving from post to post in a family with inadequate support. They touched on themes of premature teenage sex, problematic boundaries, secrets about sexuality and aggression, and fear of parents' lack of approachability, lack of understanding, and likeliness to retaliate.
>
> The group questioned whether I would do more to provide comfort for them than they had seen the family get. They wondered whether I would hang back or move in too quickly. Remembering her emotionally distant father, one group member cried openly and reached for tissues, much as the young women in the family on the video had done. The boyish looks of the mother and two of the girls on the video reminded another woman of her clinical work with a boyish woman. The group member said that this client had unconsciously filled the place of her twin brother, about whose death at birth she had not been told. Another, who worked with abused children, sadly expressed how her feelings get paralyzed when fathers come for therapy. As she told us how she could not reach out to them, she realized how over-identified she was with the hate coming from their deprived or neglected wives.
>
> Group members also talked about mothers in negative terms. They felt that mothers were weak and required their daughters to protect them. They

resented mothers and at the same time feared leaving them and losing their love. They saw female children as depressed and frightened of their dependency needs and therefore having to act out to be seen and get the attention they need. Then turning to fathers, they found them absent, aggressive, stiff, or dead.

As they spoke, I kept thinking of the group's longing for emotional bonding with a safe paternal object. Could the filling of my empty chair at the beginning of the group mean making up for lost parenting? Could it represent the wish to bond with a figure who was identified as a sexual man and yet was there in a nonsexual role to help with growth and development? Was the group supporting the woman's initiative in taking my seat because through her the group could express its wish to have its desire satisfied by bringing together a male-female amalgam in the leader's chair? Was the group unconsciously trying to create a male-female pair to make possible a baby who would get held and nurtured by everyone in the group? The group had agreed that this had been the unconscious function of the baby in the family video. I now thought that the group might be identifying itself as a baby to get unspoken needs met.

I was able to have all these thoughts but not to respond as the group needed. I felt deadened. I felt like the father in the family—able to be thoughtful about his family duties as a parent but unable to be there for them emotionally. Being the institute cochair as well pushed me to experience role strain that I had not had in previous small groups. I now felt perceived as an absent male authority, as Dr. David Scharff had been experienced, and I identifed with the perception. I felt anxious about when to interrupt the flow of the abreaction to the video and whether to interpret the transference to me as a stiff father.

Speaking from my experience of helplessness, I decided to comment on the traumatic effects of the video and the members' identification with the helplessness of the teenaged daughter. I said that I felt that I was being asked whether the group was in safe hands in terms of both the family in the video and the group in the group room. One of the women in the group held this remark in contempt. She said that I was lecturing the members when they wanted to be cared for. In fact, she said, I was not there! She insisted that the trouble with analytic work is that it is too cognitive and that people want empathy.

The group did not concur with the woman's objections and said that her comment was uncaring in itself. The group silenced her and yet unconsciously seemed to be in agreement that empathy was lacking in men in general. The members went on to express the view that men are burdens on women, who hate them for giving them children to raise alone. United in anger at ineffective fathers, the group was developing a transference to me both as a man who lacks empathy and as a woman who has been left with the children and hates her role as leader.

The only other male member of the group was sitting apart with a space between himself and the rest of the group. He raised the issue of sexuality by sharing a fantasy of having sex with the five women members. He realized that this was his incestuous identification with the longings of the teenager in the video, who was preoccupied with sex as a substitute for parental nurturing. He admired the liveliness of the women in the group, and he found that it was promoting erotic feelings in him. I asked whether he was bringing in sex to stimulate a discussion of longings that he alone felt or whether these were longings stimulated in other group members. No one else picked up the theme. The man went on to say that he was feeling tired and cut off. He was thinking about his wife, who was in the other group, and about his adolescent daughters, who were quite a challenge for him. It was so much easier to be a baby, like the one on the video, who had only to raise her arms or show distress to get noticed by her sisters.

I mentioned that the whole group seemed to be wanting me to notice their needs and not be a stiff or dead father to the group or a resentful mother. I said that I thought that the group's filling an empty spot by sitting in my chair was an indication of the group's longing to have something of me. Following my intervention, the members developed a group concept of my chair as the "seat of power."

The group then went on to discuss faculty members who encourage women to compete and get what they want. The group expressed ambivalence as to what it would get. A lonely quality emerged in the tone of the group. Group reactions to Drs. Jill and David Scharff, who, though married and paired as codirectors of the host institution, came and went separately as teachers at this institute and who were rarely seen together except at the plenary meetings, brought out the group's longings for a fertile couple. The empty chair became the symbol for this fertile couple, idealized but not realized by the group—an empty seat of power. They attempted to get symbolic possession of this longed-for ideal by having one of them take my empty chair for a moment before the beginning of the group.

One member now felt confused by the discrepancy between my consistency as solo leader of the small group and the inconsistency in my diverse behaviors in different pairings in my cochair role. Seeing me with different partners, male and female, produced more of a desire to sit next to me or to take my chair. Some wanted to pair off with me. Others wanted to compete with me. They wanted to associate with my phallic power or to take it from me. Someone else wanted to possess the therapeutic level of efficacy that she now thought I had shown in getting the group to deal with these issues.

In this institute, I was working alone as a small-group leader, and I was paired as the "other spouse" of my cochair, Dr. Jill Scharff. This left the members wanting to be the "other spouse" to me, to take over the "chair" from me, and to leave me alone by leaving a "chair" empty next to me. Their perception that the Scharffs did not appear together despite being married altered the group's image of the ideal parental couple into a frustrating, unavailable couple of two distinct individuals doing their own thing. The small group then viewed me in my cochair role as a surrogate husband and father, keeping the abandoned woman cochair happy and keeping the family together. The group itself was experienced as the single-parent family that was so much a part of some of the members' clinical practices and personal life situations.

As the group continued, however, the theme of missing the mother who could be emotionally in tune was again drowned out by the topic of the missing father. Women could take charge at home, but often they had no choice, because of weak, abusive, or absent men who left them to work things out with the children. Gaining power that way was a troublesome issue for women both as clinicians and as wives and mothers. How could they feel loving as well as competent instead of being powerful and resentful of it? Learning from cognitive and affective experience in the small group and working collaboratively in the median group at this institute gave the women group members a feeling of empowerment that ran contrary to the dominant view of women in the culture of their families of origin and those of the families that they treat.

The group used my shifting roles to explore its relation to authority in the institutional, parental, and paternal sense. The group members could then apply this learning from inside their own experience to their understanding of and work with families of various configurations in different situations.

The Small Group Responds to the Presenter Role

On the fourth day of the institute, I took my turn to present and so filled yet another role in the institute. I described my combined play–talk–draw approach to therapy with a family with two latency-age sisters. The artwork was vivid and revealed a good deal of the family unconscious. For example, one drawing portrayed the child's preoccupation with her mother's genitals as dark, robotic, and deadly depressing. The progression in the children's artwork reflected change accomplished in subsequent stages of the therapy.

> In the group session following the case presentation, there was discussion of the deadliness of depressed mothers and the distancing behavior of husbands and fathers. In contrast to her view of the parental sexual relationship as robotic, the index child's liveliness impressed the group. Several members who had been struggling with whether I could be emotionally present as leader of the small group opened up with praise and delight at how warm and engaged they saw me in my role as therapist with the family I had presented. One said that warmth was a gift that the children were receiving in therapy. Another said that she saw another side of me, as a caring and loving man with the girls. A particularly pessimistic member who had been severely critical of me remarked at having a new take on my capabilities for passion and presence. She cried, feeling that she had been tough on me during the week. She now felt that her harsh attitude was undergoing a change. The group was admitting to having loving feelings about me, fully expressed without inhibition or despair. There was powerful identification with the needs of the children—to be attended to, to be nurtured by two parents—feelings engendered by a difficult family therapy case but one with a hopeful outcome.
>
> The group felt possessive of me and proud that I was their leader. I noted that my role as presenter and the image of me as a therapist had accelerated group movement to the depressive position. Members asked me how I had received their responses. I thanked them for their comments, which were helpful to me, and I appreciated their praise. I felt proud of their input at the presentation, and I was pleased by their willingness to share with the larger group. The group noted its emotional impact on me, the supposedly distant and impervious leader.
>
> The group accepted my case presenter role much more easily than my cochair role. The experience improved their ability to integrate their perceptions of me in the role of authority as cochair. The group's shift to the depressive position enabled me to escape from the projection of stiffness and deadness with which I had been struggling. My gratitude at being released from the stiff, dead projection was profuse. It revealed to me the strain that I had felt in broadening my range to encompass the multiple functions of the cochairing role.

The institute was coming to an end the next day, and in this penultimate session the group used its experience of me as a presenter to resolve ambivalences about me as a small-group leader and cochair. Members agreed that their excitement in responding to the case presentation created movement in their ability to resolve ambivalent feelings and enabled them to let go of their projections of the unavailable object. They also discovered that there had been considerable tension over the wish to be the only child to Drs. Jill and David Scharff (the codirectors), to Dr. Jill Scharff and me (the cochairs), and to me alone (the small-group leader).

The directors' work in managing the host institution and providing for all of the attendees made them seem too busy to be present as the groups wished, and they became a target for dissatisfaction—which they were used to dealing with in role. In my role as both small-group leader and cochair, I became an even more available target for complaint and longing, which, unlike them, I was not used to handling. The sense of deprivation, even while being given to, found its echo in the small group's sense of me as being too busy in my role as cochair. This impression created a demand that I be devoted only to the group members (which I could not do) and be emotionally present (which was a struggle, as I was on a rapid learning curve in my new chairing role).

My case presentation, in contrast, revealed that I could give of myself in ways they could take in as the good, nurturing experiences for which they longed. My having an administrative role emphasized the teaching aspects of my role as small-group leader and drove the group toward a heightened experience of longing for the group to be more like a therapy group. This was a defense against dealing with their ambivalence about me in my ambiguous position as their teacher, colearner, and authority figure all at once.

> In the final small group, jealousy and rivalry about not getting the ideal teaching family of "one-child-with-two-parents" receded. These feelings were replaced by an attitude of hopefulness. The group moved on, from feeling stuck as an overburdened child having to learn family therapy without enough support to feeling like a satisfied child who got sufficient parenting and mentoring from me and my colleagues. Members acknowledged the limitations of their previous way of clinging rigidly to their wish for a couple to show them the way. They now recognized this as a shared, unconscious basic assumption that had been determining their group experience. I received appreciation and gratitude for my efforts in the institute as well as in my role as leader for my small group.

The group moved from a dependent, infantile level to an autonomous, self-motivated one, empowered by the understanding that had evolved through the group process.

SUMMARY

I have illustrated the powerful effects on a small group's experience of having their group leader cochair the institute. Working on institutionally induced transferences at times led me, as the small-group leader and as cochair, to feel guilty that the group was unfairly subjected to forces outside their control, leaving so much more for them to process. One result was that I felt more depleted. At the same time, I felt elated by taking on more responsibility for the institute because it gave me the opportunity to provide more for the participants, extend my own learning curve, and demonstrate my competence. I felt challenged to integrate the group's transferences to my multiple roles into the already full dynamics of the small group. I worked to recover from a slight degree of defensive emotional constriction in myself in response to both the group's projections into me and my own projections into myself as I took on new learning in various roles.

The small-group members worked together with me to understand the psychological relation of the intrapsychic, the interpersonal, and the larger culture of the institute. My experience as small-group leader and cochair was open for examination both from direct observation and from inference based on its effect on the dynamics of the small group. All institutional experience was available for discussion, for obtaining clarification of interpreting and containing functions, and for working systematically through problems of multirole functioning. The small-group leader's multirole experience tested the flexibility of the teaching model and its applicability to the multiple functions that the members attending the institute face as therapists and human beings in their daily lives.

The two illustrations support several conclusions. The therapist–patient paradigm of abstinence, anonymity, and neutrality does not suffice in framing and working with the added dynamics, nor is the idea of participant-observer sufficient. The group leader must first experience the strain of the reality of multiple roles. He can then develop hypotheses about how this pushes on the microtask of the small group. The small-group-leader-as-cochair's "real world" of multifunctioning in a variety of roles presses members to speak to their own multiple roles.

The multiplicity of roles when the small-group leader also serves as cochair is a challenge for him and for the group. Seeing and hearing their leader in role as cochair in the larger institute creates ambiguity for the group. This affects the internal object relations of the small-group members. It produces longings and ambivalence arising from projections fueled by rage at deprivation. It raises issues of competence and adequacy for the members. It requires them to assess their functioning in their own multiple life roles. The usual impact on the learning of the small group in response to case materials, presenters, invited guests, and institute faculty during the week is augmented when the leader also has a cochairing role.

19
Supervision in the Learning Matrix

THE TRADITIONAL MODEL

It is often assumed that the good therapist will also be a good supervisor. A newly assigned supervisor might receive supervision as a safety check on competence, but that is not always required. Once their appointments are made, supervisors do not have their supervision work supervised. They function autonomously in an area that is unscrutinized, almost as separate from seminars as therapy should be. This means that supervision, an important educational activity, is relatively unexamined. Although some supervisors and their supervisees have welcomed the opportunity to present supervision processes for study at international psychoanalytic meetings, most have not. Ignorance of the meager literature and the assumption that skill as a clinician automatically transfers to teaching clinical skill combine to limit supervision to the unexamined arena of the supervisor–supervisee dyad. These factors restrict the effectiveness of supervision, rob supervisors of support groups, and compromise the development of a comprehensive theory of supervision.

In many institutions, supervisors also evaluate competence with a view to deciding the supervisee's future. This can make supervisees secretive or duplicitous in order to avoid criticism or delay in progression. It can destroy individuality, spontaneity, and creativity if students suppress their independent thoughts in the name of getting through the program. In our view, the student is more free to learn if the supervisor is not required to certify competence against a standard. We agree that the supervisor must evaluate and intervene, but without the burden of having a judgmental or gatekeeping function.

THE LEARNING MATRIX MODEL

We propose a model that provides supervisors with a matrix in which to study supervision. In this model, supervisors relate the supervisory process to the social unconscious and the professional culture in which the treatment is taking place and connect it to the supervisee's learning in the total institution. Gains from the supervision experience are then fed back into the matrix.

What do we mean by supervision? Individual and group supervision are learning settings in which supervisors and supervisees focus on the clinical case and the dynamics of the therapist–patient relationship. Supervision establishes an initial condition within which the development of knowledge can occur.

As chaos theory shows, the organism's sensitivity to initial conditions is acute (Gleick 1987, D. Scharff 1998, 2000, J. S. Scharff and D. E. Scharff 1998). The organism develops a pattern that is shaped by its proximity to a more organized system. The organism in turn influences and is influenced by other patterns of relatedness in neighboring systems that are then said to exert a *strange attractor* effect. The patient–therapist relationship brought to a supervision setting comes in contact with the powerful organizing system of the supervisor's greater experience and superior knowledge that operates like a strange attractor. The dynamic system of the supervisee–supervisor relationship reflects the patient–therapist system and at the same time shapes and guides the supervisee's development and its impact on the patient–therapist relationship.

Supervisors have described a *parallel process* in which issues in the therapeutic relationship are reenacted between the therapist and the supervisor (Arlow 1963, Searles 1965b). We prefer to conceptualize the parallel processes found in supervision in terms of chaos theory. We see parallel process as a *fractal*, a similar pattern created in a different level of scale, a dynamic footprint of the therapeutic interaction being described. By its self-similarity to the image of the therapeutic system, the fractal image created in supervision provides a clue to the nature of the therapeutic relationship and the form of the transference and countertransference in the treatment that is being studied. The chaos theory concepts of fractals and strange attractors help us conceptualize how individual patterns of thinking, feeling, and behaving (shown in treatment) interact with others (shown in supervision) and reverberate in systems of mutual influence.

Supervisors oversee the progress of the case and help supervisees extend the range of their clinical understanding and skill. If they discover that the range is limited by a lack of knowledge of theory, they may suggest remedial reading or courses of study, but they do not focus on teaching theory. Supervisors are responsible primarily for providing supervisees with an opportunity to learn technique with a view to developing their therapeutic efficacy. This requires that they think that their work as therapists is good enough to be helpful to the patient, but not optimally so, and that they feel safe enough in the presence of their supervisors to acknowledge those areas of expertise that need to be developed. Supervisors assess these weaknesses of the therapists and find ways of addressing them.

As supervisors, we are there as guides, helpers, supporters, and mentors. Admittedly, we are also there as delegates from the faculty of the institution, and we do need to evaluate the supervisee's learning progress in relation to institutional goals. We must identify dumb, weak, and blind spots for further discussion or analysis (Gross-Doehrman 1976, Szecsödy 1994, Wallerstein 1981). This duality in responsibility sometimes leads to ambiguity and conflict, both of them made worse when supervision evaluations are kept secret and when the institution has a certifying task. We do, however, value the idea of making evaluations, but only if they are standardized and mutual: Evaluations follow a known checklist, they are filled out both by supervisor and supervisee, and the results are openly discussed.

An additional balancing mechanism is provided to counteract dumb, blind, or weak spots in the supervisory function. The supervision experience is open to discussion in faculty meetings. Other faculty members who know of the student's learning style in small- and large-group settings or who have already supervised the student may help the supervisor design interventions to improve the student's application of concepts to the clinical situation.

As supervisors, we maintain a focus on the therapist's view of the patient–therapist relationship. We look at how the patient's psychic structure and unconscious object relations make their impact on the personality of the therapist. We notice how the therapist responds and communicates understanding to the patient on the basis of the appreciation of the transference gained by monitoring and analyzing the countertransference.

Just as the affective learning group may veer toward the therapeutic, the supervision process may by filled with inappropriate affect and unconscious fantasies that are difficult to manage. All the behaviors that arise in the group in response to anxiety about the concepts may be brought into the supervision as well. The supervisee may identify with the patient's unanalyzed aspects and act them out in relation to the supervisor in a parallel process of fractal similarity (Arlow 1963, J. S. Scharff and D. E. Scharff 1998d, Searles 1965b) or may aggressively identify with the admired or envied supervisor and then import aspects of the supervisor into the treatment (Sachs and Shapiro 1976). We find it helpful to comment on the supervisee's behavior toward us if it illuminates or interferes with understanding the patient. Recurrent transference issues toward the supervisor or the patient may need to be referred for treatment if self-reflection by the supervisee is not sufficient to get past the difficulty.

Recognizing the tendency for trainees and supervisors to become vague, abstract, overly supportive, or critical of each other in reponse to the anxiety of the supervision setting, Szecsödy (1997) recommends managing the discomfort by the careful maintenance of the frame of supervision, analogous to the holding frame of therapy. He describes three aspects to the frame. First, the stationary aspect refers to the management of the learning environment in terms of time and place of meeting, payment, and methods of reporting. Second, the mobile aspect of the frame refers to the continuous, reflective review of the working together. Finally, the focusing aspect of the frame concentrates on the patient–therapist interaction.

We enlarge the focus of the frame by reviewing the supervision process at a faculty meeting not only to improve our teaching but also to address the overlooked issue of how clinical skill is learned (Szecsödy 1990). To the supervisor's report of progress and difficulties in supervision, other faculty members add their reviews of the student's way of working in previous supervision or in the small- and large-group at conferences. This generates a broader understanding of the student's learning process and development as a therapist. To our observations concerning the reflection of the therapy process in the supervisory relationship, we add that the nature of the therapist's contribution to the therapeutic relationship is reflected in the small- and large-group process. There is fractal similarity between the supervisee's patterns shown in therapeutic relationships, supervision, and group interaction.

In the example that follows, a supervisor describes her struggle to help an advanced woman student overcome a learning block that is preventing her from recognizing, gathering, and interpreting the transference. The woman is bright and affectively engaged, and so the faculty is puzzled as to why she has a learning block in this one area. We want to show how the supervisor thinks about the problems to be addressed in the supervision and how she is helped by input from faculty who know the student in other settings.

The supervisor describes the stages in the learning process and her use of faculty help as she and the woman work together on their blind and dumb spots supported by the learning matrix. Resistance and blocking give way to recognition of the transference. The example finishes with a brief follow-up on the supervisee's later work with the transference as a supervisor with her own supervisees.

SUPERVISION OF ADAIR

I was assigned as the third supervisor for Adair, a well-trained university teacher of graduate students in an analytically oriented social work school. Adair is highly motivated, well prepared, punctual, and well organized. She is nice, charming, beautiful, and kind. She knows analytic theory, and she is a senior clinician. She is thoroughly professional. Her patients make a good alliance with her, and they get symptomatic improvement. To an analyst, however, her clinical work lacks unconscious resonance. Perhaps others at the university sensed this, for she remained a classroom teacher and had not been authorized to do clinical supervision in the field.

The Faculty Discusses Adair's Supervision Needs

Adair was enrolled in the second year of the two-year program of affective learning and had chosen to have supervision as well. She had been in supervision with an individual supervisor and with a group supervisor. At a faculty meeting, her individual supervisor reported that he was frustrated in his attempts to help Adair. He asked the faculty for help. He said that Adair gave her clinical account in detail and then had nothing else to say. She could not free-associate to the material. He had done some free-association himself to show her how to do it, and she got better at letting thoughts come to her mind. He said that she tended to fill in the blanks with thoughts but never with feelings.

One of the faculty who had been Adair's small-group leader commented that this fit with his impression. Adair had always formulated her thoughts on the concepts clearly and willingly, but she had tended not to share her emotional responses to the clinical material. Although she engaged in group discussions as a valued member, she did not bring in personal reactions linked to the group experience. He remained puzzled by his personal response of liking her very much but at the same time not feeling connected to her.

The supervisor responded by saying that it is easy to connect to Adair through the positive, but the negative is not there to relate to. That is what gives the feeling of something missing. The supervisor went on to tell the faculty that Adair is comfortable with the positive transference that goes along without interpretation but that she does not interpret, welcome, or even notice a negative transference. He said that he had learned that an influential teacher at the university had established a professional culture in which countertransference was always regarded as evidence of the therapist's infantile neurosis. He had the impression that Adair had been trained to suppress responses as if they were improper. The faculty agreed that when therapists learn in their formative years that personal reactions in the therapeutic context are always seen as pathological, it is hard to persuade them that countertransference is the centerpiece of treatment.

Then Adair's group supervisor spoke. In group supervision, he said, Adair was easily the most competent student and therefore was less aware of how much she had to learn than the others. The group supervisor felt that Adair's needs were getting lost. She recommended that Adair end the group supervision and concentrate on individual supervision. But the individual supervisor felt stymied. He valued Adair's mature personality, intelligence, commitment, and university experience, and he really wanted her clinical work to advance, but he felt thwarted in his attempts to work in the transference.

The faculty knew that Adair's working group wanted her to become a clinical supervisor, but no one could imagine that Adair could teach how to work with the transference if she could not work with it herself. The faculty thought that Adair was floating between two supervisions, neither of them taking hold of the problem. The faculty recommended concentrating the supervision effort in one place. They referred her to me, hoping that, with the information gathered from her previous individual and group supervisions and from her small-group experience, I could help Adair fill in the missing piece in her learning. My supervision task was to focus on helping Adair recognize and gather the transference and to use her countertransference as the fulcrum for transference interpretations.

Adair's Supervision with Me

Adair presented to me her individual therapy with two adult cases. The first was a middle-aged mother whose last child would soon leave for college. The second was a 23-year-old woman who had just left her mother to live independently. She chose to focus on the first case, the same one that she had had in supervision with the other supervisor.

ADAIR'S FIRST CASE

Adair introduced the first case, the 45-year-old wife of a German diplomat and mother of two whose only son was about to leave home. Adair spelled out with medical precision the woman's four different types of medication that were prescribed for her during home leave in Germany. These are monitored by a local psychiatrist who also treats the husband. The woman has had a phobia of having sex with her husband since angrily suspecting him of an affair that he denied. If she finally had to be sexually involved with him, she froze. At times of extreme stress, she became quite disturbed. Adair's interpretation was that the woman tended to dissociate and become incoherent when she couldn't express the rage that she felt at her husband's continual lying and outrageous, neglectful behavior.

A Missing Countertransference

Adair had been away on vacation. She began supervision with me by reporting the first session with the patient after her return. She told me that the woman complained that her husband doesn't understand why she is not happy. He doesn't see that it's because of him. When Adair was away, he had upset her so much that she became incoherent. He's always asking why she's still in therapy and asking whether she will finish soon. When the woman became incoherent, he took her to his psychiatrist to diagnose her state of mind and get the proper medications. Adair reported all this to me in a calm, coherent, precise way.

I started to make connections. Adair was away. Her patient became incoherent. Her patient thinks she is angry at her husband, but she has trouble expressing her anger. I'm thinking to myself, "The woman must also be angry at Adair who is away, and so she goes to a man to get the anger suppressed with medications, which her husband wants." I wanted to see whether Adair could make the connection, so I said, "Can you think about it some more? Why do you think she went to the psychiatrist?"

Adair answered, "Her husband took her because he knows the psychiatrist, too. They used to see him for couple therapy, but the husband stopped going. When it happened once before, they went to that psychiatrist because he does a good job and he speaks German."

The more factual answers Adair gave me, the more upset I became. I was thinking that if my patient went to someone else, when I was away, I would definitely have questions. I might be upset to hear that she had trouble. I might be angry that she went to someone else. I might feel unsure of her commitment. I might feel guilty that I had not worked on this beforehand so it would not have happened. But not Adair. She was quite accepting of her patient's actions. Adair was completely calm, and I was completely upset.

I said to Adair, "I find that I'm feeling upset by this, and I notice that you just accept the way it is. I'm just wondering why there would be this difference in our reactions?"

She answered, "Well, he's not going to the couple therapy anymore."

I couldn't see what that had to do with it. I simply asked Adair to tell me more.

She continued, "And I know that the patient has a strong tie to me, so why would I worry if she goes to the psychiatrist?"

I said that since the tie was strong, separation must mean something to the woman. I asked Adair what had been discussed about her impending vacation. She told me that, naturally, she would expect the woman to go to the psychiatrist she and her husband already knew. What Adair said made sense in practical terms, but I felt uncomfortable with the reasoning and the certainty. I realized that my main discomfort was not so much with the specifics of the arrangement as with Adair's total neglect of the issue of separation and attachment.

Adair then explained to me, "The patient likes to talk a lot, so if I'm not here to talk to, she'd want to go talk to the psychiatrist. And, in a way, the psychiatrist is better because he speaks the patient's native language, so the patient can tell him things she might not want to tell me. She forgets she has told them to him and not to me."

There is a split in the transference here that Adair is quite accepting of and not concerned about because she is so sure of the woman's basic attachment to her. Adair is unable to see or to think about any difficulty that mars the positive transference. This is a blind spot.

Adair said, "So do you want me to tell you about the next session?"

And I said, "No, I can't go on. If this happened to me, I tell you, I'd be really upset."

She said, "No, I wasn't. I was grateful there was someone she could trust that she could turn to."

That made sense. It sounded mature and generous. I felt ridiculous. Why was I upset? I thought it over. As the supervisor, I hadn't seen the patient, and I didn't know whether she really needed medications. I didn't know whether this was the best referral for her. What I did know was that Adair was accepting practical explanations rather than searching for emotional meanings. I began to think of how to help Adair get more in touch with the emotions of the transference.

"Tell me again how you understand what is happening," I suggested.

Adair gave me her formulation. "This woman dissociates the feeling from the situation she is in, and she blocks being close. She doesn't want to get too attached to her husband. She can't really express anger at her husband, who is always traveling. It reminds her of when her father left. She doesn't want to suffer. So, really the main issue is a blocking of anger. That's makes her feel crazy. And that's why she takes the medications."

What Adair said made sense. It was not formulaic. It was a sophisticated understanding of the woman's dynamics. I respected that, and it fit with my estimation of her advanced level of training. But it was not emotionally engaged. I began to wonder whether Adair was relieved that the woman has a psychiatrist to go to who will give her a substitute attachment of a person from home and a drug so that she doesn't get so angry that she goes crazy.

At this stage in our supervision work together, the closest thing to an interpretation that Adair reported was saying to her patient, "You were upset that your husband went away, and it felt overwhelming because it reminded you of when your father went away. It's a re-creation of the trauma of that early separation." This seemed correct, but it totally ignored the related information that Adair was gone on vacation for three weeks. The connections were not being made to the transference. I realized that Adair was not having the feelings I would expect a therapist to have. The countertransference was not being experienced. It was being projected, perhaps into the patient and certainly into me.

If this were therapy, I might conceptualize this problem in terms of a resistance or an impenetrable defense against a childhood trauma of some kind. But in supervision, I find a different orientation helpful. I saw Adair's difficulty as a failure of notation (Bion 1962). She could not notate the *selected facts* that I presented to her concerning work with the transference. She could not see that the patient's anger at her husband served to prevent her from recognizing her anger at Adair for being away. She could not notate her own emotional response to the patient's flight to a new object. While unable to notate these facts, she was, however, able to project her countertransference into me. My introjective identification allows me to notate her countertransference and describe the patient's transference, which makes a start toward understanding. But Adair's failure of notation blocks that understanding, and I cannot get verification of the validity of the fact.

Working with my countertransference got us nowhere. It just increased the distance between us. Presenting the carefully thought-out facts did not help. So I had to avoid thinking and analyzing and simply ask Adair how she felt about whatever the patient might say or do.

Blocking the Transference to Absence

In a session after another vacation some months later, Adair was still dealing with the woman's rage at her husband. She reported that the woman said that he was outrageous, that he was like her father, and that she was as angry with him as she had been the day she heard that her parents were to be divorced. Adair convinced me that the husband had earned her patient's righteous anger. But the thread of the associations this time tied the woman's rage to what just happened in the therapeutic relationship, as it always did, especially obvious at times when Adair had been away or was about to go away. Again, it was obvious to me but not to Adair.

> I asked, "Don't you see the thread? The woman is worried that when you go away you'll be leaving her so as to avoid her and her craziness that her husband can't stand and that you'll be going off to have a trip with your husband, who wants to be with you. You and he are the couple she's referring to when she tells you how enraged she was when she heard her parents were having a divorce."
>
> Adair replied, "Well, that's interesting to think about, but I'm not convinced. Because when her husband is away, she feels free."
>
> I thought to myself, "When Adair is away, she must imagine that the patient is feeling free. Therefore, she won't have to feel guilty. She can't imagine herself being with her husband causing this reaction. So she blocks the communication and blocks the connection."

Although I could think my way through this more easily at this stage of our working together, I felt hopeless about saying any of it. I felt that Adair blocks, blocks, blocks. It was hard for me to deal with. I began to think that there was a treatment issue here, but that was not it. Adair was a well-adjusted, likable person with a stable family life and no inhibitions. Her own attachments to friends, family, and colleagues were strong and devoted. Everyone liked her. I went back to thinking over the material. Adair did not harvest the split-off, regressive, dissociated fragments that got put into the mother tongue and left with the psychiatrist. When the patient got very depressed and sounded fragmented, Adair stood by while she sent herself to the psychiatrist, who squashed it. There was nothing wrong with Adair's ability to feel empathy for her patient and to resonate with her rage at the object. Perhaps she got scared of the underlying sadness and craziness and had to block it.

> As I thought of this blocking, Adair now said that when she gives one of her formulations, the patient blocks it and cuts her off somehow. I said to Adair, "The woman is worried about being disconnected from the person she's attached to, her husband, and she freezes him out. I think she's also worried about you leaving. This separation anxiety gets acted out as a cut-

ting off of your ideas. The disconnect happens now, before you actually leave her."

Adair replied, "Yes, but I've been through more difficult ideas than this with her."

I said, "Adair this *is* the difficult idea, and I feel *you* are cutting it off with *me*." Having pointed out the fractal similarity between the therapeutic and the supervisory process, I said, "Now I'm thinking about how to deal with this with you. How am I going to get to this?"

I talked with her about what was happening between her and me, thinking that she would learn to do that with her patient. But it worked no better this time than it had before. So I resolved to return to my earlier strategy of asking how she feels about things. I followed my intention at first, but then I reverted. "In the transference material about her husband never listening, constantly traveling, and telling her to take her medication, we can see the transference. She doesn't want to give you her feelings because she's afraid you'll banish her or maybe send her to another therapist."

Adair responded, "Yes, she's angry at her husband and at her last therapist." Adair confirmed the value of the idea of displacement of the transference to her, but the idea of gathering the transference to herself was cut off again.

I said, "You know that this woman is full of fury and despair. Right now she thinks of you as a good object in a sea of mistrust and disappointment. But rage is such an issue for her, it's bound to be directed at you at some point if you manage not to block it. And when that happens, you might possibly get filled with it, and it may spill over in relation to me. So if you notice stirrings of angry feelings towards me, please talk about them."

Well, of course, she didn't, but I made it clear that this could happen.

In response to my comment, Adair showed that she connected anger at the husband to anger at the previous therapist but not to herself. Now we have established the connection between craziness, anger, interrupted attachment, and anger at a therapist. But I was always left with the feeling that the pieces weren't coming together. Adair said things that were absolutely right on, and yet there was this disconnect.

The inability to recognize the impact of absence continued even when premature termination came into view. Adair found out that her patient would have to move back to Europe in six months because her husband was being reassigned to fill a vacant diplomatic post. In the months following this announcement, there were many missed sessions because of travel to Europe for interviews. Adair reported many details of their discussion about whether the patient and her husband would be sent to this country or that country in Europe, which type of residence they would prefer, which college to select for their son, whether he should be educated in the United States like his sister, or in Europe where his parents would be, and so on. I was getting the facts but none of the emotion.

> I asked Adair, "What do you feel as you face losing her?"
> Adair said, "Well, I'm just feeling I haven't done enough for her."
> I said, "I'm feeling like you. I can't do enough for you. And I really want to help you because you are so good in so many ways."

Support from the Learning Matrix

In a faculty meeting, now six months after beginning my work with Adair, I described the problem. A colleague pointed out that my feelings about Adair mirrored those of her previous supervisor. Some faculty members were filled with the sense of hopelessness and frustration that I was conveying. Others felt that there was some progress in that Adair was now able to link the patient's reaction to her husband with anger toward the patient's previous therapist. On the other hand, she could not see her patient's anger as transference to herself, she could not see her countertransference, and she could not relate to my fractal image of the countertransference in the supervisory relationship.

Adair was getting closer, but there was still a long way to go. One of her small-group leaders said that he had had the same experience of Adair being so close and yet so far from getting it. Her former supervisor suggested that the block of Adair's career path was causing her to block her thinking. Perhaps he had a point, but I knew that until her thinking was freed up, her career path would not open up either. I said to the faculty group, "Adair will never be a supervisor until she can put the elements of the transference together in her clinical work." The group shared my dilemma of how to go about enabling this to happen. While the group was talking, I felt encouraged, and suddenly I knew what to do. I should tell Adair in a positive tone that to be a supervisor she needed to learn how to work in the transference and that I was working toward that goal.

> I went back to the next supervision session and told Adair, "You are so good at so many aspects of therapeutic work. If you could just get this transference piece of therapeutic skill, the whole thing would come together, and you could be a clinical supervisor." Adair said that she really wanted to get it and that she would try.

First Recognition of the Transference

In the next supervision session, Adair reported the patient's ruminations on details about the move, the uprooting, the house relocation, the planting, and the furnishing of the new residence. Adair concluded, "She is her husband's entire support system, so she has to go arrange the move, buy the house, furnish it, and replant the garden. Now that he's leaving, she has to go uproot. She's missing this place so much, and she's feeling overwhelmed at how much she will have to do to re-create a home and a beautiful garden."

Then Adair said to me, "You know what she said? She said, 'I wish I could take my orchids with me.' This was really amazing because I love orchids too, and I have them in my office. So I knew what she meant. I said, 'Maybe you wish you could take me, too.' Then she started laughing, and she said, 'I know it's impossible.' And so we started talking about how to transfer her to another therapist once she gets there. But she wants to get the details of the move settled first."

When Adair recognized the patient's longing to keep her with her, I experienced a glimmer of hope that Adair had got it. Here was a flicker of recognition that confirmed that Adair had taken in what I had been saying. But she let go of it quickly. When she switched to the topic of referral, I felt that the transference was cut off again. Even so, I felt some excitement that I carried in to the next supervision session.

Obliterating the Transference

In another session, the patient expressed negative feelings that I thought clearly contained her transference to Adair. So I said to Adair, "Here is another opportunity for recognizing and gathering the transference."

This time Adair said, "No. I really don't think it's there. When I supervised this case with my first supervisor, there really were far more frequent transference issues. They're not really in the material here."

I said, "Adair, I know you don't see it. But if I see it, I have to show it to you, and I will continue to do that."

I realized that the positive transference was now in Adair's line of vision but not the negative transference. I looked for an intervention that expressed my positive transference toward Adair as a clinician and at the same time showed her the negative side. The comment that I was about to make was actually almost the same as the one that the faculty had encouraged me to say. I had said it already, but this time I said it more directly, with greater conviction, and at a core-affective moment.

I said, "The reason I keep going after this is that we find you to be a very senior clinician and teacher, and this is a little piece that is missing. For you to be a clinical supervisor, which is something that we really want for you, you need to get this piece of understanding. You can't do this work at your best until you've got it."

Adair responded positively to this. I think it really helped her to listen to me when I said that I needed her to achieve her full potential rather than asking her to recognize and make up a deficiency. I related to her through the acceptable positive transference in order to have her become an attractor for organizing the negative transference.

Before we could complete the supervision task, the patient terminated. I talked with Adair about where we had gotten to in supervision. Adair was still using the psychiatrist to deal with the depression medically, she was still unconvinced about the transference, and she still neglected to interpret the impact of her absences and the patient's premature termination. Adair did now interpret the patient's positive transference, but she still could not see the negative transference. Unhinged from its aggressive counterpart, the positive transference to Adair operated like an exciting object relationship that then left the patient at the mercy of her rejecting object relationships. I sensed some improvement in the recognition of transference but not enough. All the same, I felt encouraged that I could approach her blind spot from this area of enlarging vision.

ADAIR'S SECOND CASE

I asked Adair to find another case that was ongoing. I said that my goal would be to intensify our focus on learning from the coutertransference and recognizing the transference. I knew that Adair would need me to come at it indirectly.

Adair's second case was a young woman with a depressed, suicidal, raging, intrusive, violent mother and a remote, neglectful, intellectual father. Her boyfriend treated her badly. The mother was psychotic, the father was absent, and the boyfriend was hopeless. The young woman was trying to win the right to live independently.

Adair's account of her treatment conveyed the tumult and crisis in the young woman's family relationships—my mother this, my father that, I'm going to college, I'm quitting my job, my boss is abusing me, frantic phone calls, horrible emergencies, mother's instrusive phone calls, boyfriend's cheating, and so on. I felt overwhelmed by the material, but Adair remained steady and supportive. She did not draw any negative expressions toward herself. Adair made good interpretations more frequently now. She saw that this young woman's abusive relationship with her boyfriend repeated the experience of being with a disturbed mother who abused her. Adair's observing ego was continuing to develop, but a fully engaging, affective ego was still missing.

> So much of this young woman's material had to be full of transference, but now I couldn't see it either.
>
> I said to Adair, "I can't find the transference in this. It's got to be there, but there's so much material, all of it urgent, realistic, and external. There are so many awful things going on. There are no dreams to help us. I just can't see it."

I had set my aim at working with transference, but the case that Adair chose was overwhelming my preferred way of working. I asked the faculty meeting for help again. One of my colleagues wondered why Adair would choose that case and suggested that perhaps she wanted to try to keep me away from the transference as well. Adair's former supervisor noted that she had presented a similarly disorganized situation to him. Another colleague had the idea that the young woman's transference was to the total situation. She deposited that with Adair, who then conveyed it to me without metabolizing it because of not sensing the negative transference. Someone else pointed out that Adair's self was gratified by being able to locate badness in the object. Again I said that I couldn't understand why the material bothered me more than it bothered her, and I wondered whether she was really far more bothered about it than she showed.

The man who had been her individual supervisor thought that Adair might be completely terrified about being in touch with anger in her therapeutic relationships. He reminded me that the culture at the unversity was to suppress emotions. Perhaps Adair was afraid that if she showed an intense feeling, I would pathologize it. But she knew that I didn't think that way. After all, I had shared my feelings of upset when her first woman patient referred herself to a psychiatrist instead of working on her grief and rage in the transference. Adair gave me the impression that there was no need for anyone to feel that upset about it. Talking about this challenge with my colleagues gave me more distance from the problem. I began to think more positively about my progress in confronting the learning difficulty.

It was clear to me and to Adair that this young woman valued her sessions highly. Adair did nothing intrusive or hurtful toward the young woman. On the contrary, she was solicitous, was responsive to occasional phone calls, and sometimes gave advice that was based on maternal feelings of wanting the best for her. The young woman's mother was so destructive that Adair was wonderful in comparison, the kind of mother to have. Adair did see the positive transference. For example, she recognized the transference significance of the patient's reference to a sum of money that was approximately twice Adair's therapy fee. Adair made the inference that the woman was wanting to see her twice a week instead of once. This told me that she recognized the positive transference but didn't know to remark on it. She used the positive transference to the patient's advantage, but she could not think about it. Not being able to make transference thinkable, she could not note it as a selected fact, and therefore she could not take the next step of interpreting it.

The patient continued to have so much to say and so much to do. This meant that there was always a long story for Adair to tell me, a passing through from Adair to me of the patient's transference to Adair as a willing ear, a sponge—an attentive, detoxifying mother, one who must not comment on the negative transference for fear of identifying herself with the abusive mother.

Affect Enters the Supervision

I had not met with Adair the previous week because she was on vacation. She began the next session by reporting the usual kind of material. The young woman told her that the boyfriend doesn't have enough time for her, the boyfriend doesn't understand her, and the boyfriend changes the plans. The young woman was angry with him, but not as angry as he was. He was so angry with her for what he imagined that she had done to him that he went off with another woman. She thought that she would have to break up with him because he was in such a rage.

This reminded me of Adair's first patient, who fled to a new object. I said to Adair, "I think the patient is talking about the boyfriend's anger instead of talking about her own anger, not just at him but also at you because you were on vacation again. Tell me, why would she need to do this?"

Adair replied, "She doesn't want the other person to get angry with her. She wants the other person to care about her and her family."

I noted that Adair's answer came through in the displacement. She resonated with the tendency to focus on what the other person will do or feel, but at least she was acknowledging someone's fear of being the recipient of negative feeling.

I said, "Look Adair, she's telling you how you shouldn't leave her. She's saying, 'Look how upset people get when they are dropped or when someone is off with someone else instead of the person they've abandoned.'"

Adair said, "I agree with you. Yes, I agree with you."

Adair accepted it this time. It still felt as if she had been persuaded intellectually, until suddenly she said, full of feeling, "I know I'm really all she's got."

That was a big move for Adair. To me, that was gratifying. I realized that she was still more in touch with need, attachment, and love than with frustration, rejection, and hate, but now I felt that we would get there, too.

The Moment of "Getting It"

Now that Adair was in touch with affect and recognizing that she functions best in an intellectual mode, I gave her material to read about the transference (J. S. Scharff and D. E. Scharff 1998c). Adair did her homework.

Adair said, "I've thought a lot about transference, countertransference, and the therapeutic instrument. And now I've got it!"

I was skeptical, and I waited for the proof in her clinical account.

Adair told me that now the young woman was thinking about her graduation, her new apartment, her problem with the mother, and her ex-boyfriend. Adair went on. "She complained to me that she had been in therapy a long time and the problems were still there. I said, 'I think that you're thinking and feeling that I'm not doing enough to help you.' "The woman said, 'Yes.' "And I said, 'Talk to me more about this.'"

"Talk to me more about this"! How many times I had used those very words to her! It was gratifying to hear her use them with her patient and encourage the expression of negative feeling. Indeed she had got it, but I waited to see whether it would remain with her and not get cut off.

In the next supervision session, Adair reported that the young woman talked about how horrible her reality is, how alone she feels, and how she hopes for a prince to save her. She described fully how hard it is for her when Adair goes on vacation.

The patient was in a direct discussion of the transference, and I looked to see how Adair dealt with it.

Adair said to me, "Do you think she's relating this fantasy of a savior-prince to me?"

I said, "Yes, I do. I think she sees you not just as a good mother but now as a prince who could rescue her."

Adair said to me, "So you see, I really can see the transference now."

And I said, "Yes, I think you can." I asked Adair what she thought was in the way of it before.

Adair replied, "I really couldn't believe that it was about me. I didn't want to feel grandiose. But now I see I'm just an instrument."

Now it was my turn to have an insight. Adair taught me something about resistance to working in the transference. Some people may feel that they cannot matter that much to somebody. Others may imagine that they are displacing the real objects in a patient's life by becoming transference objects and diminishing the reality of the original objects.

Using the term *instrument* might suggest reaching out cognitively into the material rather than containing it, but this use of the term appealed to me because it captured the sense of the therapist as a tool used by the patient in getting the work done (Fleming and Benedek 1966, J. S. Scharff and D. E. Scharff 1998c). I do think that Adair was demonstrating a containing function. What she was gathering in the transference was becoming more tolerable, more able to be thought and felt. Adair proved to me that she could now see the positive and the negative transference. Nevertheless, the emotions she was able to connect with were still mostly in the area of need, idealization, and longing. As an instrument for receiving rage, Adair was not yet finely tuned. Still the winds of change were blowing, and the next step would be to help her make her transference interpretations directly to the patient.

Interpreting the Transference

Now that she understood and accepted her importance to the patient, Adair rapidly became able to interpret the transference significance of her patient's destructive relationships.

> The young woman got involved in a highly destructive, humiliating reunion with her ex-boyfriend the next time Adair was away. When sessions resumed, the young woman was ashamed and felt like quitting treatment. Adair recognized that this was not just the patient's turning to a boyfriend with whom to repeat the abuse she suffered from her mother. She now realized that this was her patient's way of letting her know how desperate she felt when Adair was on vacation, as if to say, "See what happens when you leave me."

At last, the turning of anger at the object against the self was delivered into the treatment situation, and Adair interpreted it thoroughly. Once the patient was able to acknowledge and work through her anger at Adair, she became able to find a better job and a new boyfriend who treated her with respect. But the young woman found that she did not find this decent young man sexually appealing. Adair knew that sexual guilt was troubling this patient, but she tended to accept the patient's resistance to discussing her sexuality. When Adair pressed the issue, with my encouragement, the young woman expressed a lot of anger at people in her life, so that the topic of sex was not addressed.

Adair reported, "I said to the patient, 'The anger you are feeling about everybody takes up all the time and diverts us from discussing sexual feelings. I think you are angry at me for raising this issue because you are afraid of looking bad in front of me.'"

Adair now not only saw the transference but also understood how to use it as the fulcrum for change.

Adair as a Supervisor

I was pleased to learn that the university promoted Adair to a clinical supervisory role. She presented two of her individual supervision cases to me. She did an excellent job of establishing a good alliance with her supervisees and asking them to look at transference manifestations. She was particularly good at helping her supervisees notice their enactments of good-mother transferences that covered over bad-mother identifications. She discussed with me her observations and her strategies for how to approach problem areas. I was especially gratified to notice how often she asked her supervisees to tell her more, to tell her what feelings the patients aroused, and to ask them to look at the transference. She told me that she is glad that she is now better able to accept rage expressed toward her in the transference and is still working on it. I was gratified when Adair told me that learning in supervision had convinced her to work on dealing more directly with her own anger as a therapist and a teacher.

When colleagues read this chapter, they confirmed that they had noticed the same changes in her group participation. They agreed that Adair had recovered from her state of faulty notation. The blind spot was no longer there.

When Adair read this chapter, she gave her own view of what made the difference in her ability to see the transference. She said, "I couldn't see it before because I didn't know how to think it. All the supervisions helped me a lot, but they hadn't gotten me to notice the transference. I wish you could have just given me concrete examples or told me what I was doing wrong and shown me how to do it right. I didn't know that I was looking in the wrong place. I was still looking for transference as the patient experiencing me as a reedition of a particular family member. Recognizing the countertransference was easy because I know what I feel, but I couldn't find the transference in it because I never believe that my feelings have that much importance.

"Sometimes I need something concrete. So reading the paper on how to think about the geography of the transference helped me (J. S. Scharff and D. E. Scharff 1998c). Then in supervision I got it! You wanted me to take my feelings, connect them to the theme of the session, and see how my feelings and the theme were expressing the patient's hidden thoughts and feelings about me. So then I knew what to look for and what to do. It was when the second patient was able to admit to her feelings about me that I finally got it. It has made a tremendous difference in my work with patients and students and in my group. I can see it even helps me in my own family."

20
The Internal Couple in the Group Mind

THE IMPACT OF THE COUPLE

As codirectors, we (David and Jill Scharff) have dealt with the large group's unconscious fantasies about us as a couple so that it does not interfere with the learning task. In fact, elaborating on them is part of the task because it leads to awareness of the impact of feelings about a couple. We have experienced these reactions among students and faculty as they work with us in our roles as directors, senior coauthors, and coeditors. Together we have studied them as a source of information about the impact of the internal couple on the institution and on the learning and teaching process.

In every educational institution, there are many actual couples. There are dyads of director and codirector, teacher and student, analyst and analysand, and supervisor and supervisee. In these role relationship dyads, there is a power gradient. Then there are cochairs, codirectors, cotherapists, and coleaders. Assuming equality within these dyads, the power gradient operates not within the dyad but between the dyad and the others who are being led, directed, or treated. The dyad is experienced as an augmented authority, reminiscent of the parental pair.

When the codirectors are married, the resemblance to the parental couple is more immediate, and authority is magnified. The image of the married couple provokes unconscious fantasy about the couple as an authoritative pair and as an intimate partnership. The actual couple is the embodiment of a pairing basic assumption group that supports and subverts the task. The actual couple stimulates the emergence into consciousness of a composite internal couple that is embedded in the unconscious life of the group.

In this chapter, we concentrate on the resonance of the actual couple with the internal couple in the group mind. The pervasive, unconscious effect of the internal couple has become conscious on a number of occasions, most notably during weeklong institutes when both of us were teaching and most recently following a presentation on the use of the affective learning model. We begin with a few short examples and later give a longer example of the effect of the internal couple on the teaching and learning of the conference institution.

The Woman Submerged in the Couple

An example of the impact of the couple on the large group's response to a talk that Jill Scharff gave when David Scharff was in the chair is described in Chapter 13. The image of us as a couple leading the conference institution preoccupied the members and it obliterated the content of Jill Scharff's talk. In that institute, women group members preferred to think of her as one of them or as a group leader or a cochair paired with a faculty member. They found the image of her being a couple with her husband upsetting because it disturbed their enjoyment in seeing her together with other women faculty members with whom they felt identified.

In one of the small groups, a woman member saw the Scharffs as a weak man together with a strong woman and felt annoyed at a couple like that. One man saw a facilitating man with a competent woman and admired that. One woman saw a powerful couple and envied that. One woman saw a respectful couple and wanted to emulate that. Whatever their valency for perceiving the nature of the couple relationship before them, each of these participants was preoccupied with that male–female, married couple, not with the woman's ideas.

The Exciting and Rejecting Couple

Another example, described in Chapter 18, is taken from the experience of a small group during a different summer institute in which we were present in our adminstrative capacity as codirectors of the institution. Both of us were teaching one session each day but not together. In one small group, members were excited to see us at plenary meetings and occasionally at presentations by other faculty members. They felt disappointed that we did not teach as a couple. The small group experienced considerable frustration over the wish to have us as a couple to themselves.

At this stage, the group members viewed the couple as ideal, and they jealously wanted the ideal teaching family of one child with two parents. When we were too busy as directors to be present together all the time as the group wished, we became a target for dissatisfaction. When we did not appear together despite being married, the group's image of the ideal parental couple changed into a frustrating, unavailable couple of two distinct individuals doing their own thing. Our individual appearances had the effect of reminding the group of the absence of the couple that they desired.

The Attacked Same-Sex Couple

When the small group is led by a couple, the group reacts more intensely to their relationship than to them as individuals. When the couple is a same-sex couple, the group members struggle to construct the pair in a familiar image that fits with their internal couple.

In Chapter 13, we show how the group tried to split the female-female coleading team by thinking of one woman leader as male and denigrating the other. The group created alternative couples in and out of the group as a way of defusing and yet gratifying their preoccupation with the leaders' pairing. The group members did not want to see the women leaders as a collaborative couple, each operating with equal authority. If they had to recognize them as women, then they preferred to imagine them as a nursing couple or as a supervisor–supervisee couple, rather than as a pair of equals.

The Couple Relationship in the Institution

We believe that, when an educational institution is led by a couple, their professional partnership has to be available as a subject for discussion because their couple relationship will be on the minds of both students and faculty, in resonance with the universally present internal couple in the individual and in the group mind. Whether admired or envied, idealized or denigrated, heterosexual or homosexual, the presence and the absence of a couple may operate as an interference with learning. On the credit side of the ledger, it may lead to exploring feelings of exclusion, envy, and gratitude in relation to the couple and finding one's own position in relation to the integration of affect and cognition.

When the group deals with an actual couple, the members see before them a representation of their fantasy of a couple. The existence of the couple implies that both individuals have renounced their parental objects in favor of a nonincestuous object. They have identified each other as a source of goodness. The group imagines that each of them has refound a lost good object in the partner and enjoys a blissful reunion with the ideal mother. Supposedly, they have resolved issues of libido and aggression so that they are in balance. Because they were each found acceptable to the other as an ideal object that combines the exciting oedipal object and the tender preoedipal mother, it is imagined that they feel no inadequacy, no loss, and no injury (Bergman 1987).

The successful partnership represents daring to identify with the oedipal couple and overcoming the oedipal barrier at the same time (Kernberg 1980, 1995). If the couple lives together and works together as well, it is assumed that, in successfully linking erotism and idealization, they have recruited aggression in the service of love, which implies that they have the potential for creating a new object relationship in depth (Kernberg 1974). They appear to have achieved a healthy balance between the conscious and unconscious object relations sets of husband and wife (J. S. Scharff 1992b). They have become a couple, which means that others are excluded from the possibility of creating a couple with either one of them.

As therapists, we are familiar with oedipal feelings of rage at betrayal by the mother who turns to her husband for sexual pleasure and refuses to gratify her child's erotic desires to possess her. As parents, we have become aware of the persistence of oedipal fantasy as a problem in family life. As teachers in an institution led by a couple, we need to recognize the impact of the actual couple in the minds of the faculty and students. To work with this, we need the concept of the internal couple, an important psychic structure and pervasive unconscious fantasy (J. S. Scharff 1992a, J. S. Scharff and D. E. Scharff 1998d).

The Motivating Fantasy of the Internal Couple

Klein (1952) introduced the controversial idea that the infant has a fantasy of the parents in intercourse. The infant imagines that each parent possesses the other's sexual parts through oral, anal, and genital routes as early as four to six months of age. When the infant is frustrated, he thinks that it is because the father or mother is in a state of constant enjoyment of the mother's breast or the father's penis that he wishes for. The child relates not only to its mother separately but to the father-in-mother and to the mother-in-father (Ogden 1986). The infant already has a vivid appreciation of the integration of male and female elements both in the individual human personality and in its interpersonal expression in the couple relationship.

As the child grows, the fantasy is infused with derivatives from oral, anal, and phallic stages. The lap baby imagines the parents in a feeding frenzy. The toddler in the anal stage of development views intercourse in fantasy as a battle for control and domination over the object or as a way of holding on instead of letting go. A child in the phallic stage sees intercourse as a display of urethral competence and muscular strength. Oral, anal, and phallic trends blend into a fantasy of penile penetration, possession, and ultimate gratification.

The child who is maturing in terms of the psychosexual stages is also becoming more sophisticated in perceiving and distinguishing between ways of relating and in recognizing the relationships between objects of affection. On seeing his parents kiss, the toddler may feel jealous and excluded. For the child, this is the hated rejecting couple. Equally likely, he may get between their knees, not attempting to pry them apart and repossess his mother but hoping, with his arms around their knees, to be included in the loving embrace. For the child, this is the inclusive loving couple.

As the child grows, this loving yet rejecting couple becomes a source of conflict. The child needs and loves the security of it but hates the rejection. The child loses the feeding, soothing breast and the caring person of the mother when she moves away from her bodily preoccupation with her child to relate to her husband erotically. Aware of nighttime separation from both parents who guard their privacy, the child feels painfully excluded from their relationship. Increased genital sensation in the phallic and oedipal stages drives the wish to enjoy sexual pleasure as the grown-ups do. Accompanying fantasies of sexual possession lead to the fantasy of killing the rival, which provokes guilt and anxiety about stealing, spoiling, hurting, and ultimately losing a loved and needed parent. This is how the internal couple becomes a conflicted internal object.

Once the child learns to resolve the unbearable conflict by renouncing claims on the desired opposite-sex parent in favor of maintaining the parents as a loving couple, the internal couple is more important than each individual internal object. This stage of development obviously goes much better if the parents really are a secure couple, able to withstand their child's assault. If the couple loves each other despite disagreement and has been able to deal firmly but lovingly with the child's sexual drives, then a loving, flexible couple will be internalized. If the couple is barely together, the child's naturally disruptive oedipal wishes may be released full force or may be massively repressed. If the couple is securely together but in a sadomasochistic or fatal attraction, the internalized internal couple will then be of that type. If the couple is actually divorced, the child faces an arduous task of maintaining the fantasy of a potentially loving couple without distorting the reality of the parents' broken marriage. In this case, the internal couple may remain a fractured object, or, if it is formed, it is one built on loss and yearning.

Again the internal couple undergoes further development as the child builds onto it experience with other couples—the grandparent couple, the uncle and aunt, remarried parents, and male-female work couples at school, or at the doctor's office, or romantic couples in movies. Eventually, the internal couple is overhauled during the resurgence of oedipal issues in adolescence. Sufficient trial couple relationships with peers allow for modifications that lead to an independently conceived internal couple.

The internal couple is a psychic structure based on the child's experiences with the parents' relationship and other couples of significance. It affects marital choice and the long-term quality of the couple relationship that the adult creates. It has the generative capacity to create and interact with future object relationship systems in various personalities as children are added to the family system. Here is an example from the clinical situation. The therapist's account of his assessment of a patient whom we will call Mrs. A shows the power of the internal couple on a spouse and on a therapist.

The Internal Couple in the Clinical Situation

Mrs. A. had been married for twenty years to a man with whom she also had a successful business run from their home. He had had some trouble with the IRS, but that was before she knew him, and he had reformed. Both of them were tax attorneys, and they employed a small staff. Unknown to her, her husband had subcontracted a job to an accountant, Mr. B. To Mrs. A.'s astonishment, she and her husband were accused of fraud, arraigned, jailed, and interrogated. She was released after a week when it was established that her husband and Mr. B., who she now found out was also her husband's homosexual lover, had colluded in fraudulent billing. Her husband was indicted, the lover had fled the country with the assets, her firm owed thousands of dollars, her bank account was frozen, her husband was in jail, and she was worried that he would commit suicide in his despair.

Mrs. A. told this macabre story in a highly dramatic, incredibly entertaining way to a therapist. She did not seem upset, however, because she had faith in God and knew everything would work out. The therapist was filled with a mountain of fear, anxiety, and desolation. He was flooded with the horror of shame and social exposure. All he could think was, "Why is she so trustful? She's an attorney! How could she not have known about the money? How could she not have known about the lover in her own house? How can she rise above such horror?"

The therapist noted a disparity between Mr. and Mrs. A. in which she had the business integrity and faith while he had the delinquency and despair. The therapist also noted a peculiarity in his own coupling with Mrs. A. in which Mrs. A. had the narrative competence and the therapist had all the feeling. This insight led the therapist to ask Mrs. A. about her parents' relationship.

Mrs. A. explained that her mother was a tax attorney, too. She ran her legal business from her home, managed a horse farm, and raised four children. She knew how to "squeeze a nickel." She was optimistic, capable, and controlling and seemed uninterested in romance. Her father, who had worked his way up in the world from nothing, used the money from her two businesses to invest in high-risk ventures that necessitated constant travel. He was full of energy and excitement, always on the road or out with his male friends. His wife had no idea what he was doing or how they would cope with his latest business crisis, but she always managed somehow. They were held together by their firm belief in God and by their passionate commitment to the Catholic Church.

Mrs. A. had chosen a husband who had been on the edge of business crisis and delinquency. Once they were married, he was always home, unlike her father. His daily presence repaired the loss of her paternal object and filled a hole in her perception of her parents' relationship. But like her father, her husband was now in crisis again, and he was always with a male friend. Like her mother, she was left running the business. Like her mother, she maintained an optimistic attitude and overlooked major problems. This was a marriage united by faith in God, intensity coexisting with distance, abundant optimism masking fundamental desertion. Mrs. A. had created her marriage in the image of her internal couple.

The therapist examined his own anxious response and associated to his own internal couple. His parents, who were always worried about paying bills, dealt with their financial anxiety by paying early. Like his parents, the therapist dealt with his anxiety by feeling it early and in full measure. Once he had thought of this similarity, the therapist felt his anxiety lessen, and he became able to think. He began therapy with the patient by showing her the link between her way of dealing with her marriage, her current experience, and her view of her parents' relationship.

The Internal Couple in the Institution

The internal couple affects how other couples are perceived and treated in systems outside the family. In the institution, it affects how various couples are dealt with in actuality—institution codirectors, program cochairs, and small-group coleaders. Beyond that, it influences how well individuals can create a couple to get their needs met—student and dean, supervisee and supervisor, learner and teacher.

The Absence of the Internal Couple

The absence of a couple may be equally problematic. The next example of failed coupling comes from a conference plenary review meeting for weekend-only participants in the program. The topic of the weekend was hysteria.

> Preceding the plenary, an experienced therapist presenting in her student role, had given an excellent, lucid, detailed account of a clinical case, to which the main presenter consulted. Normally a lively person, she gave her account in a deadened way of which she was quite unaware. The presenter commented on it and detected a hysterical mechanism at work in her. He said that this was evidence of a countertransference response to her patient's hysteria. The woman seemed taken aback by his comment and might have been hurt. She realized, however, that it was accurate and expressed appreciation for the insight into the case.
>
> The main presenter had addressed the topic of hysteria from the separate points of view of the mother, the father, and the child before pulling his ideas together in a final session. The oedipal triangle had been split up into its components, and the integration had not yet happened by the time the plenary occurred. The presenter extended the terms *mother, father, couple,* and *intercourse* as metaphors to differentiate image-based, word-based, and integrative styles of thinking. He presented the creative internal couple as an antidote to hysterical patterns of relating conveyed by a mother and a father who do not express sexuality. Discussion of this point generated annoyance and incredulity that got in the way of understanding what he was saying. These reactions had to be addressed in the plenary review that followed. (The invited speaker does not attend the plenary meeting.)
>
> The plenary began with expressions of concern. Someone wondered whether the student presenter was alive and well after the male featured speaker who was consulting to her case presentation had shown her how she was deadened by hysterical mechanisms. The small groups had been deeply into the issues and had difficulty joining in the tasks of plenary. At least one member from each small group was missing. We learned that this was because of unmanageably intense feelings of anger and loss at missing fathers. These feelings were stimulated by the speaker's focus on Freud and fathers

in his discussion of hysteria that day, the members' experience of the speaker as an elusive object they could not easily connect with, and the intensity of the brief immersion in the topic. Rather than stay to learn from their pain and the impact of "Father Time," these members shortened the time and took their pain outside the area of discussion. One member pointed out that skipping the plenary meant that some feeling or idea was being acted out rather than thought about, and that we could not really know what it meant if those who were absent were not there to talk about it. Following on her idea, a faculty member said that there was a group hysterical mechanism of dissociating from pain associated with the father so that it could not be thought about.

The missing people were women. One small group reported that the group had split along gender lines. The men had sat together and carried all the affect for the group. Members in another small group had been upset, remembering that a female faculty member who tried to engage the speaker in a debate about male and female ways of thinking was not responded to (see Chapter 17). None of them had managed to be in a creative couple relationship in dialogue with the speaker, and neither could she. The plenary group concluded that with so much talk about fathers, with affect being expressed only by men, and with the example of the female faculty member being cut off, female members could not speak of their perceptions and so were more likely to act them out. The difficulty in sustaining a multilogue persisted. Some small groups were not represented in the discussion at all.

Participants complained that something was missing in the plenary group. Overemphasis on men, fathers, the silence of women, and the hysterical absence of pain combined to diminish the flow of dialogue in the plenary. The intimate experience of the small group was pulling against joining in the intellectual inquiry of the plenary to make sense of the total experience. The plenary group appeared not to want to know about the experiences contained within it or to engage in a fruitful interchange, much as the hysterical personality does not want to know about intercourse.

What was missing in the plenary was a groupwide creative intercourse. The members were primed to feel deprived of an internal couple by the design of the presentation and the nature of the discussion: The speaker had split up the male and female elements of his idea and had not yet presented his integration, and he did not couple in debate with the female faculty member. The small groups had been splitting intellectual and affective experience along gender lines. They were splitting off pain and projecting it into individuals. Together in the plenary, the small groups were re-creating a group enactment of a family in which there is no vital couple and in which hysterical mechanisms substitute for the reality of sex and generativity. The plenary group demonstrated failed intellectual intercourse and embodied the splitting of the generative couple. The members felt unable to imagine or sustain creative intercourse in the emotional and intellectual activity of men and women studying together. In short, the plenary was suffering from the lack of the internal couple.

The presence or absence of the internal couple has a pervasive influence that is too often overlooked. We avoid it because of discomfort with ambivalence about the couple, wishes to destroy what one cannot have, fear of reactions to the gratification of being in a couple relationship, and fear of exposure of weakness that could threaten one's own couple relationship. Nevertheless, the issue has to be addressed as a subject from which to learn.

Faculty Discussion after Presentation by the Couple

At a weekend conference in April 1999 on the theme of the relationship of individual to institution, we made a joint presentation of our paper "The Individual and Group Affective Learning Model" (J. S. Scharff and D. Scharff 1999a). At the fourth large-group event of that weekend, this presentation put forth our method. The model had already been experienced, modified, criticized, and embraced by many of the participants in the large group, but they had not heard a comprehensive presentation of the ideology until then.

Following the discussant, the large group reflected on the use of the model by individual learner and teacher within the institution in the here-and-now. Some reactions to experiencing the presenters as a couple were intense enough to obliterate the content of what we had said. This led us to think more about the impact of the actual couple as leaders and presenters on the institution and on the learning. These reactions appear as part of the group discussion reported in Chapter 21.

Here we concentrate on the work done in the faculty review meeting in which small-group leaders reported their groups' responses after our joint presentation. We will refer to ourselves by our first names, David and Jill, but we will give the faculty members the pseudonyms Art, Belle, Brett, Don, Elise, Erin, George, Hank, Linda, and Martin to protect the identities of small-group members they mention. At the beginning of the faculty meeting, both Don and Hank said that they needed help with their groups because of interference with the study task arising from anxiety about relating to the couple. Don was given priority.

Themes of Oedipal Exclusion

Don began, "The group continued the pattern from previous meetings of focusing on one person. This time Nancy held the floor and pursued the argument that she had taken up with David Scharff in the large group. She insisted that this supposedly democratic organization really isn't, because it has a hierarchy from which she is excluded. She thought, as she had said in the large group, that students should be allowed to attend the faculty review meetings. It soon became clear that, as she listened to the presentation by the Scharffs, she felt like a child excluded from the parental couple. The group kept on discussing her point of view without much progression. I said that the group members were focusing on an individual in order to avoid shared anxieties, and I wondered what each of them might be feeling.

"Now Dominique tearfully said that she had overexposed herself and that the institution should spit her out. The group worked with her shame, but the more she worked, the more ashamed she became. Nancy was trying to connect with Dominique, but she kept pushing Nancy away, as if Nancy were representing the institutional authority she had been arguing with in the large group. In response to my commenting on this, the field of participation widened to include the others. Dominique began to settle down, and she asked the group members what they liked about her. Some members of the group responded, but it was difficult for Dominique to take in their positive comments. Her shame and poor self-esteem has been impeding the group's process the entire year. I think she felt more vulnerable because of idealizing the competent couple presenting to the large group.

"I said that when she and another member, Karen, both begin to experience their vulnerabilities, they encounter a strongly shaming internal object. Karen agreed and said that she appreciated the opportunity to work through some of this in the group context.

"The room was awfully hot, and we had maintenance come in to reset the thermostat, but it did no good. Having problems with overhearing the groups on either side of us, too, we wondered how much of what we were saying could be heard by them. We kept hoping for a better tomorrow when the hotel gets organized to give us back our usual room. The group ended with members addressing their issues and concerns about malevolency, envy, and anger. The members do feel that the group is becoming much safer."

Now, in the faculty review meeting, other faculty members joined in the discussion of Don's group.

Elise said, "I am troubled by the theme of hot and cold. Don's group was too hot, and he had to call the technician. Erin's group this morning was too cold, and she had to call the technician, too. Now I wonder about the dynamics of these two groups, if there is some . . ."

Hank finished her sentence for her: "Some need for consultants to help with the environmental holding."

Brett said, "We can see these groups functioning as thermometers for gauging the level of participation."

Belle, who had chaired the Scharffs's presentation and large-group discussion, said, "In the presentation this afternoon, first it was too hot, and then it was too cold. As the chair, I didn't notice, but others did and asked me to call maintenance twice. I think we're having problems in awareness and emotional regulation."

Discussion of Don's Group Process and the Theme of the Internal Couple

The implications of the struggle with the internal couple are not made fully explicit in Don's report or even in the faculty discussion of his group. This is, of course, the nature of the work: Understanding grows with rethinking. We can now see that the presentation by the couple in the large group affected the entire small-group experience by provoking conflict with the group's internal couples. Don was aware that Nancy's feeling of exclusion by the couple prompted her idea that students should not be excluded from the faculty meetings, a proposal she made *as though the feeling of exclusion could be solved by taking an action.* Don understood that her idea captured the group and diverted her and the others from studying her affective experience. The group does not have space for thinking about the couple and therefore cannot find space for examining the individual position in relation to the couple (Britton 1998). In a different personal reaction to the couple, Dominique's feeling of shame and exposure speaks for a sense of inadequacy before the image of the powerful couple from which the group is excluded.

Two members of the group (Nancy and Dominique) speak for the painful sense of exclusion by the couple. The group tries to form working pairs of its own—Nancy and Dominique, Dominique and Karen—and even though no specific couple is established, the process of trying to do so opens space for thinking and working in the group, which is then closed by settling on the action theme of correcting the environmental problems. The group tries to find a working couple within the group itself both to compensate for the painful exclusion and to embody the way of working that they admire and envy. In this process, they do find dialogue, but along the way they feel the "heat" and the intrusion of other groups talking in nearby rooms, both of which represent the lack of environmental holding that is associated with the feeling of exclusion. That action does no good, but they do manage to return to the study task.

Belle remembers that the large-group presentation was also dogged by poor temperature control. This was difficult for her to recognize while she was in the presence of the Scharffs as a couple. As directors, we are ultimately responsible for environmental factors, just as parents are even while they are attending to other functions or even when they are absent. In this way, Belle links her experience of the atmosphere in the large group when the couple was presenting with the small group's preoccupation with the couple. The actual couple is an external presence that resonates uncomfortably with the internal couple in the individual, the small group, and the large group. The internal couple leads to difficulty with awareness and regulation of affect on this occasion.

Idealization of the Primal Scene:
Destructive Envy or Creative Identification

Hank asked whether we could move on. He said, "My group started out with a complaint about the ambiguity in the model. One of the women kept saying, 'Why do they say we should get regressed, and then they say we're bad for being regressed?'" He shook his head and said, "So much for listening. She couldn't hear what you said at all. She wasn't the only one. Lorna said that the words weren't important. I still don't understand why the words of the presentation fell away. They were not as important as the communication of the image of the couple presenting them. She said that, for her, it was like three years of learning came together through your gestures. I said, 'What is that—gestural integration?' I guess I couldn't imagine what gestures could possibly carry the conceptual material. I asked her to explain it to me.

"Lorna then said that actually she was upset by the words. I said, 'You mean like if Fred and Ginger were dancing and they started talking about their shopping list or something?' She said, 'No, no, no, not that at all. You're really misunderstanding me.' Then Paul said, 'I didn't like the words either because I thought about the fact that David and Jill were getting along too well, and that didn't fit with my experience of David upsetting some of the women with one of his jokes.'"

Hank began to formulate his experience: "The words of the presentation were being attacked by idealization and negativity. The content was being destroyed by their experience of the primal scene. It was as if the couple presenting were saying that this was how they made children, why they go about it this way, and how they raise them. The conceptual integration was too difficult in the face of the excitation associated with having parents explain the grand scheme.

"I kept trying to explain to Lorna that while this felt positive to her, it seemed to me that her way of saying that only the gestures and the physical presence of the couple mattered devalued their ideas. She felt injured and attacked by me, and she kept saying that I didn't understand. This is supposedly three years of integration coming together for her, and she believes it comes to her without words! She also said it was as if she could see the words as David and Jill spoke them. I said to her, 'When you see words, that's indicative of some regression.' She retorted, 'This is supposed to be an interpretation-free zone.' I felt as if I had injured her. Normally, I can take the students' not agreeing with me, but I felt that I had to fight her on this. I got stuck on this issue with her. I got trapped re-creating a pair with her, and it wasn't full of agreement like the presenters were."

Erin, noting that Hank was perseverating on the subject of Lorna, asked, "Where was the rest of your group?"

David answered for Hank with another of his jokes. "They were watching the couple fight!"

Elise disagreed with Hank's understanding of his group's experience. She had a positive view of Lorna's reponse. She said, "There are times when the picture is worth a thousand words. Could it be that what Lorna saw helped her locate an internal couple that was more creative than before?"

Art agreed, "It wasn't the usual meaning of the primal scene. Lorna saw a creative coupling, and something clicked for her. I think it was helpful for the two presenters to talk about the overall model. It made it clear that we (the couple) and we (the faculty) are all working to provide the best possible environment for the participants. We're working on all these different factors, and we're thinking about a lot of aspects. This might well have actually coalesced into a positive reaction that could have overcome paranoid fantasies of the primal scene."

Erin returned to helping Hank think about her point of view. She asked him to address the specifics of the words not mattering to Lorna. "Wouldn't it suggest that the words could destroy the reality?" she asked.

Art replied, "I'm glad you bring us back to that. What I'm describing is healthy. What Hank described is not. He was most aware of the unresolved idealism of the wordless, wonderful communication from the couple being used to deny aggression about exclusion."

Elise also continued to see the positive. "I don't see it as denial of aggression," she reasserted. "If a person locates inside of herself an internal couple as a more creative object, that's what she is doing at that particular time. She is not paying attention to the words actually being said because she is in a healing process."

Hank could not agree. "I didn't feel that it was healing," he insisted. "I felt that it was idealization masking envy and preventing resolution."

David Scharff, now in role as the solo leader of the faculty review process rather than as part of the presenting couple, saw the value of both points of view. "It's both good and bad," he said. "There's something good that Lorna's getting, but in the process of getting it, she has to destroy part of the experience. The question is whether she and the group can think about that. When you ask her to, she says you're just being nasty. When you confront her, you feel she's feeling destroyed. She gives you the message that you're doing something terrible."

Hank was able to own his projection into Lorna. He acknowledged, "As I think it over now, my vulnerability was probably based on my own feeling of dissidence [sic] in seeing David and Jill make the presentation. I found it very difficult to think during the presentation."

No one remarked on Hank's slip. David simply asked whether Hank had said that in the group.

Hank replied, "Yes, I actually did say that. They asked me, 'What did you think during that presentation,' and I told them, 'I experienced a difficulty in thinking.'"

Erin said to him, "I thought you were trying to do some integrating, and I thought there was a resistance to your doing that, both in the large group and in the small group. You were thinking. You were addressing the tension in the model and the resistance to doing the integration."

David asked him, "Could you say more about experiencing difficulty in thinking?"

Hank continued, "I assume it has to do with my own reaction to the primal scene. I felt as if I was watching Fred and Ginger work out their choreography. I had to work extremely hard to hold on to the ideas. So, I think that's why I was susceptible. Perhaps I was looking to Lorna and trying to pull out of her the destructive component so that it would validate my experience."

David said, "It's as though you lodged the problem in her."

Jill, in role as a member of the faculty review meeting, agreed, "In that group, yes." Then she went on to focus on Hank directly. "But usually it lodges in Hank. I've noticed that it's always Hank who relates the impact of the presence of David and me as a couple to primal scene anxiety. And he never really gets support for it. I've noticed that before. It's always a relief to me when Hank raises the issue, but then it never goes anywhere. As a group we don't know how to deal with it. I confess I'd rather not have to, but I know it's important."

George asked, "Important to deal with you two as a couple?"

Jill replied, "Yes, as a representation of the internal couple."

David knew that she hated this topic. "That's what you dread, Jill," he said.

She agreed, "Oh, I dread it. Of course I dread it."

Art was puzzled. "Why do you dread it?" he asked.

Jill responded, "I don't like the exposure."

Continuing to explore her reaction, Art asked, "You mean the exposure of being seen as a couple personally, while working together professionally?"

David said, "This is the view of the couple that was troubling to Nancy and Dominique in Don's group."

Belle understood in part because she had been dealing with feelings about her recent remarriage. "Being a couple invites so much envy," she said sympathetically.

Elise objected. Speaking for the integration of positive and negative responses, she said, "But there are two issues here. One is that you were performing, showing off. The other is that you were creating. One is upsetting. The other is giving."

David said, "The way we usually experience this reaction is that Jill dreads it, and I'm oblivious to it. But she's right: We have to try and look at it because it clearly contains a dynamic which is blinding to people in the institution. I link this to Nancy's saying, 'You don't let us into the faculty meetings, and you really should.' Although I took it up with her on a literal level about the institution's need for a protected space for faculty to think, I realize that at the personal level, she is making a request to be in on the primal scene. And that idea literally scares the wits out of all of us, and we can't think clearly. So it's a continual dynamic more present in this institution than in many because there is a couple leading it. Hank, you asked Lorna to start thinking about it, which she experienced as destructive because the group would have to destroy the idealization. One reason Lorna might resist is that you are actually trying to get her to do it for you because you find it so difficult."

Hank agreed, "It's such a preoccupying question for me. I think you're right, Jill. I have a valency toward talking about it."

David reassured him, "I don't experience it as an intrusive idea. Your talking about it is valued. The problem is that we get stuck with it. We don't take it anywhere. We are having trouble moving on it."

Martin, a new faculty member who did not know Hank well, asked him, "If it's not in keeping with the feelings of the faculty, why do you keep doing it over and over?"

Hank said, "I don't know. But you're right. It's this Johnny-one-note song that I sing with regard to that particular scene."

Associating to Martin's mentioning the feelings of the faculty, Art pointed to the effect that the faculty's discussion of the couple issue was having on him. "When there was a lot of back-and-forth in our discussion in the large group, I found that tremendously enlivening," he said. "There was a joint creation that everyone was sharing in with David and Jill as the two presenters."

Brett was able to get right to the point. "The presentation was experienced as your making love," he said directly to Jill and David. "This takes me back to Elise's closing statement in the last group, which was about the love that is expressed in teaching. I think that your collaboration in making the presentation was blinding those who wish for a generative couple."

Erin elaborated on this, adding, "And it might be worrying them that the couple could be destroyed if they invite envious attack by continuing to present the results of their collaboration."

Suddenly, Elise recognized that the good and the bad aspects of experiencing the couple were represented in the metaphor of the temperature changes. She exclaimed, "That's the hot and cold!"

Discussion

In this faculty discussion, the effect of the couple on the learning task is made explicit. In Hank's small group, Lorna begins by describing her experience of the teaching couple and the effect it has on her. Then there is a debate between Hank and Lorna about the nature and meaning of her experience, about which Hank is incredulous, although other faculty members find it understandable as a moment of affective integration. This results in the faculty group doing its own work on the effect of the couple on the student group and, more important, on themselves as a group. In this discussion, Hank gets help from the faculty to air his own issues about the codirectors as a couple and their effect on his capacity to think and learn. As the discussion unfolds, the faculty develop a space for their shared thinking that subtends a generative process. It is not only Hank who finds this helpful, but we do as well.

As the actual couple who are always being considered in the group mind for their implications for group and individual internal couples, we often find our capacity to think about these dynamic effects constricted by the powerful dynamics of the institution and the subgroups that it contains. We need the cumulative experience in Hank's small group, the large-group experience that preceded it, and the faculty discussion afterward to stimulate Hank and the whole faculty to think through the specific effect that we have as an actual couple on the groups and to see more clearly the implications for internal couple dynamics at various levels of the institution.

In Hank's group, we see that Hank and Lorna form a couple that is characterized by misunderstanding and disagreement—a dissident couple, we might say, making use of Hank's slip. It is an aggressive mirror of the couple that we form. In the affective experience of the group, it feels destructive and combative, but that does not mean that it will be destructive of learning and growth. Just as aggression is a necessary part of growth and development and dissidents are essential for political reform, aggressive encounters in groups are necessary to new learning. New learning comes from chewing on, and often destroying, what is previously understood. The object of study has to be "attacked" in order to be digested, and that process often feels dangerous or destructive, even when it yields new and powerful lessons.

The same sort of process happens in parallel in the faculty group. As various faculty members deconstruct Hank's understanding of his own experience—which they are able to do, secure in their respect for his work— they arrive at an understanding of their experience with us both as an actual couple and as the pair in the institutional role with the valency for attracting many fantasies of the internal couple. The faculty members examine differences in perception, open the space for thinking, and strengthen their capacity for tolerating idiosyncratic responses and uncertainty about what is happening in order to arrive at a comprehensive understanding of the issues. Then faculty members can take this level of understanding back to their small groups.

The remaining leaders whose small groups were not experiencing turbulence gave their accounts briefly. We abstract the portions of their reports that pertain also to the resonance between the actual couple and the internal couple.

The Coupling of Affect and Cognition

Brett said of his small group, "One person reported studying in an institution where she was told, 'You have to be a cognitive thinker, or you're not going to get your doctorate.' Another who studied at a training institution in Britain reported that her teachers said, 'We don't want any references to research or quantitative work because we want you to stay with the transference.' These two points of view speak for the split between cognition and affect, but the group itself represents two halves of the whole that we are trying to think about. I thought that the presenters came out with a model for integration that people could think about consciously. And some people want to remain unconscious about the model. So it scared some of them to see it presented clearly."

Brett had another comment about his group. "I've never had a weekend group that talked about termination so soon. The only thing one of my group members said was, 'If I really start getting into this and then I have to leave Sunday, what am I going to do?' His conclusion was this: 'Destroy thinking about it. Don't discuss it. Don't connect with the ideas.' He wanted to destroy the experience of coupling with the group. That way he could end the thing that raises hope and fear."

Discussion

Brett's group provides two brief examples of the issue of the internal couple in the small group. The first describes constraints against linking affect and cognition in the back-home situation. Group members discuss their difficulty with the integrative task in which affect and cognition are "coupled." Here they are referring to the content of the presentation rather than to their experience of the presenting couple. In the second part of the group, one man is reluctant to engage with the group when it will be gone after only three days. The allure of the learning is tempered by the disappointment of the group's ending. This operates as a powerful disincentive to coupling with the group for the learning task.

The Decoupling of Process and Content

Art then described his small-group dynamics. "In the two-year group that I led there was a split. The group members liked David's way of presenting, but they attacked Jill's style, even though they appreciated the content of what she was saying. They felt that her facial expressions were condemning and awful. It seemed to me that the group attacked her, and through her David and the model, because of anxiety stirred by the evidence of a good containing function that was shown in the content and in David's style of presenting it. If there is such a good container, the deeper feelings that are feared are going to come out. As they heard the model, members felt even more support and understanding and then began talking about their fears of their own deeper feeling states emerging."

Art added a note of caution about an individual. "I just want to sensitize people to the fact that Cassandra is going to be really hurting and may feel fragile. Everybody in the group was heaping on her all the negative feelings they never told her before, and the group ended before much could get done past that."

Art was sensitive to the pain that an individual might be feeling as an individual. The group had not yet worked on understanding the use of her as an object of projection—a defeated object of shame in relation to the oedipal couple.

Arriving at a Position of Authority

Erin's group of advanced participants had enjoyed the presentation with less conflict. "My group felt positive about having words put to the experience in a way that they hadn't heard spelled out before," she said. "They felt that they were invited into the thinking about this rather than just the experiencing of it. Then they talked about whether there was any other place to go in this institution. Are there just two roles: the student role and the faculty role? They continue to come back for more learning because the presentations are always at the cutting edge, but they would like to have a separate role with an acknowledged status from which to make their contribution. They talked about their struggle with envy and inadequacy and their wish for an enhanced institutional role in order to feel better about themselves."

Brett was sympathetic to their situation. "I wonder if the presentation of the model instilled shame in them," he mused. "Here we are presenting something quite robust, quite narcissistically fulfilling, and tying it together for them. The model values the participants so highly that they may feel the institution can't exist without them individually. Here's this wonderful presentation that says who we are and how we're developing, but the model and the institution can't survive without them."

George began to explore the parallel to family process, and a rapid, witty interchange followed.

George: "It's as if they felt that if one of them were to leave, Mom and Dad may fall apart, or get divorced . . ."

Erin: "And certainly wouldn't have any more babies."

Martin: "Or *would* have more babies."

Brett: "Is it primal or is it . . . ?"

David: "Terminal?"

Conclusion

The child wants room within the family where it cannot split or destroy the parental couple. The grown student, like the one in Erin's group, wants to know whether there is room in the institution for them. If there is space for them, will it include room for their own creative coupling, or will it just be a basement apartment in which they are allowed to board until they leave the institutional family? These and other questions about the internal couple can be fruitfully explored if faculty and students are given room to do so. While the exploration is often uncomfortable, it is crucial to the development of space for thinking.

21
Risks, Advantages, and Applications

This chapter is drawn from a large-group discussion at a conference on the individual and institutional dynamics at which Dr. Anton Obholzer, from the Tavistock and Portman NHS Trust in London, was the featured speaker. As codirectors of the institution, we made the first presentation on the individual and group affective learning model based on our co-authored paper (J. S. Scharff and D. E. Scharff 1999a). We used a dialogue format to introduce the theoretical and technical aspects of the model elaborated on in Chapters 2, 3, 5, and 6. In Chapter 20, we reported on small-group and faculty-group responses to that presentation as a dialogue that had evoked the unconscious internal couple. Now we report on the large-group discussion of the content, led by Dr. Anton Obholzer. Following the presentation, the discussant, the presenters, the students, and the faculty focused on the advantages and disadvantages of using the model, the risks involved, and future applications. This discussion rounds out the presentation of the group affective learning model as a whole object for contemplation.

THE DISCUSSANT'S RESPONSE

Integration

Anton Obholzer summarized his view of the model and went on to elaborate: "What the model is trying to do is to put together all the various fragmented bits that have been nicely polished by others but kept separate. In the large group, you integrate them in the way you talk to each other. If you carry on talking together back and forth like that, working like that for weeks and months and years, you come a long way toward integrating some of these ideas, and you reach a model like this. It's striking that when I look at not only the concepts but also the reading list, I see you've integrated the work of people who certainly don't speak to each other and who most of us don't even think about within the same framework. So, that in itself is not only courageous but breaks the mold and allows for new ways of thinking."

The Need for an Interpretation-Free Zone

Thinking about the Scharffs as a couple presenting the model, Obholzer continued, "A memory came to mind of an analytic colleague who spoke with some feeling about his early childhood. Both his parents were analysts, and he recalls what seems to me (at least from the British perspective) a singularly Californian childhood of driving along in his parents' pink Cadillac convertible with his two analyst parents in the front seat and himself in the back seat and the parents attempting to control him through a variety of interpretations released over the shoulder as they were driving along in the California sunshine. Now, the point of this story is to raise the question: 'Should there be such a thing as an interpretation-free zone?' Not only for little boys in the backseats of their parents' cars, but should there be an interpretation-free zone for students? That I think is a key question. I think the answer is that there should be. One should have a space where one is free of comment and therefore free of being pushed into a rigidly held role identification."

Splitting or Integration of Interpretation and Education

"On the other hand," Obholzer continued, "if there is such a thing as an interpretation-free zone, then there is splitting, and the various sectors don't meet. So, that's the price of it. The traditional way of attempting to deal with this in psychoanalytic education has been by splitting education and analysis. You have either teaching, which supposedly has nothing to do with analysis, or analysis, which has no contact with teaching. The truth is that it's not like that because the connection continues to operate anyway, now on the basis of a nod and a wink. Nothing is said, but somehow or another inferences are made nevertheless.

"At the Tavistock we have attempted to deal with this using a variety of models. We have a group relations event which students go to, and we have got tutors who are supposed to integrate individual therapy and teaching experiences. The truth is, it doesn't often work. The tutors themselves have not had that integrated experience, so the problem remains. The affective learning model is revolutionary."

Safety in the Primary Task

Obholzer came to his main point. "It seems to me that perhaps the important concept, and one that you have taken for granted, is the concept of the primary task. Everything you are doing is in the service of the learning task. It is reassuring to students to know what the task is and why you are doing it in this reflective way. They also need to know what safeguards there are to stop this reflective process getting out of hand.

"It is important to assess the risks in the model. One of the safeguards is to ask what is going on in relation to the task. One does need to have a whole series of interlocking safeguards from various perspectives at all levels of faculty and participant that one can monitor from time to time."

In conclusion, Obholzer said, "The affective learning model comes a long way toward pulling together things that need integrating. It comes a long way toward addressing some of the problems in psychoanalytic education. If others might wish to take up and use this way of teaching and learning themselves, they will need help from the model to overcome institutional defenses and envy in order to begin incorporating some of these ideas."

THE LARGE-GROUP DISCUSSION

When Obholzer concluded, the discussion widened to include all the participants, presenters, students, and faculty.

Dual role relationships

An advanced student said, "In training as a systems family therapist, we are really drilled about avoiding dual relationships. For instance, if you were my small-group leader and also served as supervisor to me, that would be a dual relationship. Here in this model, dual relationships (a) exist to some extent and (b) seem not to be a problem. Could you talk about that some?"

David Scharff corrected her impression. "We avoid creating certain dual relationships, too. For instance, a participant who values the small group might request individual supervision with the same group leader. We have to refuse because the leader whose responsibility is to relate to the group can't work well if energy is siphoned off to focus on an individual. This would disrupt the group process. On the other hand, a small-group leader may be selected as a supervisor once the group is over. We would inquire into the reason for the choice, and if it made sense, we would agree, provided the supervisor and supervisee will keep the overlap in mind and examine how one relationship affects the next one so as not to live out the old role in the new one.

"We do not necessarily avoid a role relationship now that existed within a different role relationship formerly, but we ask that the influence of these factors be subject to investigation. That type of analysis is missing in systems therapy. Then all you can do is have rules about what you can and can't do. We do avoid some role conflict, but our guiding principle is that you look into what is happening before deciding."

Dealing with Resistance

A two-year program student mentioned that the group could be too effective in reducing resistance and therefore might suppress useful argument while appearing to encourage it. She said, "There is a risk that I have imagined associated with this type of learning, and I have spent the year protecting myself from it. This month I have been thinking about whether or not this is a necessary protection for me.

"I came to this institution as somebody who very much wanted to learn about object relations developmental theories, not so interested in analytic treatment, and yet wanting to open myself to the experience of hearing the argument for analytic treatment. One of the ways I've allowed myself to hear that argument is to assume it's going to take at least two years to make a good argument to me. I don't want to start arguing back, but the integrative task of the small group invites me to bring up the resistances I am working pretty hard to set aside while I listen to the argument. A particular lecture or particular weekend isn't long enough for me to engage in my debate because I'm a good arguer and I can convince myself to stop listening. And so, in the small-group task I have noticed myself avoiding talking about analytic treatment models because in some ways I'm too quick to realign my own system and I'd like to wait until the argument is more full. Without the small group, there are doors I would have closed already while thinking I was keeping an open mind."

The Regressive Pull of the Small Group

Another two-year program student, who teaches psychology to graduate students, spoke. "At a personal level, I find the small groups particularly helpful with the subjective responses stimulated by the material. At a professional level, I can observe an experienced facilitator, see how interventions are made, and find out which ones work. Now that I've experienced those advantages of the model, I've tried affective learning with my classes in graduate school.

"But as an instructor, I experienced dissonance using the model because the students I'm teaching are at different emotional, developmental, and cognitive levels than the students I learned with, all of them being trained therapists already. I have difficulty with my graduate students maintaining the small group as a learning experience versus a going-into-therapy experience. It's a very hard line to hold with students while succeeding in holding the group from walking away from the experience."

Jill Scharff responded to the issue of the regressive pull of the small group. "I think this links to the issue of the interpretation-free zone. Can a group maintain its work mentality, or is it inevitably going to express basic assumption functioning? It's inevitable that a work group will also express basic assumption functioning. This is a problem if a leader is overwhelmed by a group's propensity for basic assumption functioning or prefers to keep a group in the area of basic assumption functioning. Another problem occurs if the leader is so comfortable doing group therapy that she adheres to that familiar old model instead of following the integrative task. Similarly, preference for didactic instruction interferes with the capacity to engage with the unknown of the new model.

"Why is there a regressive pull? It arises from the propensity of the leaders and the character of the group. The size of the small group tends to be experienced as the family or the little home that those who like small places retreat into as a safer place to go than the large group. For those people, the regressive pull takes them to the area of longing, affiliation, and depending. For those who are frightened of a small group because it is too intimate, the regressive pull takes them into the area of fear, rejection, fight/flight, and connecting in the large group through hate.

"The integrative task is one that has to take into account cognitive and affective aspects of learning. There is no way it can be otherwise. Entering a group is itself an affective experience. If that is denied, the group experience is then one of frozen affect. The group is never affect free. No relationship is affect free. All small groups experience affect or suffer from the lack of it, and they regress at times as they proceed with the task. They have to if they are to do their work. The various forms of regression can then be recognized as patterns—as defensive processes to be worked on.

"Bion noted that critics of group methods say that a group in the grip of a basic assumption is one that can do no work at all. But Bion held that such a group can become one capable of a high order of intellectual functioning because the affective experience has been brought to consciousness and is now available for work. Once that is done, the group can progress to a new level of capability for dealing with regression, using that regression in the service of the learning task, and recovering from it."

The two-year program student who teaches psychologists continued, "As I said, I've experienced problems trying to integrate this group affective learning model into the classroom in a school system where other teachers aren't teaching this way. It has set up a splitting and devaluing of other professors' teaching methods. There is some concern in my mind that that dynamic could be destructive to the overall institution."

David Scharff agreed with her assessment of the risk: "If students come to idealize this method, they may devalue other methods and other teachers, and of course that's destructive. That particular split isn't a noticeable feature within this institution because those who don't choose this method go elsewhere to study. We don't yet know how well this kind of method can be applied to other institutions or how they might react to it.

"The pull for the affective learning group to become like a therapy group is the point of exposure that leads to the most frequent criticism of the method by students who don't make a commitment and by guest presenters who are there for one weekend conference only. It's the area in which we ourselves most frequently criticize our work. We have done a lot of thinking about it in the process of this writing and review. There is always tension between the task of integrating experience in the group with clinical experience, theoretical learning, and personal responses which we value highly. In a group that's working, it will pull more in one direction at some times than at others and then return to a state of balance. The group that veers off into an unthinking, unintegrated affective experience is of great concern to us."

A faculty member defended the usefulness of the regressive movement when if it is controlled in the service of learning. He said, "An affective experience might be therapeutic for a particular moment for a particular individual.

Without it, the learning may not proceed. The group might usefully pull in the therapy direction, and then the group leader has to refocus the attention on the group process of learning the concepts."

Containment of Anxiety

Following this discussion of the need for regressive experience, another faculty member addressed the wider issue of the mental health care context. He commented, "This institution is attended by people looking for containment because of the lack of containment both in private practice and in institutional settings these days. There is a demand placed on the institution to contain the anxiety from our individual settings and that sets in motion the unburdening and projection of anxiety rather than taking in, containing, and thinking about concepts and experience. That is an obstacle to be negotiated each time we come together. Anxiety has to be transformed into contained, metabolized experience and then fed back in a titrated form that enables participants to feel safely held by the institutional structure so that they can learn from within themselves rather than simply rejecting or accepting views that have been put on them. One of the greatest difficulties facing the institution that offers group affective learning stems from its being an oasis in an otherwise dry landscape."

The Anti-Task Group

Anton Obholzer rejoined the discussion. He thought that the risk of the small groups becoming therapy groups is one of the most obvious pitfalls into which a group leader might be pulled. He said, "Leaning toward therapy is an example of a flight from the task achieved through spotting and exploiting the vulnerabilities of the small-group leaders. I have in mind particularly a patient where it took me years to discover what she was up to because from time to time she would bring me the most delectable dreams. Usually, there were no dreams, and then there would be basketfuls of the most delectable dreams. It took me a long time to realize that these were actually brought in order to distract me from what was going on.

"The same applies in the small groups. Some members are going to bring bits of delectable pathology to small-group leaders who spend their life as therapists. They tempt them with these morsels in order to get them off the task. This anti-task staff baiting happens all the time for legitimate reasons of apparent compliance. If it's not picked up in time, it can become problematic.

"In other settings where the small-group leaders aren't clinicians, clinical pathology would not be half as tempting. Something else would be needed to put on the hook that grabs the consultant off task—perhaps an educational, methodological, or philosophical question to tempt a group leader who was trained as a teacher or philosopher. So, a comparative study is needed. The group affective learning model needs to be tested in an institution not teaching therapy to assess the risks and advantages over traditional methods in that setting."

Jill Scharff agreed that pathology could be used as a distraction from the task. From time to time, however, we are actually *studying* pathology. So she asked, "How can you study pathology except through the lens of your own pathology as well as through your pathology-free zones? To some extent, demonstrating pathology *is* the task. What determines whether that becomes anti-task is the degree to which it is used, not in the service of the learning but in the service of distraction, and the extent to which a subgroup formation crystallizes around an individual's pathology, is maintained that way, and is not subjected to examination."

Anton Obholzer concurred. "It is a matter of proportion. It is when the group perseverates on individual pathology that it becomes a problem."

Jill Scharff concluded, "We do find that each small group finds the balance between affect and cognition, individual and group, in a somewhat different place along the continuum of possible interpretation of the task.

A faculty member objected to designating the discussion of an individual's pathology anti-task. He said, "I think that people feel criticized when they're found to be off task. There is a built-in wish to shift back to intellectual understanding when our anxieties are opened by the presentations and can't be dealt with as fully as by a therapy group. Participants who are struggling with anxiety about the ambiguity inherent in the task project their anxiety into the group and then identify the group as a critical conscience. I think this phenomenon gets magnified when we limit emotional openness and availability for process and review."

Imperfections and Limitations of the Model

In response to a question about whether the group can always deal with every type of participant, Jill Scharff acknowledged, "The model doesn't always work well. It just doesn't suit some people. They try it, but they're too anxious to benefit from this way of working. Others want to hear the theory, but they don't want to connect to it affectively. So they will not join in the small-group functioning, or they come to one session and quit. They interrupt the process and take away from the learning of the group. The most disappointing experience of failure occurred when a small group's difficulty making a commitment to affective learning spread by contagion from one member to another. A nidus of difficulty in that group could not be addressed because of the limitations of our knowledge at that time and the constitution of the participants in that particular group."

A student who was in the first year of the two-year program said that she wanted to pick up on the experience of feeling criticized for not modulating the amount of affect in therapy-like material that comes in. But what she actually talked about was her own criticism of the faculty's actualization of the model. "This is a model of learning from peers in a group process setting," she began. "The hierarchy is also operative, however. Our awareness of the faculty review meeting is evocative of oedipal conflict. The idea that everything is out there and available for us to work with is not really true. I think there is some paranoia engendered by the falsity of the idea that there is no hierarchy and everything is open. I sometimes wonder if we could integrate this factor in our discussion. I suppose the answer would be that the institution can never be perfectly attuned to any individual student in the same way that a mother can't be with an infant. Perfect isn't perfect, anyway."

Anton Obholzer responded sympathetically and provided an alternative for the faculty to consider: "There is always ambivalence toward faculty meetings. The feeling of being excluded may be unpleasant, or it may be a relief. In the group relations conferences to study group dynamics that I organize, in some events the staff do work in public, about everything. Although at the beginning it feels really quite awkward for the staff, it actually works very well. We feel it is good for both the staff and the members. So there's an alternative way of working that faculty could consider."

"Anton Obholzer is describing one version of an interesting model," David Scharff agreed. "But I'm not sure we want to move to that degree of openness, however. Our teaching and learning model has some overlap with group relations conferences in terms of underlying theory, but they have a different primary task. Group relations conferences are not ongoing over two years. There the small groups do not have a task of integrating didactic material with personal and group responses. Conferences for studying group relations offer the faculty group as one of the groups to be studied. Our task is to use the group process in the service of our primary task, which is to facilitate learning and clinical application, not to study group process.

"We do have a hierarchy. We don't claim that everything is done in the open, and we don't want to eliminate private areas for working. Faculty have their own space for discussing things that may or may not get talked about in the large group. Participants also have their own spaces. They go off and talk about things which they may or may not bring up in the large group. Our guiding principle is that anything *can be talked about*, not that everything *has to be done* in public. People do need bounded spaces, some of them hierarchically arranged, so that they can process things in various ways. Later, they can talk about their process or their conclusions in the open. Whether they do so or not, the arrangement and its consequences are open to examination."

"If the institution is untouchable," a faculty member cautioned, "the small group carries the anxiety of spinning out of control. The structure of the institution has to be open to examination, and the design of every conference or institute includes a specific place where that occurs. I'm referring to the plenary review meeting where the faculty does work in the open with whatever the student body wants to raise. That is unlike most other psychotherapy or analytic training institutions."

The Use of Time

Another faculty member changed the topic. He said, "My comment takes us in a different direction. I'm referring to our use of time, which adds to the power of this particular learning model. We use time in these weekends and in the two-year program in a way that has a powerful effect. For instance, we start on time and end on time, and this puts a boundary on our work together. We learn in masses of time, three-day weekends when we don't do much of anything other than attend these meetings and a week in the summer. That way of learning is quite different than two or three hours a week for ten or twelve weeks."

Jill Scharff followed. "We keep time boundaries to let us know within what frame we're working, when the end is, how much time we have, and how to pace ourselves. It derives from respect for the opinion of the group—the whole group. There will be enough time to hear not just from the designated presenter but from the people who have come supposedly to learn but who also have previous knowledge and the current experience of learning to share."

David Scharff added, "Starting and stopping on time, respecting the integrity of each event, including informal occasions to meet, creates varied spaces for thinking."

A first-year student compared her current experience to previous learning. "At another institution, I listened to a presenter who spoke all the way to the end of her time," she recalled. "I felt that there was no time for the audience to do what we're doing here. It was such a disappointment. She stirred up ideas, but we didn't have a small group or any kind of open discussion like this to deal with them. I realized what a richer experience a lecture is if there's time for people to free-associate."

Learning from the Third Position

One of the advanced students who had attended many conferences connected theory and experience. "I'd say that one of the benefits to me from continued participation in the conferences using this model has been the emphasis on affective linkages," she began. "I'm aware of the difficulty of maintaining the linkages and establishing the perspective of 'the third position'— which it seems to me is the basis of the integrative affective task." Working from the impact of her current experience on the concept of integration that she was describing, she continued, "We are sitting here in the audience facing the couple who presented. They are seated with the chair, so altogether we are facing a threesome. In a visual form, we are literally facing the embodiment of the intellectual and affective task that we are presented with."

Jill Scharff agreed that the integrative task calls for the ability to work from the third position. "I'm glad you're referring to Ron Britton's work," she responded. "At an earlier conference using the affective learning model, Britton (1998) spoke about being able to hold the third position within the oedipal triangle by tolerating the pain of maternal and paternal aspects coming together in a fruitful and creative intercourse or, by analogy, to tolerate affect and cognition coming together in a creative intercourse within the mind of oneself and any others within the group. (The impact of Britton's [1998] lecture is reported in Chapter 13.) Many classical analysts think that object relations theory has to do with preoedipal dependency. On the contrary, we are well aware that sexuality, aggression, and curiosity infuse both preoedipal and oedipal relationships. In affective learning about object relationships, we study all these aspects from every developmental position. The integrative task calls for a person to work from the third position, a position of oedipal resolution."

Linking the previous speaker's comment with other aspects of the discussion, Jill Scharff continued, "Your comment about literally facing the couple and the threesome is reminding me of two other comments: one about the child in the back of the Cadillac with the analytic parents and the other about the dual relationships that appear to be tolerated here. The most obvious example of the dual relationship is that David and I are work partners in developing and using the affective learning model, and at the same time we are husband and wife in our family. There are other husbands and wives in the membership. Are these couples and dual relationships going to be interferences with our capacity to work from the third position? Or are they situations that are open to examination as to the effect they have on one's fantasy life and one's capacity for identification with the task?"

Following on that, Anton Obholzer stated, "It seems to me that in speaking about this affective learning model you have been clear about how it began, how it's taken in by the individual through personal introjection, how it lives on externally by repeated attendance at conferences, and how it creates for the participants a personal membership in an ongoing inner-world training institute."

Extensions of the Model

A student in the second year of the two-year program asked, "Is this teaching model specific to the therapy model that is being taught, or does it have applications to other types of psychoanalytic education? Could it be applied in education broadly?"

"It's specific to the teaching of object relations theory," Jill Scharff replied. "Could it be applied to analytic theory of an eclectic type? I think so. But I haven't seen it happen, so I can't really say for sure."

David Scharff referred to his school's consultation work. "School teaching is done in groups. Teachers learn about groups to the extent that this will improve their teaching technique and their capacity to maintain discipline, but they don't usually value the group for life-skills education. Our first attempt to use affective learning was with students and teachers in high school and elementary school, and later in college, to help them be more thoughtful about the emotional aspects of teaching and learning (see Appendix). Affective learning models could be useful in other educational and work settings."

Jill Scharff added, "I hope there's a place in general education for the kind of integrative task that we are doing. I believe that this kind of group work would offer children a place for learning how to process life experience. This would encourage adaptibility, which to my mind is the single most useful human skill for times of rapid change. I'd like to see children assigned to groups that meet weekly to talk about their roles as pupils, the content they have to learn, their feelings about that, and their learning process together in the small group and in the large group in the classroom. I think that would raise a healthier, more reflective generation of children."

A student who taught high school added some information that supported this hope. "Back in 1922," she began, "John Dewey was writing about how you can't separate emotion from intellect in the learning process. His ideas were largely ignored for years, but many teachers and scholars in education now believe that the field needs to move in this direction." She continued, "In the university where I trained, the emphasis was on educating teachers to develop artistry and reflection. We were to reflect on what we were doing while doing it (Schön 1983, 1987). In other words we were supposed to learn from our experience while teaching and to help our students to do the same.

"For instance, a lot of elementary and high school teachers in various disciplines are asking students to keep portfolios of their work including their drafts and their accounts of their learning processes. In Britain this kind of portfolio assessment of process as well as product has been mandated as part of the national curriculum in some subject areas. Not only that, but children are being taught to work collaboratively in groups. Even at the Ph.D. level, groups are used to provide a place of support for learning research methodology, undertaking research, and writing theses—and a place for reflection on the group process (Ely et al. 1991). How you think about the question and how you work together to get the answer is becoming more important than the answer alone. So, I think the affective learning model in psychotherapy training is consistent with the trend in general education today," she concluded.

Associated Models

A student who was about to graduate was thinking back to her earlier professional education: "In medical school, the faculty wanted us to have some of the same experiences as the patients so we would have a better understanding of what it was like to be on the other side of the doctor–patient relationship. For instance, students had to have nasogastric tubes put down our noses, or have bleeding tests done on us, or wear hospital gowns and be exposed physically."

David Scharff reminded her of Michael Balint's application of psychoanalysis to family practice consultation and medical education (Balint 1957). "There is now a worldwide system of Balint groups for family doctors," he said. "They use a related methodology for groups based on clinical case presentation in which family doctors process their experience. Some of these groups have been held for medical students.

"That's a much less literal way of processing experience than the way you had to do it in medical school. In Balint groups, medical students can talk about their traumatizing experiences, such as being ill, experiencing a medical procedure, or treating ill or dying patients. The group contains their anxiety and gives them a secure place in which to metabolize their experience. They learn how to use the wisdom of the group to help them face future challenges."

Maturation of the Model and the Host Institution

An advanced student was appreciative. "This particular learning model is perhaps the most useful one that I have come across," he began. Looking ahead, he went on, "And I would like to continue to utilize it, but with recognition of my advanced status. 'Veteran' participants find it problematic to recapitulate ground that newer participants need to cover to establish a small group. When a small group has only veteran participants, certain kinds of issues can get addressed that can't be touched in other contexts. These veterans would like to participate together at the advanced level, continuing to learn and contribute to the model. Through the generous use of the self in teaching and learning, the model facilitates our growth in a loving way. But the issue isn't always how to receive love, it's also how to give love."

Another advanced student who had attended many conferences said, "My personal experience in terms of role identification in which I have felt stuck as a perpetual student leads me to wonder how this model is going to mature over time."

Embracing the unknown of the potential of the model, David Scharff replied, "The first program we did using a precursor of the affective learning model was ten years ago. I had no idea then what it would evolve into when we put together the original ideas from our previous work. It's become much more than anything I thought of. It's developed a life of its own. It continues to place demands for evolution through questions like this and suggestions that students and faculty make. We know it takes some steering to stay on track, but not so much that we limit our direction. After all, we can't know what we'll be steering through. I've come to realize that the thing to do is to let go and see what happens."

Epilogue

As the program director, I represent the educational task. I have the responsibility for overseeing and directing the program, for ensuring that the teaching is effective, and for keeping the learning environment free of anxiety and corruption. I exercise this responsibility within the learning matrix of support and feedback to which I contribute and from which I receive my course corrections. The more I am informed by the faculty's pooled wisdom, the better the work of the institution. To the extent that I manage not to become defensive and constrict the process, openness recycles from director to faculty to students again. The resulting non-linear fabric of connectedness builds a matrix of continual learning and teaching in a setting of trusted and examined relationships.

We value learning from experience at every level—listening to the information given through lectures, workshops, and readings; sharing in the emotions of the group; and finding meaning in relationships. As students, if we are willing to be open about ourselves and receptive to others, we can move together into areas in which we do not yet know our way. As faculty, we take responsibility for creating a dependable learning environment and for having something to teach, and at the same time we join in the exploration of shared areas of not knowing.

Affective learning is an integration of the affective and the intellectual. The affective learning model uses multiple perspectives that give dimension to the thinking process. Emotional responses, interpersonal behaviors, and fantasies, which in the world of therapy are often pathologized, are depathologized by being experienced in a group where they are processed and reviewed empathically from multiple vertices in many settings and by overlapping group compositions. Actions and feelings that are narrowly construed as difficult or abnormal can be examined from conscious and unconscious perspectives, amplified and objectified by the magnifying lens of several small and large groups, and eventually detoxified and understood.

A single comment, a dream, a small-group theme, a clinical presentation, or a multilogue in the large group—each is a fractal of the overall learning process. A small part of the pattern in one dimension is repeated in other dimensions and reflects the overall pattern. From any small part, a complete hologram of the total experience can be constructed. For example, discussion by the faculty group is like a hologram of the learning process of the whole institution. The faculty brings information from the large and small groups to its shared examination with a view to understanding the whole pattern. The resulting faculty process reflects images of the institutional culture that have penetrated into each of the groups and then generates enriched images that have ramifications throughout the institution.

In this book, we have offered many examples of the faculty's small-group process. The faculty is the small-group that the program director leads. The small group leaders reporting to the faculty group bring with them the experience of the whole institution. Faculty group discussion leads to an enhanced understanding of the problems of a particular small group, of a theme arising in the discussion of the large-group presentation, or of the projection of group and institutional issues onto an individual. When several faculty members report on a shared group event—as in a large-group presentation, a plenary, or even a coffee-break discussion—their pooled experience virtually always exceeds the wisdom of the director who is leading the faculty group. In these discussions, the group joins in problem-solving, in peer supervision of their group work, in giving essential feedback to the program director and supervising his work, and in coconstructing an image of the learning process.

Object relations teaches that the need for relationships is the fundamental, sustaining condition of living and growing. The more open we are to relating, the more we have to offer and the more we can take in cognitively and emotionally. This principle works in psychoanalysis and psychotherapy. And it works in the teaching and affective learning of psychotherapy.

Appendix

Appendix
Teaching and Learning:
An Experiential Conference*

INTRODUCTION AND PURPOSE

A conference has been designed using an experiential group format for studying the relationship between experiential and cognitive learning, and the interrelationships of the personal processes of teaching and learning within both groups and individuals. The aim of the conference is to provide a vehicle for the examination of the way in which teaching and learning are related to personal experience. The conference design provides a number of varied group settings and calls for a range of consultant role behavior, so that the individuals will have several contrasting modes of experiences in which to study both their own and others' attempts to teach and learn and to examine the effects of the contexts.

Throughout these varied group settings, there is a constant task for each participant: the examination of the processes of the individual's attempts at achieving learning—that is, the *student* role—and at facilitating learning for others—the *teaching* role. The personal and group factors that impede and facilitate teaching and learning are both an object of study and a means of understanding more about these reciprocal processes within the self.

*"Teaching and Learning: An Experiential Conference," by David Edward Scharff and Jill Savege Scharff, reprinted courtesy The A. K. Rice Institute, from *Journal of Personality and Social Systems* 2(1):53–78, 1979.

It is also assumed that the primary experiential mode of such a conference, largely stripped of any readily apparent cognitive structures, will give the participants a chance to examine the relationship between their own cognitive knowledge and the knowledge derived from experience.

The examination of the relationship between cognitive and experiential learning is further heightened by specific elements of conference design that focus on this, such as a lecture event, which is chiefly an opportunity to study the experience of trying to learn within the constraints of a lecture format.

Furthermore, the study task of the conference focuses on the ambiguity of the current experience and maximizes the disorganized foundations of knowledge within the individual and the group, much as the blank screen stance of the psychoanalyst maximizes the unconscious elements of individual patients in an analogous study task. This provides an opportunity to study the unconscious, interpersonal, and group processes in essentially a laboratory setting, unfettered by the needs for specific performance, the pressures of outside evaluation, or practical expediency.

This paper will describe the design of such a conference that we have tried several times, emphasizing the structure and rationale as it has evolved to date. We will then have a limited opportunity to discuss some of the themes and fruits of the conference, illustrated by issues that arise for work in the setting provided. It becomes obvious that the issues that may emerge are infinitely varied, as complex as the structure of individual experience and knowledge multiplied by the variety of interpersonal factors in human groups, and that one could never hope to know, explain, or encompass them all. But we do have a beginning toward understanding the kinds of experience that can emerge, and we will share as many of them as space permits.

RATIONALE FOR THE USE OF A GROUP RELATIONS FORMAT IN THE STUDY OF TEACHING AND LEARNING

A person may experience relationships in a number of ways:

a. One brings to the conference a background of prior personal and institutional relationships that constitute previous experience with people and with teaching and learning.
b. One has an opportunity to experience oneself in relation to other individuals and groups of individuals in the conference itself.

c. One can experience oneself and groups of individuals in relationship to the subgroups and parts of organizations existing within the conference as a temporary institution.

d. One may experience oneself and the temporary conference-as-institution in relationship to other organizations or kinds of organizations or institutions within and after the conference.

Thus, there is a microcosm–macrocosm continuum of learning experience that extends from the individual's internal group representing the sum of internalized prior experience to the groups outside and beyond in current and future concerns. When we speak of group experience, we include the smallest earliest groups in the continuum—specifically the mother–child group and the family group of three or more—as not only the individual's original experience with group life but also the earliest experience of learning and teaching.

This microcosm–macrocosm continuum is capitalized on in the conference by a continual focus on the struggles to learn and teach together yet maintaining the need for separateness during the personal task of learning. This is illustrated in the way individuals use and abuse each other and themselves, in the relationship of the group and the individual to the consultant or teacher (who is defined as a colearner as well), and in the attempt to use the various structures of the experience either to learn or to maintain secure relationships at the expense of learning.

Much of the model of group relations work that follows derives from our experiences in the Tavistock Model group relations conferences, developed by the late A. K. Rice and offered by the Tavistock Institute of Human Relations in Great Britain, and by the A. K. Rice Institute in the United States (Rice 1965). This conference is based on a task of the study of authority and leadership in several group settings. In turn, the understanding of group phenomena rests on Wilfred Bion's ideas (Bion 1961, Rioch 1970b).

Bion described group life as consisting of two elements: the work (or task) group, which coexists with the basic assumption group (or group unconscious). Basic assumption group life follows one of three major themes: dependency, fight/flight, and pairing. In a dependent group, members rely on the leadership, as in a religious group; in a fight/flight group, they engage in aggressive or fleeing behavior, as in the army; and in pairing, two or more members band together to bring forth a messiah who will save them, as in a family having a baby as a way out of difficulties.

Our use of this set of ideas has been modified by the differing nature of our task. But we continue to draw on this previous experience, as well as on our consultation work to schools (Savege 1974a,b, D. E. Scharff 1975a,b), research into transitions of adolescence (D. E. Scharff 1980, 2000, D. E. Scharff and Hill 1976), our training and teaching experience in individual child and family therapy (D. E. Scharff 1977), the creative therapies (Savege 1975), and their literature.

What Is Meant by "Learning" and "Teaching"?

With the understanding that learning and teaching are open to diverse definitions, an attempt is made to keep the operational definition in the conference at as deep and general a level as possible and at the same time, simply stated. This is done with the idea that the conference experience forms a basic science laboratory experience in education and growth to be widely rather than narrowly applied by each individual. The very definitions, then, of teaching and learning are open for examination by the individual and the group. What can one learn from the current experience about external life and about oneself, and what can one teach about it?

In the here-and-now conference, learning is generally defined as the ability to experience emotionally and cognitively the events that take place, and to increase understanding of the nature of the individual's place in them. As the lesson is unstructured, it values complexity, involvement, and integration. While learning implies intellectual understanding, it should not be at the expense of emotional involvement. The learning strived for in general, then, is an integrated human experience probably closest to emotional growth or mature understanding that tolerates complexity, integrates feeling and thought, and tolerates the eternal experience of the unknown—of never being able to know everything. And this learning intimately involves other people, not symbolic abstractions, even when the learning is about an apparently more concrete subject, for example, a conference institution that purports to further the pursuit of knowledge or of specific learning–teaching relationships. Even then, much of the learning is about the nature of human interaction. The individual can hope that light will be shed on his characteristic attempts toward and defenses against teaching and learning in a way that is analogous to a patient who learns about characterologic style and defense in the psychoanalytic process.

Teaching within the conference is best defined as the attempt to facilitate the learning of others. This includes several kinds and levels of verbal and nonverbal behavior in an endless variation of ways of facilitating others' learning. Teaching may be a sharing of one's own learning or confusion, a questioning of another, a posture that indicates acceptance during stress, or a confrontation around ambiguity or defensiveness. At its most profound level, teaching and learning take place when two or more people share the vulnerable areas of their personal unknowns without shutting each other out but without attempting to do the work for each other unnecessarily.

The Consultants

In the Tavistock conference, throughout its various group settings, the consultant consistently leads the group to its task of the examination of leadership authority in relation to the consultant as an authority. In our conference where authority is *not* the central concern, the consultant is primarily a teacher and a colearner who has the task of learning and teaching about what is still being learned, including how to teach that. Because of previous experience and skills developed for this task, the consultant is also an authority but deals with authority issues in the group as they interfere with or are substituted for the learning process. The interpretations and problem solving are in terms of the struggles to learn and to teach within the group and for individuals. However, the consultant is interested primarily not in the individual but in the group's experience. Since modeling and identification are two important modes of learning, the processes of the consultant's work in relationship to the group are available for examination and exploration.

Furthermore, the teaching *style* of the consultant is available for examination as one of the variables of great importance in teaching and learning. In the conference structure, a deliberate attempt is made to vary the style of consultancy and to make this variation an object of study. The range varies from the style of a small study group, in which the consultant frustrates individual dependency needs, to the directive style of psychodramatic role-play, to the formal role as lecturer.

Some of the unstructured events require an impersonal consultancy style where the membership learns to listen to what the consultant has to say rather than how it is said. Other events later in a conference require a more relaxed and *apparently responsive* style. We say "apparently responsive" because our experience is that the type and content of interventions remain fairly constant. This deliberate varying of style has a purpose. The matrix of consultancy roles offers a variety of object relationships, some of which will be personally more relevant than others for individual members of subgroups.

The Conference Format

The format of the conference is still in evolution and presumably will never be frozen if we, as consultants, hold to our task of learning from each conference and applying the learning to the design of the next conference. We have more experience with the original events than with the newer ones and have conceptualized some that at the time of this writing we have not yet had a chance to try. Various adjustments are required from one conference to another, depending on the length of time available and the needs of the sponsoring institution. Such adjustments are made consistent with the principle of weaving a pattern of alternating media and nonmedia, small and large group, intimate and anomic teaching and learning situations through which the individual will pursue the task of the conference. A basic shape of familiar, tried events has emerged and is illustrated here by the program of a two-day conference.

First Day

a. Opening Plenary (10 minutes)
b. Small Group (90 minutes)
     Coffee
c. The Individual in the Large Group: Psychodramatic Format (120 minutes)
     Lunch
d. Large Group (90 minutes)
     Tea
e. Lecture–Discussion (1 hour)
f. Small Review Group (90 minutes)
     (Same grouping as Event b for all small groups)

Second Day

a. The Small Group in the Large Group: Art Media Format (90 minutes)
     Coffee
b. Small Group (90 minutes)
     Lunch
c. Final Plenary (or Large Review Group) (90 minutes)
     Tea
d. Small Application Group (90 minutes)

The overall conference forms an organic whole with problems, issues, and themes growing from one event to the next, some continuing and being magnified and others submerging to resurface later. This sense of continuity needs to be borne in mind during the discussion of each event. In the ensuing discussion, we will draw examples primarily from one conference in an attempt to give a sense of that organic quality as it grows through experience, and in doing so, recapitulates the movement of human growth and development through learning.

The conference staff consists of the consultants, the director, and the administrator. The conference membership consists of participants drawn from one institution for teaching and learning. So the members have preexisting role relationships as students, student–teacher, teachers, or senior teachers that they import to the conference from the institution. Since to date the conference is offered to individuals rather than to the institution from which they come, we assume individual members are present in similar conference roles as conference members and not as student, teacher, and so on. These preexisting roles in the institution contaminate their conference role relationships and are worked with.

To keep this clear in our report, we have used the following conventions: We refer to the institution where the membership was from as the original institution to differentiate it from the conference institution; we use quotation marks when mentioning the individuals' preexisting roles as "student," "teacher," and so on in the original institution. For reason of confidentiality, we have changed members' names and have not specified from which conference or which institution our examples are taken.

The Individual Events

The Opening and Closing Plenaries

These two events form the boundaries between the membership as a whole and the staff as a whole. In addition to having certain formal properties, these events form a kind of skin around the conference, even though, as we have designed the conference, the closing plenary is the second-to-last event. This schedule leaves a review–application group to defuse some of the charged atmosphere of the seemingly inevitable climactic confrontations between members and staff to further the assimilation of the organic whole of the conference experience and its carry-over to the individual's professional life.

The opening plenary is a brief gathering of all participants: members seated in rows facing conference staff, including consultants, administrator, and director. The planned content has been the introduction of staff, the reading of a statement about the task and format of the conference, and the answering of any questions of such an opening meeting. In the early part of the ensuing conference, it serves as a focus on the struggle with the understanding of task and structure.

Example 1

A conference member, Arthur, challenged the right of the conference director to tape record portions of the conference. Although our intent to tape for subsequent review and learning was described in the advance brochure, Arthur, who held an advisory position in the original institution, insisted that he had not known this and would withdraw his membership, supported by the loyalty of many members who would follow. We decided that it was more important to forgo the tape recording, losing that opportunity for our learning, than to win the confrontation about our authority and lose the membership with whom we wanted to teach and learn. The effects of the challenge to and the exercise of authority in the learning situation, as seen in this plenary and later in the conference, were examined as interferences to the process of teaching and learning. A major theme of that conference was evaluation and theft of knowledge by teachers as well as withholding from teachers the opportunity to learn.

The closing plenary shares some of the characteristics and themes of the unstructured large-group event, although it has a different task. The physical setting, therefore, is also different in that we recently have begun to arrange the chairs so that the staff group faces the membership as in a panel discussion or lecture. This enhances the feeling of confrontation, magnifying the chance that a staff-membership division will be one of the objects of study as the conference experience is reviewed and examined. This is part of the theme of the evaluation of learning and teaching that seems to be an integral part of the process of teaching and learning. The physical arrangement underscores the need for membership and staff to evaluate not only each other but also their own performance. This does not mean evaluation in any formal or reporting sense but in the more profound sense of the need for individual evaluation of the value, impediments, and gains of experience. This personal and institutional self confrontation may be derived and projected so that the conference staff is seen as the object to confront.

Example 2

In a closing plenary of another recent conference, the members began the event by changing the chair arrangements to a large circle. In subsequent examination, they were able to describe the wish to form a pseudo-democracy not only to submerge the conference staff among the membership but also to hide and protect the member who was the senior administrative teacher of their original institution. They hoped to avoid confronting us and him with their feelings about our and his work. This also would have protected themselves from evaluating their own work in the conference and original institutions.

The Small Group

The small group is a cornerstone experience of the conference. Its format is similar to the study group derived from the work of Wilfred Bion and is somewhat similar to the small groups used in the Tavistock Human Relations Conferences developed and described by Rice (1965). For those not familiar with the format, we begin with a brief description of the similarities.

The small group consists of between seven and eleven members optimally, with a single consultant. The group meets for an hour and a half several times during the conference. If the conference extends over three to five days, the small group might meet six to eight times, while in the briefer conferences we have run, it has met in modified form four times in two days.

The consultant behaves prototypically as described previously, acknowledging no direct questions, commenting on the general issues in the group that underlie the manifest content and that are contributing to or impeding the pursuit of the study task. This has the effect of magnifying aggression, frustration, and feelings of self-deprecation early in the group experience. It brings into focus for study a shifting maze of group behaviors that are various defenses against the study task. Simultaneously, the consultant is reflecting a personal struggle with the role and with the experience as a teacher and learner in the group. Here again the consultant's behavior provides a model for the personal examination of an individual's own processes. This might be described as a group being steered toward the Socratic method, with all the anxiety inherent in such a method of study.

The interventions, and perhaps even the style, of the consultant differ from the traditional Tavistock small group in the orientation, focus, and underlying theory. Comments are aimed at examining small-group relations, not as in the Tavistock intervention around the themes of authority and leadership but of doing so in the pursuit of the teaching and learning tasks. What this means specifically will become more apparent in the following sections that describe some conference experiences. The interpretive interventions focus on the uses of defenses and the nature of work in the conference.

Example 3

Two group members, themselves teachers in the original institution, began to tell others who were students in that institution what they might learn in the conference. The students assumed the posture of not knowing anything and of expressing the confusion on behalf of everyone. This polarization of knowing and not knowing as defined traits of participants kept the group from the collective anxiety of not knowing what *this* experience would hold in store for them and of sharing the unknown together.

Another important set of small-group events involves the relationship between the group members and the consultant who is often put into the role of teacher who should be in the know and is then vilified for not telling or passing on this knowledge, as though the current experience could be foretold. This set of interactions provides an arena for the examination of dependence–interdependence–independence issues as they impede and facilitate the teaching and learning. This aspect of the relationship of the group to the consultant continues throughout all events but is often most intense in the small-group, where members may vacillate between seeking and avoiding the identification of their own teaching and learning parts. It is, therefore, crucial that the consultant serve as the model for the middle ground of the overlap between teaching and learning where study takes place.

The Large Group

We have generally staged this event in a series of widening concentric circles of chairs, just enough to accommodate membership and staff, taking a cue from our own experience in Tavistock conferences. This emphasizes the confusion and anxiety experienced in a group of such size, designed to be large enough so that no one visually takes in the total experience of the group. It emphasizes the nature of the complexity of such an experience, underscoring one of the things that must be coped with even in more simplified and direct group experiences. Coming early in the conference experience, ideally as the second major event after an introductory small group, the large-group event tends to underscore the family nature of the preceding small-group experience and in contrast presents a kind of chaos of the outside world. It echoes the developmental step from the family to the wider world of school in the educational growth of the individual.

Example 4

In one large group, there were two seats left for us, David Scharff in the center near two female conference members, who were students in the original institution, and Jill Scharff on the extreme periphery. At first this was seen as representing a hole in the middle of the group's learning, to be filled by the sexualized pairing of the female "students" with the male director/consultant, and an attempt to exclude the female consultant, denying the work and personal pairing of the two consultants. Later it was also seen as an attempt to evacuate the center of the working group by placing there "students" who were expected to substitute emptiness for the digestion of knowledge. By keeping out of the center those members who were "teachers" in the original institution, the conference maintained the illusion that only "teachers" could know enough to do the central work.

The group dynamics of the large group extend the teaching and learning task to the conference institution as a whole, offering the opportunity to examine the role of the larger group to generate, express, facilitate, and frustrate the individual's study task at a time when, simply because of the size of the group, other individuals are not answerable to each other. One individual may ask a question of another, or react to another, but be unable to respond because their dialogue is cut off. The study of what can be learned or taught in such a potentially confusing atmosphere is important in regard to individuals who seek to work, teach, or learn in institutions or organizations. If the small group represents and elicits the experience of the family or intimate group of peers, the large group operates at the level of the wider world in which one is answerable to forces beyond the control and answerability of these intimate relationships. In the world of fantasy, these correspond to the difference between family myths and society-wide or religious myths. It is in the large group that we have the best opportunity to examine the origin and use of the reverberation of myth in the struggles to learn and to teach. Psychological, social, and religious myths have a useful expressive and experiential life here: The consultant leaders are deified and villainized, while the "mob" is dependent, on the rampage, or keenly and worshipfully hopeful. Individuals emerge from the chorus like Greek actors on platform shoes taking the role of hero, guide, leader, man, woman, parent, child, victim, or has-been. The challenging and unnerving attempts to give form to the chaos of inner-life and group experience in this setting are precursors of the development of drama and media as aspects of human communication and expression. The large group sets the stage for the ensuing events that try to make sense of the experience of chaos.

The Individual in the Large Group

Psychodramatic Format

This is the first departure we made from the Tavistock group formats and was designed to provide an alternative to the intergroup events that we felt not to be directly applicable to our task. It also provided an approach to the use of drama as a teaching vehicle.

In this event, using the psychodramatic format modified from psychodrama described by Moreno (1946), the membership and staff sit in a large continuous circle. One of us (J. S. S.) is the director of this event, and the other (D. S.) is her assistant. A member who volunteers to share a problem connected with the conference experience is chosen to be the protagonist.

The director of the event then assists the protagonist in setting a scene that expresses this issue, either real or fantasized. In order to engage in the enactment of the protagonist's problem, other group members are chosen by the protagonist to take other significant roles. As the action proceeds, the director's assistant stays physically and emotionally close to the protagonist, speaking as the inner voice of the protagonist at blocking points when feelings cannot be expressed to allow the protagonist to explore further. Technically, this is called *doubling*. Other members of the group are encouraged to join in the doubling, either for the protagonist or for the support roles. They can, thereby, facilitate the action exploration and later discuss their experience of partaking in or viewing the action. This is an action format, and the action is essential to the teaching and learning aim.

Example 5

In this conference, after a number of members volunteered, one female undergraduate called Anne mentioned her struggle with valuing honesty and openness while fearing both adverse evaluation by her teachers and her own capacity to offend fellow students with her bluntness, a characteristic conflict for her that had emerged in the previous small group. She re-created a situation in which a student had painted a picture of a small child and asked others what they thought of it. Anne had wanted to say, "That's terrible. The colors are not good." Instead, she said, "Gee, that's nice."

In the role play, Anne was able to exchange places with the other girl, to begin to understand what fears she was projecting onto the others in protecting her from her own criticism, and to examine the sources of her own inhibitions in that prototypical teaching and learning problem. In particular, her own fears of vulnerability had kept her from developing a tactful form of critical teaching. Others who had been present in the same or similar exchanges were able to share, to provide differing perspectives, and to join Anne in this personal issue that bore a direct relationship to the theme of evaluation within the conference.

After a series of related minidramas are developed by the member–protagonist, the group as a whole discusses and processes their experiences, observations, feelings, and reflections. It is crucial to allow sufficient time for this part of the event, for without it, the experience tends to remain interesting but not to be integrated with the rest of the conference. Since additional time is required, this event tends to run two hours, while others are an hour and a half.

One aim of this event is study the ways in which the concerns of the individual speak for the group as well as the ways the group reflects the concerns of its individuals. The interaction between these two can only be examined in one or two sample dramas within a conference, but once the principle of the reciprocity of the group and the individual has been illustrated, it can be studied further in other events without being so graphically delineated. The other aim is to study how teaching and learning are affected by the involvement of the self in physical action as well as verbalization and reflection. The physical creation of emotionally charged events bears a definite relationship to learning and the growth of each of us individually and is worth recalling and pursuing in this special format.

The Small Group in the Large Group

Art Media Format

This is designed to explore the use of media as aspects of human expression and communication. The large group is instructed to divide into subgroups consisting of the small group membership and is told that each small group should paint its experience in the conference in relation to the other groups in the conference (meaning in relation to the other small groups, the staff group, and the large group). The group has twenty-five to thirty minutes to complete its task and is supplied work space and art materials (large paper, paint and brushes, or pastels). The consultants are available on request but so far have not been requested. At the end of the specified time, the groups reassemble as a large group to describe their paintings and the process by which they made them and to elaborate on the themes presented. Only after the group presents its work do the members of the large group question, reflect, criticize, and comment. An attempt is made to discover what parts of the conference experience are represented by each of the groups and what can be learned by the process of taking all the creations of the groups as a total statement about the conference experience.

Example 6

At one conference, some members were not present for the instructions, and when they retired to their private group areas, one of the conference members who was on the faculty of the original institution repeated the instructions, leaving out the phrase "in relation to the other groups." Although another member who was a student in that institution corrected him, this was overlooked, which later led to an exploration of the distortion of not listening to those in a student role and its meaning for learning and teaching.

The two groups worked differently: The group that had worked earlier with D. S. looked like a working group with several members engaged at once. The other group that had worked earlier with J. S. S. looked like a series of individuals with one member at a time using the brushes for the most part. Both groups were unable to return to the large group on time until we began to comment in increasingly louder voices on the stretching of boundaries, speculating on the wish to play and to avoid the work of examination of their products. The illustrations below are the products.

J. S. S.'s group described how they had drawn a large and a small rhinoceros (Figure App.–1), arising from the thought of drawing a unicorn which somehow did not fit. These two rhinos both had wings and were both pregnant with twin unicorns. The sky was blue with a black cloud on which a smiling face had been drawn, and the cloud was emitting rain and lightning. One rhino stood on muddy ground and the other on the grass. This represented the belittlement of the student and the aggrandizement of the teacher, with some appreciation that these roles *could* change. They then displayed their second painting (Figure App.–2) which they had done with a lot of giggling but could not say much about it.

Figure App.–1

Figure App.–2

D. S.'s group then spoke about its painting, which had begun with a flower design (Figure App.–3). Each petal represented an individual's view of the group, while the center, which was originally supposed to be the large group, had in fact become the small group. It contained a summary of each individual's small-group experience. The images in the center were described as a series of signatures. The middle signature was a yin and a yang sign (also an upside down

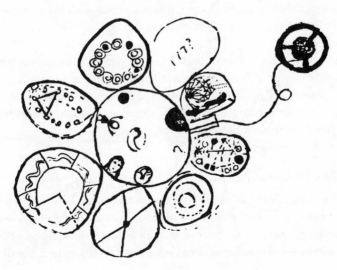

Figure App.–3

"S", the consultants' shared initial). The stem of the flower changed during its production to become something of a string attaching the flower to a tape. This tape represented the dominant theme of whether the director would persist with recording the conference and intrude on the privacy of the members. The one who drew the tape felt he had given up his invaded feeling but then appreciated that *he* had *become* the tape recorder of the group in his silent passive observing stance. One woman suddenly realized that the flower looked more like a bomb.

In the discussion phase, several themes surfaced in what became a rich but conflictual discussion. Attention focused at first on the rhino symbol, with questions as to whether this was a male and female that might be pairing or a mother and a daughter, both of whom were pregnant. Had the pregnancy been immaculate, caused by the rain and lightning from the happy cloud? The sexuality once recognized, the group responsible for the rhinos defended them from critical study, as in defense of the play of the group. Comments were taken not as group work but as a spoiling of the play. A call from the consultants to work with the material was met with resistance, one member saying he knew how it felt to be a patient being treated by a psychiatrist. However, the groups were able to talk quite a bit, both here and in the later review groups, about the uses of covert sexuality, the need of a horny fantasy beast that could stand up to the hard critical knocks while protecting the frail unicorns, unborn and full of creative promise, who might have sharp horns (critical comments) but who also might have a creative mythical magic. The other group came to recognize and play with the ambiguous picture of an explosive, intricate flower that represented the intellectualizing defenses against a wish to fuse rather than grow and a fear of evaluation that kept them sharing only a small part of their inner experience.

Interpretations of the symbols of the group experience are not intended to be absolute or right. They arise from the interaction of painted image and fantasy responses leading to further explorations of the experience. They reflect only the understanding actually achieved about the conference, through the conference media, not about the art productions.

The Lecture-Discussion

This event, with all the hallmarks of a traditional educational format, has turned out to be one of the most thought-provoking of the conference. Its form is direct: Within a one- or one-and-a-half-hour event, a lecture of twenty to thirty minutes is given. So far it has been done by the conference director

(D. S.), but any of the consultants could be designated. Originally, we thought the lecture could deal with either a theoretical model of teaching and learning, or a theory of educational and personal development, or organizational theory as applied to institutions of teaching and reaming. All of these would be relevant. But so far, we have given lectures that focus on aspects of the lecturer's personal experience (including the struggle to teach in a lecture), of his own struggles to learn and to teach, and of his experience with previous conferences (including the Tavistock model from which this one is derived) and previous consultants, leading only secondarily to some theoretical notions about teaching and learning.

The results have been dramatic and stimulating, ranging from those in the audience who despair to learn what the lecturer has said to those who say with obvious relief that they know all that despite the fact that the bulk of the lecture is about the *lecturer's own experience* and is not theoretical. What comes first, so far in our attempts, is the rage, despair, relief, and other affective responses to the experience, with very little attention to the content of the lecture.

Example 7

When, on one occasion, the lecturer stepped aside from the podium (purposely used to underscore the formal nature of the lecture) after the lecture for the discussion, one listener said he had the fantasy the lecturer was going to hit him, while another thought to himself, "Ah, now I will be able to hear what he says." Another reported being unable to listen and being forced to look out the window, while another member reported "hoping the 'students' would get what the director had to say" since he [a faculty member in the original institution] "knew the theory already."

It is worth noting that the original institution of the group we are reporting on in this example eschewed formal learning settings like lectures, but its students did have to take more traditional courses at other times and places, and most of its faculty could sooner or later be expected to function in such settings.

The affective barrage aimed at the lecturer afterward has led him (in other conferences) to ask that another of the consultants chair the event, with responsibility for focusing on an understanding of the interaction between the lecturer and the conference membership. Although perhaps formally not necessary, since the role of all the other consultants is to make whatever interventions they feel help in furthering the task, even without the formal designation of the chair, the independence of the chairman has proven to be a valuable addition in focusing on the total task.

Review and Application

The Review Group

Each review group, consisting of the same membership as the small group, is asked to begin reflecting on the conference experience both as a whole and through a perspective of some distance on the particular events. We have focused on comparison of the effectiveness of the different formats for each individual in which he has been asked to teach and learn. The review group has been used to pull together the experience of the conference before a break.

Example 8

One member of the review group had been in J. S. S.'s review group the previous year. J. S. S. noticed a change in that he was much more responsive and talkative throughout the conference. During review, she commented on finding him newly communicative and responsive and would be interested in anything he had to teach her and the group about that. He confirmed her impression and said that he had learned during the last year's conference that being involved in silent thinking for yourself did not teach others. He previously thought others knew what he was thinking and where he stood. Realizing that, he had been trying to say what was his mind and had been able to take a more effective leadership position in the original institution and in this conference.

Then he remembered that he noticed a change in the consultant since the year before. She did not seem to be as strictly concerned with task and defenses. She thought this was accurate and had been worried about sloppiness and not doing as well as before. He, however, now found her more helpful. This might have been because she was more freely entering the area of unknown herself this time, undefended by well-tried interpretation and focus.

The Application Group

The closing event of the conference is the review and application group, which leaves the individual participant started on the continuing task of using what has been learned in this work situation. To date, we have elected to restrict the application focus to that of the conference experience of the individual's own problems around teaching and learning. The expectation is that this focus may bring changes in each individual's role and functioning in the original institution.

Example 9

In one final review and application group, a member with a faculty position in the original institution discussed a problem around defensiveness in his "students," working on his own need to talk at them. Another member who was one such 'student' began to explore some of the ways he personally had felt threatened by him and others in the conference and in his work, while another person began to explore areas of personal vulnerability in her own teaching situations with children in her role in the original institution. As this was going on Anne, the "student" who had volunteered as protagonist, in the psychodrama group previously described, began to draw (Figure App.—4). Her drawing, she said, would have become a man falling off a cliff, while someone with a microphone pressed him to "speak a little louder, please." She was illustrating

Figure App.—4

both the threat felt by several members and her own vulnerability exploited for others' conference learning while leaving her feeling hurt and desperate.

This example shows that the focus of application was on the personal teaching and learning of the self in any work situation. The learning is not applied to the original institution from which the members come. Because of this, there tends to be some overlap in areas of discussion between review and application groups although their tasks are differentiated.

DISCUSSION

In the discussion, we would like to briefly consider four areas, recognizing that a fuller examination of them will have to await another publication. They are

a. the role of relationships in the study of learning and teaching,
b. the role of groups in the study of learning and teaching,
c. the role of media in the study of learning and teaching, and
d. defenses against learning and teaching.

Relationships in Teaching and Learning

This conference is, above all, a chance to study the role of personal relationships in education. Developmentally, learning occurs for an infant when a neurological/physiological substrate in the infant is prepared to accommodate and be shaped by experience. From the first, these experiences relate to a primary person in the child's life, the mother, even in the case of the intra-uterine learning potential that has recently been demonstrated. In the view of many, the need for attachment to other people is the primary and organizing theme of human development (Bowlby 1969, Mahler et al. 1975, Winnicott 1965). It follows that the role of attachment and its complementary opposite, the need to be separate-but-attached, will have a major, organizing role in learning and teaching. Initially, we learn in order to be fed, protected, and loved by another, while others learn to do (and teach) these things in order to feel worthy. But we must separate from that other person in order to do these things for ourselves, and the separation process must be matched by a reciprocal letting go. In the process, we come to treasure knowledge because (a) it is a part we take in of those we love, (b) it is a mastery of how to be separate and get along on our own (that is, become the caring figure to ourselves), and (c) it gives us a way of giving part of ourselves to, or doing for, those we love, thus securing and renewing the bond of attachment-in-separateness.

An example is provided within this kind of conference or in the teaching-and-learning situation, when someone supplies an insight or piece of information that helps another. The bonds between those two are usually strengthened, acting as adult substitutes for the original primary bonds between mother and child. While the learner is at that moment close to dependence, paradoxically the learning experience equips the learner to be more independent from that moment on. This leads to the eventual shared loss of the mutually dependent relationship in which learner depends on teacher and teacher depends on learner for a sense of worth. But this loss, optimally, leads the way to a mature interdependence in current future relationships.

But this relationship between personal attachment and the facilitation of learning often does not work this way, and when it does not, it becomes one of the important inhibiting forces to teaching and learning. Relationships built on the wish to detach or the fear of loss will not facilitate learning. For instance, envy between two people can powerfully inhibit teaching and learning. A "student" envying a "teacher's" position of knowledge can refuse spitefully to learn, either consciously or unconsciously. And a "teacher" envying a "student" (perhaps for youth, intelligence, freedom, opportunity, or lack of restriction) may fill the relationship with bitterness, condescension, or control, thereby making learning by the "student" unlikely. We will discuss some of the defensive positions in the attempts to learn and to teach shortly. *It is not that nothing can be learned in these impasses*, but the learning is about the causes and defenses of the impasse, and any learning or teaching beyond that is in spite of these destructive or impeding factors, not because of them. This conference maximizes the attempt to study the defensive positions, including the use of defined student or teacher role, their causes, solutions, painful feelings, and consequences.

Finally, we emphasize not only that we include current relationships with individuals but also the vast number of old relationships still alive for each of us. These relationships with people and parts of people often idealized or distorted are constant companions who help and hinder us constantly and who are given a new life within the conference to be studied, learned about, and learned from still.

There are a series of complex underpinnings of personal interaction that are available for study within the conference and that have general relevance to learning settings. The emotional state is one of the crucial and constant variables. In the experiential setting, we can explore the amount of anxiety, depression, enthusiasm, or anger that helps or hinders learning. What human underlying needs are represented by these affects? When do they accompany vulnerable or defensive positions? When do they prepare the ground for new learning, sharing, or insight?

Another of these issues is the role of authority and leadership in facilitating or impairing teaching and learning. What is the constructive use of one's own or another's authority? Whom can one trust or depend on? What relationship, both to nominal leadership and to leadership exercised by peers, will help or hinder one's own progress? These questions represent aspects of what might be called the management of behaviors in the learning situation, the experiences that relate to the whole area of the use of discipline in education, discipline both of oneself and of others. For instance, although conference activity is largely verbal behavior, it brings up the same boundary issues to be dealt with in physical and verbal behavior in other settings, for there is still the opportunity for invasion of private space, for verbal violence, for destruction of structure, and for constructive rebuilding, cooperation, and sharing. Consultant behavior is one that members will study, attack, emulate, ignore, and depend on. The question available for study is, How does this help or hinder the task?

Groups and Learning

The conference is, in part, a group relations conference, although one with a particular task around teaching and learning. In presenting several learning settings, it provides an opportunity to compare differing learning vehicles, but it also forms an institution with a thread of group experiences in which the dynamics of groups have a chance to influence and be part of what is studied and at the same time give each member a chance to teach about and through them. All the vicissitudes of conscious and unconscious life, as best described perhaps by Bion (1961), can be taken on in mortal combat. In life we learn in groups. The group life, therefore, needs to be part of what is studied about teaching and learning.

And then, as we have said, the conference as a temporary, sample institution becomes a model for the larger patterns of the ways the original institution facilitates or hinders teaching and learning. This aspect is one that we would like to explore more directly in future extended conferences, as described in our final comments in Section IV.

Media

A part of the experience of the conference with wide application to the field of applied teaching is the study of the teaching-and-learning task with the use of the various teaching aids or media. Within the conference, we have noted that memory for media and action events is more prominent than for other events. Furthermore, in presenting this work to professional audiences, we have found the same overrepresentation of these events in their discussion. The vividness of the visual presentation and its creation involves the childhood roots of the sensorimotor body in action, picture, and drama. From this developmental viewpoint, it is clear enough why words and verbal experience are harder to make as graphic and memorable. Yet the understanding and analysis of each of these events still rests on verbal processes to understand or make sense of the experience. We have begun to wonder whether the facilitating effects of media and action in teaching and learning mask a process of avoidance of learning. Is something better remembered, but without the fine sense of detail and introspection? Does the resistance to critical inspection that we saw tell of a problem that is part of these modes? The possibility has occurred to us that the visual–motor clarity of these events may actually *detract* from the learning since the sense of experience can overshadow the sense of understanding. But then it may also follow that the experiences themselves remain consciously available longer for follow-up reflection.

Defense against Teaching and Learning

From the earliest moments of the conference opening, there is evidence of defenses and resistances to the task of studying, of teaching and learning by oneself and with one another. These defenses form a network of interrelated balances that shift constantly in pattern and weight, some diminishing while others rise against the development of a learning attempt. After interpretation of the defenses, there follows a period of work and clearer confrontation with basic anxiety about teaching and learning, and a new equilibrium between various defenses and anxieties results, weaving a pattern unique to that conference and to that collection of members and staff.

As described by Bion (1961, Rioch 1970a), the group has its own basic assumptions that represent its collection of unconscious forces. Personal "valencies" or tendencies lend the individual on behalf of the group to the expression of varying basic assumptions in what is for each person a unique pattern. In a complementary way, through studying the overall pattern of conference work and resistance, one can hope to learn more about one's own work and resistance, roles in various events, defenses against teaching and learning, and recurring thought and feeling patterns, all of which either may provide or block insight. While we will be presenting discrete descriptions of some of the common defenses (and by no means all of them), it should be borne in mind that these are but the single units or building blocks out of which the organic understanding of a conference is built.

Example 10

During the small group, a conference member on the faculty of the original institution explained at length, giving something of a lecture, while another member, who was a student at that institution, asked questions, expressing that he felt he could never know such things. On closer examination, the "student" had disagreed with the "faculty" member but was denying his own experience and his own knowledge out of awe of the idealized teacher, thereby depriving the "faculty" member of a new learning experience as well. This, in turn, could be seen to protect them both from the more ambiguous and painful experience of sharing in not knowing and from the need for further exploration.

The "faculty" member, who defensively "lectures" "students" about his subject while being unable to hear their probing questions, is hiding his vulnerability and possible lack of knowledge but at the same time is exposing his need to be in control not only of his information but also of the people who are the objects of his teaching. He presumably needs respect and confirmation as a "teacher." In a reciprocal manner, the "student" who feels unsure of what he knows stays in control of the anxiety about knowledge by maintaining that he knows nothing compared to his "teacher," comforted in feeling that there is someone else who knows, perhaps with the hope that he will get there someday but does not have to be responsible for his learning now.

In the group process, then, the opportunity can be presented for these reciprocal positions to be exposed as a collusive effort of this "faculty–student" pair to fend off the necessity of each individual in the conference to explore the known, the unknown, and the teaching each has to offer the other in the process. In subscribing to this more profound task, the reciprocal defenses become an object of study. They become vehicles in the descent into the substrata of underlying need, defense, and fear of the unknown.

Example 11

The silence at the beginning of the female consultant's small group was broken when one of the members (who had the role in the original institution as one of the more senior teachers and administrators) gave an erudite, extremely intellectualized account of teaching and learning. He suddenly realized no one was relating to him and felt set up, pleading with others to explain why this kept happening. Others obligingly responded by keeping him in focus and attacking him for this self-centered behavior and for ways in which he wielded his authority in the institution.

We worked on the defensive aspects of this at a number of levels. There was the obvious defense of intellectualization stating the known to fend off the unknown situation that still had to be learned about. There was the polarization of knowing it all into a conference member who was also a senior "teacher" while others attacked this defensiveness in him, even while relying on it and perpetuating it.

The female consultant began to feel irritated and excluded, and it occurred to her that the group might be displacing feelings and anxieties about her and her role onto this member.

Here the group was defending itself by confronting the known "teacher" rather than the unknown consultant. It was dealing with him as an authority rather than as a "teacher," again out of anxiety about dealing with the nature of the female consultant as teacher or authority. When this was interpreted, the group tried hard to pair the member with the consultant, so that the consultant would be wedded to him (and through him to the group) instead of the task. Here the defense of pairing was in use, at the same time giving expression to need for intimacy that was to come up so many times.

Example 12

a) The membership confronted the conference director in the plenary about his previous plan to tape the conference, so that his first impact on the membership was in the role of the authority who had to make a decision in face of protest.

b) In small groups, there were attempts to set up a member with a senior role in the original institution as an authority figure and then work on feelings about authority.

c) Throughout the early phase of the conference, the word *authority* kept appearing in the membership.

It became clear that the membership had heard that this would be a Tavistock-type group conference and assumed that the work would be the same as in other previously attended group relations conferences on authority and leadership, ignoring the facts of the conference brochure titled "Teaching and Learning—An Experiential Conference." Here the conference membership was defending itself by substituting the known rather than grapple with the unknown. This original skewing of focus persisted, however, and we became aware that many times authority issues were magnified and worked on as if to free up the process of teaching and learning by improving relations, when it was equally likely that the focus on authority issues was a defense against getting on with the process.

Example 13

During the art media event, one group produced the painting of the rhinos. Then excitedly and messily it did a colorful, blurred finger painting (see Figure App.–2). During the discussion, the group was incoherent about this second painting, except to mention there was a yellow duckie and that the blue was happy in among the green. Attempts by others to discuss it were fended off or experienced as hostile criticism.

It was not possible to fully understand and verbalize what was represented in any way that could be worked with and learned from in a reciprocal, reality testing way. We guess that the preverbal regressive needs for expression, mess, pleasure, feeling, and body contact were split-off from central conference control and gained primacy over the task. Here play, which was part of the work, became a defense against further teaching and learning. A paranoid defense was also in use, where criticism and anger were felt to come from outside persecutors trying to destroy the fun.

Example 14

A large review group consistently avoided reviewing the conference experience. Instead it seemed to be re-creating a previous large group learning situation. There was a lot of talk about the loneliness of the learner whose passive wishes to be taught were thwarted and who had to do it alone. Then there was a question about the need for intimacy as a prerequisite for teaching and learning. A longing for more real relatedness to each other was expressed. Then the membership described a number of special interest groups that had sprung up in the original institution but finally dwindled down to just one or two people, who then gave up the groups.

The review task was not followed in order to avoid feelings about the end of the conference. The experience of being a lonely, longing learner was very much alive but was not being examined in the here-and-now of the ending of the conference. After this interpretation, the issue of intimacy was raised, partly as an objective way of dealing with the jealous feelings toward the paired consultants but also as an entry into speaking of needs for continuing attachment. The longed for intimacy and attachment were defended against by intellectualization, but then again the very issue of attachment was used as a defense against loss of attachment to a teaching and learning task.

These defenses operate in a complex way, and the treatment of them as a complicated interpersonal process is one major example of the conference's focus on the management of complexity and ambiguity. They operate as boundaries between individuals, while communicating personal need, a need to be dealt with in a certain way, to be allowed privacy, a request for respect, a sign of feeling vulnerable. Rather than treat them as pure *barriers* to interaction, we have chosen to see them as *vehicles* facilitating interchange, operating at the interface between people. They are opportunities to interact; they *are* the interaction, and if treated as objects of study, they function as ways in to one another, as ways for individuals to explore themselves in relation to others. In studying their own defensiveness, members may be more able to study from within the relationship between the teacher and the learner inside the self.

Each unitary defense speaks of both an underlying need and an underlying fear. Then there is a reciprocity of need and defense between conference members. For instance, one will have a student defense, while another will have a teacher defense, and they will collude to act a combined role *as though* teaching and learning are going on. Therefore, the interrelatedness of unitary defenses leads to a series of role relationships. In our conferences for groups from an original institution of teaching, these role relationships have been developed and institutionalized prior to the developed. Defenses and role relationship systems brought to and developed de novo within the conference are treated as vehicles to knowledge, not as barriers, as semipermeable membranes, allowing access while providing a boundary. In the truest sense, then, the roles and defenses are the object of the learning and teaching. They are the subject that the unstructured lesson of the conference is about.

FINAL COMMENTS: IMPLEMENTATION AND CONFERENCE DEVELOPMENT

This conference works toward an experience of interlocking development and growth. In educational settings, much richness occurs from the sharing of experience by people at different stages of their life sharing in the interlocking of their life crises, life hopes, and life fears. How each of us copes with the current state of our life, learns from it, and defends against its particular pain is of vital importance. It is this piece of human ecology and growth that we have hoped to focus on in developing this conference model.

We have much to learn about and through this model. We hope it offers a way to teach through the sharing of a process, to reach others and to enable them to share in the exploration of the constant and ever-receding unknown. So far, we have had the opportunity to try the design over relatively brief periods. Although the conference has been offered to memberships drawn from teaching institutions, we have not tried to extend the model to apply in an organizational consulting sense to those institutions, partly because the conferences were so brief and partly because we wanted to remain conservative in our aim at this stage in our experience with the design. Instead, we have focused on the consultation to individual members around their own teaching and learning, which had to include interferences from institutional role relationships that were also present in reality at the conferences.

We hope the conference experiences provided opportunities for learning for the individual, as described in Examples 9 and 10. At a feedback session some months after that conference, the director of the original institution attributed to the conference an improvement in staff–student morale. This might have been the sum of individual changes affecting the shared institution, but it seems more likely that it was also due to a sentient effect or perhaps an oblique effect, as if the conference *had* been an organizational consultation. Actually, there were many expressed wishes that this should be offered, which we regarded as attempts to change the task.

In developing the design, we would like to try longer conferences that would give the opportunity to deal with patterns that recur over longer intervals, allowing more in-depth work and learning. In a longer conference, most of the events would take place several times. Small-group meetings might meet twice a day, large group daily, and the other one to three events per day would use the art, psychodrama, or lecture formats. We would also include two events that were not used in the conferences reported here but that we have tried since.

These events are:

"The inner group in the small group"; a personal process recall method is used to extend the range of the teaching and learning experience to include the inner world of the individual and his past.

"The small group in the large group." The use of the teaching technology, audiovisual, and other nontechnical ways of presenting and recording informa-

tion and experience is examined as it facilitates or impedes learning for the small group in its task of sharing its experience with the large group.

We anticipate that the level of complexity of theme and interpersonal development in such an extended conference setting would be well worth the added investment of time, adding to the richness of the experiential fabric, the depth of exploration, and the amount of carry-over into life after the conference.

With an extended conference, we would also be interested in focusing more directly on the application of the model as an organizational consultation to the teaching institution. We know already that an organizational effect can be increased by specific attention to the organizational consultation task, although it is possible that the earlier organizational impact happened precisely because the focus was not the organization but rather the individuals involved in its work.

We would be interested in comparing this conference of homogeneous membership with one offered to a heterogeneous membership from several institutions with shared but different educational goals, methods, and environment and without previously developed role relationships. It would also be interesting to compare these conference experiences with one offered to an educational institution that also has a service task, such as a department of psychiatry or other medical university department.

SUMMARY

In this paper, we have tried to present the conference as a structure, but one with an open and evolving content. Content and structure are, after all the vehicles for the process of learning about and through one another. The conference focuses on that process as the essence of teaching and learning.

Note: We are grateful to our colleagues, the late Margaret Rioch, Ph.D., for her support in the early steps of our conference development; the late Charles B. Ferster, Ph.D., and Ken Roy, M.A., for joining us as consultants in the last conference and sharing in the development of the conference conceptualization; to all of them for their critical reading of this paper; and finally to the institutions of the American University Learning Center and the Mark Twain School for asking us to work with them.

References

Ainsworth, M. D. S., Blehar, M. C., Waters, E., and Wall, S. (1978). *Patterns of Attachment: A Psychological Study of the Strange Situation*. Hillsdale, NJ: Lawrence Erlbaum.

Alvarez, A. (1993). *Live Company: Psychoanalytic Psychotherapy with Autistic, Borderline, and Deprived and Abused Children*. London: Routledge.

Anderson, R., ed. (1992). *Clinical Lectures on Klein and Bion*. London: Routledge.

Anzieu, D. (1988). Foreword. In *Psychoanalysis and Group*, ed. D. Rosenfeld, pp. ix–xiv. London: Karnac.

Arlow, J. A. (1963). The supervisory situation. *Journal of the Amercian Psychoanalytic Association* 11:576–594.

———. (1972). Some dilemmas in psychoanalytic education. *Journal of the American Psychoanalytic Association* 20:556–566.

Ashbach, C., and Schermer, V. L. (1987). *Object Relations, the Self and the Group*. London and New York: Routledge.

Balint, M. (1957). *The Doctor, His Patient and the Illness*. New York: International Universities Press.

Bennet, M. J. (1989). The catalytic function in psychotherapy. *Psychiatry* 52:351–364.

Bergman, M. (1987). *The Anatomy of Loving*. New York: Columbia University Press.

Bernfeld, S. (1962). On psychoanalytic training. *Psychoanalytic Quarterly* 31:453–482.

Bertalanffy, L. von (1950). The theory of open systems in physics and biology. *Science* 111:23–29.

Bion, W. R. (1961). *Experiences in Groups and Other Papers.* London: Social Science Paperback, 1968.

———. (1962). *Learning from Experience.* New York: Basic Books.

———. (1965). *Transformations.* London: Heinemann.

———. (1967). *Second Thoughts.* London: Heinemann.

———. (1970). *Attention and Interpretation.* London: Tavistock.

Bollas, C. (1987). *The Shadow of the Object.* New York: Columbia University Press.

Bowlby, J. (1969). *Attachment and Loss. Volume 1: Attachment.* New York: Basic Books.

———. (1973). *Attachment and Loss. Volume 2: Separation.* New York: Basic Books.

———. (1977). The making and breaking of affectional bonds. *British Journal of Psychiatry* 130:201–210, 421–431.

———. (1980). *Attachment and Loss. Volume 3: Loss.* New York: Basic Books.

Briggs, J. (1992). *Fractals: The Patterns of Chaos.* New York: Touchstone.

Britton, R. (1998). *Subjectivity and objectivity in borderline states.* Paper presented at the "Object Relations in Britain" conference of the International Institute of Object Relations Therapy, London, July 27–31.

Britton, R., Feldman, M., and O'Shaughnessy, E. (1989). *The Oedipus Complex Today: Clinical Implications.* London: Karnac.

Budman, S. H., and Gurman, A. S. (1988). *Theory and Practice of Brief Therapy.* New York: Guilford.

Chiang, F. (1979). Father. In *In the City of Contradictions*, p. 50. New York: Sunbury.

De Maré, P., Piper, R., and Thompson, S. (1991). *Koinonia: From Hate, through Dialogue, to Culture in the Large Group.* London: Karnac.

Dewey, J. (1922). *Human Nature and Conduct.* New York: Henry Holt.

Dicks, H. (1967). *Marital Tensions.* London: Routledge & Kegan Paul.

Eitingon, M. (1923). Report of the Berlin Psychoanalytical Polyclinic. *International Journal of Psycho-Analysis* 4:254–269.

Ely, M., Anzul, M., Friedman, T., et al. (1991). *Doing Qualitative Research: Circles Within Circles.* New York: Falmer.

Ezriel, H. (1950). A psychoanalytical approach to group treatment. *British Journal of Medical Psychology* 23:59–74.

———. (1952). Notes on psychoanalytic group therapy II: interpretation and research. *Psychiatry* 15:119–126.

Fairbairn, W. R. D. (1944). Endopsychic structure considered in terms of object-relationships. In *Psychoanalytic Studies of the Personality*, pp. 82–136. London: Routledge & Kegan Paul.

————. (1952). *Psychoanalytic Studies of the Personality*. London: Routledge & Kegan Paul.

Falzeder, E. (1999). *Profession: psychoanalyst, an historical view*. Unpublished paper.

Fleming, J., and Benedek, T. (1966). *Psychoanalytic Supervision: A Method of Clinical Teaching*. New York: Grune & Stratton.

Fonagy, P., Moran, G. S., Steele, H., and Higgitt, H. C. (1991). The capacity for understanding mental states: the reflective self in parent and child and its significance for security of attachment. *Infant Mental Health Journal* 13:200–216.

Fornari, F. (1966). *The Psychoanalysis of War*. New York: Anchor.

Foulkes, S. H. (1948). *Introduction to Group-Analytic Psychotherapy Studies in the Social Integration of Individuals and Groups*. London: Heinemann.

————. (1964). *Therapeutic Group Analysis*. London: Allen & Unwin.

————. (1974). *Group Analytic Psychotherapy: Method and Principles*. London: Gordon and Breach.

Foulkes, S. H., and Anthony, E. J. (1957). *Group Psychotherapy: The Psychoanalytical Approach*. London: Penguin, 1965.

Freud, S. (1921). Group psychology and the analysis of the ego. *Standard Edition* 18:69–134.

————. (1926). Inhibitions, symptoms and anxiety. *Standard Edition* 20:77–172.

Fromm-Reichmann, F. (1950). *Principles of Intensive Psychotherapy*. Chicago: University of Chicago Press.

Galatzer-Levy, R. (1995). Psychoanalysis and chaos theory. *Journal of the American Psychoanalytic Association* 43:1095–1113.

Gleick, J. (1987). *Chaos*. New York: Viking Penguin.

Gross-Doehrman, M. J. (1976). Parallel processes in supervision and psychotherapy. *Bulletin of the Menninger Clinic* 1:9–105.

Guntrip, H. (1969). *Schizoid Phenomena, Object Relations and the Self*. New York: International Universities Press.

Hopper, E. (1977). Correspondence. *Group Analysis* 10(3):9–11.

————. (1996). The social unconscious in clinical work. *Group* 20(1):7–42.

————. (1997). Traumatic experience in the unconscious life of groups: a fourth basic assumption. *Group Analysis* 30:439–470.

Hoyt, M. F. (1990). On time in brief therapy. In *Handbook of the Brief Therapies*, ed. R. A. Wells and V. J. Gianetti, pp. 115–143. New York: Guilford.

Jacques, E. (1955). Social systems as a defence against persecutory and depressive anxiety. In *New Directions in Psycho-Analysis*, ed. M. Klein, P. Heimann, and R. Money-Kyrle, pp. 478–498. London: Tavistock; New York: Basic Books.

Jones, M. (1952). *Social Psychiatry: A Study of Therapeutic Communities*. London: Tavistock.

Kernberg, O. (1974). Mature love: prerequisites and characteristics. *Journal of the American Psychoanalytic Association* 22:743–768.

———. (1980). Love, the couple, and the group: a psychoanalytic frame. *Psychoanalytic Quarterly* 49:78–108.

———. (1986). Institutional problems of psychoanalytic education. *Journal of the American Psychoanalytic Association* 34:799–834.

———. (1995). *Love Relations: Normality and Pathology*. New Haven, CT: Yale University Press.

———. (1998). *A concerned critique of psychoanalytic education*. Paper presented at the Swiss Psychoanalytic Society, Geneva, October 3.

Klein, M. (1946). Notes on some schizoid mechanisms. In *Envy and Gratitude and Other Works 1946–1963*, pp. 1–24. London: Hogarth, 1975.

———. (1952). Some theoretical conclusions regarding the emotional life of the infant. In *Envy and Gratitude and Other Works 1946–1963*, pp. 61–93, London: Hogarth and the Institute of Psycho-Analysis, 1975.

———. (1975). *Envy and Gratitude and Other Works 1946–1963*. London: Hogarth and the Institute of Psycho-Analysis.

Kreeger, L., ed. (1975). *The Large Group: Dynamics and Therapy*. London: Constable.

Lifschutz, J. E. (1976). A critique of reporting and assessment in the training analysis. *Journal of the American Psychoanalytic Association* 24:43–59.

Lonie, I. (1991). Chaos theory: A new paradigm for psychotherapy? *Australia and New Zealand Journal of Psychiatry* 25:548–560.

———. (1992). The princess and the swineherd: some applications of chaos theory to psychodynamics. *Australian Journal of Psychotherapy* 11(1):47–59.

Lorenz, E. (1963). Deterministic non-periodic flow. *Journal of Atmospheric Science* 20:130–141.

Mahler, M., Pine, F., and Bergman, A. (1975). *The Psychological Birth of the Human Infant*. New York: Basic Books.

Main, M., and Solomon, J. (1986). Discovery of an insecure/disorganized/disoriented attachment pattern. In *Affective Development in Infancy*, ed. T. B. Brazelton and M. W. Yogman, pp. 95–124. Norwood, NJ: Ablex.

Mandelbrot, B. (1982). *The Fractal Geometry of Nature*. San Francisco: Freeman.

Menzies, I. E. P. (1960). A case study of the functioning of social systems as a defence against anxiety. *Human Relations* 13:95–121.

Miller, E., and Rice, A. K. (1967). *Systems of Organization: The Control of Task and Sentient Boundaries*. London: Tavistock.

Milner, M. (1987). *The Suppressed Madness of Sane Men*. London: Tavistock.

Moreno, J. L. (1946). *Psychodrama, Vol. 1*. New York: Beacon.

Neri, C. (1998). *Group*. London and Philadelphia: Jessica Kingsley.

Ogden, T. (1986). *The Matrix of the Mind: Object Relations and the Psychoanalytic Dialogue*. Northvale, NJ: Jason Aronson.

————. (1989). *The Primitive Edge of Experience*. Northvale, NJ: Jason Aronson.

————. (1994). *Subjects of Analysis*. Northvale, NJ: Jason Aronson.

Palombo, S. (1999). *The Emergent Ego: Complexity and Co-Evolution in the Psychoanalytic Process*. New York: International Universities Press.

Pichon-Rivière, E. (1977). *El Proceso Grupal. Del Psicoanalisè a la Psicologisa Social*. Buenos Aires: Nueva Visiòn.

Piers, C. (2000). *Character as self-organizing complexity*. Unpublished paper presented at the winter meeting of the American Academy of Psychoanalysis, New York, January.

Pines, M. (1979). Group psychotherapy—frame of reference for training. *Group Analysis* 12(3):210–218.

Quinodoz, D. (1994). *Emotional Vertigo: Between Anxiety and Pleasure*, trans. A. Pomerans. London and New York: Routledge, 1997.

Quinodoz, J.-M. (1991). *The Taming of Solitude: Separation Anxiety in Psychoanalysis*, trans. P. Slotkin. London and New York: Routledge, 1993.

————. (1997). Transitions in psychic structure in the light of chaos theory. *International Journal of Psycho-Analysis* 78(4):699–718.

Rice, A. K. (1965). *Learning for Leadership*. London: Tavistock.

Rioch, M. (1970a). Group relations: rationale and technique. In *Group Relations Reader*, ed. A. Colman and W. H. Bexton, pp. 3–9. Sausalito, CA: Grex, 1975.

————. (1970b). The work of Wilfred Bion on groups. *Psychiatry* 33(1):56–66. Reprinted in *Progress in Group and Family Therapy*, ed. C. Sager and H. Kaplan, pp. 18–32. New York: Brunner/Mazel, 1972, and in *Group Relations Reader*, ed. A. Colman and W. H. Bexton, pp. 21–33. Sausalito, CA: Grex, 1975.

Sachs, D. M., and Shapiro, S. H. (1976). On parallel processes in therapy and teaching. *Psychoanalytic Quarterly* 45:394–415.

Salzberger-Wittenberg, I. S., Henry, G., and Osborne, E. (1983). *The Emotional Experience of Learning and Teaching*. London: Routledge & Kegan Paul.

Savege, J. (1973). Psychodynamic understanding in community psychiatry. Proceedings of the Ninth International Congress of Psychotherapy, Oslo. Reprinted in *Psychotherapy and Psychosomatics* 25:272–278, 1975.

———. (1974a). Thomaston School pupils' group. London: Tavistock Institute of Human Relations Centre for Applied Social Research Document CASR 1031, October.

———. (1974b). Tutors' pastoral care consultation group at Thomaston School. London: Tavistock Institute of Human Relations Centre for Applied Social Research Document CASR #1031, November.

———. (1975). Role and training of the creative therapist. In *Creative Therapy*, ed. S. Jennings, pp 199–227. London: Pitman.

Scharff, D. E. (1975a). Aspects of the transition from school to work. In *Between Two Worlds: Aspects of the Transition from School to Work*, ed. D. E. Scharff and J. M. M. Hill, pp. 66–332. London: Careers Consultants.

———. (1975b). The transition from school to work: groups in London high schools. In *When Schools Care*, ed. I. Berkowitz, pp. 329–339. New York: Brunner/Mazel.

———. (1997). *Teaching and learning about children in groups*. Paper presented at the annual meeting of the American Association of Psychiatric Services to Children, Washington, DC, November.

———. (1980). Between two worlds: emotional needs of adolescents facing the transition from school to work. In *Responding to Adolescent Needs,* ed. M. Sugar, pp. 215–233. New York and London: SP Medical and Scientific Books.

———., ed. (1996). *Object Relations Theory and Practice.* Northvale, NJ: Jason Aronson.

———. (1998). *Chaos theory and self-organizing systems.* Unpublished lecture at "Separation Anxiety and Psychoanalysis" conference, International Institute of Object Relations Therapy, Bethesda, MD, December.

———. (2000). *The taming of psychological chaos: Fairbairn and self-organizing systems.* Paper presented at "Fairbairn and Relational Theory Today" International Conference, Lisbon, October. Reprinted in *Fairbairn and Relational Theory Today*, ed. F. Fereira and D. E. Scharff (in press). London: Karnac.

Scharff, D. E., and Birtles, E. F., eds. (1994). *From Instinct to Self. Selected Papers of W. R. D. Fairbairn*, vol. 1. Northvale, NJ: Jason Aronson.

———. (1997). From instinct to self: the evolution and implications of W. R. D. Fairbairn's theory of object relations. *International Journal of Psycho-Analysis* 78:1–19.

Scharff, D. E., and Hill, J. M. M. (1976). *Between Two Worlds: Aspects of the Transition from School to Work*. London: Career Consultant Publications.

Scharff, D. E., and Scharff, J. S. (1979). Teaching and learning: an experiential conference. *Journal of Personality and Social Systems* 2(1):53–78.

———. (1987). *Object Relations Family Therapy*. Northvale, NJ: Jason Aronson.

———. (1991). *Object Relations Couple Therapy*. Northvale, NJ: Jason Aronson.

———. (1999). *Advances in object relations theory and practice: chaos theory, attachment research, object construction, and transference geography*. Workshop, American Academy of Psychoanalysis, Washington, DC, May 15.

———. (2000). *Deterministic chaos theory: a new paradigm for psychoanalysis*. Paper submitted for "Chaos Theory and Psychoanalysis" panel at the International Psycho-Analytic Association meeting, Nice, July 2001.

Scharff, J. S. (1989). *Foundations of Object Relations Family Therapy*. Northvale, NJ: Jason Aronson.

———. (1992a). Projective and introjective identification, love, and the internal couple. *In Projective and Introjective Identification and the Use of the Therapist's Self*, pp. 133–157. Northvale, NJ: Jason Aronson.

———. (1992b). *Projective and Introjective Identification and the Use of the Therapist's Self*. Northvale, NJ: Jason Aronson.

———. (1995). Psychoanalytic marital therapy. In *Clinical Handbook of Couple Therapy*, ed. N. S. Jacobson and A. S. Gurman, pp. 164–193. New York: Guilford.

———. (1999). *The role of the Chair in psychoanalytic education*. Unpublished manuscript.

Scharff, J. S., and Scharff, D. E. (1998a). Chaos theory and fractals in development, self and object relations, and transference. In *Object Relations Individual Therapy*, pp.153–182. Northvale, NJ: Jason Aronson.

———. (1998b). Five dreams: fractal of an analysis. In *Object Relations Individual Therapy*, pp. 589–598. Northvale, NJ: Jason Aronson.

———. (1998c). Geography of transference and countertransference. In *Object Relations Individual Therapy*, pp. 241–281. Northvale, NJ: Jason Aronson.

———. (1998d). *Object Relations Individual Therapy*. Northvale, NJ: Jason Aronson.

———. (1999a). *The individual and group affective learning model*. Unpublished lecture at the "Effects of Unconscious and Group Processes on Individual and Institutional Functioning in Work Settings" conference, International Institute of Object Relations Therapy, Bethesda, MD, April 10.

———. (1999b). *The group affective model: an alternative model for learning psychoanalytic group therapy*. Unpublished pre-circulated paper presented at the American Psychoanalytic Association winter meeting, New York, December.

————. (2000). *The group affective model: a new training paradigm for psychoanalytic education.* Workshop, American Academy of Psychoanalysis winter meeting, New York, January.

Schön, D. (1983). *The Reflective Practitioner.* New York: Basic Books.

————. (1987). *Educating the Reflective Practitioner.* San Franscisco: Jossey-Bass.

Schore, A. (1994). *Affect Regulation and the Origin of the Self: The Neurobiology of Emotional Development.* Hillsdale, NJ: Lawrence Erlbaum.

————. (2000 in press). Freud's project and current findings on brain correlates of affective development. In *Freud at the Millennium*, ed. D. E. Scharff. New York: The Other Press; London: Karnac.

Searles, H. (1965a). *Collected Papers on Schizophrenia and Related Topics.* Madison, CT, and New York: International Universities Press.

————. (1965b). Problems of psychoanalytic supervision. In *Collected Papers on Schizophrenia and Related Topics*, pp. 584–604. Madison, CT, and New York: International Universities Press.

Shapiro, R. (1979). Family dynamics and object relations theory: an analytic group-interpretive approach to family therapy. In *Adolescent Psychiatry: Developmental and Clinical Studies*, vol. 7, ed. S. C. Feinstein and P. Giovacchini, pp. 118–135. Chicago: University of Chicago Press.

Slade, A. (1996). Attachment theory and research: implications for the theory and practice of individual psychotherapy. In *Handbook of Attachment Theory and Research*, ed. J. Cassidy and P. R. Shaver, pp. 575–594. New York: Guilford.

Sonnier, I. L. (1989). *Affective Education: Methods and Techniques.* Englewood Cliffs, NJ: Educational Technology Publications.

Spillius, E. (1988). *Melanie Klein Today, Vol. 1: Mainly Theory*, and *Melanie Klein Today, Vol. 2: Mainly Technique.* London: Routledge.

Springmann, R. (1976). Fragmentation in large groups. *Group Analysis* 9(3):185–188.

Spruiell, V. (1993). Deterministic chaos and the science of complexity: psychoanalysis in the midst of a general scientific revolution. *Journal of the American Psychoanalytic Association* 41:3–41.

Stadter, M. (1996). *Object Relations Brief Therapy: The Therapeutic Relationship in Short-Term Work.* Northvale, NJ: Jason Aronson.

Stadter, M., and Scharff, D. E. (1999). Object relations brief therapy. In *Brief Therapy Strategies with Individuals and Couples*, ed. J. Carlson, in press. Redding, CT: Zeig/Tucker.

Sutherland, J. D. (1963). Object relations theory and the conceptual model of psychoanalysis. *British Journal of Medical Psychology* 36:109–124.

———. (1980). The British object relations theorists: Balint, Winnicott, Fairbairn, Guntrip. *Journal of the American Psychoanalytic Association* 28(4):829–860.

———. (1989). *Fairbairn's Journey to the Interior.* London: Free Association Books.

———. (1990). On becoming and being a person. In *The Autonomous Self: The Work of John D. Sutherland,* ed. J. S. Scharff, pp. 372–391. Northvale, NJ: Jason Aronson, 1994.

Szecsödy, I. (1990). *The Learning Process in Psychotherapy Supervision.* Stockholm: Karolinska Institute.

———. (1994). Supervision—a complex tool for psychoanalytic training. *Scandinavian Psychoanalytic Review* 17:119–129.

———. (1997). Framing the psychoanalytic frame. *Scandinavian Psychoanalytic Review* 20:238–243.

Turquet, P. (1975). Threats to identity in the large group. In *The Large Group: Dynamics and Therapy,* ed. L. Kreeger, pp. 87–144. London: Constable.

Van Eenwyck, J. R. (1977). *Archetypes and Strange Attractors: The Chaotic World of Symbols.* Toronto: Inner City Books.

Wallerstein, R. (1981). *Becoming a Psychoanalyst: A Study of Psychoanalytic Supervision.* New York: International Universities Press.

Wells, L. (1985). The group-as-a-whole perspective and its theoretical roots. In *Group Relations Reader 2,* ed. A. D. Colman and M. H. Geller, pp. 109–126. Washington, DC: A. K. Rice Institute.

Westen, D. (1990). Towards a revised theory of borderline object relations: contributions of empirical research. *International Journal of Psycho-Analysis* 71:661–693.

Winnicott, D. W. (1945). Primitive emotional development. In *Through Paediatrics to Psycho-Analysis,* pp. 145–156. London: Hogarth, 1975.

———. (1951). Transitional objects and transitional phenomena. In *Through Paediatrics to Psycho-Analysis,* pp. 229–242. London: Tavistock, 1958; Hogarth, 1975.

———. (1960). The theory of the parent–infant relationship. *International Journal of Psycho-Analysis* 41:585–595. Reprinted in *The Maturational Processes and the Facilitating Environment,* pp. 37–55. New York: International Universities Press, 1965; London: Hogarth, 1965.

———. (1963a). Psychiatric disorder in terms of infantile maturational process. In *The Maturational Processes and the Facilitating Environment,* pp. 230–241. London: Tavistock/Hogarth, 1965.

————. (1963b). Dependence in infant care, in child care, and in the psycho-analytic setting. In *The Maturational Processes and the Facilitating Environment*, pp. 249–259. London: Tavistock/Hogarth, 1965.

————. (1965). *The Maturational Processes and the Facilitating Environment*. London: Tavistock/Hogarth.

Wolf, A., and Schwartz, E. K. (1962). *Psychoanalysis in Groups*. New York: Grune & Stratton.

Yalom, I. D. (1970). *The Theory and Practice of Group Psychotherapy*. New York: Basic Books (3rd ed. 1985).

Zinner, J., and Shapiro, R. L. (1972). Projective identification as a mode of perception and behavior in the families of adolescents. *International Journal of Psycho-Analysis* 53:523–530.

Index

Adjunctive therapies, brief therapy, 89–90

Affect, learning matrix model, 328

Affective learning experience, 71–84
  group as maternal object, 73
  group work (clinical example), 73–84
    aggressive affect, 78–81
    intimacy, 81–84
    stranger anxiety and projective identification, 74–78
  overview, 71
  theory base, 71–72

Affective learning groups (student reflections). *See* Student reflections

Affective learning model, 21–43
  in allied professions, 28
  associated models, 367–368
  background for, 29–30
  concept overview, 21
  discussant's response, 355–357
  extensions of, 366–367
  faculty small group, 37–38
  group experiential learning, 30–31
    small groups, 33–35
  group leader, 37
  innovations, 28–29
  International Institute of Object Relations Therapy, 22
  large-group discussion, 357–368
    anti-task group, 361–362
    anxiety containment, 361
    dual role relationships, 357–358
    regressive pull of small group, 359–361
    resistance, 358
  large groups, 31
  limitations of, 362–364
  maturation of, 368
  median groups, 31–32
  multiple faculty roles, 38–39
  philosophy of, 23–25
  program design, 22–23

Affective learning model (*continued*)
  regressive pull, 36
  subgroupings, informal, 33
  supervision, 39–40
  task in large and median groups, 32
  therapy groups contrasted, 99–107
  third position, learning from,
    365–366
  time use, 364–365
  traditional education contrasted,
    25–28
Affective learning small groups,
    143–160
  boundaries, 152
  couples and oedipal exclusion,
    153–156
  envy, defenses against, 153
  examples, 147–148
  functional dynamics, 143–147
  paranoid-schizoid and depressive
    positions, 150–152
  separation anxiety, 156–160
  vulnerability, hatred of, 148–150
Affect regulation, object relations
    theory, 59
Aggressive affect, affective learning
    experience, 78–81
Ainsworth, M. D. S., 53
Alliance development, brief therapy,
    86–87
Allied professions, affective learning
    model, 28
Alvarez, A., 132
Anderson, R., 133
Anthony, E. J., 30, 51
Anti-task group, affective learning
    model, 361–362
Anxiety, containment of, 361
Anzieu, D., 47

Arlow, J. A., 25, 27, 314, 315
Art media, conference format, small
    group in large group,
    385–388
Ashbach, C., 30
Authority
  couple effect, 352–353
  female, chair challenge, 292–294

Balint, M., 53, 186, 367
Bell, D., 211
Benedek, T., 330
Bennett, M. J., 90
Bergman, M., 336
Bernfeld, S., 26
Bertalanffy, L. von, 30
Bion, W., 10, 11, 28, 29, 30, 35,
    49, 50, 53, 58–59, 74, 81,
    133, 135, 138, 141, 142, 143,
    145, 147, 211, 247, 280, 299,
    360, 375, 394, 395
Birtles, E. F., 60
Bollas, C., 53, 136
Boundaries, affective learning small
    groups, 152
Bowlby, J., 57, 73, 392
Brain research, object relations
    theory, 59
Brief therapy, 85–97
  adjunctive therapies, 89–90
  alliance development, 86–87
  change in learning, 92
  didactic and dynamic focus, 87–88
  historical material, 88
  institute administration, 93–97
  interpretation, 89
  new attitudes, 92
  overview, 85–86
  personal learning, 93

relational issues, 89
serial courses, 90–91
Briggs, J., 59, 61, 65
Britton, R., 206, 222, 344, 366
Budmann, S. H., 90

Chair, 279–295
  activities of, 281–286
  authority of, 280
  challenges to, 286–295
    container for projections, 289
    easy-to-prepare presentation,
      ‑286–287
    female authority, 292–294
    group dynamics, 291
    interpretation, 289–290
    transformation by support for,
      294–295
    unconscious, 287–289
  functions of, 280–281
  need for, 295
  overview, 279
  small-group leader as, 297–311
    general reactions to multiple
      roles, 300–302
    institute supports, 302–303
    multiple roles, 298–299
    overview, 297–298
    personal issues, 299–300
    responses to multiple roles,
      303–310
Chaos theory
  individual/couple as objects,
    168–171
  object relations theory, 59–69
Chiang, F., 13–14
Conference, 203–234, 373–401
  day 1, 206–210
  day 2, 211–215

day 3, 215–223
day 4, 223–229
day 5, 230–234
design of, 203–204
discussion of, 392–399
group relations format, 374–392
  consultants, 377
  evolution of, 378–379
  individual events, 379–380
  individual in large groups,
    383–385
  large groups, 382–383
  learning and teaching,
    376–377
  lecture-discussion, 388–389
  review and application, 390–
    392
  small group in large group,
    385–388
  small groups, 381–382
implementation and development,
  399–401
overview, 373–374
schedule for, 205
small-group task, 204–205
Containment
  affective learning, 141
  chair challenge, 289
Countertransference
  affective learning, 141
  learning matrix model, 320–326
Couple effect, 333–353
  authority, 352–353
  examples, 334–335, 340–342
  faculty discussion, 342–352
  impact of, 333–334
  institutional setting, 335–336,
    339–340
  motivating fantasy, 336–339

Couples, oedipal exclusion and,
affective learning small groups,
153–156
Couple therapy institute, student
reflections, 198–200
Creative identification, couple
effect, 345–349
Culture
group analysis and, 51–53
women, 15–20

Defenses
against envy, affective learning
small groups, 153
against learning and teaching,
conference format, 395–399
De Maré, P., 31, 50, 51
Depressive position, paranoid-
schizoid position and, affective
learning small groups, 150–152
Dewey, J., 366
Dicks, H., 19, 53, 68, 69
Didactic focus, brief therapy, 87–88
Displacement, from transference, 6–
10
Dorey, R., 26
Dream analysis, group unconscious,
116–120
Dual role relationships, affective
learning model, 357–358
Duncan, D., 230
Dynamic focus, brief therapy, 87–88

Education, interpretation and,
affective learning model,
splitting or integration of, 356–
357
Eitingon, M., 26, 28
Ely, M., 367

Emotional vertigo, individual/
couple as objects, 166–168
Envy
defenses against, affective learning
small groups, 153
destructive, couple effect, 345–
349
Experiential learning
group, affective learning model,
30–31
small groups, 33–35
object relations theory, 69–70
Ezriel, H., 30, 35

Fairbairn, W. R. D., 19, 30, 53,
54–55, 60, 111, 147
Falzeder, E., 25, 26
Family system, women, cultural
pressures on, 17
Fantasy, motivating, couple effect,
336–339
Fears, of uncertainty, overcoming
of, 3–6
Female authority, chair challenge,
292–294
Fisher, J., 215
Fleming, J., 330
Fonagy, P., 53
Fornari, F., 144
Foulkes, S. H., 28, 30, 51
Fractals, object relations theory, 61–
62, 67–69
Fractal scaling, transference and
therapeutic action, 65–67
Fractal splitting, object relations
theory, 61–62
Freud, S., 10, 25, 29, 74, 81, 111,
241
Fromm-Reichmann, F., 85, 184

Galatzer-Levy, R., 65
Gleick, J., 30, 59, 61, 62, 64, 314
Gross-Doehrman, M. J., 315
Grotstein, J., 187
Group analysis, 46–51
  culture and, 51–53
    institutional matrix, 53
    small affective learning groups,
      52
  group definition, 46–48
  small and large groups, 50–51
  small/median/large group
    characteristics, 48–49
  small/median/large group
    differences, 51
  small work group and basic
    assumption group, 49–50
Group-as-a-whole phenomenon,
  teaching applications, 11–15
Group dynamics, teaching
  applications, 10–15
Group unconscious, 109–123
  coleader reflections, 120–121
  composition and themes, 110–111
  postconference working through,
    121–123
  structure and context, 111–120
    dream analysis, 116–120
    dynamics, 111–116
    training and, 109–110
Guntrip, H., 53, 92, 188
Gurman, A. S., 90

Heisenberg principle, 60
Hill, J. M. M., 29, 30, 376
Historical material, brief therapy, 88
Holding on, letting go and, affective
  learning, student reflections
  on, 131–133

Hopper, E., 49, 50, 51, 211, 214,
  215
Hoyt, M. F., 90
Hwa-byung, women, cultural
  pressures on, 18–19

Identification, creative, couple
  effect, 345–349
Individual/couple as objects, 161–
  171
  acknowledging the object, 162–
    164
  chaos theory, 168–171
  clinical work, 164–166
  emotional vertigo, 166–168
  overview, 161–162
Infant observation, responses to,
  affective learning, 139–140
Initial conditions, sensitive
  dependence on, object
  relations theory, 62–63
Insanity, sanity and, affective
  learning, student reflections
  on, 133–136
Integration
  affective learning model, 3
    55–356
  of interpretation and education,
    affective learning model,
    356–357
Internal couple. *See* Couple effect
International Institute of Object
  Relations Therapy, 22
Interpretation
  brief therapy, 89
  chair challenge, 289–290
  education and, affective learning
    model, splitting or
    integration of, 356–357

Interpretation-free zone, need for,
    affective learning model, 356
Intimacy, affective learning
    experience, 81–84

Jacques, E., 30
Jones, M., 28, 30
Jung, C. G., 25

Keats, J., 35, 136
Kernberg, O., 26, 27, 28, 29, 336
Klein, M., 19, 30, 53, 55–56, 74,
    81, 133, 142, 147, 150, 336
Kreeger, L., 49

Learning, teaching and
    conference format, 376–377
    object relations theory, 45–46
Learning matrix model, 313–332
    example, 317–332
    overview of, 313–316
    traditional model compared, 313
Letting go, holding on and, affective
    learning, student reflections
    on, 131–133
Lifschutz, J. E., 25
Lonie, I., 65, 66
Lorenz, E., 62, 64

Mahler, M., 392
Main, M., 53
Malan, D. H., 186
Mandelbrot, B., 61, 67
Maternal object, group as, affective
    learning experience, 73
Menzies, I. E. P., 30
Miller, E., 30
Milner, M., 136

Moreno, J. L., 383
Mother, as desired object, affective
    learning, student reflections,
    128–131
Motivating fantasy, couple effect,
    336–339

Neri, C., 46, 47, 48
Neuroscience, object relations
    theory, 59
New objects, 173–181
    comparisons, 180–181
    importance of, 173–174
    reflections on, 178–179
    situational dynamics, 174–178,
        179–180

Oberholzer, E., 25
Obholzer, A., 355, 356, 357, 361,
    362, 363, 366
Object relations theory, 53–70
    affect regulation and brain
        research, 59
    attachment research, 57–58
    Bion, 58–59
    chaos theory, 59–61
    experiential learning, 69–70
    Fairbairn, 54–55
    fractals, fractal splitting, and self-
        similarity, 61–62
    fractals and, 67–69
    interpersonal expression, 69
    Klein, 55–56
    sensitive dependence on initial
        conditions, 62–63
    sensitivity to transition at edge of
        chaos, 63–65
    sources of, 53

teaching and learning, 45–46
transference and therapeutic
    action, 65–67
Winnicott, 56–57
women, cultural pressures on, 18
Oedipal exclusion
    couple effect, 343–344
    couples and, affective learning
        small groups, 153–156
Ogden, T., 53, 65, 132, 336

Palombo, S., 65, 66, 67, 69
Papadakis, M., 214
Paranoid-schizoid position, depressive
    position and, affective learning
        small groups, 150–152
Pasolini, P. P., 193
Penis, object relations theory, 68–69
Pichon-Rivière, E., 48
Piers, C., 65
Pines, M., 28, 30
Piper, R., 50
Presentation(s), 249–263
    account of, 249–262
        dialogues, 254–256, 260–262
        patient history, 250–251
        sessions, 251–254, 256–260
    chair, 279–295. *See also* Chair
    discussion, 262–263
Presentation preparation, 237–248
    clinical presentation preparation,
        240–245
    preceding group effect, 245–248
    presenter mentoring, 239–240
    presenter selection, 237–239
Presentation reflections, 265–276
    learning process, 268–273
    presenter reflections, 273–276

subsequent group impact, 265–
    268
Primal scene, couple effect, 345–
    349
Projection, chair challenge, 289
Projective identification
    stranger anxiety and, affective
        learning experience, 74–78
    women, cultural pressures on, 18
Psychodrama, conference format,
    383–385

Quinodoz, D., 65, 110
Quinodoz, J.-M., 110

Regressive pull
    affective learning model, 36
    of small group, affective learning
        model, 359–361
Relational issues, brief therapy, 89
Repetitive patterns, historical
    material, brief therapy, 88
Resistance, affective learning model,
    358
Resonance, with self and objects,
    affective learning, student
    reflections on, 138–142
Rice, A. K., 28, 29, 30, 375
Rioch, M., 28, 375, 395

Sachs, D. M., 315
Safety, affective learning model, 357
Salzberger-Wittenberg, I. S., 30,
    107
Sanity, insanity and, affective
    learning, student reflections
    on, 133–136
Savege, J., 29, 30, 376

Scharff, D., 10, 19, 25, 29, 30, 50,
    51, 53, 60, 62, 65, 66, 68,
    69, 85, 90, 110, 222, 235,
    277, 280, 297, 298, 304,
    306, 309, 314, 315, 332,
    333–353, 355, 356, 358,
    360, 363, 364, 366, 367,
    368, 376
Scharff, J., 10, 16, 19, 25, 29, 30,
    50, 51, 53, 56, 62, 65, 66,
    68, 69, 85, 90, 222, 223,
    279, 280, 297, 298, 303,
    306, 307, 309, 314, 315,
    332, 333–353, 355, 356,
    359, 362, 364, 366
Schermer, V. L., 30
Schön, D., 367
Schore, A., 30, 53, 59, 63, 137
Schwartz, E. K., 30
Searles, H., 48, 314, 315
Seinfeld, J., 188
Self-similarity, object relations
    theory, 61–62, 65
Sensitive dependence, on initial
    conditions, object relations
    theory, 62–63
Separation anxiety
    affective learning small groups,
        156–160
    emotional vertigo, individual/
        couple as objects, 166–168
Shapiro, E., 188
Shapiro, R., 56
Shapiro, S. H., 315
Slade, A., 53, 57
Solomon, J., 53
Sonnier, I. L., 107
Spillius, E., 135
Spitz, R., 25

Splitting, of interpretation and
    education, affective learning
    model, 356–357
Springmann, R., 49
Spruiell, V., 66
Stadter, M., 53, 85, 87, 90
Steiner, J., 187
Strange attractors, transference and
    therapeutic action, 65–67
Stranger anxiety, projective
    identification and, affective
    learning experience, 74–78
Student, as teacher, affective
    learning, student reflections
    on, 136–138
Student reflections, 127–142, 183–
    201
    on affective learning, 127–142.
        See also Affective learning
    comments, 200–201
    couple therapy institute, 198–200
    letting go and holding on, 131–133
    mother as desired object, 128–131
    resonance with self and objects,
        138–142
    sanity and insanity, 133–136
    student as teacher, 136–138
    weekend synopsis, 183–198
Supervision
    affective learning model, 39–40
    faculty satellite roles, 40
    learning matrix, 313–332. *See also*
        Learning matrix model
    practicalities, 40–43
    traditional, 109
    transference, displacement from,
        6–10
Sutherland, J. D., 53, 55, 68
Szecsödy, I., 315, 316

Target, M., 223, 224
Teaching
    affective learning model, 21–43.
        See also Affective learning
        model
    group dynamics applied to, 10–15
    learning and
        conference format, 376–377
        object relations theory, 45–46
    student as teacher, affective
        learning, student reflections
        on, 136–138
Therapeutic action, transference
    and, object relations theory,
    65–67
Therapy groups, affective learning
    group contrasted, 99–107
Third position, learning from, 365–
    366
Transference
    displacement from, 6–10
    learning matrix model, 320–326
    therapeutic action and, object
        relations theory, 65–67
Turquet, P., 49

Uncertainty fears, overcoming of, 3–
    6
Unconscious, chair challenge, 287–
    289. *See also* Group
    unconscious

van Eenwyck, J. R., 69
Vulnerability, hatred of, 148–150

Wallerstein, R., 315
Wells, L., 11
Westen, D., 56
Williams, A. H., 215
Winnicott, D. W., 30, 53, 56–57,
    72, 134, 137, 138–139, 140,
    188, 280, 392
Wolf, A., 30
Women
    cultural pressures on, 15–20
    female authority, chair challenge,
        292–294

Yalom, I. D., 30

Zinner, J., 56